ॐ

सोऽहम्

PĀTAÑJALA YOGA SŪTRA

Sanskṛta Sūtras with Transliteration, Translation & Commentary

By

Dr. P. V. Karambelkar

KAIVALYADHAMA

Swami Kuvalayananda Marg,

Lonavla, Dist. Pune - 410 403,

(Maharashtra, INDIA)

First Edition -1986
First Reprint - 2002
Second Reprint - 2012
Third Reprint - 2017
Forth Reprint - 2020
Fifth Reprint - 2021
Sixth Reprint - 2023
Seventh Reprint : 2024

ISBN 97881 894 85177

₹ : 700/-

Published by :
O. P. Tiwari, Secretary,
Kaivalyadhama,
Swami Kuvalayananda Marg,
Lonavla, Dist. Pune-410 403,
(M.S.) INDIA

Printed by :
ACE Enterprises,
Madhu-Raj Nagar, C1-6 & 25,
137/A, Paud Road, Kothrud,
Pune-411 038,
(M.S.) INDIA

Swami Kuvalayanandaji

Founder Director Of Kaivalyadhama, Lonavla

(1883-1966)

Swami Digambaraji (1903-1990)

Chairman / Director Kaivalyadham, Lonavla
(1966-1990)

INTRODUCTION

It gives me immense pleasure in presenting this English Commentary on Yoga Sūtras, the most important ancient text of Yoga, composed by Maharṣi Patañjali. The science of Yoga does not originate with Patañjali. It was prevalent long before the emergence of Patañjali, who only systematized it, which is evident from the very first aphorism of Pātañjala Yoga Sūtras (P.Y.S.) **'atha yogānuśāsanam'** (see commentary on P.Y.S. I. 1.)

Thus in modern times we owe to Maharṣi Patañjali for the systematic presentation of Traditional Yogic lore embodied in the Indian scriptures prior to Patañjali.

Patañjali has presented this ancient Yoga Vidyā (the Knowledge of Yoga) in such a Scientific and Rational way that every theory, hypothesis and principle put forth by Patañjali can be tested through most rigorous modern scientific methodology. Perhaps this is the reason that modern Spiritual trends seem to have their roots in Pātañjala Yoga Sūtras. This provides the Pātañjala Yoga Sūtra a status of Yoga Śāstra to be studied by every Scientific Student of Yoga.

It will not be out of place here to mention about how and why I was prompted to write a commentary on Yoga Sūtra.

Pātañjala Yoga Sūtra was prescribed as one of the subjects in Kaivalyadhāma's G.S. College of Yoga and Cultural Synthesis right from its inception in the year 1950.

The teaching of the subject required not only the knowledge of Sanskṛt but also the practical knowledge of Yoga. It was true that I was a practicing Yoga Sādhaka but I never considered that my knowledge of Sanskṛt language is sufficient enough to teach the subject in the college. But I had a keen interest to study Pātañjala Yoga Sūtra in detail and I was moved by its scientific way of presentation of the matter, as I was basically a student of science and working as a scientific researcher in the field of Yoga. This intense desire of mine was soon materialized as I had an apportunity not only to understand and learn the Pātañjala Yoga Sūtras for myself, but also to teach the same in the college. The only hindrance in teaching the subject, as I felt, was with regard to my insufficient knowledge of Sanskṛt which, I could overcome due to two of my colleagues Dr. M. V. Apte (the then Medical Officer and also Scholar of Sanskṛt) and Tarkatīrtha Raghunātha Śāstri Kokaje (a great Sanskṛt Scholar and Yoga Researcher in the Philosophico-Literary Research Department) who not only appreciated my knowledge of Sanskṛt, but also encouraged and helped me towards my teaching of Pātañjala Yoga Sūtras. In the beginning, for four - five years, I had to study almost all Traditional Sanskṛt commentaries as well as other modern commentaries on Pātañjala Yoga Sūtra before lecturing on the Sūtras of Pātañjali in G. S. College of Yoga.

In this endeavour, after about 5 years of studying and teaching, with my practical experience of Yoga and scientific background I began to feel that the subject can be understood more scientifically and rationally, albeit profitably, with the explanations and interpretations that I could develop during these years.

Naturally, I began to present these new explanations in my lectures on Pātañjala Yoga Sūtras in the Yoga College. No doubt, I used to present the views of the earlier commentators to the students and then I presented my own explanations, giving reasons for the difference of opinion I had from earlier commentators. Also, I expected that my explanations of Sūtras should be presented by the students in their examination answer books. The students, especially some of the foreign students, approached me and expressed that whatever I was teaching as my explanation of the Sūtras could be understood by them very well, when I was giving them lectures. But these new explanations could not be found anywhere in any book; so, after sometimes of teaching, they became rather hazy in the minds of the students. Hence, they requested me that I write my own commentary of Pātañjala Yoga Sūtras. Some research staff members of our Philosophico-Literary Research Department also approached me with the same request. One of them namely Shri. Gyan Shankar Sahay offered to take my dictation of this commentary on Pātañjala Yoga Sūtras. Thus this commentary ultimately came into existence. It was published in installments, each of 40 pages, in Kaivalyadhāma's Quarterly Research Journal 'Yoga Mīmāṃsā' and some extra copies of the pages were simultaneously printed. Thus the first edition of Pātañjala Yoga Sūtras with Translation and Commentary according to me, appeared in book form. This edition had no Preface or Introduction. The copies of the same are almost exhausted and so this second edition of the book is being presented alongwith Preface and Introduction.

Maharṣi Patañjali, as is well known, has rendered Yoga Darśana in the form of Sūtras i.e. aphorism. Though the word Sūtra primarily means **'thread'**, it has acquired unique connotation, namely **'writing in a precise and condensed form'**, which has been reflected in the following oft quoted verse in this regard :

अल्पाक्षरमसन्दिग्धं सारवत् विश्वतोमुखम् ।
अस्तोभमनवद्यञ्च सूत्रं सूत्रविदो विदुः ।।

"According to the knowers of Sūtra, the Sūtra composition essentially should be precise, not giving rise to any doubt, presenting essence of many thoughts, coherent and blemishless." The Sūtra, in this sense, is a most condensed statement of something, which may take several words or pages in writing. The utmost possible brevity is the special and prominent characteristic of Sūtra way of writing. There is a saying in Sanskṛt, which states that if a Grammarian could cut down even one mātrā (alphabet) of the original Sūtra, he would be happy, as if he has got a son. This shows how much importance is given to brevity in Sūtra. In this book itself it could be seen in many Sūtras that this principle of brevity is followed by Patañjali to the utmost degree, because, according to most of the scholars, who have studied Pātañjala Yoga Sūtras, Patañjali is one of the best, almost an ideal Sūtrakāra. One example of this is the Sūtra I:23, which is at least apparently a single word 'Īśvarapraṇidhānādvā'. To explain this very brief one word

Sūtra, I had to give thirteen lectures, when I was teaching in the Yoga College. Even in the present book, as can be seen, the commentary on this Sūtra takes about five pages.

This type of writing became, probably necessary, in the old days, even when mode of writing was known to man, and books could be written, they were not easily available as of today. In fact every thing was taught by the teacher verbally to his students in the old Gurukul system. However, after finishing his studies at the Gurukul, the student returned to his home and he had forgotten something out of what the teacher had taught him, he could not refer to any book etc. as a student of today could do. Even supposing that he went back to his teacher's place, it may very well happen that the teacher may not be alive, where then to solve his difficulty. To over come such an eventuality the Sūtra construction probably was devised.

Another characteristic, again simulating a thread, is continuity in all the Sūtras, just like the continuity of different component fibres entwined in a thread. Thus every Sūtra is logically bound with its preceding and following Sūtra and the whole Sūtra compilation forms a compact unity.

We find that almost in all ancient Śāstras, such Sūtra constructions were composed in the former times.

Pātañjala Yoga Sūtras is very often popularly referred to as Yoga Darśana. The word 'darśana' means 'seen'. The idea behind the word seems to be that, that the views presented in the 'darśana' were actually 'seen' i.e. inspired in the mind of compiler of the 'darśana'. And that they were not a result of mere thinking and deliberation, as usually is the case in some new theory or presentation. Patañjali's Yoga Sūtras are actually very probably a result of such inspiration.

In the Pātañjala Yoga Sūtras, Patañjali has presented the science of Yoga, in a most scientific manner as already said, both from ancient (traditionally) as well as modern scientific outlook. The Sūtras are presenting not only the philosophy and science of Yoga in mere theoretical manner, but for actual practice, through which the ultimate goal of Yoga viz. according to Pātañjala Yoga Sūtras, the Kaivalya, is reached. In fact according to my understanding each word of each and every Sūtra has this aim of following its instruction for practical purpose.

A word with regards to some of my new explanations will be opportune here, the details of which can be seen at their respective places in this commentary.

All the old commentators as well as modern commentators except Dr. C. T. Kenghe (Author of "Yoga as Depth Psychology and Para - Psychology" (1976), Bharat Manish, Varanasi) have assumed **'Samādhi'** as the substantive for the adjectival word **'Samprajñāta'**. Dr. Kenghe, perhaps is the only author, who has objected the use of 'Samādhi' as substantive for 'Samprajñāta'; but has not given any solution to the problem. After giving sufficient thought to this problem, I came to the conclusion that the proper substantive for the adjectival word 'Samprajñāta' should be **'Yoga Pradeśa'** i.e. the sphere or region of Yoga and not 'Samādhi' (Ref. pp. 38 - 51).

Similarly, almost all the past commentators have coined a

technical term **'Asamprajñāta'** as opposed to Samprajñāta for the term **'Anya'**. According to my opinion, coining of such a technical term and superimposing it on the term of Patañjali is uncalled for or unwarranted. Patañjali, himself being a scholar of Sanskṛt as well as Yoga, could have easily given this term. If Patañjali has not used the term, it means that he had some definite purpose in avoiding the use of such term and explained the **'Region of Yoga'** as **'Anya'** (for details Ref. pp. 51 - 54).

I have already stated in the earlier passages of this preface that Patañjali was a Scientific exponent of Yoga and thus, he is very consistent in the use of the terms. One term used and defined at one place contains identical connotation, wherever it has reappeared in the Aphorisms. Terms like **'Vitarka'**, **'Dhyāna'** are some of the examples for this. The term 'Vitarka' has been used in P.Y.S. I. 17; II. 33 & 34. While commenting on such places, I have continuously tried to maintain consistency in their meaning.

Just as the above mentioned claim that one and the same term cannot have two meanings, even if used at the different places in the same text; similarly two different terms cannot have identical meaning, as it will amount Patañjali to be inconsistent in his presentation which is against the norms of composing the Sūtra. The words **'Samāpatti'** and **'Samādhi'**, have been used by Patañjali in the very first chapter viz. 'Samādhipāda' of Yoga Sūtra. Unfortunately, almost all the past Commentators have not been able to differentiate these two terms and therefore, considered them as having similar meaning. As I proceeded with the commentary of the text, I could find a logical difference in these two terms as **Samāpatti** standing for process, whereas **Samādhi** is the result of that process (for details Ref. pp. no. 130 - 152).

In the context of Prāṇāyāma, as against the general and popular understanding of identifying **'Gaticcheda'** with Haṭhayogic Kumbhaka it has been pointed out while commenting on P.Y.S. 11:49, that **'Kumbhaka'** is **a form** of 'Gativiccheda' but not **the only form**. Thus the 'Gativiccheda' would mean any alteration in the rhythmicity or regularity of breathing (that makes the breathing finer) and the Kumbhaka type will be a variety of Patañjali's 'Gativiccheda' of Prāṇāyāma and not identical with it, as has been claimed by some Haṭhayogic Texts (Ref. pp. 282 - 285). Besides this specificity, the present commentary deals the topic of Prāṇāyāma in the context of some of the modern scientific findings on the topic discovered in Researches at Kaivalyadhama and at other places.

In order to make this commentary Sādhaka friendly a special chart is given (after pp. 124) showing the inward journey of Citta. This is an attempt to map out the experiential process and is expected to comprehend the Yogic experience in terms of **'Yoga - Pradeśas'**, **'Processes'** and **'States'**.

The Yoga presented in Pātañjala Yoga Sūtras, as said in the text itself, can be named properly as Aṣṭāṇga Yoga or Pātañjala Yoga. According to me, as it is sometimes called, it is not correct to refer to it as Rāja Yoga. Swāmi Vivekānanda, first used this designation for Yoga of Pātañjala Yoga Sūtras, very probably. But there is no any base in Pātañjala Yoga Sūtras itself, to designate this Yoga as Rāja Yoga. On the basis of the understanding of Rāja Yoga as explained in Haṭha Pradīpikā also (see Upadeśa I of H.P. published by Kaivalyadhāma, Lonāvlā) the Yoga in Pātañjala Yoga Sūtras can not and should not be called Rāja Yoga. However if the name Rāja Yoga which means **'King of Yoga'** is taken to mean the superlative Yoga system, then definitely the Yoga of Pātañjala Yoga Sūtras can and may be called as Rāja Yoga.

As stated above the aphorisms in Pātañjala Yoga Sūtras are primarily for practising Yoga, I hope that the readers of this commentary of mine would be inspired to practise Yoga in their life and not study the Sūtras merely as a theoretical and philosophical subject. For this reason I am indebted to Kaivalyadhāma for bringing out this Edition of Pātañjala Yoga Sūtras again into light. I hope that many people will be inspired to the practice of Yoga.

I end this Preface with the famous salutation to Patañjali :

योगेन चित्तस्य पदेन वाचां
मलं शरीरस्य च वैद्यकेन ।
योऽपाकरोत्तं प्रवरं मुनीनां
पतञ्जलिं प्राञ्जलिरानतोऽस्मि ।।

(yogen cittasya padena vācāṃ
malaṃ śarīrasya ca vaidyakena ।
yo'pākarottaṃ pravaraṃ munīnāṃ
patañjaliṃ prāñjalirānato'smi ।।)

TR. : I salute Patañjali, the highest among the Munis (sages), who has presented the remedies for removing the impurities of the body through his treatise on Āyurveda (Caraka Saṃhitā, an ancient Indian Medical Science) and of language through his treatise on Grammar (Pātañjala Mahābhāṣya) and the impurities of Citta through his treatise on Yoga (i.e. this Pātañjala Yoga Sūtra).

- Dr. P. V. Karambelkar

PREFACE

It was a long standing demand from everyone associated with Kaivalyadhāma to prepare a commentary on Pātañjala Yoga Sūtra (P. Y.S.) on Scientific lines and understanding Dr. P. V. Karambelkar (Ph.D. in Bio Chemistry) whom we lovingly call **'Kākā',** the then Joint Director of Research and a very close associate of the founder Director of Kaivalyadhāma Swāmi Kuvalyānandaji, took the task of writing a Commentary on P.Y.S. Kākā has a very long experience of teaching Yoga Sūtras in our G.S. College of Yoga and Cultural Synthesis. His interpretations of Sūtras emerge not only from his Scientific researches in the field of Yoga but also from his personal experiences of yoga Sādhanā, both immensely contributing towards the worth of the work which it has presently assumed. Initially the whole commentary was serialized and published in Yoga Mimāṃsā (a Quarterly Research Journal) Published by Kaivalyadhāma, Lonavla. Simultaneously, around one thousand extra copies of each serial were printed, which were later combined and given the shape of a book. The book was received vehemently even without any introduction or index. Due to the increasing demand for this commentary, the book soon became unavailable for many readers, and hence the need for the publication of its second edition was greatly felt. Fortunately for all the Yoga lovers, Kākā, the commentator himself, went through the whole book again and changes/ corrections wherever necessary were made by him for the present edition.

A few words about the originality of the present commentary will be opportune. Kākā has at his credit several original interpretations on many central issues of Pātañjala Yoga Sūtras, which have featured in his introduction too. The Interpretations, such as, of Samāpatti, its relation with Samādhi, of the number of Samādhis advocated by Traditional as well as Modern commentators differ in important respect, as rightly claimed by Kākā. I hope that the yoga lovers will be enriched and enhanced in their understanding of P.Y.S. by these interpretations and they themselves will appreciate the scientific approach of Yoga Sūtra of Patañjali.

The responsibility of giving this book a final shape- prior to publication -was given to our Philosophico-Literary Research Department and the staff members of the Department painstakingly took care of every aspect of its presentation along with adding an exhaustive Index for the facilitation of the readers. The Institute appreciates the effort made by them.

We have no words to express our feelings of gratitude to Shri O. P. Tiwariji, Secretary, Kaivalyadhama, Lonavla, who has really dedicated his whole life for the sake of this Institute and his contribution can best be termed as an example of a Karmayogi.

Our thanks are due to Mrs. Pushpa Mandke, Office Superintendent, K.S.M.Y.M. Samiti, Lonavla, for providing link between the Institute and the Printer.

Mrs. Nazima K. Saudagar deserves our thanks for the typing work related with Index etc..

We thank Mr. Nitin Tanpure, the Prop. ACE Enterprises, Pune, who has taken pains towards the type setting and printing work of the present book within the stipulated time.

We thank all our ashramite co-brothers and sisters for their constant inspiration and appreciations.

Last but definitely not the least, we humbly request our learned readers and practitioners of yoga to communicate their valuable suggestions and comments, if any, which will be appreciated and incorporated in the next edition of this commentary.

स्वस्तिरस्तु ।

- Swami Maheshananda

SCHEME OF TRANSLITERATION

अ -- a; आ -- ā; इ -- i; ई -- ī; उ -- u; ऊ- ū;

ऋ -- ṛ; ॠ -- ṝ; ऌ -- lṛ; ॡ -- lṝ; ए -- e; ऐ -- ai;

ओ -- o; औ -- au; अनुस्वार -- ṃ; विसर्ग -- ḥ;

क् - k; ख् - kh; ग् - g; घ् - gh; ङ् - ṅ;

च् - c; छ् - ch; ज् - j; झ् - jh; ञ् - ñ;

ट् - ṭ; ठ् - ṭh; ड् - ḍ; ढ् - ḍh; ण् - ṇ;

त् - t; थ् - th; द् - d; ध् - dh; न् - n;

प् - p; फ् - ph; ब् - b; भ् - bh; म् - m;

य् - y; र् - r; ल् - l; व् - v;

श् - ś; ष् - ṣ; स् - s;

ह् - h; क्ष् - kṣ; त्र् - tr; ज्ञ् - jñ;

Plan of Arrangment of Subject Matter :

SS. = Sanskṛta Sūtra.
TL. = Transliteration.
WM. = Word Meaning.
TR. = Translation in English in full sentences.
CE. = Comments and Explanations.

१ समाधि पादः

1 SAMĀDHI PĀDAḤ

(Section of Samādhi)

SS. - **अथ योगानुशासनम् ।।१:१।।**

TL. - atha yogānuśāsanam - I:1.

WM. - atha = now;
yogānuśāsanam = a systematic discipline of yoga.

TR. - Now (begins) the systematic presentation of the discipline of yoga.

CE. - Some traditional commentators have tried to see behind the word 'atha' (Now), a kind of auspicious invocation or prayer. This is because, in the old Indian tradition, particularly originating from Vedic tradition, a treatise, even on a non-religious and worldly subject, was having such an auspicious prayer or salutation to some deities and this was usually called 'maṅgalācaraṇam'. Books written on topics closely related with religious matter and tradition, therefore, had such a maṅgalācaraṇa as an essential part. In the orthodox and traditional view point, yoga was looked upon as closely related to religion i.e. Vedic or Hindu religion, so much so, that it was considered as an essential and integral component of religious practices. On account of this, to the old orthodox commentators, it would seem almost a sacrilege that a work on yoga like Patañjali's "Yoga Sūtras" is having no maṅgalācaraṇa. To remove this deficit or fault, they looked upon this word 'atha', which is no doubt an introductory word, as the maṅgalācaraṇa and have imagined that a lot of hidden meaning of that nature lies behind the word. But this outlook is merely sentimental, the meaning given in this way being only arbitrary and it is very doubtful whether the author Patañjali had all that idea in his mind when he used that word.

'Atha' which means 'now' is generally used as an introductory word when in some discussion suddenly a new and important topic is to be opened. In this way this word also indicates that prior to the presentation of the new topic, there was already going on a discussion or talk, very probably on a closely related subject matter. Looked in this way, this first word of Yoga Sūtra indicates to us that these yoga sūtras were probably taught to the students by the teacher, when some prior knowledge or information about yoga had already been imparted to the students. In other words Yoga Sūtras are not to be looked upon as a text for teaching the knowledge of yoga to a complete novice. In fact, they are meant for a person, who has learnt and practised a lot in this discipline. They are thus, like a book of pointwise notes for rapid recapitulation and reference by a person, who is an expert or at least a fairly advanced student of yoga.

In the ancient tradition the knowledge was imparted by the teacher to the student through direct verbal teaching. Books were probably not existent or at least were very rare and therefore, difficult to obtain. Yet when the knowledge began to increase, it became gradually more and more difficult to remember all that one had learnt through such verbal teaching. It became necessary to find some way to preserve this knowledge about a particular discipline in some very condensed form, so that when need arose, the adept could easily retrieve and get access to the information, which he probably had, but which was obscured during a long interval. The mode of sūtra construction was invented at such a time. So, sūtras in general and Patañjali's Yoga Sūtras in particular are meant for such ready retrieval by an advanced student having learnt well the science and art of yoga, both on philosophical and practical lines. A modern student and aspirant of yoga should not expect that he can use Patañajali's Yoga Sūtras as an introductory text on yoga. In fact he has to learn and practise yoga for a long time and then approach the sūtras, no doubt taking help from commentaries and living teachers, if fortunately available, to understand the whole science of yoga as systematised and presented by Patañjali for getting guidance for development and perfection in yoga.

The word yoga as understood by Patañjali is defined hereafter in its different aspects in a number of subsequent sūtras, especially in the next two i.e. I:2-3.

The word 'anuśāsana' is made up from the main word 'śāsana', which has a general meaning of good organisation or arrangement. The prefix "anu" has a sense of 'following'. The whole word has nearly a meaning expressed by the word 'śāstra'. Probably instead of using this shorter word, which would have been more proper as per rules of sūtra construction, Patañjali has used the longer word to indicate that what he is presenting is no doubt a systematic exposition of a complete discipline of yoga, but that what is presenting is not completely new, but follows the old tradition as had come down through ages up to his time. In this way Patañjali has given us a hint that he is not the founder of the yoga system, as is very often believed to be popularly. There are clearcut indications in the body of the Sūtras itself that Patañjali has rather brought together in an orderly manner and in a very condensed form a lot of knowledge about the science of yoga and especially its practical aspect. This fact has been noted by a number of scholars both Indian and Foreign. In his compilation Patañjali has been very catholic. He does not seem rigidly bound to any particular dogma, even Vedic or Hinduistic. As has been opined by some scholars he has not hesitated to include ideas and elements belonging more to non-vedic school such as Jainism, Buddhism etc. At places it seems very probable that he has not been loath even to borrow words and phrases from such non-vedic sources. A prominent example of this is probably sūtra 1:33 'maitrikaruṇā'- etc., which is found exactly in the same form in Buddhist sources. However, it does not necessarily mean that Patañjali is the borrower of Buddhist or Jain ideas everywhere, where a parallelism is seen in his system and other such systems. The most plausible explanation seems to be that at this period, i.e. about 500 B.C. to 200 A.D. there was a very strong tide or movement emerging in India, when a number of thinkers and seekers of spiritual truth had arrived at closely similar way of thinking. Therefore, it is quite probable that none borrowed the ideas from the other systems, but all had taken these from the common pool of thought that was current and widely defuse at the time.

One fact seems to be quite certain that Patañjali is mainly a compiler and not a founder of the system of yoga, not even of the aṣṭāṅga system as expounded in the Yoga Sūtras. According to many texts some Hiraṇyagarbha is said to be the originator of yoga śāstra. Who is this Hiraṇyagarbha is a very uncertain thing. May be that there was some sage of this name, who first systematically expounded the science and practice of yoga. But it is also quite probable that there was not any real historical person of this name. The name Hiraṇyagarbha is also an epithet of the Almighty God and as is the popular and orthodox belief, the source of all knowledge is ultimately the Supreme Divinity. In this sense this Hiraṇyagarbha may mean this Supreme Entity. Anyway, there are quite good indications that there were Yoga Sūtras existent even prior to Patañjali's Yoga Sūtras. These are almost completely lost. It is quite probable that Patañjali might have used the main frame-work of this ancient Yoga-Sūtra text to compile his present work. Some of the existent sūtras might have been borrowed literally by Patañjali in his compilation. (see on this Kolhatkar 2nd ed., Śaka 1881, Bhumikā, p. 164).

SS. - **योगश्चित्तवृत्तिनिरोधः ।।१:२।।**

TL. - yogaścittavṛttinirodhaḥ - I:2

WM. - yoga = yoga;

citta = citta;

vṛtti = functional modification (of citta);

nirodha (ḥ) = bringing to complete cessation.

TR. - Yoga (is) bringing to complete cessation the functional modifications of citta.

CE. - This sūtra in a way defines the meaning of the word 'Yoga' as a practical method or means. The next 1:3 sūtra, in contrast, explains the meaning of yoga as the goal. The sūtra in a very broad manner tells what Patañjali thinks of yoga as a means for achieving the goal. The individual members of the practical path of Patañjali's yoga are described in the 2nd pāda, which is therefore, justly named Sādhana pāda i.e. pāda (Quarter section) of sādhana i.e. means or techniques. Particularly sūtra II: 29 and II: 1 give the enumeration of such means.

There is no exact equivalent in English and other Western languages for the word citta. Many English commentators have translated the word with the English word mind, but this is not precise and correct. Probably the Sanskṛt and yogic equivalent for mind is 'manas'. Patañjali definitely differentiates between 'citta' and 'manas' as can be seen from the sutras I:33 and 35. The idea that citta is not the same thing as mind has struck some former commentators also. Therefore, to make a distinction between the two, they have rendered citta by some such expression like 'mind-stuff' etc. But also this is not very satisfactory, particularly as it does not clarify the notion behind the word citta.

The word citta is formed from the verb root 'cit', which means to incite, to enlighten, to make aware etc. Adding the suffix 'ta' the word citta becomes a past participle adjective used as a noun. The literal meaning of 'citta' would thus be, 'that which is incited, enlightened, made conscious etc.' Citta according to Sāṃkhya viewpoint is a product of prakṛti. Prakṛti of its own self is 'jaḍa' i.e. unable to act or become conscious. The mere presence of puruṣa, in some mysterious way influences the prakṛti and leads it to act and enables it to become conscious. So from this basic meaning, we should understand the sphere of citta to be all that, where consciousness becomes manifested in the human organism. Viewed in this way the citta is active right from gross body level, where sensation of the sense-organs is present, right up to the mind, inclusive of its subconscious and unconscious levels, and even beyond mind to Supra-conscious level. Thus mind forms only a small fraction of the sphere of citta. However, the part of citta with which the common man is normally conversant is mind, more particularly that portion of mind which is active in wakeful consciousness. Further, in the beginning of yoga practice, when the sādhaka (aspirant) enters upon the inward going practices like dhāraṇā, dhyāna etc. the region from which he has to start is usually this conscious mind. Therefore, very often, at least in the beginning, the word citta would have to be equated approximately to the mind and even will have to be translated in such a case by the word mind.

The word vṛtti is derived from the verb root 'vṛt' which means 'to behave' and also 'to revolve in a circular motion'. With the suffix 'ti', indicative generally of a process or movement, the word vṛtti here would mean the behavioral mode of citta. The word is usually translated by most of the English commentators as modification. A better translation indicating this behavioral tendency of the citta would be functional modification. Vṛttis rise in citta one after another like the circular waves moving in the disturbed water and this similarity with the water waves is also often implied in the word vṛtti. In fact some commentators have used a simile of a disturbed water reservoir for the citta having successive vṛttis arising in it. So also the controlled and tranquillized citta is often compared with undisturbed water of a lake or a pond.

The word 'nirodha' has the verb root 'rudh'-to stop by obstruction, the prefix 'ni' may be looked upon as a short form of the word 'niḥśeṣa' meaning 'without remainder' i.e. total or complete etc'. Thus the word nirodha will mean stopping completely. As said above the verb 'rudh' has a sense of obstructing a process or movement, using an opposite force. But it may be emphasized here that the word nirodha here should not be understood in this sense. The stopping of the functional modifications (vṛttis) of citta is not to be brought about, at least in Patañjali's system, by any forcible means or method. The nirodha will be spontaneous, brought about automatically by the practice of all the aṣṭāṇgas (Eight limbs or members) of Patañjali's practical yoga system. In fact, every yoga should be and is a nonviolent smooth pacific process. Yoga is passively active - Patañjali's yoga method is particularly so. So we may understand by the word nirodha the coming to a cessation of the process of vṛtti-arousal in the citta, achieved through a pacific and smooth process.

SS. - तदा द्रष्टुःस्वरूपेऽवस्थानम् ।।१:३।।

TL. - tadā draṣṭūḥ svarūpe 'vasthānam - I:3.

WM. - tadā = at that time, then;

draṣṭṛ (uḥ) = of the draṣṭā i.e. seer;

sva	=	one's own;
rūpe	=	(in) the form;
avasthānā(m)	=	re-establishment.

TR. - Then the seer will be re-established in its own form.

CE. - This sutra explains the meaning of 'yoga' according to Patañjali, as the objective or end. The word 'tadā' = then, thus means, 'at the time the vṛttis of citta are brought to a complete stand still'. What is achieved in this condition is return back of the seer principle in its original pristine (śuddha) state.

It is generally believed that Patañjali's yoga is closely allied to the Sāṃkhya Darśana. Many scholars even are of the opinion that Patañjali's Yoga Darśana takes its stand on the Saṃkhya, so far so, that Sāṃkhya and Yoga (which usually means Patañjali's Yoga Darśana or Philosophy) are sister philosophies and are almost similar in their metaphysical and philosophical standpoints. It is also believed that Patañjali has accepted all the principles or "tattvas" of Sāṃkhya completely, though a clear evidence for this cannot be obtained from the yoga sūtras directly. Probable close relationship with Sāṃkhya may be postulated from the sutras II:17 to 23. The main difference from Sāṃkhya is an explicit inclusion of a new principle-Īśvara. It is on account of this that very often yoga i.e. Patañjali's Yoga Darśana is referred to as 'seśvara Sāṃkhya'. Another element which is different in Patañjali's Yoga from Sāṃkhya is the notion of citta, which is absent in traditional Sāṃkhya.

Sāṃkhya has postulated two eternal and primordial elements puruṣa and prakṛti. Prakṛti is usually translated in the English commentaries as matter, but prakṛti is not very precisely mere matter. Matter, of its own self, is dead and therefore non-acting, while prakṛti, as its name indicates (pra = prakarṣeṇa i.e.. intensely, kṛti = action) is potentially able to act, in fact all activity is an attribute of prakṛti from amongst the two primordial principles. However, it can do so only in the presence of puruṣa. The word "Puruṣa" has a usual meaning in common language as a 'male person' or 'individual'. But the Sāṃkhya term puruṣa should not be understood in this sense of person. It is an elementary primordial principle, which is said to be immutable under any circumstance. This, therefore, automatically means that it will not be able to act or do anything of itself. It is even described as 'akartā'; i.e. no doer; 'heturahita' = having no desire or will (to do anything). The action and, therefore, change is an attribute only of prakṛti. But prakṛti is jaḍa i.e. inert. It can act by the mere presence of puruṣa, though the puruṣa remains totally unaffected and uninfluenced in the happening. The activation of prakṛti caused by the mere presence of puruṣa is technically called 'puruṣa-prakṛti-saṃyoga' or 'saṃyoga' for short. The word 'saṃyoga' usually means joining, union, coupling etc. But this saṃyoga is a very mysterious and mystical phenomenon, very difficult to explain and understand. However only on account of this saṃyoga the prakṛti is excited and begins to evolve and the whole phenomenal world whether material or psychical, manifested or unmanifested is an evolution of prakṛti. It should be again emphasized that in this saṃyoga the puruṣa and prakṛti still remain completely unrelated and independent. Anyway puruṣa at least is not at all 'involved' in this evolution and remains unaffected and unchanged throughout. In one way the ultimate achievement after completion of yogic process is the undoing or the end of this saṃyoga, which had really never taken place factually. The direct and actual realization of this purity of puruṣa principle in its pristine state is the aim of yoga. Thus yoga is realization of the total separateness of the primordial principles-puruṣa and prakṛti, and in this way yoga is not joining together but separating or at least realization of the complete separateness of these two primordial entities. Strangely, in this sense yoga is really viyoga-separation, disunion.

As said above puruṣa, by its nature, cannot do anything. Therefore, it cannot perceive either and so it would be not precisely correct to call it a perceiver or seer i.e. draṣṭā. The perceiving entity is in truth the citta and therefore the real draṣṭā is citta and it should be understood so. But citta is an evolute of prakṛti and therefore it cannot perceive of its own accord. It is due to presence of puruṣa that the citta is incited or enlightened and becomes able to perceive and to act in other ways. In this sense puruṣa is the ultimate source from where citta gets its potentiality to become conscious and thus to perceive. Understood in this way the ultimate seer-principle or potentiality is puruṣa. In the present sutra the word draṣṭā is used in this sense and stands for puruṣa, though it must be again pointed out that this epithet is not precisely correct and strictly should not be applied to puruṣa. Briefly we can say that the word draṣṭā is indicative of a wrong identification of puruṣa, the ultimate cause of the consciousness potentiality, with citta, the actual conscious perceiving entity. 'svarūpe' literally means in one's own form. Here it should be understood as in its unsullied, pristine, primordial state or condition.

SS. - वृत्तिसारूप्यमितरत्र ।।१:४।।

TL. - vṛttisārūpyamitaratra - I:4.

WM. - vṛtti = functional modification (of citta);

sārupya(m) = literally, same-formness i.e. identification;

itaratra = elsewhere, at other occasions or times.

TR. - At other times (than the state of svarupāvasthā of the draṣṭā) there is total identification with the vṛtti (that may be present in the citta at that particular time).

CE. - This sūtra tells the state in which the common man thinks that the draṣṭā principle in him, i.e. in fact the puruṣa-tattva in the man, is existing. As explained above under sūtra 1:3, the draṣṭā i.e. puruṣa really is forever immutable. Therefore, in truth, he can not undergo the changes or modifications of vṛtti. These modifications are taking place in citta, but as already explained, there is a false identification of puruṣa with citta, an evolute of prakṛti. A common man is not really aware of puruṣa and has no clear concept of the complete separateness of puruṣa and prakṛti, especially in its evolute in the form of citta. This clear realization is the ultimate goal and achievement of Patañjali's yoga, and therefore, only the yogī, who has reached this perfection can only realise this thing. Till then whatever happens to citta is misconceived as happening to the back-ground of consciousness of citta i.e. puruṣa.

The word 'sārūpya' is an abstract noun derived from the adjective 'sarūpa' (sa = it, the same, rūpa = form i.e. state or condition). Thus sarūpa means of the same form or state. The suffix 'ya' along with the conversion of 'sa' to 'sā', as per rules of Sanskṛt grammar gives us the abstract noun showing the state. Thus 'sārūpya' means having the same form or state, or better still, identification.

SS. - **वृत्तयः पञ्चतय्यः क्लिष्टाक्लिष्टाः ।।१:५।।**

TL. - vṛttayaḥ pañcatayyaḥ kliṣṭākliṣṭāḥ - I:5.

WM. -

vṛttayaḥ	=	plural of vṛtti, therefore vṛttis (functional modifications of citta);
pañcatayyaḥ	=	five kinds or types;
kliṣṭa	=	involving kleśas (afflictions); difficult to remove;
akliṣṭāḥ	=	not involving kleśas, not difficult to remove.

TR. - vṛttis (the functional modifications) of citta are of five types, some of them are difficult to remove, while others are easily removable.

CE. - Vṛttis are classified by Patañjali into five types, which are enumerated in the next (I.6) sūtra. It may be felt that this typification is quite inadequate, as occasion may arise, when there comes a question whether a particular vṛtti could be satisfactorily relegated to any one of these five types. A very precise and clearcut classification, as is usually expected in a scientific classification, is not the objective of Patañjali here.

Patañjali's sūtras are meant more for practising yoga, than presenting yoga merely as a theoretical science, the application of it becoming of secondary importance. The main purpose of this practical path is to do away with these vṛttis, by bringing their functional aspect to a cessation. For this objective the precise classification has little value, because whatever be the type of a particular vṛtti, ultimately the aim is to stop its function. Therefore a rough classification is quite enough for Patañjali to reach this practical end. Even sometimes it may be felt difficult to decide in which of these five types depending on the predominant nature of that vṛtti, even though it may have some aspect related to another type. If on account of difficulty in deciding the exact type of the vṛtti, a sādhaka assigns it to some class or some type erroneously, it would not be very harmful from the practical point, as ultimately whatever the type of vṛtti, it is to be done away with.

However, to understand broadly the nature of these vṛttis, a classification of them must have seemed desirable to Patañjali. But as said above for his purpose, merely to help the sādhaka to understand the nature of vṛttis, this classification need not have to be very elaborate and precise. At the same time the number of types should be large enough to make it possible to classify any vṛtti in one or other of these types. Such a suitable number seems to be near about five. Further Patañjali seems to have a liking for the number five in the same way as that of Sāmkḥya and so he might have classified the vṛttis into five types.

The word 'kliṣṭa' is the past participle adjective of the verb root 'kliś'- to irritate, tease, give pain etc. The noun 'kleśa' (see sūtra II:3) is also derived from the same root. These kleśas are the primordial and ultimate cause of pain and misery. The word 'kliṣṭa' would therefore mean painful or misery-causing, on account of the association with one or more of the kleśas. As will be clear from the discussion about the nature of the kleśas (see under sūtras II:3-12), they are never completely done away with. Consequently the vṛttis which will be associated more closely with kleśas will be so much more difficult to do away with. In this way the kliṣṭa vṛttis, which are associated with kleśas, are also difficult to remove.

Though the vṛttis have been broadly said to be kliṣṭa and akliṣṭa, these terms should be taken as relative. In fact there is no vṛtti which is totally akliṣṭa i.e. completely disassociated with kleśas. Every vṛtti will have at least some trace of kleśas associated with it, however subtle it may be. The word akliṣṭa therefore should be understood in this sense, 'involving relatively very little of kleśas' and not as having complete absence of all kleśas. So kliṣṭa means very intensely affected by kleśas and akliṣṭa means affected little with kleśas.

As said above, depending on the intensity of the kleśas in the particular vṛtti, it may be more difficult to remove it.

SS. - **प्रमाणविपर्ययविकल्पनिद्रास्मृतयः ।।१:६।।**

TL. - pramāṇaviparyayavikalpanidrāsmṛtayaḥ - I:6.

WM. - pramāṇa = true and therefore acceptable data;
viparyaya = wrong or false knowledge;

vikalpa = Imagination, fantasy;

nidrā = (sound dreamless)sleep;

smṛtayaḥ = plural of 'smṛti' which means memory or recollection; plural of smṛti is used not because there are many smṛtis, but because the whole is a compound word, enumerating many things and should be in plural form.

TR. - (These five types are) knowledge based on true and acceptable data i.e. right knowledge, false knowledge, imagination, dreamless sleep and memory.

CE. - The first vṛtti in this sūtra is denoted by the word 'pramāṇa', which means true fact or data accepted as true. This fact or data is not the vṛtti, because these are outside of citta and are presented to the citta. The vrtti is the knowledge, which arises in the citta based on that fact or data. Therefore the full name of the first vṛtti should be 'pramāṇajñāna-vṛtti' and the word 'pramāṇa' should be understood in this sense and therefore is interpreted as right or correct knowledge (agreeing with the actuality). The three varieties of pramāṇas mentioned in the next (i.e. I:7) sūtra are also indicating facts or data, which are valid and acceptable to this Darśana. From this Patañjali even understands the basic meaning of pramāṇa as true fact or data, but seems to have used the same word, probably for the sake of brevity, also for the knowledge (which is a vṛtti) arising out of it in the citta.

SS. - प्रत्यक्षानुमानागमाः प्रमाणानि ।।१:७।।

TL. - pratyakṣānumānāgamāḥ pramāṇāni - I:7.

WM. -
pratyakṣa = literally, presented to the eye (prati = before + akṣa = eye i.e. any sense organ) i.e. senses, usually rendered as 'direct' (directly perceived);
anumāna = inference;
āgama (aḥ) = authentic and reliable testimony (plural);
pramāṇāni = plural of pramāṇa.

TR. - Direct perception through senses, inference and reliable testimony are (three) pramāṇas (acceptable facts or authentic data, on which right knowledge is based).

CE. - The word 'pratyakṣa' is usually understood as direct perception. But, the commonly so called direct perception is in fact indirect, because, the perceiver is the citta or mind (manas), which perceives through one or more of the senses. In truth the common man never perceives directly. It is only advanced yogis, who have the ability to have the knowledge really directly i.e. without the intermediacy of the senses. This direct knowledge is therefore distinguished by the term 'yogipratyakṣa' or 'yogapratyakṣa'.

The word 'pratyakṣa' is made up from 'prati' opposite or presented before + 'akṣa'. = eye. Thus, literally, it means presented before the eye (i.e. a sense organ). Eye, which is the most dominant of the five senses, is often used to indicate senses in general. Thus, here 'pratyakṣa' means perceived through (one or more) senses.

Anumāna (anu-prefix meaning 'following + māna-something measured i.e. something known). Thus 'anumāna' means an inference or a deduction based on some previous knowledge.

Āgama means that which has come to us i.e. which has been handed down to us traditionally. It is presumed that this traditionally handed down knowledge is authentic and reliable, because the ancient ones (ancestors = 'āptas') would not propound or tell what they do not know to be true. The word āgama is therefore also called 'āpta vākya' = sentence or statement of an ancestral relative. Another synonym used is 'śabda' = authentic word.

All these three varieties of pramāṇa are, in one way or other, based ultimately on direct contact or perception with the object or phenomena about which the knowledge is gained. Inference is based firstly on some observation made, and secondly, the deduction about the thing or phenomena inferred is also possible, because at some previous time that thing or phenomena was directly perceived by some person. The testimony obtained from a reliable source is also supposed to be based on some direct observation of that thing or phenomena, by the reliable person.

SS. - **विपर्ययो मिथ्याज्ञानमतद्रूपप्रतिष्ठम् ।।१:८।।**

TL. - viparyayo mithyājñanamatadrūpapratiṣṭham - I:8.

WM. - viparyayaḥ ($\rightarrow$0) = viparyaya, wrong or false knowledge;

mithyā	=	false;
jñānam	=	knowledge;
atadrūpa	=	not (corresponding to) its form (actuality, actual state);
pratiṣṭham	=	based on.

TR. - Viparyaya is based on false understanding or knowledge, not corresponding to the actuality of that (thing or phenomena).

CE. - The compound word 'atadrūpa' is made up of 'a' (not) + 'tat' (its)+ 'rūpa' (form) and would literally mean 'not corresponding to its form'. But the word 'form' should not be understood as the shape, but means here its nature or actual condition. 'It' stands for the object or phenomenon perceived.

Viparyaya or wrong knowledge is also derived through the same three means as that for pramāṇa-jñāna viz. pratyakṣa, anumāna and āgama.

The direct perception can be wrongly interpreted, as in the usual traditional example of viparyaya, viz. mistaking a rope for a snake. Here the object, rope, is actually seen by the eyes, but is interpreted as a snake on account of a great similarity in the form of the rope with that of the snake. Thus the direct perception can give a false understanding or knowledge. In the same way an inference can also lead to a wrong conclusion, thus to a false knowledge. Testimony also can lead to false knowledge, if the source of testimony, which is assumed to be reliable, may itself be wrong or false.

SS. - शब्दज्ञानानुपाती वस्तुशून्यो विकल्प ।।१:९।।

TL. - śabdajñānanupātī vastuśūnyo vikalpaḥ - I:9.

WM. -
śabda = word;
jñāna = knowledge;
anupātī = following to, dependent upon, based on;
vastu = thing (actuality), substance;
śūnya (ḥ->o) = devoid of;
vikalpa (ḥ) = imagination.

TR. - Vikalpa (imagination) is based on (mere) wordy knowledge or understanding (and is) devoid of actual substance.

CE. - The usual traditional examples of vikalpa are śaśaśṛṅga' (hare's horn), 'vandhyā-putra' (son of a barren woman). These, particularly the latter, are examples of things which can not exist anywhere anytime, but one can imagine them and at least use these expressions in speech.

The word vandhyā-putra is a self contradictory term. If a woman begets a son, she can not be called a vandhyā or barren woman. Thus this is an impossibility, which, however, is expressed in words and can be imagined. Vikalpas are thus imaginatory, ideas, which can never occur in actuality.

SS. - अभावप्रत्ययालम्बनावृत्तिर्निद्रा ।।१:१०।।

TL. - abhāvapratyayālambanāvṛttirnidrā - I:10.

WM. -
abhāva = (a = (non + bhāva = presence)
= absence;
pratyaya = experience or content of the citta (at a particular moment);

ālambanā	=	feminine of ālambana, which means a support for hanging or suspending a thing from e.g. a peg. The word ālambanā here can be rendered as having the support i.e. suppported or based on;
vṛtti	=	functional modification of citta;
nidrā	=	(sound and dreamless) sleep.

TR. - The vṛtti based on the experience of (total) absence (of any content in the citta) is nidrā (sound dreamless sleep).

OR

The vṛtti based on the (total) absence of experience is nidrā (sound dreamless sleep).

CE. - The word 'abhāvapratyayālambanā' is a compound word made up of three main words-abhāva + pratyaya + ālambanā. The whole word is an adjective of the substantive 'vṛtti'. Ālambanā-means supported or based on. The remaining part of the compound word viz. 'abhāvapratyaya' can be rendered either as pratyaya (experience) of abhāva (total absence of everything or as abhāva (total absence) of pratyaya (experience). In both these renderings the general sense of the sūtra remains practically the same i.e. in nidrā there is no content in the citta.

Some commentators have raised a question as to the propriety of considering nidrā as a vṛtti. Recently, Dr. K.S. Joshi (see Y.M vol. XIX, No. 1, page 91-95) has put forth this very point of doubt very explicitly. His argument is based on two points :-

1. That the vṛtti is a modification of citta and not its state, because the states of citta, as is well known are mūḍhatā, kṣiptatā, vikṣiptatā, ekāgratā and niruddhatā.

2. That nidrā has been defined as a vṛtti where there is abhāvapratyaya i.e. experience of (total) absence. But the total absence of everything, according to him, can not be an object of experience. The experience of the absence of a particular thing can be experienced in relation to the presence of other things. He argues that this experience of total absence is not in fact an actual experience. Rather it is an inference derived from something that was experienced before the citta entered into nidrā and the something that is experienced after coming out of nidrā. He, therefore, argues that the total absence (of everything) is merely inferred by comparing and correlating the condition of citta in nidrā with these two experiences, but the total absence is not directly experienced and can not fundamentally be a thing of experience.

Now, cittavṛtti, a modification of citta involves a change of state. It is usually not called a state, because compared to the so-called 'states' of citta, vṛtti is relatively transitory. The 'State' of citta namely mūḍhatā etc. endures for a long time. Even to transform a mūḍha to a kṣipta or a kṣipta to vikṣipta is not easy, leave aside of changing such person into ekāgra or niruddha. These natural states of the citta of an individual very often persist for the whole life.

On the other hand the citta goes from one vṛtti to another, even within an instant. But when a different vṛtti has come into the citta, the citta will have to undergo a change of state, which, no doubt, is very temporary as said above. Thus a modification of citta involves certainly a change of state though for a very short time. In nidrā also the citta must be going into such a relatively transitory change of state, since citta is not destroyed in nidrā. Even if it is argued that the postulation of condition of the state of citta in nidrā is merely deduced by inferences, it can not be denied that the citta was in some modified state and which was neither one of the remaining four vṛttis or modifications viz. pramāṇa, viparyaya etc. Therefore, viewed in this way, there is nothing wrong in calling nidrā a vṛtti.

The second argument, that the pratyaya (experience) of abhāva (total absence) is inferential and not an actual experience, would lose its weight completely if the compound word 'abhāvapratyaya' is broken up as 'pratyayasya abhāvaḥ' i.e. absence of experience. In this rendering the question whether the condition of citta in nidrā is an experience or not, does not remain valid. In this way also it is valid to accept nidrā as a vṛtti. In fact it appears that Patañjali gives more stress on the word 'abhāva' = the absence, than on 'pratyaya' = the experience.

It is worth noting that only in this sūtra out of I;7 to I:11, those describing the individual types of vṛtti, Patañjali mentions the word vṛtti, thus emphatically pressing the point that nidrā is unquestionably a vṛtti, at least according to his conception of the vṛtti. Probably Patañjali had a fore-inkling that such doubts about nidrā being a vṛtti might arise in the minds of some and that is why he might have emphatically repeated this word in only this doubt-creating sūtra of vṛttis.

Nidrā has been rendered here as 'sound dreamless sleep' from the general sense of the sūtra. In dreamy sleep i.e. dreams, there is no total absence of experience. In dream something is experienced and the vṛtti of the citta may be usually vikalpa or rarely viparyaya or even pramaṇa depending on the nature of the thing or phenomena being experienced in the dream.

There is a very close similarity between the state of nidrā (sound dreamless sleep) and that of samādhi. Even some writers have pointed out that the two states are very similar. This may be true only apparently. The physiological and psychological parameters in many cases may show complete identity in these two states. It is quite possible that the currently available methods of testing a person physiologically and psychologically may give the same kind of results in the investigation of these two states. It-is probably for this reason that the present methods of psycho-physiological testing are unable to throw much light on the various samādhis or their stages.

However, the two states are in some respect poles apart. Nidrā is a tāmasika state, while samādhi is sāttvika. In fact the highest stage of samādhi must be a triguṇātīta state i.e. a state beyond all the three guṇas and therefore, not even to be called sāttvika in strict sense. After a sound sleep a man may be physically refreshed and even psychologically somewhat in a more than usual peaceful state. But from the spiritual aspect sleep has not got any real value. There is no enlightenment nor any transformation of personality in nidrā. In contract, samādhi, though devoid of anything, which may be called an experience in the usual sense, changes the personality of the individual in a most marked manner. Further, the latter leads to enlightenment, which is often called 'Knowledge' which is of quite a different category than anything which we call knowledge about the phenomenal world. This so-called 'Knowledge' is a knowledge or an actual experience of 'The Reality', which at culmination is an experience of the Ultimate Reality, There is no such happening in nidrā. In fact, in nidrā usually there is no gain of even phenomenal knowledge, leave aside the 'Knowledge of Reality'.

As per the wording of the sūtra, nidrā is a transitory state of citta (vṛtti) which is devoid of any content, whatever way we break up the compound word 'abhāvapratyaya'. Since in dream there is some content in the citta, this nidrā of the sūtra must be a dreamless and therefore sound sleep. Recent E.E.G. investigations of the sleep state have indicated that even what is usually called a sound i.e. dreamless sleep is really not continuously so. It has been found that even in this so called sound sleep the person has alternately a dream state and a dreamless state, both lasting for very short intervals. Strictly speaking, therefore, the description of nidrā, as given in this sūtra, could be applicable only to these short intervals of dreamless sleep state. However, this knowledge was not available in the times when Patañjali compiled these Yogasūtras. This word nidrā, therefore, was used for the sleep state usually called 'sound', where there might be dreams, but whose impression or memory is not left after awakening from that sleep. Usually the epithet 'sound' is applied to such a sleep, where after-effect or memory of having dreams is not retained. So, though in fact, the state meant by nidrā by Patañjali is a state in which there are dreams, since no after-impression of these is left on the citta, it is as good as a dreamless sleep from the effect point of view. In the present translation of the sūtra the nidrā state or vṛtti has been explained as dreamless sound sleep, this explanation being placed within parenthesis to bring the sense given by 'abhāvapratyaya'.

SS. - **अनुभूतविषयासंप्रमोषः स्मृतिः ।।१:११।।**

TL. - anubhūtaviṣayāsaṃpramoṣaḥ smṛtiḥ - I:11.

WM. -

anubhūta	=	experienced;
viṣaya	=	subject or thing;
asaṃpramoṣaḥ	=	(a - Not+sam - completely + pra- thoroughly + moṣa(ḥ) - literally robbing i.e. deprivation, taking away). No total deprivation;
smṛti (ḥ)	=	memory.

TR. - Smṛti (memory) (is) (the vṛtti on account of which the citta) (does not) undergo a complete deprivation of an experienced subject (thing or incident or happening).

CE. - The word 'asaṃpramoṣaḥ' is derived from the verb root muṣ to rob or steal. From this root is formed the noun moṣa (ḥ) = stealing, robbing etc. To this noun the three prefixes, a -not, sam -totally and pra-thoroughly, have been joined, which therefore give the word asaṃpramosaḥ, which would mean 'not being robbed completely and thoroughly'. The idea seems to be that the citta has a tendency to retain anything.experienced for a very long time, but the time is the robber, which is trying to rob or deprive the citta of this possession. When in this struggle the robber, the time, is not powerful enough to deprive the citta completely and thoroughly of its possession of the experience of the thing, it is an 'asaṃpramoṣaḥ'- not complete and thorough deprivation of that experience. That is, the thing or phenomena (the subject) is not completely lost and is retained, at least partly, by the citta. Thus in this strange way the functioning of the memory is defined by this sūtra. As is evident, even a partial retention of the past experience which may not correspond in every detail to the original experience is a smṛti. As is the common experience, very rarely the memory of an incident or thing is precisely correct in every detail to the actual incident or thing.

SS. - **अभ्यासवैराग्याभ्यां तन्निरोधः ।।१:१२।।**

TL. - abhyāsavairāgyābhyāṃ tannirodhaḥ - I:12.

WM. - abhyāsa = practice, repetition;
vairāgya = disattachment, disinterestedness;
bhyām = through the two;
tat(→n) = (of) that or its;
nirodha(ḥ) = complete cessation.

TR. - The nirodha (complete cessation) of that (vṛtti) (is achieved) through the two (viz.), practice and disattachment.

CE. - Abhyāsa and vairāgya are discussed in the next four sūtras (I:13 to 16).

SS. - **तत्र स्थितौ यत्नोऽभ्यासः ।।१:१३।।**

TL. - tatra sthitau yatno'bhyāsaḥ - I:13

WM. -

tatra	=	in that, in those, out of those;
sthitau	=	in the steady state or stage;
yatna(ḥ→o)	=	effort;
abhyāsa (ḥ)	=	practice,

TR. - The effort to get steadiness in the (particular) state (or stage) is abhyāsa (practice).

CE. - Out of the two means abhyāsa and vairāgya, abhyāsa is explained in this sūtra This effort, which will be of a nature of repetition of a particular stage or state to get stabilised in that state is called abhyāsa and therefore, it is a repeated practice of a particular technique or stage of Yoga. The stage or technique has not been specified. Therefore, the statement is applicable to all stages or techniques of yoga, obviously here these stages or techniques are to be understood in the sense of the eight angas or members of the eight-fold practical system recommended by Patañjali. These particular members are enumerated in II:29.

Some commentators (see for example Kolhatkar) have mentioned the practice of a particular technique as abhyāsa. Very often these techniques do not seem to have been mentioned explicitly by Patañjali. It is, therefore, questionable whether their interpretation is valid according to Patañjali's view.

SS. - स तु दीर्घकालनैरन्तर्यसत्कारासेवितो दृढभूमिः ।।१:१४।।

TL. - sa tu dīrghakālanairantaryasatkārāsevito dṛḍhabhū-miḥ - I:14.

WM. -

sa	=	that, (abhyāsa);
tu	=	even;
dīrgha	=	long;
kāla	=	time duration;
nairantarya	=	uninterruptedness;
satkāra	=	welcoming receptive attitude;
āsevita (ḥ->o)	=	utilized, employed, here used in practice;
dṛḍha	=	firm (ly);
bhūmi (ḥ)	=	ground (ed).

TR. - Even that practice (becomes) firmly grounded when (adopted) (carried on) for a long duration of time, with uninterruptedness and with a welcoming receptive attitude.

CE. - The 'dīrghatva' (length) of 'kāla' (time duration) is not specified in any precise unit. But this length can be anything extending into years or even lives, because the final attainment and perfection in yoga is not an easy matter and in fact according to Indian view point, an affair not restricted to one life only, but to a number of successive lives devoted progressively for the development and achievement of perfection in yoga. Anyway by the term 'dīrghakāla' Patañjali has indicated the need of very determined patientness. If a sādhaka would have expectation to reach perfection very hurriedly in a short time, it would lead to frustration, which will be very detrimental to his progress. The disappointment of not reaching a particular stage of development, if very great, may lead the sādhaka to give up the effort completely. To avoid this, the sādhaka should prepare his mind to continue the practice endlessly until a desired stage is reached. If from the beginning he understands this and has a firm determination to reach the goal, no matter what time is required for this, then the eventuality of frustration and stopping of effort will be avoided.

Uninterruptedness should be understood in the sense of regularity. It is obvious that no sādhaka, how-so-ever keen and sincere he may be, will be able to practice continuously all the twentyfour hours without a break for his common needs of life. What is therefore meant is, he should practise regularly everyday for whatever time according to his own experience or as the teacher instructs. It is essentially necessary for a satisfactory progress, without having a gap of even one-day. Even this is very difficult to have in practical life. So it should be understood that he must try to have as little interruption in the daily regularity as possible. Quite obviously the greater the sincerity and keenness, lesser will be occasions of break.

The word nairantarya as explained above means merely regularity. But every yoga sādhaka comes to know from experience that punctuality has also a great importance. May be on account of habituation or conditioning, one comes to find that any practice of any aṅga of yoga becomes easy, comfortable and smooth, if one practises it at a time at which he is usually habituated to do it. On the other hand, the same practice becomes rather difficult and uncomfortable, if on some day it is to be performed at some time other than the usual. Therefore, though not explicitly mentioned or signified as such by the word nairantarya, punctuality should be observed as far as practicable and in this sense nairantarya should be interpreted as "with regularity and punctuality". Incidentally that the observance of punctuality should not be understood as a very rigid, minute to minute punctuality, because such rigidness very often creates tension, if the person, for some unavoidable reason, cannot abide with such rigid punctuality. One should not, in this respect, become a slave to the watch. A general and approximate maintenance of the same time for practice is what is desirable.

In any effort, for achieving perfection in anything, a welcoming receptive attitude is a must. If this is absent there will be laxity of purpose and lack of determination. This will lead to mediocre effort only. That is why the attitude of satkāra is very important for success in every undertaking. This is still more true in yoga. In fact all the three requirements noted in this sūtra are essential for gaining mastery in any field. They are therefore also very important for achieving success in yoga.

SS. - **दृष्टानुश्रविकविषयवितृष्णस्य वशीकारसंज्ञा वैराग्यम् ।।१:१५।।**

TL. - dṛṣṭānuśravikaviṣayavitṛṣṇasya
vaśīkārasaṃjñā vairāgyam - I:15.

WM. -

dṛṣṭa	=	seen;
anuśravika	=	heard through some person or other source;
viṣaya	=	subject or object;
vitṛṣṇa (sya)	=	(of) the thirstless or desireless;
vaśīkāra	=	perfect subjugation or mastery;
saṃjñā	=	1. name or designation; 2. awareness;

vairāgyam = vairāgya, non-attachment, disinterestedness.

TR. - 1. The vairāgya (disattachment) of one (who is) disinterested in all subjects (or objects) seen (or) heard through hearsay, is named vaśīkāra.

OR

2. The vairāgya is that in which there is awareness of having got over (all) the desires for (all) the subjects (or objects) seen (or) heard through hearsay.

CE. - Patañjali does not explain the term vairāgya as such. The sūtra describes, in fact, a very advanced stage of vairāgya. The reasons may be that the word is self-explanatory. Vairāgya is an abstract noun formed from vi (→vai) without, devoid of, etc. + rāga - (from-raj = to like, to attract) fondness or attachment, love liking + ya = a suffix indicative of state or condition = ness. Thus the meaning of the word vairāgya directly becomes obvious as non-attachment.

A mediocre vairāgya is of not much significance for a yogī and yoga. Therefore, Patañjali does not give much importance to such a vairāgya. Only a highly developed vairāgya is of any meaningfulness from this point to Patañjali. That is why he describes only this advanced stage.

The term saṃjñā has two distinct meanings as indicated. If saṃjñā is interpreted as a designation, this occurs in an enumeration of series of four stages of developmet of vairāgya: 1. yatamāna (saṃjnā or saṃjñaka), 2. vyatireka 3. ekendriya, 4. vaśīkāra..

These four terms are somewhat self-explanatory. 1. yata = effort + māna = one who has, one possessing. This is the very first stage in the development of vairāgya. For developing vairāgya the person must understand the importance and need (for yoga or spiritual development) of developing this trait. That is the desire to develop disattachment for objects and things must first awaken in the person. Then he will begin to strive for developing this attitude. As soon as he begins to try to develop this attitude of disattachment, he is in a state of yatamāna i.e. one who is endeavouring.

When he begins the endeavour, gradually the attitude of disattachment goes on growing. It is a common experience that the liking or attachment of a person for different things is variable in its force. Therefore, he will be easily able to give up some things, but to give up some other things, for which the attachment is deeper, will be difficult for him. In this second stage of vairāgya, therefore, the person has lost attachment or desires for certain things, yet is not able to do the same for other things. This stage is vyatireka, which means partial or fractional exclusion.

The objects or things are experienced and enjoyed through senses. The enjoyment leads to attachment. In the third stage the person has mastered all the (four) senses except one. The enjoyment of things through these four senses is lost. But he still has pleasure in things obtained by means of one of the senses. Which particular sense will be the last, and therefore the most difficult, to subjugate varies from person to person depending on his nature. For example one person may find it most difficult to lose the enjoyment of taste, but for another person the enjoyment for visual objects or auditory objects may be the most difficult. Thus the third stage of development of vairāgya is named ekendriya, indicating that only one sense is active and is yet to be subdued.

The last and fourth state of this series of development of vairāgya is vaśīkāra, which means having perfect mastery or complete subjugation of all the desires, which are to be enjoyed through various senses. This last stage of vairāgya is therefore, one, where the yogī has mastered all the five jñānendriyas to such an extent that he derives no pleasure through the objects or subjects either seen i.e. present before him for enjoyment or even those about which he has learnt through hearsay. Since Patañjali mentions only this last stage, probably according to him this is the stage of vairāgya which is of any significance for the development in yoga. The first three stages are no doubt to be gone through by every sādhaka and even when they are very advanced in such development of vairāgya, perhaps it carries no importance from the point of yoga progress to a satisfactory degree.

If the word saṃjñā is interpreted as awareness, the sūtra is indicating only the stage where the yogī has got confidence that he has subjugated all the sense organs to such an extent that they give no pleasure of enjoyment with the respective objects enjoyable through these senses and thus the yogī has lost all desires for all sensuous objects. Again, this is the purposeful stage for the progress in yoga as in Patañjali's presentation.

The word 'dṛṣta' (seen) includes all the manifest things of the world which are available for enjoyment of the yogī.

Anuśravika includes all such things e.g. heaven etc., which can not be seen, but which may be supposed to exist, if one believes what is stated about their existence by others.

SS. - **तत्परं पुरूषख्यातेर्गुणवैतृष्ण्यम् ।।१:१६।।**

TL. - tatparaṃ puruṣakhyātergunavaitṛṣṇyam - I:16.

WM. -

tat	=	that;
paraṃ	=	highest, maximum.
puruṣa	=	puruṣa principle;
khyāti (→eḥ→er)	=	(in) knowing, realization;
guṇa	=	triguṇas, the primordial component of prakṛti - viz. sattva, rajas, tamas;
vaitṛṣṇyam	=	thirstlessness, desirelessness.

TR. - That (becomes) highest in the realization of puruṣa (principle, when there is) complete desirelessness for the (tri) guṇas.

CE. - The highest state of vairāgya is the one where desirelessness is established in the yogī even for the three guṇas i.e. primordial aspects of prakṛti. In the vaśīkāra saṃjñā vairāgya, even though the yogī has subjugated all the indriyās, the possibility of resurgence of attachment to the sensuous objects is not completely abolished, because the senses are very dominant and a little looseness on the part of the yogī may lead to a situation where the desires for enjoyment of these sensuous objects may raise their heads again. This is what very often happens. A yogī, who has once developed desirelessness for all sensuous objects, may begin to feel that as now those objects are not giving him any pleasure, there may not be any harm if he uses them in a completely disinterested and therefore disattched manner. However, gradually the disinterestedness diminishes by continuous use of these objects and the yogī begins slowly to take pleasure in the enjoyment of these objects. Thus the attachment to them comes back again and the vairāgya disappears. Innumerable instances of such happening can be seen in actual life. Probably to emphasize this fact many stories of this nature have been narrated in Paurāṇika literature.

The perfection of vairāgya is achieved, as per the sūtra, when realisation of puruṣa-principle (in its pristine primordial nature) is established. This is as good as saying that this highest vairāgya is achieved only when the ultimate objective of yoga viz. realisation of puruṣa-principle i.e. kaivalya is achieved. In other words Guṇavaitṛṣṇya vairāgya may be looked at as a synonym for the summum bonum of Patañjali's yoga path or kaivalya. As long as the individual (yogī) has body, and citta, there is some linkage (saṃyoga) of the puruṣa-principle in the individual with prakṛti, however subtle it may be, since body and citta both are products of prakṛti. Thus it seems that this highest stage of vairāgya viz. Guṇavaitṛṣṇya is not achievable in life. The question may arise in the mind, what is then the purpose and sense in mentioning this vairāgya which is impossible to achieve in life ?

The only purpose of this sūtra seems to be to caution a yoga sādhaka or yogī to be always on the alert and never become loose in his effort to develop further and further, or at least maintain the level of the vairāgya achieved viz. Vaśīkāra. If he is a little careless and begins to make use of the sensuous object of enjoyment he may develop attachment for them as said above. Therefore he should take care that this does not happen. In fact, he should not be smugly satisfied with the development of vairāgya to the highest stage possible for him, but he should scrupulously avoid to make use of the worldly objects to the utmost, so that the possibility of attachment to the objects does not at all arise again. In other words even after vairāgya is developed to a high degree, the yama of aparigraha (II:30) should be practiced very sincerely and scrupulously.

To summarize the emphasis on vairāgya placed by Patañjali in these two sūtras, it seems that, since Patañjali does not discuss vairāgya in general nor directly gives any indication for the endeavours to be made to develop this quality, the very high development of vairāgya is only of any significance according to him for real development in yoga. Secondly even when a very high state of vairāgya like Vaśīkāra has been developed, the yogī should not be satisfied and smug, but should continue alertly to develop further or at least maintain the level of vairāgya till the end, so as to avoid entanglement in the enjoyment of worldly pleasures and the recurrence of rāga or attachment.

SS. - **वितर्कविचारानंदास्मितानुगमात् संप्रज्ञातः ।।१:१७।।**

TL. - vitarkavicārānandāsmitānugamāt samprajñātaḥ - I:17.

WM. -

vitarka i)	=	reasoning, argumentation, cogitation;
ii)	=	(without reasoning or rationality) evil thinking (evil thought, ideas and notions);
vicāra i)	=	deliberation, reflection;
ii)	=	good (rational) thinking good thoughts, ideas, notions;
ānanda	=	joy, bliss, feeling of happiness;
asmitā	=	literally (I) am-ness, pure sense or feeling of one's existence;
anugama (āt)	=	(from) following, accompaniment or association;
saṃprajñāta(ḥ)	=	known (describable) in its totality and in its all details.

TR. - 1. Saṃprajñāta (i. e. known in its totality and in its all details) (samādhi is composed) (of four component stages which are) accompanied by (respectively) reasoning, deliberations, bliss and (sense of pure) (I) am-ness.

2. Saṃprajñāta (i. e. known in its totality and all details) (yoga-pradeśa i.e. the sphere of yoga) (is composed of four sub-regions or sub-spheres formed respectively) with association to evil thinking, good thinking, bliss and (pure sense of) (I) am-ness.

CE. - The word 'saṃprajñāta' is a past participle adjective used here as a noun, which is to be understood. The word is made up of sam (prefix, indicative of completeness = sampurnatayā i.e. totally or fully) + pra(which is a prefix as abbreviation of prakarṣeṇa i.e. in all intensity or in all its details) + jñāta (the past participle of the verb root jña i.e. to know, so known); the whole word therefore here has a sense: "that which is completely known in all its details".

The substantive for this adjectival word saṃprajñāta is not clearly mentioned by Patañjali and is therefore to be found out or decided. All the old commentators, except Dr. Kenghe, have assumed this substantive to be samādhi. Some of these have actually mentioned this substantive word as 'yoga', but in their explanations they have indicated that even they mean by this word yoga nothing else but samādhi. Dr. Kenghe has explicitly pointed out that saṃprajñāta is not a designation of any type of samādhi.

The proper substantive for the adj. saṃprajñāta would be "yoga pradeśa" i.e. the sphere or region of yoga. No doubt even here the term yoga should be understood as the antaraṅga yoga or the inward going processes of dhāraṇā, dhyāna and samādhi. These meditative or concentrative processes are comparable to a journey of the consciousness towards its inner source. Part of the region through which this inward journey takes place is saṃprajñāta i.e. completely and thoroughly known or describable in all its details. The word jñāta is to be interpreted here more as 'describable' than 'known'. Just as a traveller, who has previously completed the journey through a region or province, is able to describe that region in details, so also this journey through the antarākāśa or inner mental region up to a portion can be well described. This describable inner region is made up of four sub-division which are full of vitarkas, vicāras, ānanda and asmitā. When asmitā, literally (I) am-ness, is transcended, the consciousness of 'I am' i.e. of one's own being will also be lost. So thereafter there will be no individuality left and therefore there will be no entity which can 'know' or 'experience'. In fact the ordinary 'consciousness or awareness' comes to an end. A so called state of 'Super-consciousness' will be established. The journey beyond asmitā will, therefore, be through another inner region, which is sometimes named cidākāśa i.e. the space of cit or illumination. In this part of the inward journey there is something, which for unavailability of any suitable word can be designated as "experience". This experience is of a completely different order than the common experience. In fact, no language has words to describe it. Therefore, there is no sense in giving it any designation. In this way this region, through which the consciousness (?) travels after transcendence of asmita is completely indescribable and in this sense it may be said to be 'completely unknown'. Patañjali as a true scientific expounder correctly and probably intentionally does not designate this region by any technical designation. Because in a śāstrīya exposition a name should be given only if it can give some sense. He therefore, rightly indicates it by a completely non technical word 'anya' (sūtra I:18) which merely means 'the other' (than saṃprajñāta). The word asaṃprajñāta (a = not+ sam + pra + jñāta) in contrast to saṃprajñāta has been introduced like a technical name by Vyāsa and following him practically by all later commentators. But coining such a technical designation is erroneous according to śāstra for the reason mentioned above. The word asaṃprajñāta, though not of Patañjali, would mean completely unknown i.e 'indescribable'.

As per this explanation there is no specific variety of samādhi as such, which can be called a saṃprajñāta samādhi and therefore it is not correct also to consider savitarka, savicāra, sānanda and sāsmitā as sub-stages comprising a so called saṃprajñāta samādhi. Obviously, therefore it is not correct to think of another and contrasting variety of samādhi to be called as 'asaṃprajṅāta'. However, just as a person or thing residing in or originating from or related to a particular place is named after his or its place e.g. a Bombyite, a Londoner, these inward going or meditative processes taking place in the particular region might, if at all so desired, be designated by the region in which they take place. Thus, if one so likes, one may name a saṃprajñāta dhāraṇa or a saṃprajñāta dhyāna or a saṃprajñāta samādhi. The contrasting states will be, strictly according to Patañjali, anya dhāraṇa, anya dhyāna and anya samādhi. If the old commentators' designation is to be preferred these will be called asaṃprjñāta dhāraṇā or dhyāna or samādhi. But again it may be emphasized that there is no real variety of samādhi alone which may either be called saṃprajñāta samādhi or asaṃprajñāta samādhi.

There is one more reason why saṃprajñāta and asaṃprajñāta can not be varieties of samādhi. Patañjali has mentioned three varieties of samādhi viz. sabīja, nirbīja and dharmamegha (I:46, 51 and IV:29), where, to leave no chance for any confusion, Patañjali has clearly added the word samādhi after these adjectival names. If therefore, saṃprajñāta and anya or asaṃprajñāta were also varieties of samādhi, these would be the first mention of any variety of samādhi in P.Y.S. It seems questionable thus whether Patañjali would, as a scientific expounder and therefore a logical writer, omit to mention the word samādhi after the adjectival type designation at this first occasion and only add it much later when he mentions other types of samādhi. It is worth noting that sabīja samādhi is described in sūtra I:46 of Patañjala Yoga Sūtra. From that itself nirbīja could have very easily been understood as a contrasting samādhi. Yet, when Patañjali describes it just merely after four intervening sūtras, he deliberately mentions samādhi explicitly after the word nirbīja. Slightly varying versions of Y.S. are available today, but in respect of this sūtra of nirbīja samādhi (I:51) without exception all versions are identical and the word samādhi is present after nirbīja in all of them. Looking to the special characteristic of sūtra construction, viz. of utmost brevity, Patañjali could and should have omitted very easily the word samādhi after nirbīja, it is in contrast to sabīja samādhi, any one would quite obviously have understood it (nirbīja) as samādhi. Yet Patañjali, in a way going against the rule of sūtra construction, takes care to mention nirbīja as samādhi explicitly. Therefore the assumption that Patañjali would omit the word samādhi after saṃprajñāta, which be first variety of samādhi, is not acceptable.

Another difficulty arises if saṃprajñāta is accepted as samādhi. In that case there would be five main varieties of samādhi mentioned in Yoga Sūtra. These would be :-

1. saṃprajñāta
2. asaṃprajñāta (anya)
3. sabīja
4. nirbīja
5. dharmamegha.

It becomes necessary to distinguish clearly between them,

as they should be distinct types or stages of samādhi, as they have been given even distinct and definite technical names. No commentator has clearly pointed out the distinctions precisely in these fives types and specially in the first four of these varieties. Some seem to use the word saṃprajñāta as exact synonym of sabīja, both thus standing for one single stage of samādhi. Obviously they equate asaṃprajñāta with nirbīja. In such an explanation a blame of unscientific presentation gets imposed on Patañjali, of using two technical names for one and the same thing. Even if saṃprajñāta and sabīja have part of their region common and part different, it would be necessary to explain where and how they differ. But none of the old commentators has been careful and able to make such a clear distinction or correlation between samprajnata and sabija and so also between asaṃprajñāta (anya) and nirbīja. If however saṃprajñāta is not presumed to be a variety of samādhi, then the question for distinguishing it from other types of samādhi does not at all arise and all confusion is avoided.

Dhāraṇā→dhyāna→samādhi are the stations in the inward journey of citta. These could be satisfactorily attempted to reach only after the mind is made at least somewhat steady and citta has become blissfully peaceful. Patañjali describes some very efficacious techniques for achieving both of these results, viz. manasaḥ-sthiti-nibandhana (in Sū. I:35 to 38) and cittaprasādana (in Sū. I:33,34 and 39). Obviously, therefore, he will describe the citta's inward going processes (samāpatti: closely related more to dhāraṇā and dhyāna than to samādhi, in Sū. I:41-45) and stages (e.g. samādhis in Sū. I:46 and 51) only after these. That is also a point why we think that saṃprajñāta and anya are not samādhis.

The inward journey of the citta i.e. the apparatus of consciousness takes place through the four sub-regions of the well known i.e. saṃprajñāta main region as said above. These are vitarka, vicāra, ānanda and asmitā. The word vitarka has again been misinterpreted by most of the old commentators. The English commentators have rendered this as argumentation, cogitation, (right) reasoning etc.

All these meanings seem to be based on the break up of the word vitarka : vi = viśeṣena i.e. specially with + tarka = reasoning, logic. The reason why such a significance is given to this word seems to be again the presumption of saṃprajñāta being a samādhi. It is implicit in this presumption that samādhi must be always related to good ideas, thoughts, notions and thinking etc. and therefore, vitarka is rendered as thought process specially associated with reasoning or logic. As it will be explained below, such an interpretation does not seem to agree with the meaning of vitarka as given by Patañjali himself in II:34 sūtra. Secondly such an interpretation does not clearly show what the difference between vitarka and vicāra is. Both these terms assume practically a similar significance in the usual old interpretation.

The word 'vitarka' seems to be a technical term specially peculiar to the sphere of yoga. Its meaning therefore, can not be taken loosely from common usage. Probably, being aware of this, Patañjali has actually defined the term vitarka, so that such a wrong and loose meaning may not lead to confusion.

Sūtra II:34 explains vitarkas as hiṃsā etc. The use of the word ādi (etc.) implies that the list of these vitarkas, of which hiṃsā is the first, should be and is known to the reader. Such a generally accepted list is not there, but just four sūtras before i.e. in II:30. Patañjali has enumerated yamas, of which ahiṃsā-opposite of hiṃsā, is the first. From this we get a hint that the list of vitarkas can be obtained by putting corresponding antnonyms. So, vitarkas become hiṃsā, asatya, steya, abrahmacarya, and parigraha. In the enumeration of yamas Patañjali only mentions ten yamas and niyamas. Some of these are different than Patañjali's list of these. For example mitāhāra, śama, dama, guruśuśrūṣā etc. are mentioned in yamas or niyamas by some other texts, directly or indirectly related to yoga.

Evidently their omission in P.Y.S.does not mean that Patañjali does not recognize their importance or thinks that they need not be observed by the students of his yoga path. Patañjali has mentioned five items each in yama and niyama, probably because he thinks them to be the cardinal ones and also because Sāṃkhya and Patañjali seem to have a liking to enumerate all types of things into groups of five. But it is self evident that these other good rules, worthy of being included in the observances and rules to be followed by a yoga sādhaka, otherwise said or called yamas and niyamas, are also implicitly to be followed. From this vitarkas should be interpreted as all evil things. Since the discussion is about internal practices of meditational nature, vitarka, here means bad or evil thought, notion, imagination, emotion etc.

An objection can be raised as to why Patañjali does not explain the term vitarka here itself (i.e. in I:17 or soon after). The reason is that in a way the mention of vitarka is in passing or of secondary importance in I:17 and also in I:42 and 43. At II:30-34 the comprehension of vitarkas becomes of primary and practical importance, as they are indicated to be interfering things causing difficulty in the observance of yamas and niyamas, as they are opposite of these. So, the explanation of their nature and characteristics becomes relevant there and so has been pertinently given there, in II:34, by Patañjali.

Vitarkas, as said, are evil thoughts and ideas. These are in strict reality not the attributes of objects or subjects that may be chosen for dhāraṇā-dhyāna-samādhi. In fact at levels of higher philosophy and higher yogic development, things and phenomena are neither good nor evil. It is the saṃskāras, stored in our mind or in karmāśaya in the citta, which lead to the evil or good aspects of things and phenomena. Very often even very holy and pure subjects chosen for these meditative processes give rise to appearance of vitarkas. Many sādhakas complain of such a happening and become worried, because even most sacred subjects e.g.. a deity for which one has greatest devotion or the Guru or other saintly personages chosen for meditation give rise to vitarkas. Obviously these evil things are not associated with or arising from these subjects, but they are coming from the storehouse of saṃskāras of the current or past lives.

The mind of common man is ordinarily directed outwards, trying to grasp and know about the external objects or subjects.

The evil thoughts and actions are recognized to be such and therefore undesirable even by any man with common sense. Who does not know that hiṃsā, asatya and such other things are bad, because they lead to bad results or fruits ? Yet the man, knowing this folly well, behaves in vitarkika manner. This is really irrationality or senselessness. In this sense the word vitarka would be broken up as vi i.e. vinā = without + tarka = logic or rational thinking.

In the meditational practice the mind is turned inwards. In this the situation is something like closing all the shutters of a house or room, so that the things outside can not be seen nor outside sounds heard. The mind, which is very often compared to a small child, seeks subjects from inside the space in which it is thus confined. Thus the mind, we may say, goes to search its own inner depth. The saṃskāras, which were buried in the deeper layers of the mind or citta and of which it was not actively aware, come to surface and are clearly perceived or experienced by the mind. The happening may be compared to the removal of the lid of a steam-container or that of Pandora's Box. Any subject, however good, pure, sacred, would thus give rise to vitarkas, because they are there in the citta and were held at abeyance, because citta was busy with other outside things. This is why Patañjali has mentioned that the first sphere would be the one full of vitarkas.

Patañjali, nowhere has explained how transition, from vitarka to vicāra, from vicāra to ānanda, from ānand to asmitā and from asmitā to beyond into the anya or the indescribable transcendent sphere, is to be attempted or takes place. From this and from the experience of yoga sādhakas it is to be explained that the process is self-regulated and automatic. The sādhaka can not achieve the transition by any willful effort or in a definite time. The only thing that he can do is to have abhyāsa i.e. regular practice of these meditational processes for an indefinitely long period with receptive and therefore firmly determined attitude (I:14) till the desired stage or result is achieved.

In II:33 of Yoga Sūtra, Patañjali recommends pratipakṣabhāvanaṃ i.e. cultivation of an attitude of opposite nature (to the vitarka), when vitarkas give rise to trouble. But this pratipakṣabhāvanaṃ can be and should be done only in the practical worldly life, when the mind has the ordinary wakeful consciousness i.e. during day to day activities and thoughts, in ordinary daily behaviour. This pratipakṣabhāvanaṃ can not be attempted during the meditational processes. Because in such an attempt the mind will be diverted away and dispersed from the subject chosen for meditation and the very concentrating and inward-going processes of dhyāna and samādhi would be impossible to reach.

It is a common experience that when two persons are having a dispute or quarrel, a third person i.e. an impartial witnesser, may see the wrong on one side or both sides. He then may try to bring a reconciliation or agreement by pointing out these faults of the opponent parties. Very often instead of hearing him and seeing the thing in right perspective, the parties may say that this third person does not understand or know anything of the truth or rightness, and what each one of them is saying is the right thing. They even get angry with this reconciler and ask him not to interfere. Later, when some time passes, these quarrelling persons often may realize and even openly accept their wrong stand. This happens because very often such a passage of time reduces the involvement or attachment of the person to the thing or phenomena for which he was quarrelling. Thus, when he, so to say, becomes separated from the thing, maybe by time-distance or space-distance (aloofness), he may begin to see more impartially and therefore in a greater unbiased out-look. In Yoga, in some other texts cultivation, of such an attitude or habit is recommended and is termed "sākṣīvṛtti".

Thc saṃskāras, which come up to the consciousness level, are a mental reproduction of some past experiences of this or earlier lives. The process is just like arousal of a memory, the difference being that memory is aroused on account of stimulation of a particular saṃskāra by certain external or even internal factors. While the vitarkas (evil thought etc.) and vicāras come up without any such specific stimulation, so to say, spontaneously, because the lid or partition of these deeper parts of citta is opened or removed. When they will come to actuality, there will be very little or practically no attachment or involvement of the meditating person, because the thing is long past and may be geographically far removed and also the force of emotion caused by it when the incident actually happened is also enfeebled. In this way the vitarkas, so to say, lose their power and gradually disappear. In this, the more evil the saṃskāra the earlier and more often it will come up to the consciousness level, when the person repeats dhyāna, samādhi day after day.

Vitarka and vicāras are both mental activities and in the karmāśaya, saṃskāras giving rise to both these are stored. Out of these the vitarkas, and as said above the more evil ones, will rise first because they have a greater force behind them. It is also very probable that vicāras also will try to rise up. But it is our common experience that we become more aware of the more troublesome or evil person or thing than of a less troublesome or a good person or thing. In the same way in this inward going process vitarkas are felt more than the vicaras and that is why Patañjali has mentioned them as the first occurrers of sphere of experience.

As explained above this inward going process itself will gradually weaken and lead to the disappearance of vitarkas. After this the thoughts will be more and more rational and therefore they may be aptly termed vicāras, but as the practice continues, even these vicāras gradually lose their power and disappear. Here, thus the active intellectual thinking comes to an end, but the consciousness goes further and enters a province of mere experience, which has no active thinking. In a way, we may say in common language that the emotional part of the mind and citta becomes more dominant. And what is experienced can be described only as ānanda i.e joy, pleasure, happiness, blissfulness. The person therefore has here a feeling or consciousness i.e. very pleasant and peaceful. The person thus may feel "I am blissful". But this state is also relative, because happiness, joy, blissfulness etc. are associated with their opposite. Therefore here the possibility remains that this pleasantness may turn into unpleasantness. So this state also should be transcended. Therefore in the next stage or sphere the consciousness is only of "(I) am". This condition of consciousness of being merely without any qualification or attribute is of asmitā i.e. '(I)-am-ness'. The consciousness will continue its journey further and in this transcendence, (I) am-ness is also lost and there ends the region designated as saṃprajñāta. Whatever happens further can not be called experience in the strict or usual sense. There is no 'I' and therefore there is no experiencer, at least in the sense that an experience should be describable. But as the 'I' -consciousness has itself dissolved, who will experience and who will be able to describe it even if the state is experienced in some subtle way or on different order. To give any designation to it is also, therefore, meaningless and so it is very correctly indicated by Patañjali by a word of common usage as 'anya' = the other (than saṃprajñāta).

SS. - **विरामप्रत्ययाभ्यासपूर्वः संस्कारशेषोऽन्यः ।।१:१८।।**

TL. - virāma-pratyayābhyāsapūrvaḥ saṃskāraśeṣo' nyaḥ - I:18.

WM. -

virāma	=	end, cessation, complete stop;
pratyaya	=	experience at the moment of citta; content of citta;
abhyāsa	=	repeated practice;
pūrva (ḥ)	=	preceded by/followed by/ preceded as well as accompanied by;
saṃskāra	=	impression, effect, influence;
śeṣa (ḥ->o)	=	residuum, remnant, remainder;
anya (ḥ)	=	(the) other (is).

TR. - The other (region traversed by the super consciousness part of citta after transcendence of (asmitā) is) preceded by (followed by/accompanied by) the repeated practice of total cessation of experience (by citta), (yet) leaving a residual effect.

CE. - This sūtra attempts to describe, as far as possible, that other transcendental region in which the process of meditation viz. dhāraṇā, dhyāna and samādhi, continues after the asmitā has disappeared from citta. As said above in notes on I:17 of Yoga Sūtra really this region or stage of meditational processes is totally indescribable. Yet as we often do, such things beyond description have to be described perforce, because without doing this it would be impossible to make people even aware of the existence or possibility of existence of such things. No doubt, the description will fall far short of the actuality and may even be completely inadequate and unsatisfactory. The expounder may himself by fully aware of it and yet he has no other way of making the persons, who are desirous of knowing about the thing, to know and understand at least something in some way about that thing. On the same lines, therefore, Patañjali has to describe this indescribable region in some way.

The word 'pūrva', as indicated, can have three meanings. The interpretation of this sūtra with each of the different meanings will be completely different. It is very difficult to decide which is the correct interpretation according to Patañjali. But there is a solace in this dilemma for us. Even if one accepts a wrong meaning of pūrva and so, a wrong interpretation of the sūtra, it would not matter much it would not be very harmful, because the region and the happenings in that region are in fact only to be "experienced" or "gone through".

Since, as already indicated under I:1 of Patañjala Yoga Sūtra, after the asmitā has dissolved, whatever citta undergoes cannot be really called "experience". At least this experience will not be of the same category as ordinarily understood by the word 'experience'. Ordinary experience can be described at least partially, so that the audience gets some idea about it. But the experience of this anya region is not describable in any way. Thus, this anya region comes after the practice, perfected by repetition of complete cessation of any ordinary experience or of having any content in mind, has been accomplished.

If the word pūrva is interpreted as 'followed by', then cessation of any experience or having any content in citta would have to be understood as coming after, i.e. at the end of the journey through the anya region. In this case the expression virāmapratyaya is obviously to be understood as vṛttinirodha. It may be pointed out that there is a difference in the expression virāmapratyaya and vṛttinirodha. The former is cessation of pratyaya i.e. in other words, total or complete vṛttinirodha; in Sanskṛt; therefore it can be explained as sarvavṛttinirodha. But vṛttinirodha itself can also be partial when vṛttis are partly controlled, but all vṛttis are not completely abolished.

Pūrva can be here understood like the word pūrvaka. Both these terms strictly mean 'preceded by', but if the anya region or anya yoga is preceded by virāmapratyaya, obviously this virāmapratyaya must continue during the whole journey through this anya region i.e. through out this anya antaraṅgayoga. Thus pūrva here also is to be understood as accompanied by.

A question may arise about the worthwhileness of this

journey through the anya region or anya antaraṅgayoga, if it leads to no experience, which then would be as good as voidness. But as already said, this yoga is not leading to voidness, but to an experience, which is of a completely different and superior order. Being beyond words it is also indescribable, yet it leaves an impression or effect or influence on the sādhaka. Thus a sādhaka who has entered and traversed through this region, no doubt by means of his citta, when he returns to the ordinary consciousness at the end of the abhyāsa, he would carry a residuum of the effect of this 'super-normal experience'. In a way he will be a transformed personality and this transformation will be lasting permanently and will go on becoming perfect as the abhyāsa or repetition of the practice is continued day after day, till the ultimate perfection i.e. the objective of yoga i.e. Kaivalya is attained. Thus this anya antaraṅga yoga is not futile and purposeless. This remnant of the effect of the practice is indicated by the phrase 'saṃskāraśeṣaḥ anyaḥ'.

SS. - **भवप्रत्ययो विदेहप्रकृतिलयानाम् ।।१:१९।।**

TL. - bhava-pratyayo videha-prakṛti-layānām - I:19.

WM. -

bhava	=	process of becoming, birth and life, saṃsāra;
pratyaya	=	experience;
videha	=	without body i.e. gods or deities;
prakṛti-laya	=	dissolved or merged in (mūla) prakṛti;
ānām	=	suffix of sixth or possessive case, meaning 'of'.

TR. - (This journey or yoga) of the bodiless gods and the yogīs merged in prakṛti leads only to experience (again) of birth and life.

OR

(This journey or yoga) of the bodiless gods and the yogīs merged in prakṛti (is a) congenital experience (in their case).

CE. - The present commentator has a firm conviction that Patañjali is presenting a very complete and scientific system of yoga, which is mainly for practising and achieving benefits out of this practice. Thus the sūtras are more for practice than for mere intellectual understanding or philosophical discussion. Though some of the sūtras may have a directly practical purpose, while others may have more theoretical and philosophical aspect, all the sūtras are ultimately meant to serve and help in the actual practice of yoga. The present sūtra, as seen above can be interpreted in two ways, dependent on the two meanings given to the expression bhavapratyaya. But in both these interpretations the practical utility of the sūtra does not become easily obvious. In a sense both the interpretations lead to a conclusion that the yoga, so far accomplished by the highly advanced yogis has however not helped them to achieve the real goal, that of kaivalya.

Bhavapratyaya-bhava is a gerund from verb 'bhū' to become, thus bhava basically means becoming from which the two meanings noted, namely, birth and life and creation, are derived. Pratyaya means experience. Thus one meaning of bhavapratyaya is to get the experience of being born and consequent life. This is the meaning accepted in the first rendering of the sūtra.

The second meaning is obtained by expanding the compound as "experience from birth" i.e. a congenital ability or development of going into higher meditational yogic states. The significance of such inborn yogic developments in others for a beginner yoga sādhaka is explained below.

Videha--the minor gods, which are manifestations of the various potentialities or aspects of one Supreme Divinity or God, have in reality no form or body. The various forms ascribed to various deities are just imaginary. Therefore the epithet videha or bodyless is applied to gods.

There are two peculiarities to be noted about the forms imagined for the various gods. The form is never exactly human. Some grotesqueness, at least four arms, is always present. Sometimes it, for example, verges on monstrosity e.g. Gaṇeśa, Narasiṃha. This seems to be deliberate and with a purpose. Various methods are recommended for meditation. But for a person newly entering this province, the most suitable way would be to choose a subject or better still a concrete object and try to keep his mind attached to it as long as possible. In this the chosen object should be one for which the mind would have a natural inclination to stick to. That means the sādhaka should have a liking or love and respect or devotion for the object, Things and persons of the day to day world would not be very suitable in this respect as subjects of meditation, because with these the person may have evil associations which would cause a greater interference in the process of meditation than if the subjects were without such associations. Various gods would, therefore, serve the purpose best. But to meditate upon a formless god or object would be a difficult thing, at least for a beginner. So, a form or body imagined for this deity becomes desirable and helpful. Secondly, if this form or body is exactly human, there lurks a danger that the subject may be easily transposed by the form or body of a person in the actual life of the sādhaka. The invariably present grotesqueness or monstrosity of the bodies of gods serves as a deterrent against this. This seems to be the reason that really bodyless gods have been imagined to possess such grotesque bodies or forms.

Yoga can be looked upon as a process of 'counterevolution' i.e. reversing the process of evolution as propounded by Saṃkhya and probably accepted wholly or substantially by Patañjali. Thus in the development of yoga the consciousness from the gross stage of viśeṣa goes backward to aviśeṣa and then to liṅgmātra and further to aliṅga (see II:19). But this is not the desired goal of yoga which is Kaivalya or puruṣakhyāti or svarūpapratiṣṭhā of puruṣa. It can happen that for some reason the progress on the path of yoga may be interrupted at some stage. But then it will in a way, not serve the purpose as the 'śeṣaḥ anyaḥ' real and the final objective is not achieved. The highest such stage in this counter-evolutionary progress, which a yogī can reach without fulfilling the objective of yoga is the stage of merger of consciousness into aliṅga i.e. into pradhāna or mūlaprakṛti. Such a yogī would be called a prakṛtilaya or one who (whose citta) has dissolved into mūlaprakrti. Thus this yogī is a very highly advanced yogī, so to say, one who has reached the penultimate stage prior to

Kaivalya. From the real yogic point of view even this very high and valuable progress is still purposeless as he has yet not reached the final goal, the ultimate and real objective of yoga (viz. Kaivalya). From this the sādhaka is indirectly told not to compare his own progress with any other co-traveller on the path of yoga. This tendency of comparing one's progress with that of others' is a natural tendency of every human being. Such a comparison often leads to competition and very often as a consequence to jealousy, hatred enemity etc. These things are completely to be avoided in the field of yoga whatever the sphere of yogic activity a person may be involved in. Still more harmful is the further consequence of these things, viz. frustration. Very often in such comparison when one finds that some other sādhaka seems to have attained a much greater progress within a short time or with much less effort, while he himself is lagging far behind in spite of a very sincere, arduous and longer effort, one gets disappointed and disheartened. This usually leads to a diminution of zeal and interest, which may be sometimes so grave that the sādhaka may totally give up the practice of yoga. To avoid such an unfortunate and undesirable eventuality Patañjali through this sūtra has probably indicated indirectly to avoid comparison in yoga practices with others, saying that even the great achievements on the path of yoga of videhas and prakṛtilayas are not to be envied. According to the first interpretation their progress really leads to nothing valuable, because these advanced yogīs will have to undergo again the experience of birth and life i.e. of suffering (as per sūtra 2:15)and later go in the same path of yoga as is open to every sādhaka until they attain the Kaivalya.

According to the second interpretation the achievements of these advanced yogīs, which are inborn, may seem to be an accident or a favour or gratuitousness of nature or God. But the sādhaka should bear in mind that this apparent congenital advancement in yoga is a result of the practice of yoga performed in previous life or lives. From this he has to take a lesson that he can also go to the same heights through his own efforts as very probably these yogīs must have done yogābhyāsa in their previous lives. These seem to be the only purpose and significance of this sūtra for a practical sādhaka. Otherwise, the sūtra is of no significance and need not have at all appeared in a sūtra composition on yoga.

SS. - **श्रद्धावीर्यस्मृतिसमाधिप्रज्ञापूर्वक इतरेषाम् ।।१:२०।।**

TL. - śraddhā-vīrya-smṛti-samādhi-prajñāpūrvaka itareṣām - I:20.

WM. -

śraddhā	=	firm faith;
vīrya	=	vigour, energy;
smṛti	=	memory,reminder;
samādhi-prajñā	=	intellectual ability to comprehend the yogic processes like samādhi etc.;
pūrvaka	=	accompanied by;
itara(eṣām)	=	(of) others.

TR. - (This journey inwards or antaraṅga yoga of others will be accomplished well) by the help of firm faith, vigour, (constant) reminder (of the ultimate goal) and ability to comprehend the yogic processes like samādhi etc.

CE. - This sūtra, in a way enumerates the pre-requisites or factors which are essential for success in an undertaking in any field of life. They are more pertinently needed in the path of yoga for having a definite, good and rapid progress.

Obviously firm faith is the foremost requirement for achieving success. If one has any half-hearted belief and indecisiveness he would not put up the necessary effort with full zeal and sincerity. The achievement of the goal will be therefore, a questionable thing. Patañjali in sūtra I:30 has mentioned doubt samśaya as a hindrance for the progress in yoga.

Success also needs energetic effort, so vigour or energy is an essential pre-requisite, which should accompany firm faith and would in a way automatically result from it.

In the path of yoga the progress itself may sometimes be a cause of interruption or interference. A sādhaka, particularly if he has some remarkable development e.g. attainment of a siddhi, he may be diverted from his effort, and may be enticed in the exploitation of the miraculous achievement for some worldly and therefore, nonyogic gains. Such examples are quite frequent. Therefore, Patañjali has imperatively pointed out that the sādhaka should keep this memory ever alive and so go on reminding himself again and again that he should not be led astray by these diversions and should continue one-pointedly his efforts to reach the final goal of Kaivalya. This seems to be the significance of the word smṛti in this sūtra.

Some commentators have treated samādhi and prajñā as two

independent requirements for progress. But how can samādhi, which is the last stage of this eightfold practical path of yoga, be a prerequisite for the progress in yoga. It seems, therefore, better to treat this expression as a compound word, understanding it as prajñā (special intellectual ability), for understanding the process of samādhi. If a person has not an adequate intellectual level of understanding to fully comprehend the intricate and somewhat mystical processes of meditation like dhyāna and samādhi, it would not be possible for him to practise these things. That is why a level of understanding is indicated as a pre-requisite here by the term samādhi-prajñā.

These pre-requisites may at the first instance seem to be dependent on chance or luck. It may be felt that to posses śraddhā or vīrya or samādhi-prajñā may be natural characteristics for some persons, while others may not have these. But it should be borne in mind clearly and definitely by a sādhaka that all these things can be deliberately developed.

Before one takes up the path of yoga, or in a way, any undertaking, he should remove all doubts and indecisiveness about it. If he is convinced of the importance and valuableness of the undertaking, then the faith in that path will be a natural thing. More convinced the person would be about the superiority of the value of the thing, more firm will be his faith. If properly understood, yoga offers the most valuable things, viz. the eternal and highest happiness and peace for which every human being is consciously or unconsciously striving for. With this comprehension the immutable faith in the path of yoga would be a natural result in the mind of sādhaka.

Vīrya and smṛti are also things which can be developed willfully. The stronger the will, the more powerful will be the vīrya and unshakable the smṛti and the tempo of these things will be the highest, if the faith is unshakable.

It may be felt that the level of intellectual understanding, necessary for comprehending the higher yogic processes may be an innate, and therefore, chance ability, but even this level of understanding can be created by the willful and sincere effort, if the urge for achieving the aim is powerful, e.g. by reading the pertinent literature, hearing talks of the masters and having personal discussion and guidance from them etc.

'Itareṣām' means other than the videhas and prakṛtilayas, both of whom are categories of highly advanced yogīs. According to the first interpretation of the previous sūtra I:19, even they have to take birth again and continue their progress further on the path of yoga, from the stage at which it was interrupted, as explained in the sixth adhyāya of Gītā. So, in a way even for these advanced yogīs and in any case for ordinary sādhakas the only way open for achieving success in yoga is with these four prerequisites. So, we may say that the universal way for success in yoga is the one indicated in sūtra I:20.

Some commentators have presumed that the sūtras I:19 and 20 describe respectively two categories of yogīs: (i) bhavapratyaya i.e. inborn and (ii) upāyapratyaya i.e. produced through application of means i.e. through effort of training. But since inborn development in yoga is more a chance or accident and the number of such lucky (?) persons is negligible, it would not be very correct to make a separate class or category of these. Moreover, as per our understanding and the above given explanation, even these innate yogīs have to resort to practice-effort, to continue their interrupted yoga journey. So there is only one sure and final method and no other -- "nānyaḥ-panthā vidyate' ayanāya". And even bhavapratyaya yogīs have to become upāyapratyaya ultimately.

SS. - **तीव्रसंवेगानामासन्नः ।।१:२१।।**

TL. - tīvra-saṃvegānāmāsannaḥ - I:21.

WM. - tīvra = acute;
saṃvega = urge, impulse;
ānām = suffix for plural in the sixth or possessive case, of;
asanna (ḥ) = close at hand i.e. quite easily achievable.

TR. - (This yoga) of those with acute urge (for it) is quite easily achievable.

CE. - The sūtra I:20 to I:22 are in fact universally applicable for attaining success and perfection in any field of activity, though no doubt for this reason Patañjali has pointedly mentioned these in relation to progress in yoga. Evidently the success and perfection in yoga will be achieved more easily and rapidly, acuter and more powerful is the urge or keenness or desire for it.

SS. - **मृदुमध्याधिमात्रत्वात्ततोऽपि विशेषः ।।१:२२।।**

TL. - mṛdu-madhyādhimātratvāttato'pi viśeṣaḥ - I:22.

WM. - mṛdu (tva) = mild (ness);
madhya (tva) = mediumness or averageness;
adhimātratva = extremeness or extraordinariness;
a Suffix of the fifth or ablative case meaning = from, through;
tataḥ (→0) = in that;
api = even, also;
viśeṣa(ḥ) = particular.

TR. - Even in that (there is) particular (level) of development) from (i.e. dependent on the degree of) mildness, mediumness or extremeness (or extra-ordinariness)

CE. - Even if a sādhaka has a very acute urge or keen desire, unless it is accompanied by suitable efforts (success and progress can not be achieved). Thus the progress will depend on the degree of effort put into the undertaking. This is true also in the case of yoga as stated in this sūtra.

Some old commentators have made permutations and combinations of the terms mṛdu, madhya and adhimātra and have proposed six or nine categories or degrees of the progress. But this is an unnecessary elaboration of a simple statement of generally used three categories viz. below average, average and above average.

SS. - ईश्वरप्रणिधानाद्वा ।।१:२३।।

TL. - īśvarapraṇidhānādvā - I:23

WM. - īśvara = īśvara;

praṇidhāna	=	total surrender;
āt(-d)	=	from, through;
vā	=	or.

TR. - Or (the same goal of yoga can be achieved) from (through) total surrender to īśvara.

CE. - Most of the English commentators have translated the word īśvara by the English word God. Almost all the commentators use this word with varying connotations, probably not acceptable to Patañjali, e.g. Paramātmā, Bhagavāna etc.. Sāṃkhya is generally supposed to be not accepting any such entity or even the notion of it. Patañjali's yoga, as is generally believed by most of the scholars, is based on the Sāṃkhya foundation, but for this reason Patañjali has to define his conception of this new element accepted by him, namely īśvara in I:23 to I:27 sūtras. In spite of accepting this element of īśvara, the eternality of the primordial principles of Sāṃkhya e.g. puruṣa and prakṛti also seems to have been accepted by Patañjali, so prakṛti and its evolutes which are the components of the total universe, are not created by any creator. So this īśvara is not the Creator and so also Protector or Destroyer of the Universe. Even many other attributes of God, Paramātmā, Bhagavāna etc. are not applicable to Patañjali's īśvara. The acceptance of the additional element by Patañjali seems to be because it serves some practical purpose for a good and rapid progress in the path of yoga. It is like an axiomatic presumption in any science, since it serves to build up the particular science. In this light, the question, whether such an entity exists or not also becomes irrelevant. In this way the path of yoga is beneficial and open to a person who does not want to believe in any agency like God etc.

Vā precisely means 'or'. Therefore, the method of īśvarapraṇidhāna is a completely equivalent, parallel and as such effective a path for achieving the goal of yoga as the path of cittavṛttinirodha discussed so far by Patañjali. Thus, a sādhaka can resort to either of those two completely alternative and independent methods or techniques of yoga. From this it can be further deduced and supported, what has been mentioned above, that the path of yoga is open to a non-believer. He can then go to the goal of Kaivalya by taking recourse to the principle of cittavṛttinirodha, which can be achieved through practice of the aṣṭāṅgas without having any need to believe in any entity like God or īśvara.

But this kind of comprehension of this sūtra holds only theoretical significance. There may be two or more medicines for a complete cure of a disease, which are all equally efficacious and moreover not mutually contra-indicatory. Under such circumstances only one of the medicines may be given and sufficient for the cure. But if combining two or more of these would be going to give better and rapid results, it would be obviously a most sensible and desirable thing to combine the medicines in a proper manner. The same holds good for the two alternative methods of yoga viz. cittavṛttinirodha and īśvarapraṇidhāna. There is not only no contra-indication between these two methods, but they are mutually facilitatory and therefore, they can be, nay, ought to be combined. In this way the word 'Vā' instead of interpreting as 'or' should be understood for practical purposes as 'and'.

Though as the wording and presentation of sūtras indicate at the first sight that the method of cittavṛttinirodha is completely independent of īśvarapraṇidhāna, it is to be noted that the practical way of achieving cittavṛttinirodha seems to start with kriyāyoga and accomplished through the practice of aṣṭāṅgas. And kriyāyoga as well as the niyama out of aṣṭāṅgas include īśvarapraṇidhana as an essential component. So, looking to this also, we have to understand that though Patañjali seems to state that Kaivalya can be achieved though cittavṛtti nirodha without īśvarapraṇidhāna and therefore, without the need of accepting any element like īśvara, he for practical purposes clearly indicates the essential recourse to īśvarapraṇidhāna for the final success in yoga.

Praṇidhāna means total (pra = prakaṛṣeṇa = intensively, thoroughly) surrender. When this will be perfect, the individual's personality and ego will be completely dissolved. Even the pristine asmitā-bhāva will also disappear. In a way such a perfection of īśvarapraṇidhāna will be reached only in the final achievement of yoga i.e. in the Kaivalya state. As long as the faintest trace of 'I - am - ness' will remain, the surrender would be incomplete to that much extent. From this it can be easily seen that this hundred percent perfect īśvarapraṇidhāna is a very difficult thing to practise and achieve.

Quite frequently people equate Patañijali's yoga with Rājayoga. At least from the text, especially looking to its colophon, this does not seem to be authentic. The correct designations would be Aṣṭāṅga yoga or Pātañjala Yoga. Thus the yoga described in these Yoga Sūtras is not a school of yoga, which can uniquely and specifically be considered as a particular school which may be named Rāja. But if the expression Rājayoga is interpreted as the king amongst yogas i.e. supermost yoga including the essentials of all the yoga schools, then the yoga of the Yoga Sūtras can aptly be looked upon as such a one. In this light, the quintessence of Bhaktiyoga and Karmayoga, which are supposed to be two distinct and independent schools of yoga, is expressed in this sūtra I:23. Perfection of bhakti would be achieved when the sādhaka has totally surrendered to Īśvara (here taken as a general name for Divinity). So also the essence of Karmayoga viz. to do karma with an attitude that it is being done by the power of Divinity, and looking on oneself as not responsible or as merely a passive tool of the Divine Power, will also be attained to perfection when one dissolves his ego and asmitā totally i.e. one has achieved the total surrender.

Another point to be noted is that this Īśvarapraṇidhāna as exposed here seems to be very simple and easy. One gets an impression that you have not to do anything e.g. practice of Aṣṭāṅgas etc. As already stated, this is so merely in the wording and in appearance, but in practice, in fact, not easy. If Īśvarapraṇidhāna were easy, everybody would have been liberated easily and there would have been no one who was 'baddha' 'or' 'not mukta' (unliberated). Perfect Īśvarapraṇidhāna which is equivalent to total disappearance of 'I-am-ness' can be achieved with great effort, carried over for a long time, this length of time being not in days, months or even years, but may be even over several lives. Even this effort in actuality will have most certainly to include the practice i.e. abhyāsa of many or very probably all the aṅgas of yoga.

Thus, this, so said, alternative path of yoga really will have to take recourse to the practice of yoga and in this view, is not an independent path but rather a complementary path to that of citta-vṛtti-nirodha. Really what is indicated by Patañjali, through this sūtra and by inclusion more directly of īśvarapraṇidhāna in kriyāyoga and niyama, is that the citta-vṛtti-nirodha should be essentially combined with īśvarapraṇidhāna for better and quicker results.

One other importance of combining īśvarapraṇidhāna with the cittvṛttinirodha method is for very practical day to day life. The yogī, till he attains Kaivalya, has to remain in this world and human society. Even if he goes into isolation, some contact with the society is perforce to be maintained for maintenance of life or rather the body. If the yogī is adopting only the method of citta-vṛtti-nirodha through the practice of aṣṭāngas, there lurks a danger that he may develop into a hard-hearted or even callous and cruel personality. The īśvarapraṇidhāna would reduce this effect and soften him and so he will be a kind and loving personality, because īśvarapraṇidhāna implies devotion or love towards the Divinity.

SS. - **क्लेशकर्मविपाकाशयैरपरामृष्टः पुरुषविशेष ईश्वरः ।।१:२४।।**

TL. - kleśa-karmavipākāśayairaparāmṛṣṭaḥ
puruṣa - viśeṣa īśvaraḥ - I:24.

WM. - kleśa = primordial and ultimate factos or causes of misery and pain;
karma = action;
vipāka = maturation, fructification;

āśaya	=	storehouse;
(aiḥ->r)	=	plural suffix of third or instrumental case = by;
aparāmṛṣṭ(ḥ)	=	totally uncovered or not afflicted;
puruṣa	=	puruṣa (a principle, element);
viśeṣa	=	special;
īśvara	=	īsvara.

TR. - Īśvara (is) a special (case of) puruṣa completely unaffected by kleśas, as well as karmas, maturation of karmas and storage of karmas.

CE. - Puruṣa as explained under I:3 is an abstract primordial principle, which is present in each individual. Īśvara is a special case of this puruṣa principle. So, it should be clearly understood that this īśvara of Patañjali has no personality and therefore, no form or body. It would not be correct to speak of this īśvara as either he or she. The puruṣa principle in human being, though essentially ever remains unaffected and unrelated with prakṛti, yet an appearance of delusion is created that it is closely connected and involved with prakṛti, because in that human being this tattva seems to be residing in the body and acting through the citta. In fact it is always misidentified with citta or occasionally even with the gross body. This delusory impression as said under I:3, is technically called saṃyoga, in Sāṃkhya and Pātañjala Yoga Darśana (Sūtras) (cf II:23). Such a misidentification and delusion is never possible in the case of īśvara-tattva, since it never possesses a body and therefore, also, no mind nor citta, which can only work through the body. The five kleśas (sūtras II:3 to II:9) have therefore, no possibility to effect this īśvara-tattva. That is why it is 'kleśa-aparāmṛṣṭa'.

Again since there is neither body or citta, there is no possibility of action or karma. Evidently there is no question of any maturation and fructification of karmas. Since in the theory of the law of karma it has to be assumed that different karmas take different times for the process of maturation and fructification, it becomes necessary to assume that these karmas remain somewhere in some subtle form. Nowhere is it explained what is the way in which and where these karmas are stored. But the presumed 'Store-house' of these karmas is called 'karmāśaya'. Now, since the karma-vipāka is not there in the case of īśvara, there need not have to be any karmāśaya also.

In short īśvara is that aspect or puruṣa-tattva which eternally remains unaffected and in fact completely unrelated with prakṛti, while the puruṣa-tattva in a human being at least seems to be affected and even involved with prakṛti and so undergoing all the changes that take place in prakṛti.

This concept of īśvara expounded in these sūtras I:24 to I:27 is alien to all other notions of īśvara, God etc. and nowhere has it been indicated in these sutras that this īśvara is a creator etc. of the creation nor that he can bestow his grace and make the path of the aspirant comfortable or easy. The utility of the assumption and acceptance of this īśvara-tattva is indicated in sūtras I:27 to I:29.

This sūtra also indicates the plurality of puruṣas (i.e. puruṣa-tattva in each individual being a separate entity) since īśvara is defined as 'puruṣa viśeṣa' i.e. a special puruṣa.

SS. - तत्र निरतिशयं सर्वज्ञबीजम् ।।१:२५।।

TL. - tatra niratiśayam sarvajñabījaṃ - I:25.

WM. - tatra = there, in it;
niratiśayaṃ = unsurpassable;
sarvajña = omniscient;
bīja (m) = seed, source.

TR. - In it (īśvara) is the unsurpassable source of (every) sarvajña (omniscient individual).

CE. - Some versions have adopted the expression 'sarvajñatva-bījam' instead of 'sarvajñabījam'. The reason seems to be that to speak of an individual as originating from an abstract principle like īśvara or even from an īśvara imagined as having a form, seems to be absurd. It seems better or proper to speak of a potentiality viz. omniscience (sarvajñatva) as arising from an abstract principle. But we have adopted the present version because it is found in most of the manuscripts and published editions and does not cause much difficulty or distortion of the interpretation.

In the strict sense to expect and believe a person to be sarvajña in its full sense is impossible. It would mean that this individual is able to know at any and every moment all the happenings of all the times in the whole creation. But certain persons are looked upon as sarvajñas because they probably have a potentiality to know, if they so desire, a particular event or phenomena, whatever the geographical or/and temporal distance by which they are separated from that event or phenomena.

This sūtra says that even these sarvajñas have their origin

in the īśvara tattva i.e. the source of their omniscience is ultimately the īśvara. From this is indicated that the īśvara has the potentiality of sarvajñatva or omniscience. The corollary is that all knowledge ultimately originates in īśvara.

SS. - **पूर्वेषामपि गुरुः कालेनानवच्छेदात् ।।१:२६।।**

TL. - pūrveṣāmapi guruḥ kālenānavacchedāt - I:26.

WM. - pūrva (eṣāṃ) = (of) the ancients or earlier ones;
api = also;
guru (ḥ) = master, elder;
kāla (ena) = (by) Time;
anavaccheda (āt) = (from, on account of) Indivisibility.

TR. - (It, the īśvara)is the master (the eldest) also of the earlier ones on account of (it) being indivisible by time.

CE. - This īśvara-tattva being of the nature of puruṣa is beginningless and endless. So, it is unaffected by time i.e. indivisible by time. It was already existing even before the first human being, or in fact before even the Universe came into existence. On account of this and as indicated in the sūtra I:25 it being the ultimate source of all knowledge, it can be looked upon as the master or teacher i.e. the source of knowledge for all the persons, inclusive of all the ancient teachers, who have ever existed uptill now. The word guru is usually understood as teacher. But this īśvara being an abstract principle it cannot "teach" in the normal sense. Even if this īśvara be considered as personified, as probably meant in the other concepts of īśvara e.g.. God, Bhagvāna, etc., still he would not be factually teaching through verbal or written instruction to the ancient teachers and masters i.e. Ṛṣis and Munis etc. he will have to be symbolically looked upon as a teacher, in the sense that he is the origin of all knowledge. For this difficulty, the word 'guru' can even be interpreted as the eldest or the most ancient one. In a way this sūtra indicates the eternality of the īśvara (of Pātañjala Yoga Sūtras). It also reiterates the īśvara as being the ultimate source of all knowledge.

Thus it will be seen that the īśvara as conceived in Pātañjala Yoga Sūtra is (1) completely unrelated to prakṛti (I:24) i.e it is immutable and therefore, not doing any karma any time; (2) Omniscient (I:25; 26); (3) Eternal (I:26) which also may imply its Omnipresence. But it is not Omnipotent (I:24) and so, as said, neither the creator, protector, distroyer of the universe not bestowing grace on his devotees as is affirmed about the God and such other notions of Divinity.

A question then may arise in the mind of the sādhaka as in what way this īśvara would help him in his undertaking of yoga? This answer is given in the next (I:27) sūtra.

SS. - **तस्य वाचकः प्रणवः ।।१:२७।।**

TL. - tasya vācakaḥ praṇavaḥ - I:27.

WM. - tasya = Its.

vācaka (ḥ) = verbal expression, symbolic manifestation of īśvara in the form of sound and letter;

praṇavaḥ = Praṇava, the name of the sound indicated by the letter symbol ॐ (Om).

TR. - Its manifestation (expression) in the sound (and letter) form is praṇava (or oṃkāra).

CE. - The word praṇava can be broken as pra+ṇava, pra- stands for prakarṣeṇa, meaning forcefully, rapidly, completely; ṇava is a noun derived from the verb root 'nu' which means (1) to praise, (2) to lead to a particular direction or goal, so ṇava will mean praying as well as leading to a desired goal. So the whole word praṇava can be understood as (1) intensive praying (most devoted prayer); (2) powerful instrument which leads to the goal very rapidly. Praṇava works in both these ways. It is probably the best prayer. Usually in every prayer something is asked for or at least expected from the Divinity to whom the prayer is being offered. Even if the asking is not direct, it is present there indirectly when for example one praises God as kind, all powerful etc.. In such praising terms the person praying has at least at the back of his mind that the God should be kind and helpful to him in his difficulties and troubles. Now a prayer, which has less this aspect of asking a favour from the Divinity, is from the spiritual point a superior one to any other, which has this demand of favour in a greater extent. From this view point almost all the prayers probably in all the religions, have at least some trace, may be very indirect, of expectation of some benefit or good from the Divinity. Om or praṇava is perhaps the only prayer where this aspect is totally absent. Om is merely a sound or a letter having in reality no particular meaning. So, there is no request or even expectation of any kind of grace or benefit through it from the Divine Power. In this way praṇava can be said to be the supreme or best prayer.

Praṇava is very highly eulogised not only in Yoga Sūtra and Vedic literature and tradition, but also in religions which do not accept the authority of Vedas e.g. Buddhism and Jainism. Some people affirm that it has been even adopted in some distorted form, yet with great reverence, in religions completely alien to Hindu religion and Indian tradition e.g. the Āmen, Āmin etc. of religions of Judaistic origin. A question arises as to why this sound or letter gained such a reverential position, almost universally, in the religious spiritual movements ?

Om is said to be composed of three basic sounds or letter or mātrās e.g. a (अ), ū (ऊ), m (म्). The first of these 'अ' is the first letter of the Devanāgari script, i.e. of Sanskṛit as well as most of the Indian languages. The first letters of almost all the other languages are the ones which stand for the sound indicated by the letter 'अ' e.g. Alpha of the Greek, Aleph of Phoenician and Hebrew, Alif of Middle East languages, 'A' of the most of the European languages. This is also quite the natural thing. If one tries to produce a sound from his larynx without much effort or distortion of the oral cavity, yet having a definite form, worthy of being expressed by a letter (i.e. not an inexpressible sound as produced by a dumb person), then the only possible sound would be the one expressed by the letter 'अ'.

It can be noted that Sanskṛit alphabet is probably arranged in a systematic order, based on some natural principles. The first letters (roughly nine to fourteen letters) of the Devanāgarī alphabet are vowels. In a way they can be looked upon as modifications or deviations of the first sound and vowel 'अ' but obtained by more or less marked manipulation and deformation of the oral cavity and its different parts or organs. Then begin the consonants. These are again produced by still more marked manipulation of the oral organs, specially through contact of the tongue at various parts of the oral cavity. These consonants are grouped in 5, depending on the production of their sound by the contact of tongue at a particular region of the oral cavity. The first five 'क' to 'ङ' are kaṇṭhya (gutturals), as they are produced in the gullet or larynx, practically without application of tongue pressure. The next group of five is called tālavya (palatal), which are produced by pressing the tongue at the rear part of the upper palate. The third group is mūrdhanya (cerebral) and is produced by the tongue contact further at the middle of upper palate, त्, थ्, द्, ध्, न्, are dantya (dentals) produced by contact of the tongue with on the teeth. For the last group of five the tongue has no further area to contact, and so they are produced through the mutual contact of the two lips and so are called oṣṭhya (labials). The last of these is म् (M), which being also a nasal, has a peculiarity or superiority over the other four labials that even when the mouth is closed by the lips coming together, the sound can be continued indefinitely according to the breath-capacity of the person. In a way both symbolically and practically since (1) the production of further sounds or letters becomes impracticable as the mouth is closed, and (2) the letters which follow, being in a way either deviations of some earlier letters e.g. 'य' a distortion or vikṛti of the vowel 'इ' or having no definite and distinct form, which are enlargements of hissing sound, the alphabet practically comes to an end, at least in the form of a systematic order, at the letter 'म्' 'M'. So we may say that 'अ' is the first letter and 'म्' is the last regular letter of the alphabet of the Sanskṛt language. So we can even say that, at least broadly, all the letter-sounds of all the languages of the world are to a very great extent included in the letters of the Sanskrit language.

The sound or letter AUM is said to be trimātraka i.e. made up of three mātras, or sound-time-units. These three sounds or letters are explained to be अ, उ, म्. The first and the third in these letter-sounds or varṇas are, as explained above, the first and the last letters in the orderly arrangement of the Sanskṛt alphabet. In between these in the usual alphabet there are a number of letters in Sanskṛt. All these can not be accommodated to produce a single sound and a letter e.g. 'ॐ' (AUM). So as a representative of all these the letter उ is inserted in between अ and म्. Why उ is selected as such a representative, may be because it is the first letter after 'अ' for whose pronunciation the mouth is to be manipulated and distorted markedly after the letter. For pronunciation of आ, इ, ई, the distortion of the mouth is not so very noticeable.

Thus, in a way the letter or sound ॐ, a compound of the three simple letters, is a single letter and a single sound, symbolically incorporating all the sounds and letters of Sanskṛt language, and we may even say of all the languages of the world as explained above. A gentleman sometime back has claimed that when fifty two individuals were made simultaneously to loudly pronounce one each of the fifty two letters of the Devanāgarī alphabet, the composite sound heard was the sound of ॐ, How far this is factual can not be ascertained. However, if it be so, it strongly supports the view just expressed.

We later (in May 1982) tried to repeat this experiment in our institute's laboratory. A number of tape-recordings were also made. All the observers who directly heard the joint recitation or its tape-recording, opined unanimously that the sound was not of ॐ clearly. So the claim seems questionable. The belief that ॐ includes and is the origin of all 'varṇas' can be explained only in the above manner.

The most of the prominent religious books e.g. in Vedas, in Bible etc. there seems to be an idea, expressed explicitly or implicitly, that the Divinity first manifested itself in the form of a sound or word. Obviously, it is impossible to know exactly what this sound or letter or word could be, as there was nobody to hear it nor any record of it could be made. It is also often said that whole creation came out of this Nāda-Brahma and also that all the words and letters of all the languages had their origin in this primordial sound or letter. When probably the ancient Ṛṣis deliberated on this matter and wanted to imagine what this single sound could be, they might have arrived at the sound or letter ॐ, which is discussed above, fulfils at least symbolically as well as logically, the condition of inclusion of all world-language-sounds in it.

ॐ thus is to be looked upon as the manifestation of Divinity in the sound form and thus a direct means through which the Divinity can be understood and contacted quite easily and directly. How to do this is indicated in the next I:28 sūtra.

SS. - **तज्जपस्तदर्थभावनम् ।।१:२८।।**

TL. - tajjapastadarthabhāvanam - I:28.

WM. - tat(→j) = its/ it;

japa (ḥ→s) = continuous and repeated recitation;

tat (→d) = its / it;

artha = meaning / for;

bhāvana(m) = contemplation, meditation,realization/ repeated treatment to produce a desired condition, moulding the mind.

TL. - (1) It (praṇava) (is) the japa (continuous and repeated recitation) and should be practised (with) moulding the mind for it (the sound of ॐ or praṇava).

OR

(2) (one should resort to) continuous and repeated recitation of it (praṇava) (with) meditation on its (praṇava's) meaning.

CE. - Most of the earlier commentators have interpreted this sūtra as under (2) above. In this interpretation the Sādhaka is advised to recite ॐ repeatedly and continuously, but simultaneously trying to contemplate on the meaning of the sound ॐ or praṇava.

A recent Commentary (the Yoga Sūtra of Patañjali by George Feuerstein, publisher, WM. Dawson, Folkestone, England, 1979) has given a slightly different translation "the recitation of that (syllable) (leads to) the contemplation of its meaning".

Such interpretations, according to the present commentator do not bring out the correct significance of this sūtra, specially from the practical view point. The letter or word has fundamentally no meaning. It is in fact a simple sound. Trying to look behind this sound for any meaning, such as "it is the symbol of God" etc. is arbitrary and conventional. One who is not conversant with the convention or does not accept it, would not be able to carry out the injunction of the sūtra as given by the second translation. This interpretation also does not bring out the special importance of praṇava and its japa, as probably Patañjali has in his mind, when he devotes nearly two to three sūtras to this one topic.

In the first translation, the first advantage is that twice used word 'tat' in the sūtra, which means 'it or that' is not to be changed into the possessive form 'tasya' (its, of that). The emphasis or the meaning is modified with the emphatic statement, 'It is the japa'. It has a significance that the praṇava japa is the only japa i.e. the japa of superlative merit. It means therefore, that japa of no other mantra is as efficacious as that of praṇava. This is again supported by the fact that in any mantra or stotra (prayer-in song) there is always explicit or implicit expectation of some temporal gains while ॐ is the only mantra which is merely a sound without any meaning and so without any such expectation. That is why, as explained under I:27 praṇava is the most exalted mantra for japa.

Since praṇava has no definite meaning behind it, the statements, such as "contemplate or meditate on the meaning of praṇava or leads to the contemplation of its meaning" etc, become absurd. The words "bhāvanam", "bhāvanā" etc. are derived from verb root bhū -- to become and mean "becoming" (by citta). So tadarthabhāvanam would mean '(try) becoming for it' i.e. let the citta become (for) it or let the citta be one with it; or let the citta take the form of it.

The words bhāvanam and bhāvanā in Pātañjala Yoga Sūtra seem to have a sense similar to that for the word bhāvana in Āyurveda, where, it indicates giving a repeated treatment to a medicinal substance, by which it is purified and converted into a potent remedy or medicine for alleviation or the cure of a disease. So the japa, i.e. repeated recitation, of praṇava acts like such a repetitive treatment to the citta and removes its malas leading to its purification, enabling it to proceed further for the attainment of the realization. The japa of praṇava, in this way acts like a mould for moulding the mind to go into the higher stages of concentration like dhyāna and samādhi. In the japa of praṇava thus one should make the citta to take up the form of praṇava i.e. be one with it, be itself the praṇava.

The technique described in this sūtra, specially as per second interpretation, is akin to the technique of nādānusandhāna in Haṭhayoga, specifically mentioned in Haṭhapradīpikā (IV:81 to 89, 105-106). As said in these, this technique can itself directly lead to dhyāna and samādhi and thus the praṇavajapa becomes a very important and potent technique or development along the path of yoga.

The japa, i.e. repeated recitation of mantra, is practised in three ways; (1) vaikhari, i.e. uttered by mouth in an audible tone, (2) upāṃśu i.e. pronounced in a whispering tone so that it is audible only to one's own ears, (3) mānasa (mental) i.e without producing any sound at all. In the beginning the vaikhari mode of japa is to be practised for a long time, care being taken that the pronunciation of the letter-sound (varṇa) is pronounced very correctly and clearly, the accents also being quite precise. When the mantra of the japa is uttered correctly the correctness being assured by an authoritative person or a Guru well versed in the traditional correct way of recitation of that mantra for a long time, the sādhaka may go to the upānśu mode of japa. Again after a satisfactory long practice in this way, the sādhaka can adopt the method of mānasika japa. But one thing is common to all these three modes of japa and a very important, may be the most essential point to be borne in mind, is that the sādhaka should in-between the two successive repetitions, wait patiently for some time without doing anything actively, but merely passively awaiting trying to listen to the sound of the mantra arising of its own accord from a mystical source, the so called 'anāhata (produced without anything striking against any other thing, as is usually the case with all other audible sound) - nāda' (sound). If the sādhaka is sincere, regular and persistent in his japa-sādhanā, he sooner or later certainly reaches the stage, where after he has stopped the recitation, whether uttered or mental, he hears the sound of the mantra not produced deliberately by him, even mentally, and therefore, coming from some mystical source which probably is cosmic. Once the sādhaka is able to hear this sound i.e. anāhatanāda, his citta is enticed by this very pleasing and absorbing experience. Thus the citta very easily is attached to and absorbed in this mystical sound and enters into the deep state of dhyāna and samādhi,

As already said, in contrast to all other japas, praṇavajapa has the least possibility of distraction of citta, as the sādhaka has not even to attend to the meaning of the words and sounds composing the mantra. The citta is, so to say, absorbed or dissolved (laya) in the sound of praṇava. Thus praṇavajapa facilitates the concentration of mind and citta, making it easy for citta to go to the state of samādhi. It would not be out of place to give some further practical direction for a sādhaka, who desires to take recourse to the technique of praṇavajapa, The sound ॐ is actually made up of two syllables ओ (o) and म् (m) and is some times even written as ओम् (om) or ओ ३ म् (o --m--). Obviously there are broadly three ways in which the sound can be pronounced.

1. Both syllables of equal duration ;
2. The first syllable ओ (o) longer than the second म् (M) ओऽऽऽऽऽऽऽ म्ऽऽऽ
3. The second syllable म् (M) longer than the first ओ (o) ओऽऽऽ म्ऽऽऽऽऽऽऽ

(N.B. - 's' - each sucha अवग्रह (avagraha) sign indicates the prolongation of the preceding varṇa (letter-sound) for a duration of one short letter).

All these three modes of recitation are in vogue. Usually traditionally the letters of a mantra are pronounced very slowly and in a rather elongated pronunciation, this is helped and indicated by the symbol 's', called avagraha. So ओऽऽ means that ओ is not to be pronounced very hurriedly as a very short sound, but rather the sound of ओ is to be extended for a longer duration of two or three mātras (i.e. time taken for uttering a short simple sound like अ, indicated by each 'ऽ' sign. The same is the case with म्ऽऽ indicating more elongated pronunciation of the म् sound. It may be mentioned that some people recite 'OM' very rapidly with very short ओ and म्, the whole ॐ sound also being repeated successively very rapidly, without any gap in between the two consecutive ॐ e.g. ओ मो मो मो —. However, this kind of rapid recitation of ॐ is not liked and advised by most of the authoritative and authentic Gurus.

Out of the usual three modes, the third ओऽऽऽ म्ऽऽऽऽऽ is declared by many teachers or Gurus as the best for a sādhaka interested in purely spiritual awakening and progress. The other two are said to be more for those who want to derive some mundane benefits. Though strictly speaking the ॐ japa has not even an implicit trace of asking any benefit from the Divine Power, yet many persons may and do perform this japa with an unexpressed desire in the mind for some worldly objective or advantage. In fact many other mantras e.g. Om Namo Bhagavate Vāsudevāya etc. have no explicit request for bestowal of any favour, yet it is seen that people are advised to, and resort to the performance of such mantra japas for crass worldly advantages.

The ओ in the third and spiritually best mode of recitation of 'ॐ' is to be recited 'pluta' (प्लुत) i.e elongated, more than a long (दीर्घ) letter, say up to three mātras i.e. roughly two to three seconds. Then the sound 'म्' is produced naso-labially (with the use of nose and lips), but when the lips are closed the sound is prolonged as far as possible, dependent on the breathing capacity of the sādhaka, which is indicated by म्ऽऽऽऽ. This prolongation of म् sound should not however, be stretched to such an extent as to become stressfull and discomfortable. In fact, after the sound becomes inaudible and terminated, the sādhaka should be able to remain passively restful for sometime without having any urgent need of taking in breath. Only to such a controlled and comfortable extent, the sound of ॐ should be prolonged, In the prolongation of the म् sound through the nose, there is a deep and slow exhalation (**दीर्घमंद रेचक** = dīrgha-manda-recaka). After this, when the sadhaka does not take in breath, he has an external-breath-holding, which in yogic terminology is called a Bāhya Kumbhaka. In this state the ears are sensitised to receive the subtlest sound vibrations. Therefore, if the sādhaka trains himself to remain passively restful in this bāhya kumbhaka with an attentive and expecting attitude and imagines the listening of the spontaneously and mysteriously produced 'anāhata sound', he at some stage begins to hear the same sound coming from some mysterious cosmic source. The time required for this development may vary from person to person and may be several months or even years in the case of some individuals. But yoga is a game or path of patience. The sādhaka has to be a patient in the basic sense of the word and his patience and persistence will have sure rewards. Once he hears this anāhata om or praṇava-dhvani, going to very high stages of dhyāna and samādhi will be a very smooth and easy matter for this sādhaka.

SS. - ततः प्रत्यक्चेतनाधिगमोऽप्यन्तरायाभावश्च ।।१:२९।।

TL. - tataḥ pratyakcetanādhigamo' pyantarāyābhāvaśca - I:29

WM. -

tataḥ	=	from that;
pratyak	=	Inwards, backwards to the starting point;
cetanā	=	awareness;
adhigama	=	attainment, accession to;
api	=	also;
antarāya	=	hurdle, impediment;
abhāva (ḥ->ś)	=	absence, disappearance;
ca	=	and.

TR. - From that (i.e. long practice of praṇavajapa) (results) the accession (backwards) to the origin of the awareness and also absence (disappearance) of antarāyas (hurdles or impediments in the progress in yoga).

CE. - Both the results of a persistently long practice of praṇajajapa mentioned in this sūtra are important for a spiritually interested sadhāka.

The first is that the normal outward flow of consciousness is curbed and its journey inward starts gradually and ultimately leading to an accession to its own ultimate apparent origin or primal element, which seems to be like a causative factor, viz. puruṣa. The second is the absence or disappearance of antarāyas i.e. impediments in the path of yoga, which are enumerated in the next (I:30) sūtra. The word abhāva fundamentally means absence and taking this sense, the sūtra, indicates that these impediments would not at all arise in the path of the yoga-sadhāka, if he takes recourse to praṇavajapa. The derived meaning of abhāva is disappearance. In this sense the praṇavajapa will remove the impediments from the path of yoga-sādhaka, if they have already arisen and are causing hindrance to the progress of the sādhaka. Thus praṇavajapa is like a medicine which can also cure a disease, but which can be used prominently and more beneficially as preventive for the disease.

SS. - **व्याधिस्त्यानसंशयप्रमादालस्याविरतिभ्रान्तिदर्शनालब्ध-भूमिकत्वानवस्थितत्वानि चित्तविक्षेपास्तेऽन्तरायाः ।।१:३०।।**

TL. - vyādhi-styāna-saṃśaya-pramādālasyāvirati-bhrānti-darśanālabdhabhūmikatvānavasthitatvāni cittavik-ṣepāste' ntarāyāḥ - I:30.

WM. -

vyādhi	=	disease, sickness;
styāna	=	languor, dullness;
saṃśaya	=	doubt;
pramāda	=	heedlessness;
ālasya	=	laziness;
avirati	=	a highly stubborn attachment or liking;
bhrāntidarśana	=	(bhrānti = Delusory, false + darśana = Vision, view point) Delusory viewpoint;
alabdha bhūmikatva	=	(alabdha = unattained, nonattainable + bhūmika

		= foundation, stage + tva = ness) condition or quality of inability to attain a particular stage (in the progress);
anavasthitatva	=	instability;
citta	=	citta;
vikṣepa (āḥ->s)	=	disturbances, distractions;
te	=	those;
antarāya (āḥ)	=	hindrances, impediments.

TR. - Disease, languour, doubt, heedlessness, laziness, highly stubborn attachment, delusory perception, inability to attain a stage, instability (are) the disturbances of citta (and) those (are also) hindrances (in the path of yoga).

CE. - The nine antarāyas enumerated in the sūtra are specifically mentioned to be disturbances of the citta. Some of them show the undesirable effects on body level, but these effects or symptoms are secondary happenings. In this way disease or sickness, which very often is considered as merely a derailment in the body is according to Patañjali, really having its source in citta. In other words every disease is a mental or psychological disturbance or disorder. The changes taking place and seen in the body are symptoms and secondary results of the real cause, which is psychological or an inner disturbance, which very often is not discernible or comprehended. Even modern medicine is approaching this view point and there are even today many Western medical men, who are of the same opinion that every disease has its deep root in the mind.

Patañjali does not clearly mention any method of treatment specifically for disease (of the body). But as said in the previous sūtra (I:29) praṇavajapa prevents the onslaught of diseases and probably can also cure these, since they are from Patañjali's view point fundamentally citta - vikṣepas. Whether praṇavajapa really cures and prevents diseases is very difficult to say. Indeed it would be very interesting to investigate the disease preventive and curative potentiality of mystical and psychical yogic techniques like praṇavajapa, dhyāna etc.

We may deduce the inference that Patañjali did not preclude the use of medicines for treating diseases in the usual manner, since he has even mentioned their use for attaining siddhis or miraculous powers, which are developed at advanced stages in the progress of yoga. Even there he does not prohibit such use of drugs for attaining siddhis, though he decribes siddhis actually as impediments in the path to samādhi (P.Y.S. III:37).

'Styāna' and 'ālasya' both imply unreadiness for active work, which is always a combination of the physical as well as the mental combined. In styāna the mental factor is more prominent, while in ālasya the bodily inability to work is the predominant factor.

Doubt is always an interfering factor in achieving success in any field. A yoga-sādhaka, therefore, must remove even the slightest trace of doubt about the efficacy or utility of yoga at the very start on this path. A totally unshakable faith or conviction is a primary requisite for success in yoga as already said in sūtra I:20. So any doubt about the effectiveness of yoga and its techniques will evidently act as a hindrance.

Pramāda is that tendency to do undesirable things, both of omission and commission, even when they understand and are aware of the evil results of such wrong commissions and omissions. Many people have this tendency.

Avirati has two negative prefixes - a and vi attached to rati, the main part of the word. Rati itself means liking, fondness, attachment. Virati is, therefore, the same as vairāgya i.e. disattachment. Avirati is, therefore, non-vairāgya, which again means attachment. The two negatives to express a positive meaning are used as in this case, here, to put an emphasis. So avirati should be understood as stubborn attachment, very difficult to remove. Obviously, this will work as hindrance as a total vairāgya would not be possible unless such an avirati of any viṣaya is overcome.

Bhrānti-darśana can be interpreted in three ways, all of which are hindrances. (1) Darśana has a meaning of a school of philosophy. Bhrānti-darśana would in this context mean adoption of a wrong philosophical view point. This can definitely work as a hindrance. For example, it is generally accepted by most of the scholars that Patañjali's yoga stands on a foundation of Sāṃkhya, but very often people, who are firm followers of the Vedānta school, try to interpret the Pātañjala Yoga Sūtras in the light of the philosophy of the school of their liking. This can and does interfere with their progress on the path of yoga, specially while adopting the directives of Yoga Sūtra. This point cannot be elaborated here as it will be very much space consuming.

(2) Darśana means also vision. With the development in

yoga, the sādhakas very often get the experience of strange visions e.g. appearances of different kinds of lights, visions of deities etc. If the meaning of vision is broadly taken as perceptual experiences, even mystical sounds, touch, smell and taste experiences would also be included in this darśana. These experiences, when real, serve as signposts assuring that there is a good progress in the proper direction. But more often people are led to believe that they are getting these experiences of visions merely because they have heard of these and crave for it. In such cases these visions are false or bhrānti-darśanas.

(3) With the progress in yoga many superior abilities and may be, even Vibhūtis like siddhis, are developed in the yoga-sādhaka. When intentionally or unintentionally he has occasion to utilize these potentialities, he draws respect and praise from people, naturally very often his ego is inflated and he begins to have exaggerated view about his own development and status.

This blowing up of the ego also is, therefore, an important case of bhrānti-darśana i.e. wrong view point (about oneself).

The last two antarāyas are very harmful. A sādhaka tries very hard and for long to attain a state of development e.g. that of a particular samādhi, but because of some deep-seated saṃskāras or as it is commonly said, due to his fate, he fails to reach that stage. This is the alabdhabhūmikatva. This state of affairs, when lasting over an unbearably long period, the person may get disappointed. This may lead even to frustration and consequent to the giving up of the effort or practice of yoga totally.

A still greater and dangerous frustration can result due to

anavasthitatva, where a sādhaka gets the experience of a stage e.g. samādhi once, but when he tries to attain it again by the same process, it always results into a failure. In other words the sādhaka is not stabilized in the stage and is not able to develop the mastery over the process. Again saṃskāras or fate is the unpredictable interfering factor. The frustration is still greater, because the sādhaka has once experienced the bliss or benefit of a particular stage and so a great hankering to have the pleasant experience repeatedly and permanently is created in him. But since this cannot be satisfied, the consequent deep frustration may even lead to the complete breakdown of the man.

SS. - दुःखदौर्मनस्याङ्गमेजयत्वश्वासप्रश्वासा विक्षेपसहभुवः ।।१:३१।।

TL. - duḥkhadaurmanasyāṅgamejayatvaśvāsa-praśvāsā vikṣepasahabhuvaḥ - I:31

WM. -

duḥkha	=	pain, misery;
daurmanasya	=	literally a bad state of mind, mental depression;
aṅgamejayatva	=	(aṅgam = member of the body, limb + ejayatva = trembling condition,tremoring), tremoring of the body parts of limbs;
śvāsa	=	inhalation;
praśvāsa	=	exhalation;
āḥ->a	=	indicating plural;
vikṣepa	=	disturbance;
sahabhū(->vaḥ)	=	co-existent (s), accompaniment(s),

TR. - Pain and misery, mental depression, tremoring of the body parts (and disturbances of) inhalation and exhalation are the accompaniments (sahabhuvāḥ) of disturbances (of citta).

CE. - The disturbances of citta are internal and may not be easily perceptible. But their presence can be inferred from acompanying external symptoms. These are enumerated in the present sūtra. One or more of these will always be present, when any citta-vikṣepa is there and so the presence and even intensity or the latter can be adjudged from the degree of activity if these external concomitant symptoms. Since these sahabhuvāḥ (accompaniments) are the results of citta-vikṣepas, certain techniques, which can control the former, will be helpful in removing the latter also.

The first two sahabhuvah are somewhat mental, yet they will have an effect on the body, which would, therefore, serve as easy means for the detection of the hidden and subtler citta-vikṣepas. The latter two are direct changes occurring in the body and easily noticeable.

Duḥkha means both physical pain as well as mental misery. The latter may often produce the former or at least lead to physical discomfort. Such bodily pains or discomforts can be easily detected by gestures of very frequent readjustment of posture of the person.

Daurmanasya i.e. mental depression, certainly leads to a rundown condition of the body to a lesser or greater degree. This again will be discernible by the gestures and adjustment of body postures.

Tremors in body parts and disturbances of breathing are quite objective signs. Any disturbance of citta and mind leads to a trembling of the body and some kind of modification or disturbance of the smooth normal breathing, which may affect either only the inhalation or only exhalation or both. Even temporary mental disturbances of emotions can lead to these two symptoms of aṅgamejayatva (tremors) and disturbance of respiration (śvāsapraśvāsa). The intensity of the trembling and the disturbance of breathing will be proportional to the intensity of the mental disturbance. In fact the breathing is so closely related to the state of mind and therefore also to citta, that a particular type of mental disturbance may lead to a characteristic change in the mode of breathing. It may even be possible to decide the type of mental disturbance or emotion by minutely observing the change produced in the breathing pattern. Thus in anger the exhalation becomes dominant, very forcible and rapid. This change, when marked on account of the intensity of the anger, is so peculiar that it has led to such idioms as a 'a person is breathing like an angry bull'. Disappointment leads to a prolonged and slow exhalation, Anxiety leads to short and shallow inhalations and exhalations. Great shock occasionally leads to short breath suspension. Joy also leads to similar change, but the breathing is not so shallow.

The tremors and respiratory disturbances are so intimately related with mental disturbances that they will occur without fail, everytime, whenever there is any mental disturbance.

However, if the mental disturbance is not very powerful, these two symptoms will be very weak and may not be easily discernible, unless the observer is very minutely observing. On account of this intimate relationship, as said before, the citta-vikṣepas, which are difficult to tackle, can be overcome by controlling and reducing these external symptoms by some means, which may be more practicable, as it is easyer to control the body than the mind. At least one objective of (Haṭhayogic) āsanas and prāṇāyāmas is to gain an ability to control the citta and its activity, through suppressing the trembling of the body and controlling breathing rhythm so that it remains smooth and normal. Patañjali's āsana and prāṇāyāma may also have such a purpose behind them. Patañjali in sūtras I:33 to 39 mentions seven techniques or tricks for stabilization of mind (manas) and purification of citta. Out of these, at least, that indicated in sūtra 34 seems to work on this principle.

SS. - **तत्प्रतिषेधार्थमेकतत्त्वाभ्यासः ।।१:३२।।**

TL. - tat-pratiṣedhārtham-eka-tattvābhyāsaḥ - I:32

WM. - tat = that (citta vikṣepa);
pratiṣedha = counteracting;
artham = for;
eka = one;
tattva = principle, technique, method;
abhyāsa (ḥ) = persistent practice.

TR. - 1. For counteracting that (citta vikṣepa) the practice (of) one principle (technique or method) (is advised).

OR

- 2. For counteracting that (citta-vikṣepa) (there is) one principle to follow (namely) abhyāsa (practice viz. of aṣṭāṇgas).

CE. - The significant word in this sūtra is ekatattvābhyāsaḥ. The interpretation of the sūtra will vary, depending on how this compound word is broken up and what meaning is given to the padas i.e. the component words of the compound. It is made up of three component words-eka+tattva+abhyāsa (one + principle + practice or study). The two interpretations of the sūtra, 1 and 2 above, are thus based on the break-up of the compound either as 1 - the practice (of) one principle and 2 - one principle only (to be followed namely) abhyāsa (practice). In the first interpretation of these, again there can be different senses, depending on what is understood by ekatattva (one principle). Some old commentators, who have more inclination to Advaita Vedānta, have interpreted the expression ekatattava as the one Ultimate Principle or Reality viz. Brahman. They therefore interpreted that the citta vikṣepas can be counteracted by contemplation on Brahman. This interpretation does not seem to be easily acceptable, because it depends on acceptance of Advaitism (Monism), while most scholars are of the opinion that Pātañjala Yoga accepts the dualism of Sāṃkhyas. Secondly it does not suit the context also. Some other commentators have also interpreted the expression as 'one principle', but are very vague about what specifically this one principle is. Some speak as if anything which the sādhaka may find helpful in overcoming citta -vikṣepa is indicated by this expression.

When the citta-vikṣepas would be overcome, the result would be tranquillization of citta, which again would only be possible if the mind (manas), which is a part of citta, is stabilized and tranquillized. Looking to this, the term ekatattva should be interpreted as one of principles (techniques, methods, tricks) mentioned in the subsequent seven sūtras viz. I:33 to 39, recommended for achieving 'citta-prasādana' and 'manasasthitinibandhanam'. This interpretation seems to be the most apt in this context.

SS. - **मैत्रीकरुणामुदितोपेक्षाणां सुखदुःखपुण्यापुण्यविषयाणां भावनातश्चितप्रसादनम् ।।१:३३।।**

TL. - maitrī-karuṇā-muditopekṣāṇām sukha-duḥkha-puṇyāpuṇya-viṣayāṇāṃ bhāvanātaścittaprasādanam-I:33.

WM. -

maitrī	=	friendliness;
karuṇā	=	compassion, pity;
muditā	=	happiness, joy;
upekṣā	=	indifference;
āṇāṃ	=	a plural case suffix for sixth or possessive case i.e. 'of ';
sukha	=	pleasure, well being;
duḥkha	=	misery, hardship;
puṇya	=	virtue, merit;
apuṇya	=	non-virtue, viciousness, sin;
viṣaya	=	subjects (persons, events etc.);
āṇāṃ	=	of;
bhāvanā	=	repeated treatment (to the mind or citta);
taḥ	=	case suffix of fifth case = from, through;
citta-prasādana (m)	=	process of achieving a blissful tranquil state of citta.

TR. - (By cultivating the attitude of) friendship, compassion, (participation in) joy, (and) indifference (aloofness), (respectively) towards the subjects (persons or events etc.) of (being in) pleasure, misery, virtue (and) viciousness, through repeated treatment (repeatedly telling the citta and mind to do thus) (is produced) the citta-prasādana (the blissful and peaceful state of citta).

CE. - The mind and citta are disturbed in the empirical world by such undesirable tendencies like jealousy, hatred, anger, taking demonic pleasure from other peoples' suffering etc. So a peaceful condition of citta can be achieved only by counteracting these evil or negative tendencies, undesirable for a yoga-sādhaka. To bring about a peace forcefully by some stressful impositions like suppression of tendencies, which is not pleasant to the citta and mind, would no doubt, bring a tranquil state, but is not very desirable. Therefore, the peace-fullness must also be pleasant. This is what is implied in the word prasāda or prasādanam (process of achieving prasāda). This first principle or technique recommended for achieving citta-prasāda is, in fact, the master technique for achievement of this result ultimately, even through the other six techniques described in the sūtra I:34 to 39 the citta-prasāda will be really established only if the negative attitudes mentioned above are replaced by the positive ones as indicated in this sūtra.

When an ordinary human being sees another person in circumstances, which by comparison to those of his own are happier, a feeling of jealousy is usually created in his mind about that other person. This jealousy may be very subtle, e.g.

when a mother sees the affection of her son being shared by the son's wife after his marriage and such other examples. It may also turn into great hatred in case of other persons when the feeling towards that person is openly inimical. This tendency of jealousy will be reduced, the more the feeling of love and friendship, i.e. one's ownness, is developed towards that other person. This is what is recommended in the sutra viz. to cultivate the attitude of friendliness towards persons in happier circumstances.

In the same way when a person sees another one in miserable circumstances, a feeling of pleasure or smugness is often produced in that person's mind, specially if the outlook about the unhappy man is of inimical nature. In such a case even towards inimical person an attitude of compassion or pity should be attempted to be cultivated.

Meritorious persons draw praise and respect from others. Most often, one, who does not get such praise and honour from people, again becomes depressed and miserable on account of comparing himself with that meritorious person. So, then there is a need to cultivate the feeling of happiness, as if one is sharing the praise with that other meritorious person.

Similarly one again develops a feeling of smugness or pleasure or satisfaction, when one sees some evil person being punished, since a sense may be developed in one's mind that the person deserves the punishment. But for a yoga sādhaka, such a feeling of deriving pleasure or satisfaction from seeing another person in unfortunate and painful circumstances, is harmful and undesirable. Therefore, in such situation he should try to be neutral, indifferent, neither being glad nor miserable.

The word upekṣā has been translated here as indifference. It should be understood in the sense of "an attitude and ability of not being affected adversely by emotional disturbances and to have an attitude of forgiveness, towards actions of evil persons, even when harmful to oneself". The best example of this is Jesus Christ towards those who killed him, for whom he had a prayer- "Oh God, forgive them, because they know not what they are doing". It does not indicate a feelinglessness or callousness, sometimes bordering upon cruelty, particularly when one sees other persons, for whom there is not much feeling of concern or love, in adverse and miserable circumstances. The indifference recommended here does not mean that the yoga sādhaka should not do anything to try to mitigate, as far as in his power, the misery of that other man. The indifference means not getting emotionally involved and affected in one's own mind. This is true not for only the last pair of apuṇya-upekṣā, but for the other three pairs of the sūtra also. Particularly it may be pointed out that word karuṇā has been rendered in English by pity and compassion, only because there are no other suitable English words to express even the approximate meaning., but the word pity implies mental involvement and consequent disturbing mental affectation. The word compassion is nearer to the real meaning, but as it is formed viz. com + passion, it also implies participating in the passion i.e. the sorrow of the other suffering man. But this is not what is meant by the word karuṇā. It should be understood as a softness and considerateness towards the other person without emotional self-involvement.

Though this technique is the best and really essential for achievement of citta-prasādana to perfection, it can be clearly seen that it is not easy to bring it into practice in actual life. These negative emotions of jealousy etc. can not be easily curbed and uprooted. That is why this technique may not be suitable for most individuals and keeping this in view Patañjali has recommended six other techniques.

Though hard to practise to perfection, no doubt every one should at least try to practise this method to perfection. Certainly if at the same time recourse or help is taken of one or more of the other six techniques it would give quicker and better result. In the way these seven techniques or principles of cittprasādana and manasasthitinibandhana are presented here, they seem to be quite equivalent to each other, since they are connected by the conjunction of alternation 'vā' i.e. or. From this it can be concluded that any one of them would produce the desired result in the longer run, though the time required may vary. So any one of these techniques which may be suitable and convenient for the personality of the yoga sādhaka may be chosen by him for achieving citta-prasādana. Nevertheless, it can be noted that none of these techniques is contra-indicatory with any other and so a sādhaka may advantageously take recourse to more than one of these simultaneously and parallelly to achieve the results more rapidly. In this way even if a sādhaka adopts any one or more of the remaining six techniques as the main means of attaining cittprasādana, he should at the same time try as far as possible to work on this first master technique, as it is the one which really gives or produces the result. To the extent the sādhaka will be successful in this technique, the cittaprasādana will be established to that much degree.

A doubt may arise here as to whether merely telling the mind to cultivate the positive attitude of friendliness etc. would really be effective. It is a common experience however that if the "telling" to the mind is done very earnestly and continuously, the tendency of the mind gradually is to obey these instructions given to it by its ownself. To indicate this the term bhāvanātaḥ has been used by Patañjali, which has a sense of repeated treatment which works like a mould for setting.

SS. - **प्रच्छर्दनविधारणाभ्यां वा प्राणस्य ।।१:३४।।**

TL. - pracchardanavidhāraṇābhyāṃ vā prāṇasya- I:34

WM. -

pracchardana	=	(pra + cchardana = emitting out) intensive driving out i.e. deep and forceful exhalation:
vidhāraṇa	=	(vi + dhāraṇa = holding, taking in) retention/taking in in a specific manner i.e. controlled inhalation;
vā	=	or
prāṇa (sya)	=	prāṇa (of).

TR. - 1. Or through exhalation and retention of prāṇa.

Or

- 2. Or by deep and forceful exhalation and controlled inhalation of prāṇa.

CE. - Most of the old commentators have generally rendered the sūtra as in 1. Some have rendered the word pracchardana by expiration or exhalation merely, while others have clarified it as a deep or complete exhalation. The word vidhāraṇa has been rendered as retention i.e. holding, which usually would be interpreted as holding in i.e. retention of breath in the lungs after the inhalation or (antara) kumbhaka in Haṭhayogic parlance. Others have interpreted it as retention of breath outside the lungs i.e. not taking in breath after the deep exhalation or bāhya kumbhaka.

This translation of the sūtra, specially the meaning of vidhāraṇa as retention does not seem to be very correct. Retention of breath either inside or outside, which also involves suspension of the rhythmic respiratory activity usually mentioned by the Haṭhayogic technical term kumbhaka can be, both according to Haṭhayoga as well as Pātañjala Yoga Sūtra II:49, 50, only a component part of prāṇāyāma. Patañjali is definitely not mentioning in the present sūtra a prāṇāyāmic technique. This is merely a preliminary technique involving breathing for achieving the citta-prasāda. Prāṇāyāma occupies the fourth position in the order of aṣṭāṅgas and these aṅgas are consecutively expounded in the 2nd pada of Sādhanas i.e. means. So this process can not be a prāṇāyāma, which would be out of place. So the technique would not and should not incorporate retention of breath. Further if vidhāraṇa is interpreted as retention of breath, the sutra seems to keep mum about the mode of inhalation. From this point also it seems better and more correct to interpret vidhāraṇa as (vi = viśeṣa prakāreṇa = in a special manner + dhāraṇa = taking in) a specially taken-in breath i.e. a controlled inhalation. Kumbhaka or holding of breath is a rather hazardous action. Generally the harmful effect of a wrong practice of prāṇāyāma are always a consequence of some error or excess beyond one's capacity in the breath holding part of prāṇāyāma. Sometimes the dangerous effects are so grave that the man's nervous system is completely shattered and he may even turn into a madman. So a scientific expounder like Patañjali would not take the risk of mentioning a technique involving breath-holding at such a preparatory stage. Therefore, the 2nd translation or rendering seems preferable and more correct.

There are instances (of Kolhatkar, sūtra I:34) of spiritually very highly advanced persons, who have attained the cittaprasāda by the practice of this technique viz. a very powerful and rapid deep exhalation, somewhat of explosive type like a vomiting, followed by a controlled i.e.. deep and smooth inhalation. This practice is comparable to the Kapālabhāti practice in Haṭhayoga, except the difference that both the inhalation and exhalation here are deliberate and comparatively deep. This instance (of Kolhatkar, above) also is in support that the procedure of the 2 nd translation produces actually the result of cittaprasādana and so should be the correct translation.

Prāṇa is a technical term in yoga. The basic meaning of the word is an energy or force, which is the essential force for maintenance of life. In short prāṇa can be explained as the ultimate life force and source. Without it life would be impossible. This is shown by such expression as "prāṇa has departed" used for death. This energy or force is very subtle and neither modern sciences nor ancient śastras have clearly explained its nature and characteristics. Every form of energy and force known to modern science that works in the body-mind complex of the organism is according to the ancient concept, derived from prāṇa, which is the ultimate driving force and impulse. Thus every activity and function of the body and the mind is carried out by the force of prāṇa. But those functions in the body, which are autonomous, are in this view, to a greater extent or probably solely carried out by the pranic force. Now, if we have to make a contact with prāṇa in order to tackle it or get a control over it, evidently it will be in the area of these autonomous functions that we can do it easily and best. But as the word autonomous indicates, the functions can not be controlled or tackled by volition. So, the controlling of prāṇa can be attempted in that region or function, which is governed dually, through autonomy as well as through volition. One of the foremost of such activities in the organism is respiration. Normally it goes on autonomously, but we can have a voluntary control over it to some extent. Therefore, the prāṇa can be best and conveniently controlled by controlling respiration, no doubt, judiciously. That is why, techniques having the primary objective of controlling prāṇa, which are designated as prāṇāyāma (prāṇa + āyāma = extending, lengthening i.e. both increasing the potentiality of prāṇa and also lengthening the period of its activity, which evidently can be done only if one gets control over it) are in actuality processes in which breathing is controlled in some way. So, generally in yogic parlance, unless the context does not permit it, the word prāṇa is interpreted as breath or respiration, which is evidently the meaning of prāṇa here also.

SS. - **विषयवती वा प्रवृत्तिरुत्पन्ना मनसस्थितिनिबन्धनी ।।१:३५।।**

TL. - viṣayavatī vā pravṛttirūtpannā manasasthitinibandhanī- I:35.

WM. -

viṣaya	=	subject (which also can be an object);
vatī	=	feminine suffix meaning possessor of, full of;
vā	=	or;
pravṛtti	=	tendency, inclination, intense activity etc.;
utpannā	=	produced, created;
manasa	=	mind;
sthiti	=	state;
nibandhanī	=	thoroughly binding of stabilizing.

TR. - Or a tendency (intense activity) (of mind) full of a subject, (if) produced, (is) binding the state of (steadying) the mind.

CE. - The techniques mentioned in the sūtras I:35 to 38 are, as explained in this sūtra, primarily the techniques for steadying the mind, which is a prerequisite for the prasāda of citta, since mind is a part of citta. So in a way they are techniques for achieving cittaprasādana ultimately, trying to steady the mind as a first step. In sūtra I:36 to 38 the phrase, corresponding to the meaning "binding the state of mind" is not explicitly mentioned. It is to be understood and may be added in the suitable gender form e.g. manasasthiti-nibandhanī in sūtra I:36 also, while manasasthiti-nibandhanam in sūtras I:37 and I:38.

The technique recommended in the present sūtra (I:35) is

of creating an activity or tendency of the mind which is viṣayavatī i.e. possessing or full of the subject. A query arises as to what is the exact significance of this expression, because the activity of mind will always be related to some subject or the other. Mind never functions without having any subject or basis for its functioning. Ordinarily in such functioning the subject or object, which the mind deals with, is existent or at least felt as existing in the external world or the creation. Even in a normal imagination the mind imagines about the subject, which may be an object or phenomenon, which is felt to be residing outside the mind i.e. in the external world. The subject or object referred to here is a tendency of the mind itself. The feeling created will be that that particular thing is, as if, being created internally in that mind itself. This is what is indicated by viṣayavatī i.e. full of subject, i.e. the subject is in that mind itself.

Now, the viṣayas, especially when they are objects, are cognized and enjoyed by the mind through the agency of one or more of the five senses of perception. Therefore, for enjoying the viṣaya mentioned in this technique, though created i.e. imagined by the mind and with a feeling that it is being produced interiorly, one or more sense should get the sensation or perception of that subject or object to create a feeling as if the subject or object is actually existing inside. This sensation in the case of such internally imagined objects will be most often restricted only to one sense. Thus the mind has to produce in this technique an object (subject) or thing, whose effect is felt or perceived predominantly through any one of the senses. Thus mind has to create i.e. imagine, as if, the internally existing things, could be seen, heard, smelt, felt or tasted by repeated and persistently continued contemplation of such imagined objects. They can be produced in this manner, after a shorter or longer time. On account of the usual order of dominance of these senses, the objects thus created by the mind and in the mind can be more easily produced enjoyable in that order of senses as mentioned in the previous sentence. That is why the phenomena of seeing lights and visions is experienced by the largest number of yoga sādhakas. The audition is the second in order of dominance and so phenomena of sound hearing are next in abundance in the experience of yoga sādhakas. The precise order of dominance for the remaining three senses is not definitely known, yet olfactory (smell) sense probably comes next in order and many yoga sādhakas, including the present commentator, have experienced the phenomena of creating a desired fragrance with a practice of such contemplative imagination carried over for about three to six months. For this the yoga sādhaka should sit in the squatting posture, if possible preferably a meditational posture e.g. Padmāsana, Siddhāsana etc. and try to relax to the maximum, He should be without any movement, but this should not lead to any discomfort and constraint. Then he should try to direct his attention to the tip of the nose or opening of the nostrils and imagine that he is having an odour of any flower, say rose or jasmine. If this contemplative imagination is performed concentratedly for half an hour or more daily, for a few months, the sādhaka may be able to have a feeling or experience, as if he is having that kind of odour from an actual flower or the bottle of a scent. The objects which can be felt by touch or taste can also be produced in the same manner, but probably taking a much longer time and more powerful ability of imagination.

Why such imagined objects should be able to steady the mind and not the actual objects existing in the world? The reason is that these phenomena are so remarkable and the sensation produced in the various senses is so enticing that the mind automatically sticks and remains absorbed in the strange experience. In fact, the sensation is so pleasant and attractive that the person may get an obsession and would like to remain in that experience longer and longer, just like an addict. It is to be pointed out, therefore, that the technique is to be practised only for training the mind to remain steady on one subject for a long time. Once this result of manasasthitinibandhanam is obtained and the habit to remain steady is firmly established in the mind, the sādhaka should give up this practice of the particular technique of producing a viṣayavatī-pravṛtti in the mind, though very often on account of the pleasurable feeling he may be allured to have the experience again. Otherwise, the sādhaka will have an obsessional craving for this pleasure and his further progress on the path of yoga may be interfered with.

SS. - **विशोका वा ज्योतिष्मती ।।१:३६।।**

TL. - viśokā vā jyotiṣmatī- I:36

WM. - viśokā = (vi = without + śoka = sorrow for a loss) not causing grief, serene;

vā = or;

jyotiṣmatī = (jyoti = flame, light, illumination + mati = possessing, full of), full of illumination, possessing a flame like light.

TR. - Or a griefless illuminating (light-showing) (tendency of mind) (will be steadying the state of mind).

CE. - This is the second technique recommended for steadying the mind. So the expression manasasthitinibandhinī is to be understood here also.

Patañjali isolates this particular phenomenon or experience of seeing a jyoti i.e. flame or light, which is a special case of the general technique of developing a tendency or activity of the mind to create a subject or object, which could be internally experienced, as if through a sense (cf I:35), in this case the feeling being visual, since this sense is the most dominant in almost all non-blind persons and so the experience is the most common for many a yoga sādhaka this experience is usually spontaneous and when genuine it can be very facilitatory for helping the sādhaka in advancing in the process of meditation, But it can also be a mere psychologically produced illusion. The technique recommended in this sūtra I:36 is actually to create artificially the vision of a flame-like illumination by repeatedly telling the mind that it can see the jyoti. Nevertheless, as explained under sūtra I:35 these sensations are so alluring that the mind sticks to them, so to say, effortlessly and learns to become steady. The sensation of seeing the flame or light is very easily produced and that,is why Patañjali has given this, as a special technique separately from those of sūtra I:35.

Viśokā primarily means without śoka i.e. griefless. It does not mention clearly the pleasantness of the vision of light. It, therefore, would mean a state of sereneness, but actually should be understood as pleasure giving. Instead of using a term like ānandadādtrī etc., a somewhat unfamiliar term viśokā is used by Patañjali probably intentionally. Śoka is the grief felt for the loss of a thing or person. Such a sorrow, leading to a depression of mind would not be produced through some unknown interfering factors, by the sādhaka, after experiencing it for sometime. In fact, as indicated under sūtra I:35, the practice of wilfully producing such artificial and imaginary light, sound and other sense experiences, is to be given up, once the mind is able to remain steady and cittprasādana is attained. When, therefore, the phenomena is discontinued accidentally or deliberately the loss of the experience, in this case of the flame-light does not cause a disquietude of mind, which is indicated by the term viśokā.

SS. - **वीतरागविषयं वा चित्तम् ।।१:३७।।**

TL. - vītarāgaviṣayaṃ vā cittam - I:37.

WM. - vītarāga = (vīta = transcended, disappeared + rāga = attachment, passion). One which has transcended the attachment or passion; One in which the attachment or passion has disappeared;

viṣayaṃ = subject (object, topic);

vā = or;

cittam = citta.

TR. - 1. Or (through giving) the citta a subject (for contemplation) (e.g. a person as an ideal) what has transcended the attachment (passion).

2. Or (through) a citta which has transcended the attachment for (any) subject (thing or person).

CE. - This is the third technique for "manasasthiti-nibandhanam" (neutral form of the adjectival expression, since the word citta, which it qualifies is neutral) which expression is understood in this and the next sūtra I:38.

Most of the old commentators have interpreted the sūtra meaning as the rendering No. 1 above. This interpretation should be quite acceptable, as it would surely produce a result of steadying the mind, when the mind contemplates upon the life of a saintly person, who has transcended the attachment. This bhāvanam or repeated treatment or telling to the mind, gradually would make the mind itself to adopt the ways of this ideal personage. As a result the mind will gradually become more and more attachmentless and this naturally would lead to its steady state.

However, if an attempt is made to make the mind itself passionless, again by bhāvanam or telling it to give up the passions as they are trouble-producing, the mind may and does obey such instructions. The result of steadiness would come up as the passions diminish and ultimately disappear. In this light the rendering No. 2 above is also valid.

SS. - **स्वप्ननिद्राज्ञानालम्बनं वा ।।१:३८।।**

TL. - svapnanidrājñānālambanaṃ vā, I:38

WM. - svapna = dream;
nidrā = sleep;
jñāna = knowledge or experience;
ālambana = a support (for suspending a thing from e.g. a peg);
vā = or.

TR. - Or (for steadying the mind take the) support of the knowledge gained through (1) dream (and) sleep; (2) the dreamfull sleep.

CE. - The fourth technique recommended for "manasa-sthitinibandhanam" is giving the mind the support (just as a thing is hung upon a support like a peg) of the knowledge obtained in the sleep states.

The compound svapnanidrā has been resolved by most of the old commentators as svapna (dream) and nidrā (dreamless sleep). A difficulty is at first sight felt in accepting this (i.e. 1. above) interpretation. In dreamless sleep (and it is this, which is clearly defined by Patañjali as the meaning of the word nidrā shown in sūtra I:10) there is no experience, since there is absence of pratyaya content or experience as stated in this sūtra of nidrā. How can, then, there be any knowledge, since there is no experience into the mind ? Therefore, the advice to take support of the knowledge gained in nidrā (i.e. a dreamless sleep, as is to be clearly understood, if it is to be distinguished from svapna (dream) if the interpretation No. 1 above is accepted) becomes absurd and impracticable.

To get out of this difficulty the word "svapnanidrā" has been rendered as "svapnayuktanidrā (dreamful sleep) (see Dr. M.

Sahay, Y.M. Qrty. Vol 13, No. 3 page 25), where there is some experience in dream and this can give some kind of experience, which can be called knowledge. If the objection be raised that Patañjali would have, in that case, used the shorter word 'svapna' only, it could be answered by reminding that day-dreaming i.e. wakeful dreaming or 'divasvapna' is also a condition in which the person is experiencing a state nearly like that of dreamy sleep. Again the word 'svapna' alone in common usage in Sanskṛt is used as such as a synonym for nidrā or deep sleep initself, which case the process of dreaming is not necessarily implied.

The main point about this sūtra is the detailed exact significance of this technique, especially with reference to its utilization practically for attaining the manasasthitinibandhanam.

The objective is to make the mind steady through its own efforts. The mind has therefore, to control its own wandering tendency, and any controlling is to be done deliberately. For this reason, to make use of the trick recommended in this technique, it is necessary first to develop a capacity of having dreams or sleep i.e. dreamful and dreamless sleeps at order, Then only the working of the whole technique could be under one's own control.

Everyone must have experienced that when one has to catch a railway train or a bus at some very odd-hour in the night, and the reason for which the journey is to be undertaken being of a most urgent nature, one wake up at precisely the desired time, even if there is no alarm clock or another person to awaken him. Very often this experience is so vivid that the person so awakened has a feeling as if some one has actually awakened him by something like shaking etc. in fact, when there is some such urgency, a part of citta is always alert and watching over the welfare and management of the body-mind - organism. This inner and everwakeful 'watchman' is often referred to in yogic language as the 'sākṣī'. If the person who wants thus to get awakened at a fixed time in the deeper parts of night, gives mentally an emphatic warning to his mind, just prior to going to sleep, giving the mind precise time when one should wake up, this sāksī part of the citta registers this instruction and the person wake up at the predetermined time. By practice this ability can be developed to such an extent that the person so awakes at the time exact to the minute. The feeling is gained as if someone has actually awakened him, as if by shaking. This ability can be further developed. If one tells his own mind after this in the same way to create a dream at a particular period of the night, the person actually gets a dream at that time. This can still be developed further to such an extent that the dream will be exactly conforming in all its details to a story or scenario preplanned for this dream and given to the mind. The dreams are then exact reproduction, just like a movie-film, of the presented scenario. When such a capacity of dream production is developed, the themes prescribed for the dream can be so chosen that the mind will have a very pleasant and enticing experience. The effect of such dreams, especially produced to order, is so impressive that the mind even in the wakeful part of the day afterwards, remains inwardly attached to this impression or memory of the dream. This pleasant mood automatically prevents the mind from easily getting perturbed by any disturbing troubles in the day to day life. Thus the manasasthitinibandhana and subsequent citta-prasādana can be easily obtained and firmly established by the practice of this technique, once the mastery over the dream production has been obtained. This is the way svapna or svapnayukta nidrā (i.e. dreamy sleep) knowledge is used to obtain the result.

If the nidrājñāna is taken as the knowledge of dreamless sleep, as meant in the interpretation No. 1 above, then it becomes a special case of the above described technique. The mind can be instructed in the same way to go into a sound sleep when there should be no interfering dreams. With a longer and persistent practice even this ability is developed. Since the dreams are not to arise as per instruction given to the sākṣī part of citta and so no dreams then arise, it is obvious that the sākṣī is keeping the watch over the dream arousing mechanism and inhibiting it. The sākṣī, which means "witness", is thus witnessing the whole phenomenon of deep sleep. And in this way it is an observer, perceiver or experiencer of the state of deep sleep. Though this experience can not be described, as it is impossible to describe the experience of total absence (of everything) directly, as said under sūtra I:10, the impression or effect (saṃskāra) of it is left over the mind and the mind can revive it to some extent even in the wakeful state thereafter. The degree of revival of this effect in the wakeful state goes on increasing with practice. The mind thus can remain in a peaceful state highly akin to sleep even in the waking state and this peaceful feeling is also a pleasant one i.e. sāttvika and not like the after effects of tāmasika sleep giving rise to heaviness, lethargy, dullness etc. This is the way the knowledge i.e. experience of dreamless sleep can be used for having citta-prasādana. No doubt this latter tact is much more difficult to obtain than that of producing ordered dreams. Yet one, who is keen and persistent, can definitely achieve it and the manasasthitinibandhana and cittaprasādana obtained through this technique is much effective and deeply seated than obtained through controlled dreams

The reader may be here reminded of the modern view about deep sleep, that it is actually a succession of alternately short bouts of dreams and dreamlessness. Therefore, what is called a deep i.e. 'dreamless' sleep is actually full of dreams, but these are not remembered. The deep sleep, which is mentioned in the above explanation, should be understood of as such a deep sleep, which may have dreams which leave no impression and so can not be remembered even if effort is made to do so.

SS. - **यथाभिमतध्यानाद्वा ।।१:३९।।**

TL. - yathābhimatadhyānād-vā- I:39

WM. - yathā = as suitable to, according to;
abhimata = liking;
dhyāna (ād)= (from or through) dhyāna;
vā = or.

TR. - Or through 'dhyanā' according to one's liking.

CE. - The phrase 'cittaprasādanam' is to be taken as understood here i.e. the complete sūtra would be

'yathābhimatadhyānādva cittaprasādanam'

Patañjali seems to say here that dhyāna is a technique or method of achieving cittaprasādana, which would be an absurd or self-contradictory statement. Cittaprasādana i.e. the pleasant peaceful condition of citta, is obviously a prerequisite for the meditational processes, even for dhāraṇā, which is itself prior to dhyāna (III:1-2). So, a question arises how can dhyāna be a method for achieving cittaprasādana.

There can be two explanations : -

1. The word dhyāna has been used by Patañjali here not as a technical word i.e. in the sense of the seventh aṅga out of the aṣṭāṅgas and therefore, not with the precise meaning of it as defined in the sūtra III:2; but as a word of common language and loosely having a sense of any meditational or concentrative activity of mind. But this does not seem to be much probable as Patañjali seems to be a very scientific exponent of the subject of yoga in these Yoga Sūtras. He nowhere else uses a technical word in such a loose manner i.e. using it as an ordinary word, Not only this, but he seems to be very cautious in choosing even a specific synonym of common word in particular sūtras. Thus it becomes very difficult to accept that Patañjali has used in this sūtra only, a technical word in such a loose sense. Most of the old commentators, however, have given an explanation of this sūtra as if that Patñjali has committed this fault.

2. If we do not accept such a levity on the part of Patañjali then it becomes incumbent that the word dhyāna is used by Patañjali in the precise sense of sūtra III:2. Then the explanation seems to be that this is not to be looked upon as a technique or method for achieving citta-prasādana as its result; but that it is a

mere statement of a fact i.e. that cittaprasādana in its real sense or to its perfection is achieved only when the sādhaka has attained the stage of dhyāna. The cittaprasādana obtained through the means given in the sūtras I:33 to 38 would give the cittaprasādana to a greater degree, greater the success of the sādhaka in that technique; nevertheless, even the best results of those techniques will be not as perfect as the cittaprasādana, which will be experienced when a sādhaka gets mastery over dhyāna as described in sūtra III:2.

This second explanation seems to be more correct and so preferable, because out of these seven sūtras, I:33, 34 and 39 have used the (fifth) ablative case indicating that in all these, the end result is cittaprasādhana; while in sūtras I:35, 36, 37 and 38 (the first) nominative case is used, indicating that, that particular activity of mind viz. pravṛtti, holding of viṣaya taken as ālambana, leads to the binding of the state of mind. Why dhyāna, if it were a method for obtaining cittaprasādana, should not have been mentioned immediately after the first two techniques, (of sūtra I:33, 34) for the identical result ? The reason for this discrepancy may very well be this, mentioned above, that the dhyāna is not that way a technique recommended for practice to achieve cittaprasādana as the result, but the sūtra is a mere factual statement.

SS. - **परमाणुपरममहत्त्वान्तोऽस्य वशीकारः ।।१:४०।।**

TL. - paramāṇuparamamahattvānto'sya vaśīkāraḥ- I:40.

WM. - paramāṇu = (parama = the ultimate + aṇu = a small particle), smallest particle or thing;

paramamahattva	=	the biggest thing;
anta (ḥ->o)	=	extremity, end, terminal;
asya	=	of this;
vaśīkara (ḥ)	=	complete subjugation and obedience, complete control (over something).

TR. - (There is) complete control of such a one (either the citta having prasādana or the person, who has achieved it) on the smallest particle or thing at one end (and) the biggest thing at the other end.

CE. - It can not be stated with certainty that the meaning of the sūtra is literally true, though it is believed generally by the people of devotional and religious tendencies that the perfect yogis are omnipotent and they can, therefore, do anything they like in any object, however small or however great it may be. This is what the sūtra apparently seems to say. There are stories and legends of such actions done by great yogīs and saints. But the statement may be even an exaggeration made purely for arthavāda (a purpose of bringing out the importance of a particular thing by eulogising it somewhat exaggeratedly). In that case the sūtra may be interpreted as showing a development of very great power in the Yogī. It is as good as saying that the yogī becomes omnipotent.

Even if this is not true, the power of the mind is recognised everywhere. In fact many a time even the physical force becomes ineffective if the mind does not co-operate with it. In short, a calm and quiet mind is a great source of power and may be looked upon as pre-requisite for the usage of potentialities of man in an efficient manner.

In the above comments the sense of the sūtra has been accepted as the one given by most of the translators and commentators. But the sense of the sūtra can be slightly different as indicated by George Feuerstein (The Yoga Sūtra of Patañjali, year 1979, W.W.Dawson & Sons Ltd., Folkestone, Kents, U.K page 51), where the mastery is not to be looked upon as the supernatural power to control or do anything with the object of meditation, small or big, but as the mastery to hold his mind steady upon any object or subject, however small or big. This sūtra then becomes an extension and explanation of the previous sūtra I:39 and has the advantage that involving no supernormal phenomena can be easily and rationally understood.

SS. - **क्षीणवृत्तेरभिजातस्येव मणेर्ग्रहीतृग्रहणग्राह्येषु तत्स्थदञ्जनता समापत्तिः ।।१:४१।।**

TL. - kṣīṇavṛtter-abhijātasyeva maṇer-grahītṛ-grahaṇa-grāhyeṣu tatstha--tadañjanatā samāpattiḥ- I:41

WM. - kṣīṇavṛtteḥ(→r) = (kṣīṇa = dwindled, weakened - vṛtteḥ (→r) = of the vṛtti) of the one (citta or person) whose vṛttis have become dwindled;

abhijāta (sya) = (of) the one of a noble birth, faultless, perfect;

iva = like;

maṇeḥ (→r) = (maṇi= jewel, crystal) of a jewel or crystal;

grahitṛ = apprehender, comprehender, conceiver, perceiver, grasper;

grahaṇa	=	act of apprehending, comprehending, conceiving, perceiving, grasping;
grāhya	=	(subject or object) apprehended, comprehended; conceived, perceived, grasped
eṣu	=	in (plural suffix of seventh i.e. locative case);
tatsthatā	=	isotopy i.e. condition of being in its (other's i.e. of grāhya) place.
tadañjanatā	=	(tat→d) -- its + añjanatā -- colourfulness i.e. possession of qualities), capacity and condition of taking its (of the other i.e. of a grāhya) colours i.e. qualities;
samāpatti (ḥ)	=	samāpatti (is).

TR. - Just as a faultless jewel (when placed on a surface, not only takes up its place but also its qualities), the process, of occupying the same space and imbibing all the qualities of the grāhya (subject being comprehended) by the grahītā (comprehender, citta) during the activity of grahaṇa (comprehension) in the case of the one (citta) whose vṛttis have already dwindled (so that the citta is abhijāta- highly pure and clear), is called samāpatti.

CE. - The word samāpatti has been treated as a synonym of samādhi by almost all the commentators, but this seems to be quite wrong. Both the words are technical terms in the science of yoga. If the things meant by these two terms are one and the same, it would mean that two technical terms have been coined for one thing, which should not happen in a scientific field. Patañjali particularly would have not made such a serious mistake. He would have used only one of these words if both were standing for one and the same thing. But this is not the case. Samāpatti and samādhi are very closely related, but they are different from one another. The Chart I after page 125 clearly shows the inter-relationship in between samāpattis, samādhis etc. The word samāpatti can be broken up as : sam--a prefix indicating completeness +ā -- towards or in + pat -- to fall + ti -- a suffix usually indicating a movement or process. Thus samāpatti would literally mean the process of falling (merging) into (a thing, which here would be the object or subject taken for going along the contemplative processes i.e. the grāhya) completely, i.e. the process of completely merging into a thing. Thus samāpatti is a process of merging of the citta with the subject it wants to comprehend or grasp. This is very explicitly indicated in the sūtra. Samāpatti, according to it, is that process where the grahītā- comprehender, which is the citta (or person), undergoes a process or activity in which it takes the place i.e. becomes one with the subject to be comprehended i.e. grāhya, at the same time taking all its qualities. In other words the citta gets identified completely with the subject of contemplation, the grāhya. This identification is so complete that the citta becomes the subject (grāhya) itself and imbibes all its qualities. In this identification, when it is complete, the comprehender citta and the subject of comprehension (grāhya viṣaya) become one. Then there would remain no distinction between the two viz. the comprehender and the comprehended. The process of comprehending also therefore, becomes impossible. This is what is meant by the expression : grahītṛgrahanagrāhyeṣu-tatsthatadanjañatā i.e. total identity in the comprehender, comprehension and the comprehended.

In other words the comprehender (grahītā) citta, the process of comprehending (grahaṇa) and the subject to be comprehended (grāhya) merge into one another and become one and since the comprehender, citta and comprehended, subject have become one, there is no further activity of comprehension possible. The comprehension (grahaṇa) has also, as it, merged with the grahītā and grāhya.

This total identification in which the grahītā, citta is isotopic with the subject or object to be comprehended (grāhya) and also takes up all its qualities, can take place only in the case of citta (or person) whose vṛttis have become quite weakened i.e. when they arise very rarely and even then are so feeble as not to be able to disturb the mind.

To illustrate this phenomenon the example is given of a faultless jewel or crystal (maṇi), which when placed on a coloured surface takes up the colour of the supporting material and becomes as if a part of the supporting material. This becoming one, i.e. the merger or identification of the 'maṇi' with its support, will be so much nearer to perfection, more the maṇi is without fault or blemish. If there be a maṇi without the slightest defect, the transmission of the light will be perfect, which will create an impression that the maṇi has absorbed the colour of the supporting surface totally, abhijāta primarily means born in a high family or of noble birth. In the case of a jewel or crystal (maṇi) its nobleness will be its degree of transmitting the light, because more perfect or faultless the crystal, more valuable or worthy i.e. noble it is. Even if there is a slight fault in the crystal, it does not transmit the light perfectly and its value in the market goes down. If the light transmission would be perfect, the crystal will as if merge with the background to such an extent that it would not be possible to distinguish it from the background unless one minutely observes it. Very probably in Patañjali's times glass was not known. That is why Patañjali had to give an example, to clarify this process of total identification, of the material which had the highest light transmitting ability in his times viz. a maṇi i.e. a jewel or a crystal. To find a crystal, having the least defect and so able to transmit the light as near to perfection as possible, is not an easy thing and that is why Patañjali had to qualify the word maṇi by the adjective abhijāta i.e. blemishless. In modern times very high quality optical glass is manufactured. A block of such glass would transmit the light so perfectly that on many an occasion it will not be easy to detect it and differentiate it from the surface on which it is kept. So in present times it is very easy to see how this impression, that the perfect glass, which is the transmitter or absorber i.e. grasper (grahītā) has become as if one with the object, grāhya, whose colour it is absorbing and transmitting, and if Patañjali were living in modern times he might have chosen such an illustration in place of that of a jewel or natural crystal.

Samāpatti is thus a process in which the total identification of the comprehending citta occurs with the subject or object to

CHART-I SHOWING THE INWARD JOURNEY OF CITTA AFTER PRATYAKCETANĀDHIGAMA SHOWING THE INTERRELATIONSHIP AMONGST THE REGIONS, PROCESSES AND THE STATES IN THE INWARD JOURNEY

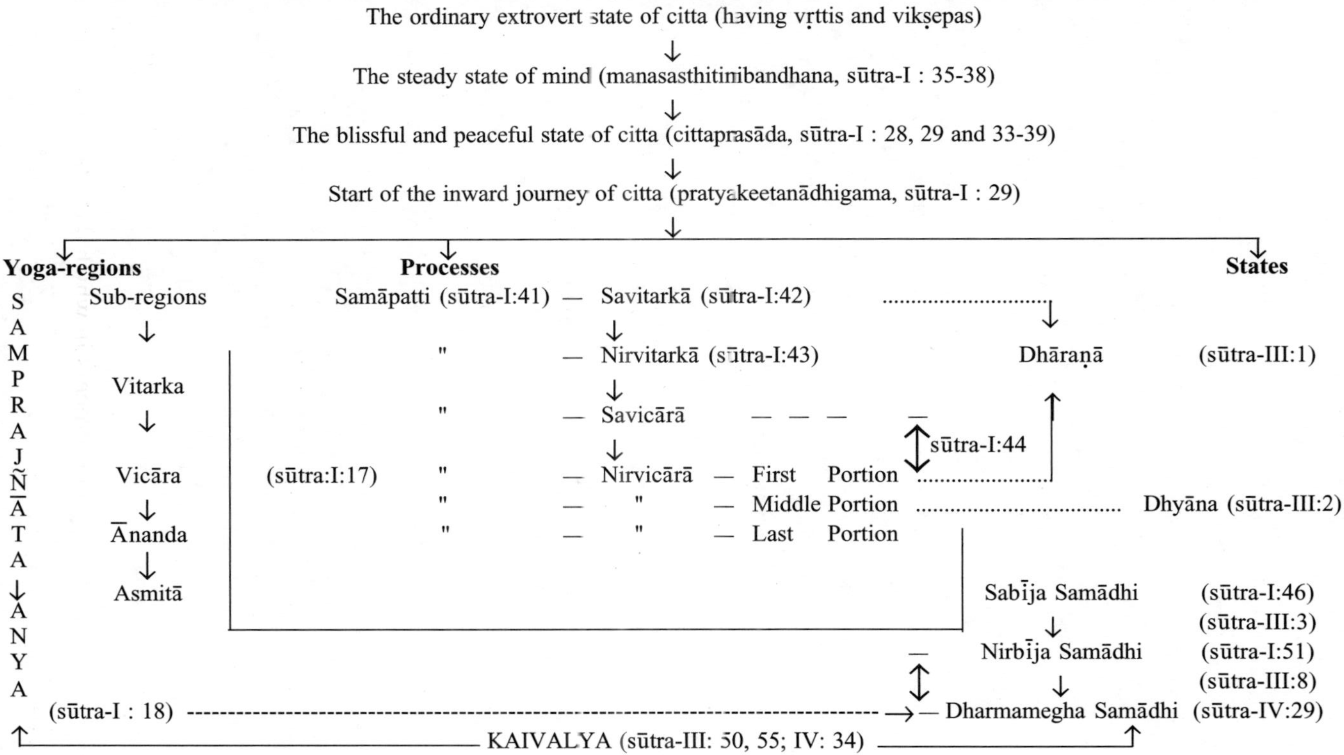

be comprehended (grāhya viṣaya). A process is a continually changing activity or condition and in such a continuous process there may be successively several changed conditions or stages. For convenience and clear understanding of the process, arbitrarily there may be designated a number of definite stages. Thus the process of samāpatti is also divided into four stages or we may say two main stages each of which has two sub-stages. Thus there are mainly two samāpattis, related respectively to vitarka and vicāra, which have further subdivisions, namely savitarkā-nirvitarkā and savicārā-nirvicārā, At the end of this whole process, a stage or state would be reached, which would remain almost unchangedly steady for sometime and this comparatively steady state is in a way an end-point or result of the process of sāmāpatti. This steady state is designated as samādhi and as indicated in sūtra I:46, this particular samādhi, which is the end point of the four samāpattis, is called Sabīja samādhi. So, we may say that the result of the processes of samāpatti is a samādhi. The converse may not be true i.e. every samādhi is not the result of necessarily a preceding process of samāpatti. Thus Nirbīja samādhi has, at least according to P.Y.S., no samāpatti preceding it.

Some commentators mention two more types of samāpattis viz. sānanda and sāsmitā. Patañjali however does not mention any of these. Nor his definition of samāpatti can be fitted to what is meant by these two samāpattis. Ānanda and asmitā are feelings or awareness of citta itself. They really are not coming from the external subject or object chosen for meditation. So, when the citta transcends the region of vicāra and enters the region of ānanda, it is not directly comprehending the viṣaya (chosen for dhāraṇā, dhyāna and samādhi) i.e. the subject chosen for the meditative processes, but is experiencing the ānanda, which is in fact arising out of itself. Therefore, there can not be now a question of merger of grahītā and grāhya and so there can not be any samāpatti. It must be clearly understood that according to Patañjali there is no samapatti after the citta goes beyond the nirvicāra samāpatti stage, and so, as said above, there is no samāpatti prior to or during Nirbīja samādhi state.

As mentioned under sūtra I:17 nowhere Pātañjala Yoga Sūtra (P.Y.S.) mentions the varieties of samādhi viz. Savitarka, Nirvitarka, Savicāra, Nirvicāra, Sānanda and Sāsmita. Only some commentators have mentioned these as stages of samādhi and substages of saṃprajñāta (samādhi ?). In fact, these words are completely absent in P.Y.S. The only words proximately homonymous with the first two of these are the designations of the samāpattis viz. savitarka and savicāra.

In Vedāntic school two other designations of samādhi are in vogue viz. Savikalpa and Nirvikalpa. These terms are totally alien to P.Y.S. The term vikalpa is technical in P.Y.S. and means fantasy or mere imagination (cf. I:9). So these two terms would respectively mean with fantasy (fantastic) and without fantasy. Some commentators inclined to Vedānta equate Savikalpa to Sabīja and Nirvikalpa to Nirbāja, but this is not correct. All the three samādhis mentioned in P.Y.S. are devoid of any fantasy, that is all are thus Nirvikalpa as per the terminology of P.Y.S.

SS. - **तत्र शब्दार्थज्ञानविकल्पैः संकीर्णा सवितर्का समापत्तिः ।।१:४२।।**

TL. - tatra śabdārthajñānavikalpaiḥ saṅkīrṇā savitarkā samāpattiḥ- I:42

WM. -

tatra	=	there, in that;
śabda	=	word;
artha	=	meaning, sense;
jñāna	=	knowledge, the experience and its interpretation in the mind (or citta);
vikalpa (aiḥ)	=	vikalpas i.e. mere imaginary things as per sūtra I:9 (with);
saṅkīrṇā	=	(feminine of saṃkīrṇā) mixed together in such a way as to cause confusion;
savitarkā	=	(sa = with + vitarkā = fern, of vitarka) savıtarkā, with vitarkās;
samāpatti(ḥ)	=	samāpatti (is).

TR. - In that (in the sūtra or in samāpatti) savitarkā (samāpatti) (is that which is) an admixture of the vikalpas of words, (their) meanings (and) (their) knowledge, causing a confusion (in perception or comprehension).

CE. - The general definition of the process of samāpatti has been given in the sūtra I:41. Its varieties or successive stages are being mentioned in the sūtra I:42 to 44. This is indicated by the word 'tatra', which literally means 'there' and is to be interpreted as therein or in that i.e. in that sūtra or in samāpatti. In this sūtra śabda, artha and jñāna are all called vikalpas. Since the present commentator firmly believes that Patañjali never uses a technical word in any loose manner, this vikalpa is to be understood as defined in sūtra I:9 of Yoga Sūtra. This means that the words, their meanings and their knowledge i.e. what we understand from these, are all three mere imaginary things having no reality. This statement is rather difficult to understand and to accept. But a little serious thinking will show that the statement is a fact. It would be easy to see this if we take the case of the name of a definite object e.g. a cap. This word in English designates an article usually used for covering the head. An Englishman has a vague belief that this word has a close and definite relation to the thing, for which it stands, but this is not true. A Hindī speaking man calls the same article a 'ṭopī'. A Frenchman would call it a 'bonnet' and a German 'muetze'. This is a clear proof that these words are in no way essentially related to the things, whose names they are supposed to be. It is by convention, which also was fixed arbitrarily, why these words have come to represent the particular article. Again in the English language itself, the word does not necessarily mean always this 'article for covering the head'. A stopper of a bottle is also called a cap and even the back part of a rifle-bullet is also called the cap. And this is not the case with the word cap only, but almost all the words, and not only in the English language, but of all the world languages. In fact that is why there is a need for the dictionaries to give different meanings of a word in the same language. In such a dictionary there will be a number of meanings given for one single word, many of which will be differing quite widely in the significance, so much so that two meanings may be even opposite of each other, i.e. the word accident usually means a (bad) chance happening, misfortune, calamity, but in a statement, "He became a rich man by accident", the same word assumes a meaning of luck or good fortune. Similarly take the word-phrase 'out of'. In a sentence 'This is out of my power', the phrase means 'outside' or 'beyond'. But in a sentence, 'Three out of seven were good'; the phrase means 'in' or 'amongst' which is exactly opposite. In Sanskrit also such examples are many. For example the verb apavṛ (अपवृ) means disclose, open up, uncover etc. as well its opposite-to cover up to hide, etc. Such examples can be multiplied and are common to all languages.

Thus we see that the word and the thing they signify i.e, their significance- 'artha' are not related naturally, but by arbitrarily created convention only.

The jñāna i.e. knowledge has also no intrinsic and real relation with the other two viz. śabda (word) and artha (meaning of the word). This can be explained again taking the same word cap. When a person says the word cap, as pointed out above, the hearer can and may think of either the article of a dress, of the stopper of a bottle or the end portion of a rifle-bullet. It may so happen that someone may tell another person, "Put on the cap". Under particular circumstances it can actually happen that the speaker wants the hearer (1) either to cover his head with a cap i.e. with a head dress article; (2) or it may mean that the hearer is to put the cap i.e. the stopper on a bottle, which is present there. Such a situation can actually occur in a place like a laboratory or a dispensary or pharmacy etc. Even it can so happen that the speaker has in his mind an idea that the hearer should cover the bottle with the stopper i.e. the covering to close the mouth of the bottle to which he is referring as a cap, whereas the hearer, under pertinent circumstances may be led to think that the speaker wants him to put a covering on his own head i.e. cap and he may do so, instead of putting the stopper on the bottle. Thus we see that the knowledge which is the result of comprehension or understanding can be different in different persons, even when arising from the same word-expression. Instances of such confusing situation can be multiplied for many words, as the reader himself may be able to do it for himself. Again it can so happen that a speaker may use a word (śabda) with a particular sense (artha) and it may be understood broadly also in the same sense (artha) by the hearers, yet the image or notion i.e. pratyaya and the consequent jñāna i.e. knowledge, which arise in each one of these hearers' minds may not be the same. Thus when a speaker may be speaking about a cap the picture or image of that cap in his mind and the images produced in the different hearers' minds may be widely differing from one another. The speaker may be having a notion of cap which is usually called Gāndhī-cap, while one of the audience may have in his mind a furcap, while, another may have a notion even of a Western type of cap, called a Felt-hat. Thus we see that these three persons comprehend i.e. get a knowledge in their mind quite differently from the same word when used and broadly understood also in the same general significance. It produces widely different kinds of images or notions i.e. the experience and knowledge in the minds of different persons is very widely varying. Thus we see that the words (śabda), their conventional meanings (artha) and the comprehension that they give rise to in the mind, which we call experience (pratyaya) or knowledge (jñāna) have really no natural relationship. But the man has usually a feeling, may a firm belief, that they are having such a real relationship. This non-existence of the relationship is indicated by the word vikalpa. This is the reason that many time misunderstandings are created. The speaker means something and the hearer understands and interprets it completely differently. Naturally this leads to confusion. Such situations arise many a time even in our normal day-to-day life. But in philosophical and yogic view point, even what we ordinarily and usually take as correct understanding from the words and their meanings, is really a mis-understanding. Because the reality of object or phenomenon cannot be truly expressed by the words. This is so, because the Ultimate Reality is beyond time and space, while the words are creations of man, both of which are limited by time and space. From this view point all our knowledge expressed through words is a misunderstanding and therefore, confusion, which is implied by the words saṃkīrṇā (mixed in a haphazard manner leading to confusion).

As explained under sūtra I:17 the word vitarka and other words derived from it, e.g. savitarkā here, are to be considered as technical terms. The meaning of vitarka should be taken uniformly the same throughout the Pātañjala Yoga Sūtra viz. evil or bad ideas, thoughts, emotions, actions etc. Therefore savitarkā samāpatti is to be understood as the samāpatti in which the arising of the vitarkā is the dominant aspect. It has been also pointed out that the vitarkas are not associated with the subject chosen for meditation, what so ever it may be. The vitarkās are rising up from the store-house of saṃskāras (impressions or residual effects) of earlier karmas stored in the citta in the store-house called karmāśaya. When a sādhaka will start with the practice of meditation, i.e. the process of directing his consciousness or citta inwards, the first experience will be of an abundance of vitarkas coming up into awareness from the storehouse, even when he might choose a very sacred and holy object or subject for this process. According to the presentation of Pātañjala Yoga Sūtras, the first part of the process will be samāpattis and even there the first one will be 'savitarkā samāpatti'. These vitarkās are closely associated with the words (śabda), their meaning (artha) and their interpretation (jñāna) by the citta and mind. In fact, vitarkās are a result of the confusion caused by the limitations of śabda-artha-jñāna usage. In higher philosophical view, things by themselves are neither good nor evil. It is a particular individual's outlook i.e. the way of understanding, which again is the consequence of the words and the significance they have behind them according to his understanding that leads to the evilness or goodness of the thing. This is the reason that the different individuals think of the same person or object or phenomenon differently either as good or as bad. A very famous illustration of this is the story in Mahābhārata, where Śrikṛṣṇa asked Duryodhana and Dharmarāja to find out respectively the most good and the most evil man from the large assemblage of sages, kings and peoples of practically all other walks of life. When Duryodhana after examining the assembly reported that every man was bad, Dharmarāja reported that every man was good in the same assembly.

How the transcendence from vitarkās to vicārās and beyond the region of (intellectual) thinking to the region of feelings viz. of ananda and asmitā and further beyond, takes place has been already explained under sūtra I:17 and may be further clarified in these sūtras of samāpatti.

SS. - **स्मृतिपरिशुद्धौ स्वरूपशून्येवार्थमात्रनिर्भासा निर्वितर्का ।।१:४३।।**

TL. - smṛtipariśuddhau svarūpaśūnyevārthamātranirbhāsā nirvitarkā - I:43

WM. -

smṛti	=	memory;
pariśuddhi (ddhau)	=	(locative of pariśuddhi = through purification), in through purification;
svarūpa	=	(sva = one's own + rūpa = form or shape etc.), one's own form or natural state;
śūnya	=	empty (of), devoid (of);
iva	=	like, almost as;
artha	=	sense, significance, essence;
mātra	=	mere;
nirbhāsā	=	(fem.), shining, having a clear appearance;
nirvitarkā	=	(niḥ→ir) = without + vitarka = vitarka) Nirvitarkā. a name of a type of samāpatti.

TR. - Through thorough purification (of) memory (results) nirvitarkā (samāpatti), (which is) as if devoid of its natural (own) form, giving a clear appearance of the mere essence (of the viṣaya i.e. subject of the meditational process).

CE. - This second stage of the samāpatti is nirvitarkā i.e. in which now there are no vitarkas coming to the consciousness level in the citta. Patañjali has merely mentioned that this happens as a result of thorough purification of the memory, but has neither in these sūtras, nor anywhere else in the Pātanjala Yoga Sūtra explained how this disappearance of vitarkas or purification of smṛti is to be practically achieved. The reason is that it happens, so to say, automatically and in what way has been fully explained under Sūtra I:17.

There it has been pointed out that the vitarkas as well as the vicāras are not associated with the object or subject chosen for meditation, which really is neither good or bad, even though the meditator may have an impression that these are associated with the subject of meditation. They are in fact coming from the deeper of subconscious level of his mind. According to yogic view they are coming from the saṃskāras stored in the karmāśaya in the citta. In the process of remembering the past experiences the revival of memory is the result of the arousal and bringing to the consciousness level of the saṃskāras from the same storehouse. As said, the difference lies in the fact that in memory there is an immediate stimulatory cause or factor, which activates and actualizes the saṃskāra, while in the processes of samāpatti the actualization is without any such immediate stimulation and therefore spontaneous. Thus in the savitarkā and savicāra samāpatti, the vaitārkika (evil) and vaicārika (rational and good) saṃskāras are brought to conscious-ness level and get exhausted in the process of samāpatti automatically. In this way the exhaustion of saṃskāras leads to the purification or cleansing of their storehouse i.e. the karmāśaya, which is also according to yogic view the source from which memories arise. This is what is indicated by the expression smṛti-pariśuddhi.

Generally in yoga and particularly in Patañjali's yoga the important results or stages come without violent effort and almost spontaneously. Yoga can be said to be passively active. Things happen and are not to be done. This in reality is also true for the aṅgas like āsana and prāṇāyāma, which are activities carried out mostly thorough the body; which, therefore, can be to some extent 'done' and it is usually spoken of them in this manner. But the perfection of āsana and prāṇāyāma (whose important and, according to some, essential part is kumbhaka i.e. cessation of breathing) is achieved only then, when they become spontaneous i.e. involve no effort. It is still more true for the meditational i.e. inward going processes. People who say that they do dhyāna, dhāraṇā or samādhi have not understood and probably have not reached these stages, at least as they are defined by Patañjali, Dhāraṇā, dhyāna and samādhi, and samāpatti, which is closely connected and is the prerequisite or a running process of these, can not be 'done', but can happen in their state of perfection.

Till then some kind of effort is always involved. Thus whether it is āsana or dhyāna, it will be perfect and ideal, only when there will be complete absence of effort. For this reason when there will be a transition of the citta from one stage of samāpatti e.g. savitarkā to the next stage e.g. nirvitarkā, it can take place only when the first i.e. savitarkā is perfectly achieved. And this, as said above, will have complete absence of effort and therefore, will occur automatically.

Though complete cessation of the arising of virtarkās in samāpatti, leading to nirvitarkā samāpatti is, as explained, automatic and so nothing much can be done to reach the further stage, some practical suggestions can be pertinently made here. Meditation without having a definite subject or even having no subject or precise directionality, is recommended by many teachers in the spiritual field. According to the understanding of the present commentator, Patañjali seems to suggest (sūtra I:41, 44, 45) to choose a definite subject for the process of meditation and does not seem to accept any process of meditation without such definite subject. As has been pointed out, however pure and sacred the subject chosen, vitarkās are bound to arise and will ultimately disappear by the process of samāpatti itself. Usually the same subject viz. a particular Deity or Saint or one's own Guru is chosen as the subject of meditation day after day. In such a case after some days the vitarkas (or vicāras in the case of savicāra samāpatti) may completely cease to arise when the citta now does not associate the vitarkās with this particular subject of meditation. If the sādhaka now chooses another subject e.g. another Deity etc. for the meditational process, it may so happen that some vitarkas, which had no occasion to get linked with the earlier subject of meditation and have therefore, not got exhausted, would now get associated with this new subject and may come up. Again after some days this second subject also does not bring up any vitarkas. Then the subject may be changed again and perhaps the sadhaka may find that some more and new vitarkas are brought up by this third subject. In this way the sādhaka should go on changing the subjects of meditation successively, until he finds that taking any new subject for meditation now does not bring up any vitarkas. This will be an indication that vitarkas of the citta have been fully exhausted and the storehouse of karmāśaya is thoroughly cleansed in this respect i.e. of vitarka or evil thinking. If the sādhaka wants to make himself sure of this thorough purification, he may try changing a sizable number of subjects and assure himself that choosing a fresh subject does not bring up even a single vaitārkika notion or feeling in his consciousness.

This practical suggestion is nowhere even hinted in Pātañjala Yoga Sūtra, nor has been referred to by any commentator as far as known to the present commentator, but it is based on his own little experience and also from similar directive seen in Buddhistic Yoga schools. As said the subject usually chosen by a yoga sādhaka, who is generally a person of religious and devotional tendencies to a lesser or greater degree, is something holy. But even such a subject can and does give rise to vaitārkika thought in the mind of the sādhaka. This has been seen actually happening by the present commentator even in the case of highly devotional persons, when meditating upon their iṣṭa devatā i.e. the deity for which they have the highest devotion and regard. However, as is to be expected, the activation and actualization and through this the exhaustion of vitarkas would not be naturally very quick. In such a case achievement of the smṛti-pariśuddhi in respect to virtarkas (and also vicāras) will need changes of a large number of meditational subjects and a much longer period, of days or years even. On the other hand, if the subject chosen is one where vaitārkika thoughts and emotions are expected to be very naturally associated by citta, the process of vaitārkika-smṛti-pariśuddhi may be accomplished probably more rapidly. In the usual tradition in Vaidika or Hindū Society, however this kind of choice of subjects naturally leading to vitarkas or evil ideas or notions is not in vogue and does not seem to have been recommended anywhere. But in Buddhistic yoga, a number of such evil subjects, explicitly and specially recommended, as for example the dhyāna on a petrifying human cadaver and that also preferably actually sitting near it. It is also recommended there that the sādhaka should take obligatorily all these evil subjects successively for his meditation. The purpose seems to be that the vitarkas in the citta (in karmāśaya) would be deliberately activated and consequently get exhausted in this type of choice of evil subjects of meditation. In fact the present commentator was at first perplexed and could not understand, why such subjects had been intentionally recommended in Buddhist yoga as would be ordinarily supposed to be not desirable objects for meditation ? When thinking over this it became clear that the purpose is that virtarkas should necessarily arise in the mind. This necessarily is the first occurrence in the process of meditation and leads to the purification of citta i.e. smṛti-storehouse or karmāśaya part of it. The Buddhists probably were struck first with the idea that this natural meditational happening could be facilitated and speeded by such a deliberate choice of vaitārkika subjects in the first part of meditation. The Buddhists have the same names, no doubt in their Pāli form, (e.g. savitakka etc.), for similar meditational processes, though they categorize it as dhyānas (jhānas). In fact this was one of the considerations, which led the present commentator to comprehend that the word vitarkā in sūtras I:17, 42, 43 is to be interpreted as evil mental activity and as is also clearly defined by Patañjali in sūtra II:34.

The resultant change or process has been described as "svarūpa śūnya iva arthamātra nirbhāsā". Svarūpa literally means one's own rūpa or form, which would mean its original or natural state or condition. In this samāpatti, the state is of total lack or devoidness of the natural form or state. Some commentators have interpreted this svarūpaśunyatā as that of 'citta' i.e. "the citta loses its own nature or subjectivity", (cf. Taimini, The Science of Yoga, sūtra I:43). But this interpretation does not seem to be correct. If citta loses its own svarūpa then any further process in it or any activity of citta would become impossible, because in this loss of svarūpa, what is intended is the loss of all characteristics of that particular entity. So, the svarūpaśūnyatā is that of the subject chosen for meditation. What we understand normally of any subject to be grasped or comprehended by the mind is the knowledge (jñāna) of that subject or thing, which we ordinarily obtain in our day to day mode of knowing things. This is again based upon and complicated with the associations that we have formed with the word (name) and its meaning, which we use for this subject. This knowledge is therefore, always relative i.e. incomplete or distorted on account of these associations and preconceptions, which we usually have in between the subject and its sabda (name), artha and jñāna, which are according to Patañjali, as explained above, false or illusory. This our empirical knowledge is far removed from the reality of the thing or subject, which we might have chosen for meditation. As the śabda (words or names), artha (significance) and jñāna (image or experience produced in the citta) gradually get dissociated from the subject in these meditational processes of samāpattis, gradually we go on getting a knowledge much clearer and nearer to the reality of the object. In this gradual approach to the reality of the subject the śabda, artha and jñāna lose their previous association with the subject existing in the citta. Our usual way of knowing i.e. comprehending of different subjects is always with the help of śabda-artha and jñāna or as Vedāntin call it, with the 'nāma-rūpa'. When, therefore, this association complicating and falsifying the understanding or knowledge, deviated from the reality of the subject, which citta had, is as if broken. The normal state or svarūpa of the subject as we understand it in our ordinary experience becomes extinct. This is what is meant by svarūpaśūnyatā.

Even then the subject is being experienced (?) in a completely different way, which so far was quite unknown to the citta. Thus in a way the citta grasps or comprehends or experiences the subject in a completely new order or level. It seems at this time to the citta that it is now experiencing the subject in its essence (i.e. real meaning or Reality), which is indicated by the word artha and this new experience or grasp of the subject is relatively so clear that the meditator even may have a feeling that he has understood the Ultimate Reality of the subject. This is what is meant by artha mātra nirbhāsa i.e. clear view of mere essence.

Here one point is to be noted. Though the sādhaka or meditator may at first have a feeling even in nirvitarkā samāpatti that he has grasped or reached the Ultimate Reality of the subject chosen for meditation, actually this is not the case. The Ultimate Reality is still far away. The journey is to be continued and the citta does continue on this journey. In further samāpattis and samādhis, the citta will have a similar experience repeated. At every successive stage a comprehension (jñāna) more clear and nearer to the Ultimate Reality would be reached, but still it will not be the Ultimate Reality. This Ultimate Reality will be reached only when the final goal of the journey on the path of yoga will be complete i.e. when the last samādhi stage will be attained and completed and the Kaivalya reached.

Another noteworthy thing is that the wording used to describe the nirvitarkā samāpatti in this sutra is almost identical with that used for the general description of samādhi in sūtra III:3, except that the order of the two main phrases in inverted. Samādhi in III:3 of Pātañjala Yoga Sūtra is described as "arthamātranirbhāsaṃ svarūpaśūnyam-iva Samādhi", which means Samādhi is that state in which there is clear perception of the mere essence (of the subject chosen for dhāraṇā, dhyāna and Samādhi) and there is as if (i.e. almost) complete loss of its form or own nature i.e. there are no distinct attributes which are ordinarily seen in that subject. This may be the reason why most of the earlier commentators equated samāpatti with Samādhi. But again it may be emphasized that the two things are not precisely one and the same. The relation of samāpatti and Samādhi as process and its end result state has been already clarified. Very often the process and the result obtained through it are necessarily to be described in the same way or by the same words, which is the case here. For example a white washing (process) of the wall results into a white washed or white wall. Though the wordings used for descriptions of samāpatti (particularly nirvitarkā and nirvicārā as per I:43 and 44) and of Samādhi (sūtra III:3) are almost same, there is a difference, which is indicative again of the fact that the former is a process and the latter is a resultant state or endpoint of the process.

In the sūtra I:43, the phrase 'svarūpaśunyevārtha-mātranirbhāsā' is the feminine adjective of the name nirvitarkā, while in sūtra III:3 the wording is 'arthamātranirbhāsam', a neutral name or description of a condition of clear vision of mere essence and also 'svarūpaśūnyam', a state of complete lack of its own form (or formlessness).

SS. - **एतयैव सविचारा निर्विचारा च सूक्ष्मविषया व्याख्याता ।।१:४४।।**

TL. - etayaiva savicārā nirvicārā ca sūkṣmaviṣayā vyākhyātā - I:44.

WM. - etayā = by these;
eva = also;

savicārā	=	(sa = with + vicārā = fern, of vicārā) proper noun meaning with vicārā i.e. with rational, therefore, good thoughts;
nirvicārā	=	(niḥ (→r) = not with + vicārā), nirvicārā, proper noun meaning without vicārā;
ca	=	and;
sūkṣma	=	subtle;
viṣayā	=	(fem, viṣayā) subject;
vyākhyātā	=	defined, explained, enunciated, expounded.

TR. - By these (same two sūtras above) are also expounded the savicārā and nirvicārā (samāpattis) with (the distinction being that) the subjects (are) subtle.

CE. - The next two samāpattis are in the region of vicarā i.e. rational thinking i.e. good thoughts and are viz. savicārā and nirvicārā. The word vicāra primarily means thinking or thought, but it most often implies thinking reasonably, rationally.

Patañjali says that the savicārā and nirvicārā samāpattis are also explained by these very (last two, I:42,43) sūtras. So, the sūtras corresponding to savicārā and nirvicārā samāpattis could be constructed simply by substituting the words savicārā and nirvicārā instead of savitarkā and nirvitarkā respectively. The distinction between the samāpattis related to vitarkā and those related to vicārā is that the latter are said to be sūkṣma-viṣayā i.e. having subtle subjects, as per the present sūtra. This has led the earlier commentators to conclude that the savitarkā samādhi, which they equate to savitarkā samāpatti, and probably including nirvitarkā samāpatti, as having the subjects gross i.e. sthūlaviṣaya (or if samāpatti then fern, sthūlaviṣayā). In contrast, they explain that the savicārā samādhi, which again is equated to savicārā samāpatti, probably including also nirvicārā, as the one having the subjects subtle. Thus according to them the mere difference between the savitarkā samādhi (i.e. savitarkā samāpatti) and savicārā samādhi (i.e. savicārā samāpatti) is of grossness or subtleness of the subjects chosen for the meditation. Their idea seems to be that the subjects of meditation can be divided into two distinct groups or categories viz. gross and subtle. Some of the old commentators do not give any further explanation of the limits of this grossness or subtleness. Others specify that the subjects are 'gross' when they are concrete and material objects, which can be perceived through the five senses, while they are subtle, when they can not be experienced through the senses, but can be imagined or grasped by the mind or citta. But in the sūtras, Patañjali does not give any such clear line of demarkation between sthūla (gross) and sūkṣma (subtle). He has in the next (I:45) sūtra merely given the ultimate limit of the subtleness. Gross and subtle are words which are only relative. A particular thing may be called gross in explicit comparison with some other things. On the other hand the same thing may be called subtle in comparison to some other things. Thus, a mental notion or an emotion is subtle when compared to a worldly concrete object, but this notion or emotion is gross in comparison to the sense of consciousness of one's being (I - am - ness or asmitā).

Any of these can be made the subject of meditation. Therefore, if we accept the explanation of the earlier commentators, it is not clear which particular samāpatti could be called savitarkā or nirvitarkā and which other could be called savicārā and nirvicārā when one of these is the subject for meditation. Thus if an emotion such as dayā (pity) be chosen as the subject of meditation it would be difficult to decide whether that samādhi or samāpatti be named savitarkā (or savitarkā) or savicāra (or savicārā).

What is meant by sūksmaviṣayā is not a particular class or category of subtle or sūkṣma viṣayas, but that any subject chosen for meditation is experienced in a subtler state in the savicārā and nirvicārā samāpattis compared to the same subject as experienced in comparatively grosser state in the savitarkā and nirvitarkā samāpattis. In fact in the progressive stages of the consecutive samāpattis and samādhi the one subject chosen for meditation and realization is to be continuously maintained the same throughout the practice of meditation at one sitting. This the same subject is experienced in different manner in or after each successive stage of meditation. The successive experiences (or knowledges) of the same subject are in each stage reaching nearer and nearer to its Ultimate Reality or Essence, but are not always the Ultimate realization of the Reality behind that subject as explained in sūtra I:43, which comes only last in Dharmamegha samādhi and Kaivalya.

An apt illustration for these meditative phenomena may be given of that of skinning of an onion. The onion has a parchment-like thick skin or rind. This is not eatable and digestable. So, when one wants to use the onion for food preparation, one has to remove this upper parchment like covering. The next inner soft layer is quite masticable, nutritious and juicy. But if the onion be kept in this condition for some days, this palatable and eatable upper layer now turns into the same narchment like uneatable skin. Again when one wants to use the onion, he will have to remove this once eatable but now unpalatable layer. Again a juicy eatable layer appears. This process can continue till the most inner core which at least apparently seems to have no easily removable layer and which is most juicy and tasty is reached. The process of samāpattis and samādhi is to a very great extent similar. According to the present commentator Patañjali seems to imply that one subject chosen for the meditational processes should be continued unchanged for fairly long time and at least for one sitting of a meditational practice. In such a progressive meditation, as explained above, at the start the meditator tries to reproduce an image or concept of that subject in his mind, which, no doubt, will have its form dependent on the associations that the meditator has in his mind about the particular subject. These association will be closely related to the words (name etc.), their meanings, and the comprehension that the meditator has for these, about that subject in his mind. This image or concept will be itself subtler than the actual subject outside in the nature, particularly if it be a concrete material object. As the citta continues its inward journey in the process of meditation, it will have to pass through various regions or levels of experience of that object, as have been indicated by Patañjali in the sūtra I:17 and 18, viz. regions of vitarkas, vicārās, ānanda and asmitā and anya, which last is transcendental and indescribable. In 4 each of these different levels the one and the same subject chosen for meditation will be experienced everytime in a different order or level. Every time, when there will be transition from one sphere to another sphere or one stage in the same sphere to the next stage of that sphere, the meditator will be, as if, having a new experience or knowledge of that same subject. He will also be having a feeling everytime in such a fresh experience that he has probably reached to the knowledge of the reality of that thing, though when the process or the stage continues for some length of time, he will begin to see that there is still further progress inwards possible. No doubt, as said before, each of these new knowledges of the subject in the consecutive stages would be more and more near to the final Reality behind the subject.

We ordinarily try to understand about any subject by the process of thinking. Naturally, therefore, the first part in the process of meditation (i.e. of the citta or consciousness going inward and trying to comprehend the Ultimate Reality or Principle lying behind the subject chosen for meditation, whatsoever it may be) is also a process in which thinking takes place. The samāpattis (two or four) take place in this first part consisting of an almost usual but very concentrated and intense thinking. Even in this thinking, as is our common experience and specially the experience of a number of meditators (sādhakas) as communicated to the present commentator, there is dominance at first of evil thoughts and notions, i.e. vitarkas. The first samāpattis are, therefore, related to and designated after the vitarkā. When the evil thoughts and notions are exhausted from the karmāśaya in the citta, the process of good or desirable i.e. rational thinking starts and the corresponding samāpattis are therefore, related to and named after this type of thinking viz, vicāra. When the citta goes beyond the region of vicāra, the process of ordinary thinking comes to an end. In thinking the process is always through the words and their meanings (names or nāma) and the comprehension or knowledge (jñāna or rūpa) of the thing through these. We are so conditioned that we can not have any thinking which is quite unrelated to words, their meaning and their understanding (śabda-artha-jñāna). Therefore, even in vicāra samāpattis, though the subject is experienced in a subtler level than in samāpattis related to vitarka, yet since the process is still of thinking, all that knowledge or understanding of the subject of meditation that is experienced by the citta is still related to and complicated by the vikalpas of śabda-artha-jñāna. That is why Patañjali says that the same sūtras of samāpattis related to vitarka are also applicable to those related to vicāra.

The process or activity of mind and citta, which we usually designate by the term 'thinking' ends, when the citta goes beyond the stage of vicāra samāpattis i.e. when the citta has traversed through savicārā samāpatti and is conditioned to remain in thoughtless or nirvicāra state in the nirvicārā samāpatti. Therefore, there is no active thinking after vicārā samāpatti, but there is a stage of feeling or experience. The citta enters into a new sphere, which is described by the term ānanda i.e. joy or happiness. The meditator, at least at first, feels as if that ānanda is arising in the citta out of the subject of meditation. This is the usual way of our looking at the so called pleasant or joyful things and experiences. We are led to believe that the source of that joy or happiness is that outside object or circumstance. But a little deeper thinking makes us to understand easily that the happiness or pleasure is not derived from any of such outside subjects. If these were the source of happiness, they should give happiness without exception every time. But our common experience is that this is not so. The source of happiness is always in our own mind and citta. Therefore, when the citta continues further on its inward journey the next region into which it enters is designable only with the help of the term ānanda. We may say it is the sānanda stage. But this or the further stage of sāsmitā can not be, and as mentioned under I:41, are not called samāpatti by Patañjali. The reasons for this are already discussed there.

SS. - **सूक्ष्मविषयत्वं चालिङ्गपर्यवसानम् ।।१:४५।।**

TL. - sūkṣmaviṣayatvaṃ cāliṅgaparyavasānam I : 45

WM. -

sūkṣma	=	subtle;
viṣayatva (ṃ)	=	subjectedness, condition of having a subject or topic;
ca	=	and;
aliṅga	=	(a = without + liṅga = symbol, mark or attribute), a state in which there cannot be any attribute and so cannot be given a symbol of designation.
paryavasāna (m)	=	culmination, endpoint (is).

TR. - And the (degree or grade) of subtleness of the subject (that can be chosen for meditation) ends in aliṅga.

The sūtra can be clearly looked upon as supporting the view point about the happenines in the process of meditation as explained under the last sūtra i.e. I:44. Patañjali here says that the subtleness (sūkṣmaviṣayatva) of the object can go up and end in the 'aliṅga' stage or category. That means the subtleness of the subject chosen for meditation as experienced during the different stages of meditation goes on becoming finer and finer till the level of experience of 'alinga'-ness i.e. total attributelessness, is experienced about that subject at the end of the perfection of meditation or in the highest stage of samādhi. Actually even this is not the ultimate, but the penultimate stage in the attainment of the goal of yoga. The final goal is one step further, beyond 'aliṅga' (mūla prakṛti or pradhāna) in the realization of the puruṣa tattva i.e. 'puruṣa-khyāti' or otherwise formally designated 'kaivalya'.

For understanding this term 'aliṅga' reference may be made to sūtra II:19, which tells that the parvas (i.e. distinct stages of development) of guṇas are viśeṣa (particular or specialized), aviśeṣa (not particularized), liṅgamātra (having merely symbol or attributedness) and aliṅga (without symbol or attribute). Though these stages of development or evolution are mentioned there as stages of guṇas, they are also the stages of evolution of prakṛti. Because prakṛti is the complex of the trial of guṇas viz. sattva, rajas and tamas. In other words, guṇas are not the components or qualities of prakṛti, as is very often spoken in their relationship but they are themselves the prakṛti. If at all we can say that they are three aspects of one thing i.e. prakṛti. That is why, as clearly explained in Bhagvadgīta XIV, no one of these three guṇas can have existence independent or devoid of the other two. The three always are together and present in everything prākṛtika. When a thing is qualified as sāttvika, rājasika and tāmasika, what is meant is not that it is fully made up of either of these guṇas, but that the particular qualifying guṇa is predominantly present. So the stages mentioned above and indicated in the sūtra II:19 are the stages in the evolution of prakṛti.

According to the sāṃkhya and very probably yoga view the elements from which the whole prākṛtika (i.e. including material, physical and mental) creation is produced are the last sixteen ones viz. five sense organs, five motor organs, manas, gross elements. These are categorized in the above classification as viśeṣa i.e. particularized or individualized, because the distinction and individualisation then is quite sharp. The previous stage of evolution viz. five tanmātras and ahaṃkāra in Sāṃkhya and asmitāmātra in Pātañjala Yoga are the six, where the individualization is not so complete and sharp. They are therefore categorized as aviśeṣa i.e. non-particularized or nonindividualized, because in pañca-tanmātrās, each gross one contains in a mysterious way the previous subtler ones. Thus the gandha tanmātrā, which is the grossest includes the other four. The rasa tanmātrā includes the remaining three and excludes gandha and so on. The ahṃkāra i.e. the sāttvika ahaṃkāra, which is merely pure 'I' -- Consciousness (and not the ego) which in Patañjali's Yoga is indicated by the term asmitāmātra (literally, merely (I) -am-ness) is also present as an essential element in everything, both living and non-living. In fact it is the asmitāmātra which gives rise to individuation. The still earlier evolute is mahat or mahān, which often is said to be cosmic buddhi. That means in individual human level the corresponding element is buddhi, which is the potentiality through which discrimination becomes possible. Here it is that the differentiation or manifestation of guṇas become apparent. This is the first evolute of mūla prakṛti or pradhāna after its saṃyoga (?) (with puruṣa). Therefore, here only the qualifications sāttvika, rājasika, and tāmasika would first become meaningful. That means here for the first time an epithet indicative of any attribute can be applied. This is, thus, the appearance of aliṅga i.e. a special mark or attribute. But this qualitativeness or attributefulness is also in its nascent form. This in indicated by the term 'liṅgamātra', having a mere symbol. Going still backward, we come to the stage of mūla prakṛti where no qualifying adjectives, e.g. sāttvika etc. even are applicable. Therefore, this state is attributeless i.e. 'markless' or 'aliṅga'.

The meditational process is in a way the process of going backward on the path of the Sāṃkhya-Yoga evolution in respect of the subject of meditation. According to Sāṃkhya and Yoga view-points anything that we can perceive or even think of is in the realm of prakṛti and has come to its present state through this process of evolution of prakṛti. In Yoga we have to go reverse on the path of this evolution or to achieve, so to say, in our consciousness, the process of counter-evolution i.e. pratiprasava (see IV:34).

Even if the meditator chooses a very concrete material object as the subject of meditation, during the progress of meditation the same subject will be experienced in its subtler and subtler stages of evolution till ultimately the subject merges into mūla prakṛti. This must and does happen with any subject whatsoever chosen for meditation. The yoga sādhaka, if his meditation goes on smoothly, well, in this way, goes to the stage of mūla prakṛti. His citta (consciousness), then has to take one last and most important jump, that of leaving the sphere of prakṛti and realize i.e. become one with the puruṣatattva. If the yogī can successfully do this, he will attain puruṣakhyāti i.e. realization of puruṣa element in its pristine nature, which is the Kaivalya. If unfortunately the yogī can not take this last jump, he will become most probably a prakṛtilaya.

The last stage of subtleness reached in the regular path of meditation or pratiprasava is therefore mūla prakṛti or aliṅga. Puruṣa can not be called subtle or gross and this last jump of consciousness to dissolve and disappear as consciousness and merge into the puruṣatattva is a special step. Īśvarapraṇidhāna, in a way, is very helpful in making the consciousness able to take this last jump. That is why Patañjali had to introduce the concept of Īśvara and include īśvarapraṇidhāna as an independent or partial, yet very important, technique in his practical yoga path.

SS. - **ता एव सबीजः समाधिः ।।१:४६।।**

TL. - tā eva sabījaḥ samādhiḥ - I : 46

WM. - tā = those;

eva	=	also;
sabīja (ḥ)	=	sabīja (sa = with + bīja = seed : with seed);
samādhi (ḥ)	=	samādhi.

TR. - Those (are) also sabīja samādhi.

CE. - The word tā (those) stands here for the four samāpattis just described in sūtra I:42 to 44. These samāpattis are also designated as sabīja samādhi. It could mean that each of the four samāpattis is a sabīja samādhi. This is perhaps the reason why the former commentators have thought the four samāpattis as being samādhis. They have, therefore, postulated the names of these so called samādhis by using the masculine form of the designations of samāpattis. viz. savitarka, savicāra etc. But we have already been emphasizing and clarifying that the samāpattis are not the samādhis. In the present sūtra itself this can be clearly seen. The words sabīja and samādhi are both in singular. From this it is clear that the four samāpattis are not all samādhis individually, but, they make i.e. give rise to one single samādhi which is sabīja. So, as previously explained, the sabīja samādhi is a condition in which citta would abide for some length of time-may be even some months or years-and is the culmination of the four processes of samāpattis.

The epithet sabīja, i.e. 'with seed', obviously indicates that something which is like a seed, that is which is small and has a potentiality of sprouting and proliferating into a tree, is present in this state of samādhi.

This seed may be either the subject chosen for meditation or the citta or consciousness itself. When the sādhaka chooses a subject for meditation, it may be a concrete or gross object in the outside world, in fact there is no restriction or limitation as to what should be the subject to be chosen for meditation and so, theoretically this can be any object whatsoever. However, an attitude of respect and deep devotion would be facilitatory and desirable for the process of meditation. Because with such a subject the mind will have a natural tendency to get attached to the subject. For this reason, usually a sādhaka is expected to choose a subject like his iṣṭa devatā or guru etc. for meditation. In such a case the sādhaka reproduces an image or picture of the iṣṭa devatā or guru in his mind. If on the other hand the subject chosen be an abstract thing e.g. Karuṇā etc. the sādhaka at the start will give some concrete form to such an abstract subject and reproduce that image in his mind. For example he may give a form of a goddess to the abstract subject like Karuṇā and then 'think' about it according to the associations and preconceptions he might have about it in his mind.

In a way this mental picture or image is itself subtle compared to the concrete object outside. At the end of samāpattis, when the citta enters into sabīja samādhi state, even this subtle mental picture dissolves, since the process of thinking itself comes to an end.

As already explained, the citta after nirvicārā samāpatti enters into the region of ānanda, which is really its own nature, but which the citta at first feels that it is arising out of the subject of meditation. Thus in sabīja samādhi the citta experiences the ānanda or blissfulness, which it feels as if coming out of the subject. We may say that the citta now experiences the subject of meditation as giving ānanda or being ānanda itself. This subtler experience of the subject in the form of ānanda changes into further stage into the 'mere' 'I' - consciousness or 'asmitā-into mātra', which again is a feeling where the I- consciousness of the sādhaka is identified with the consciousness of the subject and therefore, gives rise to a feeling that even this I - consciousness is the awareness of the subject of meditation. Thus the ānanda and asmitāmātra sensations are felt as if arising out of the subject. That is, they are, as if, an experience of the subject itself. This experience, in a way of the subject, but on the other hand, really of the citta itself, is the subtlest of all and is quite insignificant in gross magnitude as compared to the concrete subject or even its initial mental image or picture in the mind. This subtlest experience of the subject is the 'seed ' of the sabīja samādhi. When this seed is also dissolved and disappears automatically by the process of the samādhi, the citta enters the 'seedless' or nirbīja state of samādhi.

Since asmitāmātra, i.e. I-consciousness in its subtlest form, is also dissolved, there is nothing left which can have any experience. That means the experiencer 'I' is completely dissolved. Since this source of experience is no more present, there can not be again a possibility of entanglement into the empirical world and the tree of world entanglement can not sprout again from the seed.

Thus the perfection of the nirbīja samādhi would lead to liberation from the saṃsāra or world entanglement, (see 'Meditational Processes in Pātañjala Yoga Sūtra', Yoga Mimāṃsa, Vol. XIX, Nos. 1 and 2, pp. 81-99, 1981).

SS. - निर्विचारवैशारद्येऽध्यात्मप्रसादः ।।१:४७।।

TL. - nirvicāravaiśāradye' dhyātmaprasādaḥ - I:47

WM. -

nirvicāra	=	(nirvicārā samāpatti or nirvicārā state) devoid of thinking;
vaiśāradya (e)	=	(in) mastery, perfection; proficiency;
adhyātma	=	(adhi = towards + ātma = self) leading to self or spirit, spiritual;
prasāda (ḥ)	=	pleasant or blissful serenity.

TR. - In the perfection of nirvicāra (transcending thinking) state (arises) the blissful serenity of spirituality.

CE. - This sūtra tells that the sādhaka's citta really enters the region of spiritual experience when he has got perfect mastery over the nirvicārā samāpatti and the citta has been established in the state devoid of thinking. The first glimpse of the reality-principle behind the self is obtained here i.e. when the citta enters the sabīja samādhi state, which is the state of perfection of nirvicārā samāpatti. This experience of the self is very peace giving and also very pleasant. This feeling of blissfulness is also indicated by the other word ānanda and this may be called the sānanda part of sabīja samādhi. Thus here begins the real spiritual experience of the yoga sādhaka.

SS. - ऋतम्भरा तत्र प्रज्ञा ।।१:४८।।

TL. - ṛtambharā tatra prajñā - I:48

WM. - ṛta (m) = the eternal unconditional truth, the absolute reality:

bharā = fall of;

prajñā = prajñā, the special intuition-like potentiality of obtaining knowledge (directly, without the intermediacy of indriyas and manas).

TR. - There (in the nirvicāra vaiśāradya or sabīja samādhi) (arises) the prajñā which is full of the absolute reality.

CE. - In this state of sabīja samādhi, after the transcendence of vicāra i.e. thinking, there arises that peculiar faculty of the Yogī of gaining the knowledge directly. Ordinarily we obtain knowledge through senses which are like doors or windows of the mind. In a few developed persons, the knowledge may be obtained by the mind without much dependence on the senses. But even in such cases some little, at least previous, dependence on the senses would be implied. But the ṛtambharā prajñā, which makes its appearance in the sabīja samādhi is a special ability, where the citta of the yogī gets the knowledge about any object or subject without any such intermediacy of indriyas and even mind (manas). This is what is called yogicpratyakṣa. Since there is no intermediacy of senses and mind, the knowledge is not distorted and so is more conforming to the absolute reality of the object or subject. This is what is designated by ṛtam-bharā.

This (ṛtmbharā) prajñā does not give the knowledge of Ultimate Absolute Reality all at once at the first appearance of it in this early part of sabīja samādhi. This prajñā also develops gradually step by step during the advancement of sabīja samādhi and also probably through the nirbīja samādhi. Patañjali clearly mentions in the sūtra II:27 that this prajñā develops through seven steps or levels. The sādhaka will have a feeling that he has grasped the Absolute Reality at every one of the seven stages. But as he will progress in his samādhi, he will find that the Reality is still further away. The final experience of the Ultimate Absolute Reality will be achieved only at the completion of the seventh stage where the 'dharmamegha' stage of nirbīja samādhi will be perfect. This experience of mergeing into the Ultimate Reality which is the realization of the puruṣa-principle is the kaivalya, the goal of Pātañjala Yoga.

SS. - श्रुतानुमानप्रज्ञाभ्यामन्यविषया विशेषार्थत्वात् ।।१:४९।।

TL. - śrutānumānaprajñābhyāmanyaviṣayā viśeṣārthatvāt I:49

WM. -

śruta	=	heard, coming through tradition, āgama, śabda;
anumāna	=	inference;
prajñā	=	the (ordinary) potentiality of knowing;
bhyāṃ	=	from;
anya	=	other, different;
viṣaya (ā)	=	(related to) subject (fem.);
viśeṣa	=	particular, special;
arthatva (āt)	=	significance, understanding (on account of).

TR. - (This prajñā, arising with the perfection of nirvicāra state, is ṛtambharā) on account of (because it is able to give knowledge of) subjects other than those, whose knowledge can be got through words or inference (and being able to give) special understanding (of those subjects also, whose knowledge is obtainable through the other usual means).

CE. - The usual means of getting right knowledge (pramāṇa jñāna) have already been mentioned in I:7. These are the means available for man ordinarily, to get the so called right knowledge, which is in fact empirical knowledge no doubt, does correspond to the worldly actuality, as experienced by the perceiver. The knowledge, or better to say, 'realization' of a subject, got through the ṛtambharā prajñā is of a completely different order. It is much nearer to the reality of the subject and is not conditioned by the limitations of the perceiver and of the act perceiving. In other words, this is **real knowledge or comprehension of the subject.** This is why this special prajñā (potentiality of knowing) is called ṛtambharā i.e. full of ṛta or reality. It **alone**, therefore, can give the knowledge or realization of such subjects as are not amenable to the ordinary means of knowledge. This is what is indicated by anya viṣayā. For example, the knowledge about God, which a common man has, is obviously not pratyakṣa, as God cannot be perceived through senses. The only other means available are anumāna and āgama (traditional or through hearing, words of sages and wise men). In the case of God even anumāna is not valid, as for this also, previous experience is necessary, which a common man can have. So, his knowledge about God will be based on only āgama i.e. the 'heard word'. But this knowledge will be always incomplete. The real knowledge or realization would be only through this ṛtambharā prajñā, which will be developed in the meditational processes of the samādhis.

Again what we call pramāṇa jñāna or right knowledge about things and phenomena is also empirical and relative, since it is usually based on observation through senses, even when the inference or āgama may be involved. But when ṛtambharā prajñā awakens and is directed towards such worldly things and phenomena, the knowledge that the yogī would get about those very things and phenomena, would be of the reality lying behind them and therefore of quite a different order, than the ordinarily called right knowledge. This is what is indicated by viśeṣārthatva.

Out of the usual means of pramāṇa jñāna viz. pratyakṣa, anumāna and āgama (śabda) only the latter two are mentioned by the words srūta (heard i.e. śabda) and anumāna. The mention of pratyakṣa i.e. direct sense perception is omitted here, because ṛtambharā prajñā appears only after perfection of nirvicāra state, when sabīja samādhi has started. Pratyāhāra is evidently already accomplished, it being a pre-requisite even for dhāraṇā. Obviously therefore, perception through senses is out of question.

SS. - **तज्जः संस्कारोऽन्यसंस्कारप्रतिबन्धी ।।१:५०।।**

TL. - tajjaḥ saṃskāro 'nyasaṃskārapratibandhī - I:50

WM. - tajjaṃ (tat + ja + ḥ) = produced from that

saṃskāra (ḥ→0)	=	saṃskāra i.e. impression of experience or karma in the karmāśaya in citta (is);
anya	=	other;
pratibandhī	=	counter acting, preventing and removing.

TR. - The saṃskāra produced by that (ṛtambharā prajñā i.e. sabīja samādhi) is the remover and preventer of all other saṃskāras.

CE. - When the ṛtambharā prajñā awakens in the earliest part of sabīja samādhi, the yogī begins to see or comprehend things in a completely new way. He now begins to understand the reality behind things and phenomena. All the previous knowledge, which is based on the saṃskāras collected heretofore become unreal and so invalid. Thus, the effect of saṃskāras gathered so far is nullified. No doubt, no new saṃskāras can accumulate hereafter. Thus sabīja samādhi removes the effect of all the past saṃskāras. However, its own saṃskāra remains upon the citta, which is removed in the nirbīja samādhi as said in the next sūtra, 51.

SS. - **तस्यापि निरोधे सर्वनिरोधान्निर्बीजः समाधि ।।१:५१।।**

TL. - tasyāpi nirodhe sarvanirodhānnirbījaḥ samādhiḥ - I:51

WM. -

tasya	=	of that;
api	=	even;

nirodha (e) = nirodha (in) i.e. restraint, curbing;
sarva = all;
nirodha (āt) = nirodha (on account of);
nirbīja (ḥ) = (niḥ (→r) = without + bīja = seed)
Nirbīja i. e. seedless
samādhi (ḥ)= samādhi (is).

TR. - In (the condition of) nirodha of even that (saṃskāra of sabīja samādhi) on account of nirodha of all (saṃskāras), (there is achieved) nirbīja samādhi.

CE. - In the sabīja samādhi the saṃskāra produced by the realization of 'The Reality' is the only saṃskāra left, because as said in previous sūtra this saṃskāra removes the previous saṃskāras and prevents the new saṃskāras being accumulated. As already explained under I:48, this realization of the Reality is not all at once of the Ultimate Reality. This Ultimate Reality will be realized only on the Perfection of nirbīja samādhi, when, the sarva-saṃskāra-nirodha will be accomplished.

As very often mentioned before, Patañjali has nowhere given any explicit indication about the choice of the subject for meditation i.e. for dhāraṇā, dhyāna and samādhi. From this it has to be inferred that any subject may and can be chosen by the sādhaka for such meditational processes. But from the explanations given so far on the sūtras of the first pāda, the reader must have come to understand that any subject chosen for meditation ultimately leads to the ānanda and asmitā which, though the sādhaka at first may feel as if arising out of the subject chosen for meditation, are the characteristics of his own citta. Also as said before, the ānanda and asmitā dissolve and ultimately the Realization of the Reality, which is almost indescribable, takes place in the perfection of samādhi i.e. nirbīja samādhi or rather in the last part of it viz. dharmamegha samādhi. This absolute realization and so, isolation of the puruṣa tattva, which has no relation-even apparent-with the prakṛti, the latter having been dissolved in the perfection of dharmamegha samādhi, brings about the state of Kaivalya i.e. ALONENESS of the puruṣatattva or ABSOLUTENESS.

It has often been mentioned before that Patañjali nowhere gives any clear directions as to how to practise and proceed in these meditational processes, nor how to jump from one stage into the other stage. The reason is that these processes of a antaraṅga yoga are spontaneous and occur automatically. The sādhaka can not do much for having a quick attainment in any stage. "Dhyāna and samādhi" can not be done, "They happen". The only indication given by Patañjali of what is to be done for these things to happen is in the sūtras I:20 to 23. More practical directions implied are the practice of kriyā-yoga (II:1) of aṣṭāṇgas (II:29) and for preparing the internal ground (mind and citta) for meditational processes (I:13, 14, 27, 28 and 33 to 39).

Here it may be specially remarked that in this way, the yoga particularly Patañjali's yoga system can have a consonance with Advaita Vedānta also, but as is generally believed and also may be inferred particularly from sūtra II:16-26, Pātañjala Yoga

Sūtras seem to have a greater affinity to Sāṃkhya. No doubt, as a practical system, Patañjali's yoga presentation is such that it can have compromise with practically any philosophy and at least a sādhaka having any philosophical outlook can resort to Pātañjala Yoga system as a practical path for spiritual development and realization.

* * * *

२ साधन पादः
2 SĀDHANA PĀDAḤ
(Section of Means)

SS. - तपः स्वाध्यायेश्वरप्रणिधानानि क्रियायोगः ।।२:१।।

TL. - tapaḥ svādhyāyeśvarapraṇidhānāni kriyāyogaḥ - II : 1

WM. -

tapaḥ	=	austerity;
svādhyāya	=	(sva = One's own + adhyāya = portion of writing or chapter) one's own chosen reading;
īśvarapraṇidhāna	=	worship i.e. pūjana in some form (with an attitude of surrender to īśvara) of īśvara;
āni	=	plural case ending;
kriyāyoga (ḥ)	=	yoga of kriyā i.e. action (is).

TR. - Austerities, reading of chosen chapter (section of a writing) (and) pūjana offered to īśvara (comprise) Kriyāyoga.

CE. - There are innumerable varieties of austerities (tapas) described in Hindu rituals as well as in all of the religions. The sādhaka can select any one or more suitable to him and of his liking and practise them regularly. It is said that prāṇāyāma is the supreme tapas (prāṇāyāmaḥ paraṃ tapaḥ). So, a yoga sādhaka can preferably select this as the form of tapas to be practised. In fact yoga practice of any school always includes performance of prāṇāyāma as almost a compulsory activity.

The meaning of svādhyāya, usually given by most commentators, mentions that the material to be chosen for the practice of svādhyāya should be some sacred and holy book or scripture. But this much explanation is not enough. The prefix 'sva' has a sense of ownership. The sādhaka should have a feeling of such ownership towards the material to be read. Therefore, the material to be read, besides being conducive for spiritual development, must be the same from day-to-day. This will in a way produce sense of ownness about it in the sādhaka's mind. The word adhyāya, which means a chapter (fixed portion) also suggests that the matertial read should be a fixed one. Another point which has been completely overlooked by all the old commentators is the result or criterion of perfection of svādhyāya, mentioned by Patañjali in sūtra II:44, 'svādhyāyāt iśṭa devatā saṃprayogaḥ' i.e Meeting with the Īśta devatā. For this the matertial for svādhyāya must therefore be of the type of a prayer to the īśṭa devatā. How can reading any religious or scriptural material, varying from day-to-day and not addressed particularly to a deity would make the deity to appear before and meet the devotee. From this it may be stressed again that the svādhyāya should be defined as a reading or recitation of a fixed portion from a text, which has a nature of prayer implying that the deity may be propitious to the devotee. Unless this is clearly understood, the svādhyāya is not expected to produce the result mentioned in sūtra II:44, of meeting the desired deity.

Many people read successively different portions of different religious scriptures or may be of the same religious book e.g. Bhagavadgītā, from day to day as their practice of svādhyāya. But why should the first chapter of Gītā, which is merely a part of a story and has not much material of really spiritual nature should give the saṃprayoga of the iṣṭadevatā of the devotee, if the devotee be a Devībhakta and therefore his iṣṭa devatā is a Devī. Even if the sādhaka is a devotee of Lord Kriṣṇa, why the first adhyāya, or for that matter the 15th adhyāya of Puruṣottama Yoga, which is considered by many as the most important adhyāya of Gītā, should make the Lord Kriṣṇa, to appear before the devotee and shower his grace upon him? According to the present commentator the 11th adhyāya of Bhagvadgītā and specially the verses of the nature of prayer would, lead to such a result.

The third item of Kriyā yoga is Īśvarapraṇidhāna. This is usually rendered as 'Surrender to God or īśvara'. Again this explanation is not adequate. The īśvara praṇidhāna here in sūtra II:1 is a component of kriyāyoga. The word Kriyā is normally used for physical action i.e. the action to be done by the body. Sometimes the word is used for mental activity also, but then usually it is qualified by the adjective mānasika and even there the concept behind it is that the mind is a part of body. Now the surrender to God is an attitude i.e. a state of mind and not an activity of body. The īśvarapraṇidhāna, which is a part of kriyā yoga should be an activity to be done by the body. Its interpretation as īśvara pūjanādi (worship in some form of the divinity) given by some old commentators is more correct. Under Kriyāyoga the sādhaka must do some physical activity of the nature of yajana, pūjana or havana etc. by the body. How elaborate this activity should be will depend on the circumstances and the liking of the sādhaka. Too much elaboration leading merely to a mechanical routine, without the mental attitude of surrender and devotion, would not be at all desirable. Yet too much contraction or condensation is also not helpful. The mode of ritual and the time required for it should be adequate enough to develop a devotional state of mind leading to the surrender to the Divinity.

The ritual of sandhyā-vandana, which is recommended to be performed three times i.e. at sunrise, noon and sunset, or at least two times i.e. at sunrise and sunset, is a compact practice of kriyāyoga, beautifully combining all the three components (tapas as prāṇāyama, svādhyāya as praṇava japa and upasthāna and Gāyatri-japa and arghyapradāna as īśvara praṇidhāna) and requiring the minimum of time and material equipment. Condensing it also further would not be desirable, as then possibility of the desired effect being produced would be very little. Moderate elaboration, provided it does not become mechanical and a show business, would be helpful and desirable, if the time and facilities permit for the sādhaka.

Some commentators have understood the word kriyā as equivalent to karma and have given the meaning specially of īśvara-praṇidhana in kriyāyoga as doing action with surrendering of its fruit to God i.e. they have looked upon kriyāyoga as karmayoga. The words kriyā and karma, both derived from the verb root kṛ = to do or to act, have a general meaning of action and in common language they can be used inter-changeably in this sense, but in the compound names kriyāyoga and karmayoga, both have a technical meaning and the one term cannot be equated to the other, as there is a distinct difference in the precise significance of the two.

Patañjali begins the section (pāda) of practical means

(sādhana) with kriyāyoga. Its three components are again included in Niyamas. So a question may arise why this repetition and what is the distinction in this triad in these two categories, since usually in sūtra writing such apparently needless repetition is to be avoided. Moreover, why these three things are called kriyāyoga and mentioned at the very start of Sādhanapāda and then again mentioned in niyamas in sūtra II:32 has not been clearly brought out so far.

Patañjali defines yoga as the means broadly in sūtra I:2 (that yoga is the curbing of cittavṛttis). But quite surely he must have been aware that this would not be easy. The practical means for achieving this goal are to be described in this 2nd pāda and are generally supposed to be the aṣṭāṅgas, (eight members of yoga). How the practice of these aṣṭāṅgas leads to the curbing of cittavṛttis has nowhere been explicitly clarified by Patañjali or even by the commentators. The first of the eight aṅgas is yama, which comprises of ahiṃsā, satya, asteya, brahmacarya and aparigrah. As already said, unless otherwise mentioned, there is no rigid sequentiality in the yogaṅgas, particularly the first three. The practice of the later aṅgas would be more efficacious if the sādhaka has acquired adequate proficiency over the aṅgas preceding it. In this view and also as is generally believed, the sādhaka desirous of following the path of aṣṭāṅgas has to begin with the practice of yama. But the practising of yamas in actual life is also very difficult, as is evident, even from the talks of preachers, who stress the practice of yama as the essential first step of yoga, when they themselves also at the same time state that the observance of yamas, specially of satya, ahiṃsā and aparigraha is most difficult and in the present day almost impossible. Thus even the starting step for curbing of cittavṛttis would seem to be very difficult and almost impossible to practise and achieve. Being aware of this Patañjali very wisely starts the description of the practical path with a sādhana, which is very easy and open for any man, namely kriyāyoga. There need not be any person, if he is really sincere about practising yoga, who cannot practise some kind of tapas, some kind of svādhyāya and some kind of īśvarapraṇidhāna. These all are at the first stage physical actions. So there should be no difficulty doing them in the beginning. The action at the first may be only or mostly mechanical, but if the awareness and sincere desire to develop the inner attitude of mind is there, the daily regular practice of these three aṅgas of kriyāyoga would gradually produce the inner atmosphere. Only then the progress on the path of yoga and the adequate practice of yama would become possible for the sādhaka, specially if he is not inborn prepared in that way by virtue of his pūrva-karma-saṃskāras. This is indicated in the next II:2 sūtra also.

Thus, inclusion of tapas, svādhyāya and īśvarapraṇidhāna in kriyāyoga emphasizes the bodily activity aspect of these three. That tapas and svādhyāya involve activity of the body is quite obvious. But the īśvarapraṇidhāna here is primarily a thing to be done by body is mostly overlooked as is evident from its mere interpretation as, 'surrender to God'. These activities being of body can be easily practised by anybody and therefore the practical path of Patañjali's yoga begins from such easy steps accessible universally to all. The inclusion of these three aṅgas again in niyama, no doubt emphasizes their nature of bodily performance, but adds a further injunction of a regular performance of all these things every day.

SS. - **समाधिभावनार्थः क्लेशतनूकरणार्थश्च ।।२:२।।**

TL. - samādhibhāvanārthaḥ kleśatanūkaraṇārthāśca - II:2

WM. -

samādhi	=	samādhi;
bhāvanā	=	state of inner sphere;
artha	=	for;
kleśa	=	kleśa;
tanū	=	weak;
karaṇa	=	process, action;
artha (ḥ->ś)	=	for;
ca	=	and.

TR. - (kriyāyoga is to be practised) for (producing) the state of inner sphere (facilitatory) for samādhi and enfeeblement (diminution) of kleśas.

CE. - This sūtra tells the purpose or result of the practice of kriyāyoga. Since it is kriyāyoga i.e. yoga of bodily action, it is obvious that it is to be practised and through its inclusion in niyama it becomes imperative that it should be practised daily. About this enough has been said above under sūtra II:1.

The purpose of kriyāyoga is twofold. It prepares the condition of citta as it is necessary for entering into samādhi states. All the three components of kriyāyoga, no doubt, are conducive for preparing such a ground. But īśvarapraṇidhāna is the most contributory in attainment of samādhi. This has been already indicated in sūtra I:23, but more emphatically in sūtra II:45, where Patañjali says that the real perfection of samādhi is through the practice of īśvarapraṇidhāna; and in this latter sūtra, it need be stressed, the īśvarapraṇidhāna is a niyama i.e. a regular daily activity to be performed physically with an attitude of total surrender. This fact is overlooked by many sādhakas, particularly when they begin to feel that they have advanced on the path of yoga. Many yoga-practitioners have been seen saying, "Now I don't perform any pūjā etc. I devote my time more in meditation or dhyāna". But these first two sūtras of Sādhana-pāda point to the fact that even a yogī, who has reached samādhi state will have it facilitated by īśvarapraṇidhāna, which here is some type of actually performed yajana activity. In a way this second sūtra implies that some kind of īśvarapūjana is a must for the yogasādhaka from the start to the end in his journey on the yoga path. The progress on the path of yoga is not much possible unless the kleśas are cut down. As already mentioned even the first yogāṅga, namely yama, could be satisfactorily practised if the tanūkaraṇa (literally thinning-action i.e. the diminution or weakening) of kleśas has been achieved to some extent. More the kleśas are enfeebled, easier and better will be the observance of the yamas. Kleśas are not the root-cause of pain and sorrow only, but they are also the root-cause of the evil activity of man. Hiṃsā is caused through rāga and dveṣa. Asatya is caused through asmitā and rāga. Steya, abrahmacarya and parigraha are caused by rāga and abhiniveśa. These viharkas (evil thoughts and actions) or anti-yamas are done by man through the impelling force of kleśas. Therefore even the start on the path of Patañjali's aṣṭāṅgayoga needs kleśatanūkaraṇa as the first preparation. And for this the only sure and easy means is the practice of kriyāyoga. This is the reason that Patañjali starts the Sādhana pāda with the description of kriyāyoga, without which, in fact, there will be no yoga at all. This utmost importance of kriyāyoga is indicated by its mention in the sūtra II:1, so to say, going against usual conventions of sūtra construction viz. not to use or repeat unnecessary words or even letters; because its three components are parts of niyama also and they pertinently could have been mentioned only in the sūtra of niyamas, II: 32.

SS. - अविद्याऽस्मितारागद्वेषाभिनिवेशाः क्लेशाः ।।२:३।।

TL. - avidyā'smitārāgadveṣābhiniveśāḥ kleśāḥ - II:3.

WM. -

avidyā	=	(a = Non + vidyā = real knowledge worth knowing for spiritual aim) avidyā, non-vidyā;
asmitā	=	(asmi = (I) Am + ta = suffix indicating a state or condition, ness) asmitā, (I-) am-ness, I- consciousness;
rāga	=	attachment, liking, love;
dveṣa	=	hatred, antipathy;
abhiniveśa	=	(abhi = thorough + ni = deep down + veśa = entrance, entered thing, from viś = to enter) Will to live or Fear of death;
āḥ	=	suffix of plurality;
kleśa (āḥ)	=	kleśa (s) (are).

TR. - Avidyā, asmitā, rāga dveṣa (and) abhiniveśa (are) the kleśas.

CE. - The word avidyā is a technical word. There is really no equivalent by which it can be translated in European languages. In most of the English commentaries it has been rendered by words such as ignorance, nescience etc. But this gives a wrong impression. Avidyā is not ignorance. On the contrary it is what we ordinarily call knowledge, which is the empirical, worldly knowledge. That is why it has even been praised by Upaniṣads as : "avidyayā mṛtyuṃ tīrtvā vidyayāmṛtamaśnute" i.e. transcending death by means of avidyā, immortality is achieved by means of vidyā. Obviously a thing which can help in transcending death cannot be and should not be called 'ignorance'. It is the deluding aspect of the worldly knowledge, which makes it difficult for man to comprehend 'The Reality'. That is why in Vedānta it is equated to māya i.e. illusion.

Asmitā, literally translated, is 'Am-ness'. This is therefore I-consciousness present in every individual. Such a pure I-consciousness is never experienced ordinarily by a common man. The ordinary I -consciousness is always tainted. That is, a common man always has a sense : 'I am such and such'. This is what is indicated by the term 'asmitā'. Probably to distinguish the untainted, pure, root I-consciousness from this tainted I-consciousness Patañjali has some times used the term 'asmitā-mātra' (IV:4) for the former one. Asmitā as a kleśa may be understood as 'ego', which gives rise to trouble, even in ordinary life and more so in spiritual path. Very often the designation 'ahaṃkāra' is used for this troublesome factor and in this sūtra and elsewhere, when the word asmita is used as a kleśa, it is equivalent to ahaṃkāra or ego.

The names rāga and dveṣa are easy to understand, since as kleśas they have the same meaning as of common language. They can, therefore, even be translated by words such as liking and hatred.

The stem word in abhiniveśa is niveśa = (ni = Down into + veśa = Entrance from $\sqrt{\text{viś}}$ = to enter) Entrance into. The prefix abhi, which has a sense of thoroughness makes the full literal meaning of the word abhiniveśa = Thorough entrance into. Relating this to the life-process it thus indicates that thing or force, which has deeply entered into the life of an individual; in other words that force which is the impelling force of life and so makes the living possible. This force is the 'Will to live', which in its opposite aspect is often expressed as 'The Fear of death'. So the word abhiniveśa is usually rendered by these two meanings.

Some versions of Pātañjala Yoga Sūtra have the word pañcaḥ added before kleśaḥ in this sūtra. This seems to be a later addition, made by some copier, who might have felt that the terms rāga and dveṣa might be looked upon as a compound word, indicating a single entity, since very often dveṣa is looked upon and in fact is the reverse aspect of the emotion of rāga i.e.. liking, fondness, love etc. But the word pañcaḥ is redundant, because Patañjali is fond of grouping things into five and rāga and dveṣa being antipodes cannot be usually mixed with each other and looked upon as one. Moreover Patañjali unequivocally treats these two as clearly separate in the definitive sūtras II:7 and II:8.

SS. - **अविद्याक्षेत्रमुत्तरेषां प्रसुप्ततनुविच्छिन्नोदाराणाम् ।।२:४।।**

TL. - avidyā-kṣetram-uttareṣāṃ prasupta-tanu-vicchinno-dārāṇām - II:4.

WM. -

avidyā	=	avidyā;
kṣetra (m)	=	field, ground (is);
uttara (eṣām)	=	latter (pi. of);
prasupta	=	(pra = Intensely +supta = Dormant) deeply dormant;
tanu	=	thinned, weakened;
vicchina	=	(vi = in specific manner, at specific time + cchinna = broken, interrupted), occasionally interrupted;
udāra (anam)	=	generously abundant (of pi.).

TR. - Avidyā (serves as) the field for the growth of the latter (four) ones, (which exist in four states of development) of deeply dormant (ness), weakened (condition), interrupted (state, sometimes present, sometimes absent) (and) generously abundant (always vigorously active).

CE. - The latter four kleśas mentioned in the sūtra II:3 develop on the ground i.e. support of avidyā. In other words, they are, in a way, special aspects or evolutes of avidyā itself. As often mentioned, Sāṃkhya and Patañjali seem to be fond of grouping things in a unit of five. Accordingly the kleśas have been enumerated as five. But the fundamental and therefore the one single kleśa is avidyā, which takes different forms in different circumstances, of which the four mainly troublesome are mentioned in the last sūtra along with it. So if avidyā is done away with, all the other kleśas will disappear.

The latter four kleśas actively function and give trouble in our day to day life being manifested in four degrees of intensity. One thing to be noted is that in this categorisation, the total extinction of these kleśas is not mentioned. This is because even in the most advanced yogī, the kleśas are never totally absent as long as he is living in the world. Some faint trace always remains and probably should remain, because without these kleśas the practical worldly life will be impossible. For example even the greatest saint on some occasion will have to show, at least superficially some kindness or graciousness arising out of rāga or some anger or disapproval arising out of dislike or dveṣa, for correcting the wrong behaviour and demeanour of other worldly people around him, who may be seeking his guidance. Again, as indicated in the subsequent sūtra II:9, explaining the nature of abhiniveśa, this kleśa is functioning in the most learned and the wisest i.e. even in an advanced yogī, because of abhiniveśa i.e. the will to live be totally absent, the existence in the human body will become impossible.

Therefore, in practical life only these four degrees of functional intensity of the latter four kleśas can be observed. The most harmless state of functioning of these four kleśas, where they are as good as non-existent or dead, is the prasupta i.e. deeply dormant state. Just as a person very soundly asleep is as non-functional as a dead man, the kleśas in the prasupta state are for practical purposes non-active i.e. as good as nonexistent. This is the highest degree to which the kleśas can be enfeebled in the practical life and is the state of kleśa in the greatest yogīs and saints.

The next stage of reduction is tanu, which should be understood as highly weakened and therefore very rarely and very feebly functioning. This is at least the state to be achieved by a yogasādhaka, when only it will be possible for him to have a satisfactory progress on the path of aṣṭāṅga yoga. This is clearly indicated in sūtra II:2 and the best means for achieving this state is as said there, the kriyāyoga.

The last two conditions of kleśas are the ones, which are found in the common man. In the persons, who have adequate self-control the kleśas are working in the vicchināvasthā. The latter four kleśas in him may be active some times, when the circumstances are suitable for their activity, but otherwise the kleśas may be inactive or dormant. This interrupted functioning is what is indicated by the word 'vicchinna'. In uncontrolled individuals, the kleśas are udāra, which means always very actively working. Such persons will be highly reactive and may do very harmful acts, even when slightly stimulated. They are therefore very hazardous for the society. In such cases, their emotions, i.e. reactivity through the stimulation of these kleśas needs curbing, which no doubt can be best and easily done, again through the practice of kriyāyoga.

Avidyā is not included in the term uttara (latter). The reason is that it is the fundamental kleśa and in a way, it is always active in everyone's life and a gradation in its intensity is not pertinent, because even when a trace of it is present, it will cause great trouble. The real aim of yoga is to do away with this avidyā completely. But this is not an easy achievement. In fact, the total extinction of avidyā is the same thing as the attainment of kaivalya. So the extinction of avidyā will be possible when the perfection in yoga is achieved and the final objective in yoga has been attained.

SS. - **अनित्याशुचिदुःखानात्मसु नित्यशुचिसुखात्म-ख्यातिरविद्या ।।२:५।।**

TL. - anityāśuciduḥkhānātmasu nitya-śucisukhātma khyātiravidyā - II:5.

WM. -

anitya	=	(a = not + nitya = permanent) impermanent;
aśuci	=	(a + śuci = pure) impure;
duḥkh	=	pain;
anātma (su)	=	(an = Not + atma = self) not-self (in plu.);
nitya	=	permanent;
śuci	=	pure;
sukha	=	pleasure;
ātma	=	self;
khyāti (ḥ→r)	=	knowledge, understanding (is);
avidyā	=	avidyā.

TR. - Avidyā (is) seeing (understanding) permanent, pure, pleasure (and) (of the purpose of) self in (respectively) the impermanent, impure, pain (and) not (of the purpose of) self.

CE. - As per this explanation avidyā is an erroneous viewpoint or understanding or knowledge. It is a common experience that the values which are given to things and events in practical life, even by learned and so-called knowledgeable or wise men, are wrong from the standpoint of a spiritual outlook. Even when practically everyone knows that all the worldly things are changing and perishable, one thinks and behaves as if things are stable and permanent. So also things which are not pure, which do not enhance our mental peace, are looked upon and treated as if they are very pure i.e. desirable. This thinking and ultimate analysis leads to the inevitable conclusion of the final truth expressed by Buddha and even by Patañjali (II:15) that everything culminates into misery and pain, yet men are always seeking and running after these ephemeral objects and phenomena, wrongly looked upon as sources of happiness. Similarly all worldly things and happenings, which do not serve the purpose of developing highest inner consciousness and attainment of the self are looked upon as means which will give the ultimate objective of this search of the self. These wrong viewpoints are common to every man without a single exception. Even the spiritually highly developed persons, at one occasion or other, are seen to be under the influence of this kind of outlook, the same as a common man. That is why avidyā as a kleśa persists in everyone as long as he is living a human existence. In every school of Indian (Hinduistic) spiritual culture great stress is laid upon the eradication of avidyā. As already pointed out total dissolution of avidyā is the same thing as kaivalya of Sāṃkhya and Patañjali and even mokṣa of Vedānta.

All the worldly knowledge leads to all the wrong viewpoints indicated in this sūtra. That is why all such pragmatic knowledge comes under avidyā.

SS. - **दृग्दर्शनशक्त्योरेकात्मतेवास्मिता ।।२:६।।**

TL. - dṛg-darśana-śaktyor-ekātmatevāsmita - II:6

WM. - dṛg-darśana = śaktyo (ḥ->r) = (dṛg = seeing, seer + darśana = seen + śakti = potentiality + yoḥ (->r) dual case suffix, of the two). The two potentialities of seeing and of being seen (of);

ckātmatā = (eka = one + ātmā + Self, soul + tā = suffix showing state). Oneness, total identity;

iva = as if;

asmitā = asmitā, (I) am-ness.

TR. Asmitā is the (erroneous) identification of the two potentialities of the seeing (seer) and of being seen.

CE. - Every manifested thing has these two potentialities. That means everything can observe (perceive) and comprehend the rest of the world and it itself can be perceived by others. These potentialities, no doubt, exist theoretically and philosophically (at least according to sāṃkhya and yoga) in all manifested things. But in the non-sentient, the former i.e.

drgsakti, the potentiality of seeing is, for practical purposes, nonfunctional. The path of yoga is meant specially for the human beings and in him (her) both these potentialities are practically functional and they can lead to trouble, if the distinction between the two is not clearly understood and properly practised upon.

The seeing potentiality i.e. the seer principle or draṣṭā is distinct from the seen or dṛśya (that having darśana śakti i.e. potentiality of being seen). But in the common man this distinction is practically always forgotten. This leads to a wrong superimposition of the one of these over the other. The very common example of this erroneous superimposition is the feeling, which every common man has, of his self being the body. In every case in practical life, the self is thus wrongly superimposed upon something out of the seen i.e. an object of the manifest world, which it really is not. This wrong superimposition and identification leads to all the troubles in our life. In this way the kleśa of asmitā is a cause of trouble and misery. In a way, this asmitā is what is usually understood by ahaṃkāra or egotism in common language.

SS. - **सुखानुशयी रागः ।।२:७।। दुःखानुशयी द्वेषः ।।२:८।।**

TL. - sukhānuśayī rāgaḥ - II:7; duḥkhānuśayī dveṣaḥ - II:8

WM. -

sukha	=	pleasure, happiness;
anuśayi (n)	=	related as a consequence;
rāsa (ḥ)	=	attachment, liking, fondness, love;
duḥkha	=	misery, pain;
dveṣa	=	hatred, repulsion.

TR. - Rāga is a result of pleasure.

Dveṣa is a result of misery.

CE. - It is a common experience that we develop a liking, attachment or love for things and persons, which give us pleasure and make us happy and conversely despise, repulsion, hatred for things and persons giving us pain and misery. These two kleśas namely rāga and dveṣa are the emotions in the form of kleśas, which cause trouble in our day to day life. They are easy to understand and so the tanūkaraṇa or curbing of the kleśas can be easily and practically started with trying to control these two in our daily life. In fact, the best way in our worldly life to bring down the kleśas is to start controlling these two disturbing emotions. No doubt, even these can be curbed through practice of kriyāyoga.

SS. - **स्वरसवाही विदुषोऽपि तथारूढोऽभिनिवेशः ।।२:९।।**

TL. - svarasa-vāhī viduṣo 'pi tathārūḍho' bhi-niveśaḥ- II:9.

WM. -

svarasavāhī	=	(sva = one's own + rasa = juice, supporting and propelling force + vāhī = flow-er, carrier, propeller) propelled by one's own force;
viduṣa(ḥ→0)	=	learned;
api	=	also, even;
tathā	=	in the same way as;
ārūḍha (ḥ→0)	=	ridden, mounted;
abhiniveśa (ḥ)	=	will to live or fear of death (is).

TR. - Abhiniveśa (great urge for clinging to life) is (the kleśa) which functions on its own force (and) is riding (dominatively active) even in the learned, in the same way as (in the ignorant ones i.e. in unlearned).

CE. - The sūtra does not really explain what is meant by abhiniveśa. It only mentions the special characteristics of it, namely that it is its own impelling force and that it is as dominatingly active even in learned persons as in any other common man i.e. not learned or ignorant person. The exact meaning of the term is to be deduced from this description. It is a well recognised fact, particularly evidenced in the man on the point of dying, that the will to live i.e. the strong urge to cling to life is a very powerful force, which is fundamentally needed for maintenance of life. Thus this is the basic supporting power for life-continuance. This, therefore, is its own power-source, as it is the propelling power for every other life activity. This is what is indicated by sva-rasa-vāhī.

Similarly this 'will to live' is working as powerfully in a very learned man as in any ignorant person. Learned here primarily has the literal meaning of a person, who has read a lot and is at least well versed in the philosophy of spiritual knowledge and understanding, but actually it implies and points to the person in whom such knowledge has reached a very high spiritual level. But even such people are most often seen not to be ready to welcome death or in other words to have fear of death, even when they are supposed to have understood and even may be delivering impressive discourses on futility of life and worldly pleasures and inevitability of death and benefaction of the state after death. Thus from these two descriptive phrases it is to be inferred that the word abhiniveśa means the 'will to live' or in its negative form the 'fear of death'.

The basic meaning of abhiniveśa is 'stubbornly clinging to a thing'. The particular meaning 'stubbornly clinging to life' usually given to this term in Sāṃkhya and Yoga darśanas can be derived as follows. Abhiniveśa breaks up as : abhi = prefix indicative of thoroughness + ni = prefix meaning deep down + veśa = entry or a thing entered. Thus the word literally means something which has entered and has become thoroughly and deeply entrenched (in relation to a living thing). Such a characteristic thing or force working, not only in human, but in everything living, is a stubborn desire not to die and live perpetually. In this way the word abhiniveśa gets a meaning as the will to live or fear of death.

SS. - **ते प्रतिप्रसवहेयाः सूक्ष्माः ।।२:१०।।**

TL. - te pratiprasava-heyāḥ sūkṣmāḥ - II:10

WM. - te = they;

pratiprasava = (prati = opposite, counter+prasava = birth and growth, evolution); counter-evolution;

heya (āḥ) = that which is to be avoided or done away with (plural, are);

sūkṣma(āḥ) = subtle (are, plural).

TR. - They (kleśas) can be curbed down and done away with by the process of counter-evolution (and are) subtle.

CE. - As per the above rendering of the sūtra, the kleśas are said to be subtle and as such can be brought down and even perhaps completely done away with by a process of counter evolution (of prakṛti).

However the sūtra can be understood without any distortion as 'te sūkṣmāḥ pratiprasava heyāḥ' and then will be rendered : 'They in their subtle form can be done away with by the process of counter-evolution'. This second reading and rendering seems better to us. The kleśas are basically very subtle, that means that to recognise them and tackle them is not easy. Specially this is more true for the kleśas avidyā, asmitā and abhiniveśa. It has already been pointed out that even in highly advanced yogīs and saints, the kleśas, at least in very subtle trace, are active as long as he lives in this world. If the word heya is to be understood in the sense of complete extinction, these kleśas are really totally destroyed only at the time of the perfection of yoga i.e. attainment of kaivalya. Therefore the second rendering brings out this meaning more clearly and this is explained below.

The word pratiprasava means reversing the process of evolution or having a process of involution. If this general meaning of this term is taken, it can mean reversal of the process of evolution of anything. Naturally in this sūtra it strikes to the mind that this counter evolution should be related to the kleśas. In that case we have to presume and understand the process of evolution of these klesas. Many commentators have understood this term pratiprasava as such a counter-evolution of kleśas. For this, then, they have to presume a process of evolution of kleśas. Many commentators, therefore, have proposed that each kleśa in their enumeration in sūtra II:3 has been evolved from the one preceding it in that sūtra. For this they take as authority the statement in sūtra II:4. But there it is said that all the four latter kleśas grow out of and evolve from avidyā. Therefore there is no reason to presume that each one of the latter four kleśas is evolved out of the one preceding it. Obviously dveṣa is not a development of rāga. Still more abhiniveśa does not arise out of dveṣa. If at all, dveṣa and also rāga can be caused by abhiniveśa, when the latter is admixed and instigated by ahaṃkara (ego) i.e. self-pride and aggrandizement.

Moreover these commentators understand this sūtra as giving a remedy for annihilation of all the kleśas. They think that by involution and thus dissolution of a kleśa into the one preceding it in their list (sutra II:3) and continuing this backwards right through the list, all the kleśas will be totally done away with. As said, Patañjali does not seem to advise this. The commentators do not give any definite method or directive as how to dissolve one kleśa in the preceding one. Even if it be assumed that this is practicable, the difficulty still remains as to the dissolution of avidyā. In what should it be dissolved? It has not evolved from any known source. In fact, all seem to agree that it is beginningless. Its total disappearance is the goal of the yoga and of almost all the Bhāratīya schools of spiritual thoughts and development, even when the designations given to this goal may differ in different schools and the specific aspect about its nature may also be variable.

Patañjali has used the term pratiprasava in the last (IV:34) sūtra, where pratiprasava is the ultimate counter evolution of (tri) guṇas. In other words the pratiprasava is the counter-evolution of the total process of evolution, backwards from viśeṣas (viśeṣa elements or tattvas) to alinga (pradhāna or mūla prakṛti; see sūtra II: 19). Since Patañjali seems to use this term as a technical term, its meaning should be understood as this, throughout in Pātañjala Yoga Sūtra, unless otherwise clarified. In the present sūtra Patañjali does not qualify the word pratiprasava in any way, which may indicate that it is the pratiprasava of kleśas and not of guṇas. Therefore we feel that the word pratiprasava even in the present sūtra has the same meaning as in the sūtra IV:34.

If this is accepted then the present sūtra becomes merely a statement of a simple fact that the kleśas in their primary subtle state are really done away with only when the process of ultimate counter-evolution, which is same thing as attainment of kaivalya, the final objective of aṣṭāṅgayoga (IV:34), is achieved. This sūtra, therefore, does not serve as a method of curbing and abolishing kleśas, as has been assumed and implied by the earlier commentators. As shown above they do not give clear instructions as how to achieve the pratiprasava of kleśas going backwards from the last abhiniveśa to the first avidyā. Nor the method seems useful, as even they seem to think that dissolution of avidyā is very difficult, almost impossible, in our worldly life and as long as avidyā is there and active, the other four kleśas also can sprout up out of it when circumstances become suitable since it is the origin and support of those four latter kleśas (II:4).

SS. - ध्यानहेयास्तद्वृत्तयः ।।२:११।।

TL. - dhyāna-heyāstad- vṛttayaḥ - II:11

WM. -

dhyāna	=	dhyāna;
heya (āḥ as)	=	possible of being curbed or destroyed (plural);
tat(→d)	=	(of) It, its, their;
vṛtti (yaḥ)	=	vṛitti (s), functional modification(s) (of citta).

TR. - Its (or their i.e. of kleśa (s) vṛttis can be curbed and abolished through dhyāna.

CE. - As already said kleśas themselves cannot be completely done away with during our worldly existence. Moreover in their subtle state they are not much troublesome. In fact, as already pointed out, probably for maintenance of practical life, they may even be essential. They become really troublesome when they get manifested in the form of kliṣṭa vṛttis. It is here that they can be reduced, at least to such a level of weakness that they do not cause much trouble in our day to day life. This can be done best through kriyāyoga as the practice of this brings down the force of kleśas themselves. But another way of lessening and so to say completely abolishing the kliṣṭatā (painfulness or potentiality to cause trouble in the smooth working of our day to day life) of the vṛttis is indicated in this sūtra. This method is of dhyāna. The word dhyāna is not to be understood as some meditative or contemplative activity, but the precise thing as defined by Patañjali in sūtra III:2, namely a state of pratyaikatānatā i.e. a state of experience of citta, which does not vary even in the slightest manner during the whole length of time. When satisfactory mastery over such a dhyāna is achieved, the kleśas gradually dwindle and may become so ineffectual that the vṛttis do not cause any real interference or trouble in our practical worldly life.

It has already been mentioned under sūtra I:5 that the word akliṣṭa does not mean totally devoid of kleśas. The words kliṣṭa and akliṣṭa are to be understood as showing a relative involvement of kleśas in the vṛttis in comparison to some other vṛttis having less or more of kleśas. In this sense with the process of dhyāna the vṛttis become gradually less and less kliṣṭa and ultimately akliṣṭa, in the sense that they do not give any perceptible trouble in our practical life.

SS. - **क्लेशमूलः कर्माशयो दृष्टादृष्टजन्मवेदनीयः ।।२:१२।।**

TL. - kleśamūlaḥ karmāśayo dṛṣṭādṛṣṭa-janma-vedanīyaḥ - II:12

WM. -

kleśa	=	kleśa;
mūla (ḥ)	=	root i.e.. rooted in;
karmāśaya (ḥ->o)	=	karmāśaya, the repository of karmas in the form of their saṃskāras i.e. residual impressions;
dṛṣṭa	=	perceived i.e. being experienced at the time;
adṛṣṭa	=	not perceived at the moment;
janma	=	birth, life;
vedanīya (ḥ)	=	liable of being experienced.

TR. - Kleśa (s) is (are) the root-cause of Karmāśaya (and its consequences are) to be experienced in the lives, which is being experienced at present and also which are not being experienced at present.

CE. - According to the present commentator each and every sūtra in the Pātañjala Yoga Sūtras has a bearing on the practice of yoga. Yet, comparatively some sūtras are more theoretical and philosophical than others. No doubt, even such philosophical sūtras present some truth or principle, which has an essential bearing on the practice, because without proper understanding of that principle the practice may be distorted. Sūtras II:12 to II:27 are thus primarily some fundamental philosophical truths, which should be properly understood to have an efficiently fruitful practice of the yoga path of Patañjali.

Very often persons, who have a great reverence and liking for Vedānta, particularly Advaita Vedānta, claim that Patañjali's Yoga Sūtra are based on Vedāntic philosophy and they try to explain things and processes in Yoga Sūtras in the lines of such a view. We feel that Patañjali has not bound himself very rigidly to any particular school of philosophy or darśana. He seems to be so catholic that a consonance with any school of philosophy not only Hindustic but completely alien, can be easily and with very little manipulation and adjustment brought about in between it and his sūtras. However the majority of scholars are of the opinion that Patañjali's Yoga Sūtras have a greater affinity to Sāṃkhya darśana and adopts it as its own basis in a general way, so far so, that Yoga darśana, by which always is meant Pātñjala Yoga Sūtras, is very often referred to as Seśvara Sāṃkhya. We also feel that this view point is probably fairly correct. Sometimes a question is raised as to where the Sāṃkhya philosophical outlook is clearly depicted in Pātañjala Yoga Sūtras?'. We feel these II: 12 to 27 sūtras are more akin to Sāṃkhya darśana than any other.

The rendering of the sūtra as given above tells that kleśas give rise to karmāśaya i.e. the repository of the past karmas or actions, which are stored in it as saṃskāras i.e. the residual impressions or effects of the karmas. The fruits or consequences of the action (karma) of both past (and as a general truth, even of the future) as well as the present life are to be experienced (and thus the effect of the karmas is to be exhausted) in the present and future (as well as have been experienced in the past) lives. This is a statement which is one of the important postulates of the theory of Karma-siddhānta (Law of karma), which does not necessarily belong to the Sāṃkhya, but is accepted by all schools of Bhāratīya darśanas.

Both the words kleśamūlaḥ and karmāśayaḥ (→o) stand (grammatically) in case in apposition, the case being nominative case. The sūtra (first portion) can be also rendered as : 'Karmāśaya is the root cause of kleśa', the remaining portion of the sūtra rendering being the same as before. This rendering becomes pertinent because the kleśas are, so to say, eternal and because of their involvement, the karmas get stored up as saṃskāras in the karmāśaya. In a way the fundamental question "Why should the first karma in any individual's life have left a saṃskāra; in other words how and why did the process of formation of saṃskāras and their storage in karmāśaya start ?"

apparently seems to have an answer in this rendering of the sūtra. Such fundamental questions remain really without an answer and explanation forever. They are like the eternally unanswered question-whether the egg was first or the hen was first ?

SS. - **सति मूले तद्विपाको जात्यायुर्भोगः ।।२:१३।।**

TL. - sati mūle tadvipāko jātyāyurbhogaḥ - II:13.

WM. - sati = being;

mūla (e) = root (at);

tad vipākaḥ (→o) = (tad=Its+vipāka = fructification, maturation), its fructification;

jāti (y) = birth (in a species or class);

āyu(ḥ→r) = span of life;

bhoga (ḥ) = experience (of pleasurable as well as painful happenings).

TR. - (It i.e. karmāśaya) Being at the root, its fructification is birth (in a particular species), a span of life (and) the experiences (both pleasant and painful) of the happenings in life.

CE. - According to which rendering of the preceding sūtra (12) be read, 'it' in the present sūtra will mean Karmāśaya or kleśa. Nevertheless the main purport of this sūtra remains unaltered with both those renderings. Kleśas or karmas or better to say kliṣṭa karmas are the root, of which the fruit or result is the cycle of birth and death. Birth is meaningful only if the being lives at least for some time. And even if there be a very short life span, the living being has to undergo some experience, good or bad i.e. has to have some bhoga. Thus jāti, āyu and bhoga are three aspects of one and the same thing.

The term jāti has been interpreted by some commentators as a birth in a particular species or even in a particular caste i.e. social stratum. Even if this specialized meaning of jāti be taken, there is not caused much difference to the general purport of the sūtra. According to the Karma-siddhānta, the new birth in a species or caste is also a resultant of the past karmas of the individual.

SS. - **ते ह्लादपरितापफलाः पुण्यापुण्यहेतुत्वात् ।।२:१४।।**

TL. - te hlādaparitāpaphalāḥ puṇyāpuṇyahetutvāt - II:14.

WM. -

te	=	they (birth, life-span and experience in life);
hlāda	=	pleasure;
paritāpa	=	pain;
phala (āḥ)	=	having the fruit;
puṇya	=	virtue, good actions;
apuṇya	=	(a = non+puṇya) non- virtue, pāpa, vice, evil actions;
hetu (+ tva +āt)	=	purpose (+ Ness+From) = causality (On account of).

TR. - They (i.e. birth, life-span and life-experience) lead to the fruit (result), either pleasant or painful depending on its cause (viz.. the karma) being respectively full of virtue or of vice.

CE. - This sūtra paraphrases the well known truth accepted by all believers in rebirth and particularly enunciated by karmasiddhānta, that the pleasant and painful happenings in our lives are the results of our own karmas, depending on the karmas being respectively virtuous or sinful. Very often this truth is expressed in common language by saying : 'As you sow, so you reap'.

SS. - **परिणामतापसंस्कारदुःखैर्गुणवृत्तिविरोधाच्च दुःखमेव सर्वं विवेकिनः ।।२:१५।।**

TL. - Pariṇāma-tāpa-saṃskāra-duḥkhair-guṇa-vṛtti-virodhācca duḥkham-eva sarvaṃ vivekinaḥ - II:15

WM. -

pariṇāma	=	change, transformation;
tāpa	=	anguish, acute anxiety;
saṃskāra	=	saṃskāra, latent impression of past action;
duḥkha(aiḥ→r)	=	the factors causing misery (on account of, plu.);
guṇa	=	guṇas, the three fundamental components of manifested prakṛti;
vṛtti	=	vṛtti, functional modifications of citta;
virodha (at→ac)	=	conflict, opposition, opposite nature (on account of);
ca	=	and;
duḥkha (m)	=	Pain, misery
eva	=	only, nothing other then.
serva (m)	=	All, every thing

vivekin (aḥ) = the discriminating and analysing person (for).

TR. - On account of the misery caused through change, anguish and saṃskāras (latent impressions on citta left by actions) and also on account of the conflict between the guṇa (the guṇa, which is dominating in the nature of an individual) and the vṛtti (the functional modification of citta at particular moment), all is pain and misery for an analytical and discriminatory person.

CE. - Patañjali in this sūtra explains the mechanism which produces duḥkha in our life. The first channel is of pariṇāma-tāpa-saṃskāra. Pariṇāma in yogic philosophy means transformation or change. This is a cause or aetiological factor in the production of duḥkha i.e. pain and misery. We are pained when we lose something valuable or dear, e.g. at the death of a beloved person. But these results are culmination of a slow change. Everything that is created and manifested has to come to an end according to the inevitable law of nature, recognised by Sāṃkhya and Yoga in their principle that prakṛti is always changing. As long as the change does not become perceptible and we do not become aware of it, the sense of loss and consequent misery is not felt. Only when the change is advanced and definite then we become conscious that something has been lost and we begin to pine for the thing lost. Thus change, which is the fundamental characteristic of every thing prākṛtika i.e. out of the empirical world, will always lead to sense of loss and pain at some stage or other. And so change (pariṇāma) is an intrinsic aetiological factor in the production of duḥkha.

Tāpa and saṃskāra, which are enumerated here as the other two aetiological factors in the production of duḥkha are in a way only different aspects of pariṇāma itself. Tāpa = anguish or acute anxiety is a consequence of the fear of the loss of a thing dear to one and as already said, this loss is only the culmination of a process of change. Most often this close relationship is not easily recognised. Anguish or acute anxiety, therefore, seems as arising spontaneously. This, no doubt, is a distressing and paincausing happening in our life. Many people are often unnecessarily anguished about such losses and difficulties, which may come to their share in future. Therefore tāpa seems to be another important aetiological factor in production of duḥkha.

Saṃskāra is the residue in the form of some kind of impression left in the karmāśaya portion of citta by a karma i.e. action or happening. Though we do not easily comprehend it, every action or experience, which makes a saṃskāra or impression on citta, leads to a kind of habit-formation. Even if the experience was undergone only once, this process of saṃskāra leading to a small degree of habitualisation leads to facilitation, if there be occasion to repeat the experience or action again. On the other hand, if on the occasion of this repetition of experience, there is some difference or change in the nature of the experience or action, then some difficulty is felt in performing that repeated action or experience, on account of the habitualisation i.e. conditioning, which has taken place by previously having gone through that action or experience.

Thus this conditioning or habitualisation becomes a

hindrance in performance of that action, which is some what altered than before. Depending on the difficulty or inconvenience caused, the person will feel misery and pain to that much extent. Thus saṃskāras, which prove to be hindrance, when a change in circumstances is to be faced, lead to duḥkha.

In this way pariṇāma, tāpa and saṃskāra, which are different aspects of one and the same thing viz. the chain of birth and death, form a channel through which duḥkha enters into our lives. These three factors are concerned more to the manifested world i.e. the environmental external created world. No doubt, the outside here is to be understood in a particular sense i.e. outside of self. Thus even the body and mind-citta and their activity are also external in this context and the pariṇāma-tāpa-saṃskāra mechanism is applicable to all this also.

The second channel for the arising of duḥkha is guṇa-vṛtti-virodha. This guṇa is obviously the guṇa, which is predominant in the nature of an individual. This is thus the basic characteristic in the nature of that individual and is not easily changeable. The vṛttis, arising in the citta at different times, will be caused by some external things or phenomena. This external agency will have also in it predominance of some one of the three guṇas. The vṛtti aroused through this external agency will also have the some kind of guṇa-dominance as this external agency. Most often the guṇa-pattern i.e. the relative proportions of the three guṇas in the vṛtti will be different than the guṇa-pattern in the nature (in the personality, specially in the citta) of the individual. Thus a sāttvika person will be having rājasika or tāmasika vrttis arising in his sāttvika citta, this rājasika or tāmasikā being governed by the nature of thing or phenomenon, about which the vṛtti has arisen. Even if the predominance of the same guṇa be in the nature of the person and of the vṛtti, there will almost always be a difference in the guṇa-patterns i.e. the proportions of the three guṇas in the citta of the person and in that of the vṛtti arising in it. Talking in mathematical terms and assuming arbitrarily the guṇa-patterns, a person may be, say, 90% sāttvika. The external thing giving rise to a vṛtti in his citta has a 60% sāttvikata (remaining 40% being raja and tama together) and so the vṛtti is also 60% sāttvika. Thus though both the individual and the vṛtti would be ordinarily stamped as sāttvika, since out of the three guṇas the sattva guṇa is the most dominant in both, yet the vṛtti is less (60%) sāttvika as compared to the citta of the individual, which is more (90%) sāttvika. Thus, in life, practically always there is a disharmony in between the pattern of guṇa distribution in the citta of the individual and the vṛttis that arise in his citta at different moments. For example a good sāttvika man has to face in life situations, which are not in harmony with his own basic nature and so he will not like normally to do things, which he is compelled to do by the situation, but which are not in accord with his citta. This will lead to a loss of peace in his citta. In other words it will lead to disturbance or discomfort and so to misery and pain. Thus this everlasting conflict, between the guṇa-pattern of the individual's citta and that of the vṛtti, is the second channel, through which duḥkha comes into our life.

This second channel is working more internally, that is here the reaction of the citta itself leads to pain and misery.

In this way when the experiences of life are analysed by a citta, which has the ability of such discriminative thinking, it reaches an inevitable conclusion that even the things and happenings, which at first appear to be pleasure-giving, ultimately turn out to be only a source of pain and misery. Patañjali here seems to be putting forth the same truth, which has been more popularly ascribed to Buddha and is said to be one of his four noble truths: 'sarvaṃduḥkham'.

SS. - **हेयं दुःखमनागतम् ।।२:१६।।**

TL. - heyaṃ duḥkham-anāgatam - II:16.

WM. - heya (ṃ) = possible to be avoided or done away with;

duḥkha (ṃ) = pain and misery;

anāgata (ṃ) = (an = not +āgata = come), that which has not yet come i.e. future.

TR. - The pain and misery which has not as yet come (i.e. of the future) can be avoided.

CE. - The last part of the preceding 15th sūtra may lead the sādhaka to a feeling that Patañjali and that way Bhāratīya darśanas and philosophies are pessimistic in their outlook. But in this belief it is often overlooked that these darśanas only put forth the inevitability of misery as a Universal truth and a factual experience. This affirmation is made only for pointing out a way, by means of which this duḥkha can be avoided. In fact all the darśanas came into existence to fulfil the eternal desire and end the search of every human being to find the everlasting happiness (sukha) or peace, in other words to achieve the total and permanent annihilation of duḥkha. The system of yoga is not merely a philosophy or darśana, but a practical path, which gives assurance of reaching this goal through very practical means or techniques. Patañjali's aṣṭāṅga yoga shows a very well designed and clearly chalked out way of attaining this goal. This can be done through avoiding and ultimately abolishing the duḥkha.

There, obviously, is no question of doing anything about the duḥkha that has been already experienced i.e. duḥkha in the past; and even that is being experienced at present moment, since it also immediately goes into the past. The only thing a man can do is to avoid or rather do away with the duḥkha of the future. And this can surely be done as is affirmed in the present sūtra. The whole stand of Pātañjala Yoga Sūtras, according to the present commentator, is of greatest optimism and total self-dependence, which is clearly evidenced by the present sūtra.

SS. - **द्रष्टृदृश्ययोः संयोगो हेयहेतुः ।।२:१७।।**

TL. - drastr = drsyayoh samyogo heya- hetuḥ - II:17

WM. -

draṣṭṛ	=	draṣṭā (seer);
dṛśya(yoḥ)	=	dṛśya, seen (of the two);
saṃyoga (ḥ->o)	=	saṃyoga, joining, union, getting connected (is);
heya	=	that which is to be avoided and done away with;
hetu(ḥ)	=	cause (is).

TR. - The cause of that (duḥkha), which is to be avoided and abolished, is samyoga of the two, namely draṣṭā (the seer-principle) and dṛśya (seen).

CE. - Many philosophical questions are universal and yet eternally unanswerable. The cause of arising of duḥkha is also one such eternal question, because every human being, as said above, is desirous of achieving permanent happiness. Stated inversely, he wants to do away duḥkha for ever. For this he has to find out the source or cause of duḥkha. Every philosophy and darśana, implicitly or explicitly, is an attempt to find out this cause. Here Pātañjala Yoga Darśana (i.e. Sūtras) is trying to give answer to this eternal question. The apparent linking or union of the draṣṭā i.e. seeing principle or puruṣa and of the dṛśya i.e. seen or the creation or prakṛti is explained as the cause of duḥkha, which every one wants to avoid and do away with. This linkage is according to the basic concept of Sāṃkhya-yoga, not actual but is only an illusion or misconception. It is technically designated by the term sāṃyoga. As already explained under sūtra I:3, the word draṣṭā is wrongly used for purusa, which, according to its fundamental notion, can not see or perceive. Therefore this draṣṭā i.e. puruṣa is not even remotely linked with, even as a perceiver or seer of, the dṛśya, which can be only prākṛtika i.e. of prakṛti. In other words the saṃyoga, is no actual union or linking and does really never happen. It is only a delusion created in man that it has taken place and this notion is implied in this technical designation saṃyoga. Thus this apparent linking of the puruṣa tattva with the prakṛti is said to be the cause, giving rise to duḥkha.

Obviously duḥkha occurs in its two forms viz. physical pain, which can be on the body level and sorrow or mental pain, which can be on mental level. But body and mind-citta both are prākṛtika. So, if the puruṣa-tattva does not become linked with prakṛti at all, body and citta (mind) are also not linked with it in any way. Therefore it can not have any of this duḥkha. Such eternally unafflicted, pure, unsullied puruṣa-tattva is present only in one case and that is Īśvara. In every individual-here pertinently in every human -the puruśa -tattva, since it seems to reside in the body and to function through citta, it apparently seems to have got linked with these prākṛtika entities. An impression, then, is created that the pain and sorrow actually suffered by these two prākṛtika entities is, as if, being experienced by this puruṣa. Thus the puruṣa-tattva in the individual becomes the perceiver or experiencer i.e. draṣṭā and seems to get related to the things experienced by the citta and even by the body i.e. by dṛśya. In this way this saṃyoga of draṣṭā and dṛśya gives rise to duḥkha for the draṣṭā puruṣa i.e. the real self principle.

The sūtra apparently seems to give answer to the question-'why at all is duḥkha there ?'. But this is just an illusion that the question is answered. The question is eternal and so really still remains unanswered, because now there is a new question - 'why is saṃyoga there ?'. In fact, not only Yoga-darśana, but really no darśana or philosophy can really and finally explain and answer such eternal questions in the usual manner i.e. through words and so as to satisfy the intellect.

SS. - **प्रकाशक्रियास्थितिशीलं भूतेन्द्रियात्मकं भोगापवर्गार्थं दृश्यम् ।।२:१८।।**

TL. - prakāśa-kriyā-sthiti-śīlaṃ bhūtendriyātmakaṃ bhogāpavargārthaṃ dṛśyam - II:18.

WM. -

prakāśa	=	light, illumination;
kriyā	=	action;
sthiti	=	stability;
śīla (ṃ)	=	possessing the property or ability;
bhūta	=	pañca mahābhūtas, the five elements;
indriya	=	organs;
ātmaka(ṃ)	=	of the nature of, composed of;
bhoga	=	experiencing;
apavarga	=	final beatitude, absolution, liberation;
artha (ṃ)	=	for the purpose of;
dṛśya (m)	=	dṛśya, Seen (creation).

TR. - Dṛśya has the qualities of illumination, action (and) stability and consists of the (five Mahā) bhūtas (i.e. primordial elements) (and of those possessing) indriyas (organs) (and is) for the purpose of experiencing (and) final liberation (of the draṣṭā).

CE. - Dṛśya (the perceived creation) is described here. It possesses the three fundamental qualities of illumination, action and stability. These are the characteristics respectively of the three guṇas namely sattva, rajas and tamas. These three guṇas are not only three qualities, but the fundamental aspects or warp and woof of which the prakṛti is composed. All the three guṇas are thus essentially present in everything that is prākṛtika. In other words dṛśya is prakṛti itself, made up of all three guṇas : sattva, rajas and tamas, i.e. the whole creation, manifested as well as unmanifested.

Dṛśya can be divided into two main and distinct groups of things (1) those composed of merely the elements i.e. the five mahābhūtas and (2) those having organised structures i.e. possessing organs (indriyas). These two groups are clearly one of the nonsentient things, which have no functional organisation in their structure and are mere conglomeration of the five mahābhūtas; the other is of sentient or living things, who are also composed of the same five elements, but they have in them structures, which depict clear organisation having definite functions and so are called organs or indriyas. Thus the dṛśya includes all living as well as non-living things.

'What is the objective or purpose behind the creation?' is another fundamental and eternal question. A satisfactory final answer can never be found for it also. But since yoga is a system developed only for humans, in this limited context the question takes a limited and more personal form. For the yoga-sādhaka it then becomes, 'What is the utility of this creation for my objective of reaching the goal of yoga?'. This answer to this question, which is most pertinent to a sādhaka, is given in the last part of this sūtra.

The purpose which the whole creation serves for the yoga-sādhaka is to give him (i.e. apparently to the draṣṭā in him) bhoga i.e. experience of and in the world and then, only via this, finally the apavarga i.e. Ultimate Liberation or Salvation. The word bhoga is most often interpreted as a pleasant experience or enjoyment. But the word is, no doubt, used also sometimes for painful experience. Here it not only includes both pleasant as well as painful experiences, but specially in the light of sūtra II:15 it really means wholly painful suffering only. Yet the liberation (apavarga) cannot be achieved unless the individual undergoes this bhoga, with no doubt, his outlook towards it being as per sūtra II:15. Only when the sādhaka is convinced that all-even the so said pleasure-is ultimately duhkha, will he turn away from it and seek to get out of it. Thus apavarga is reached only via the road of bhoga. That is why the sūtra does not say only 'apavargārtham', but mentions the purpose of dṛśya as 'bhoga=apavargartham'.

SS. - **विशेषाविशेषलिङ्गमात्रालिङ्गानि गुणपर्वाणि ।।२:१९।।**

TL. - viśeṣāviśeṣa-lingamātrāliṅgāni guṇa-parvāṇi- II:19

WM. -

viśeṣa	=	viśeṣa (particularised);
aviśeṣa	=	aviśeṣa (a = not + viśeṣa), not-particularised;
liṅga-mātra	=	(liṅga = symbol + mātra = merely) merely a symbol;
aliṅga	=	aliṅga, not having any symbol;
āni	=	suffix of plurality = are;
guṇa	=	Three guṇas, which constitute prakṛti, so here = prakṛti;
parva (āṇi)	=	wellmarked segments or internodations such as the phalanges of fingers, or like in a bamboo, sugarcane etc. (plural suffix).

TR. - The successive stages of development, clearly separated from each other, of the (three) guṇas are viśeṣa (particularised), aviśeṣa (non-particularised), liṅgamātra (in mere symbol form) (and) aliṅga (symbolless).

CE. - Out of the sūtras II:12 to II:27 this particular sūtra most clearly links the Pātañjala Yoga Sūtras (Darśana) with the Sāṃkhya Darśana. Prakṛti, which is manifested as made up of the three guṇas, starts activity in itself, as soon as saṃyoga takes place and the evolutionary process of prakṛti begins. Originally in its mūla-avasthā or pradhāna stage the three guṇas are in sāmyāvasthā i.e. a state of balance of these three guṇas. This balance is so perfect that no one of these guṇas is discernible. In this stage, therefore, there cannot be any qualification applied e.g. sāttvika, rājasika or tāmasika. In fact the stage is one for which no adjective (= symbol, sign or emblem of any quality) can be used. That means it is a symbolless stage. The term aliṅga precisely means the same.

But since prakṛti is made up of the three guṇas, or said otherwise, prakṛti is itself the three guṇas, they get distinctly manifested with the occurrence of samyoga. The balance of the three guṇas is disturbed and either one of these gets a dominance. The next stage called mahat, which on individual level is buddhi, the discriminatory ability, is the one where the adjectives sattvika, rajasika or tamasika could be applicable, according to the guṇa dominant there. But only this much and no further qualification is possible there also. This stage is categorised as liṅga-mātra i.e. mere symbol (ic).

With further evolution the differentiation goes on becoming

more and more marked. But still it is not so sharply defined as to make the various elements quite separated from one another. There is some degree of intermingling or diffuseness. This stage is therefore named aviśeṣa = non-particularised. Ahaṃkāra (of Sāṃkhya, asmitā or asmitāmātra of Pātañjala Yoga) which may be better understood as the individuality-principle, than being rendered as ego and the five tanmātras come under it. Ahaṃkāra, which gives individualisation, is diffused in everything that is prākṛtika. Tanmātrās are also intermingled, the gross one contains all the other subtler ones e.g. the grossest gandha tanmātrā contains the remaining four viz. rasa, rūpa, sparśa and śabda tanmātrās; rasa contains the further three and so forth. Thus these elements are not very definitely separated and particularised and so they are classed as aviśeṣa-non-particular.

There are differences of opinion in commentators as to which tattvas (elements, principles) come under which of these categories, specially about distribution of the elements in aviśeṣa and viśeṣa categories. Some include tanmātras under viśeṣa. So also some group manas (mind) under aviśeṣa, since though it is an indriya according to most darśanas, they think that it is functioning through and so diffused all over the remaining ten indriyas, namely jñānendriyas and karmendriyas.

But manas (mind), specially its thinking ability, is clearly evident in humans only. For this reason and as the ancients have done, it seems proper to group it with the other ten indriyas and so put it amongst the viśeṣas. Thus the sixteen elements namely the five mahābūtas, five jñānendriyas, five karmendriyas and the master, eleventh indriya manas, being clearly distinct entities, are to be categorised as viśeṣas or particularised.

The sūtra, though pertinent here, since it indicates different levels or stages of the evolution of prakṛti (i.e. guṇas), which is the dṛśya as per preceding II: 18 sūtra, yet it does not become very clear why Patañjali presents this classification here. For this reason some commentators (e.g. I.S.Taimni, "Science of Yoga, Theosophical Society, Adyar, India) have attempted to correlate these stages with different stages of samādhis and samāpattis. Taimni was led to postulate such a correlationship on account of the mention of aliṅga (stage) as being the ultimate limit of the subtleness of the objects or subjects, which can be chosen for the meditational processes of samāpatti, (which he again equates with samādhi) which is mentioned in the sūtra I:45 and some parallelism in the various sub-regions of saṃprajñāta sphere of meditational processes of samāpatti and sabīja samādhi and the kośas or subtle bodies postulated by Vedānta and corresponding subtle vehicles postulated by Theosophy, of which he is a great devotee. But such a precisely parallel correlationship between these stages of evolution of dṛśya, the kośas of Vedāntic view and vehicles as per Theosophy on one side and the various stages in samāpattis and sabīja samādhi on the other, does not seem tenable. According to us Patañjali does not seem to accept the specialised postulates of Vedāntic view point (since Theosophy is only recent, so its views obviously were not known to him).

However there is a general relationship in these stages in

the evolution of dṛśya (prakṛti) and the regions of internal sphere, through which the journey of citta takes place during the meditational processes. The subject taken for meditation will usually be from dṛśya. During meditation as mentioned in Samādhi-pāda, the subject is experienced in its more and more subtle aspects, as the meditation progresses to higher and higher stages. As said in sūtra I:45, the ultimate limit of this subtleness of the subject is aliṅga i.e. mūla-prakṛti or pradhāna state. Here the subject of meditation dissolves completely both in its ideational and emotive aspects and citta transcends the dṛśya and enters in the Realisation (of pure puruṣa tattva), where the citta also is dissolved and this puruṣa realisation alone remains. Since the apavarga (final liberation) is to be attained through such meditational practices and these would be easily feasible, if the subjects to be chosen for these are, at least in the beginning, out of the dṛśya and have been actually perceived in life and then become available as subjects for meditation. Thus this understanding of the nature and evolvement of dṛśya becomes meaningful here.

SS. - द्रष्टा दृशिमात्रः शुध्दोऽपि प्रत्ययानुपश्यः ।।२:२०।।

TL. - draṣṭā dṛśimātraḥ śuddho'pi pratyayānupaśyaḥ - II:20

WM. -

draṣṭā	=	draṣṭā, seer, perceiver;
dṛśi	=	dṛśi, potentiality of seeing i.e. perceiving;
mātra	=	mere;
śuddha (ḥ→o)	=	pure, untainted, unblemished;
api	=	yet;

pratyaya	=	experience or content of citta;
anu	=	through the agency of, via;
paśya (ḥ)	=	one who has seen or perceived.

TR. - Draṣṭā (the perceiver) is a mere potentiality of perceiving and though pure, yet (becomes) one, who has perceived through the content of (i.e. the agency of) citta.

CE. - As explained under sūtra I:3, the term draṣṭā, usually employed for puruṣa is not precise. This is done on account of the erroneous identification of citta with it. When dṛśya is present before it, it 'sees' the dṛśya, but completely aloofly. It sees the dṛśya as though it is 'not seeing'. That means that it is in no way affected by the perception of dṛśya. In other words the dṛśya is 'merely seen' or present before the puruṣa, who thus becomes a passive perceiver, for which reason it could be said draṣṭā, but as the sūtra says, he is a mere onlooker-'dṛśi-mātra'. In this 'seeing or witnessing (sākṣitva)' puruṣa does not take any cognition i.e. does not get aware of the dṛśya. We get many a time an experience of this type of 'non-seen seeing' or 'mere seeing', even in our ordinary life. Some person or thing passes in front of us and since our eyes are open they must have surely seen it going. But if our mind is occupied intensely with something else, it does not take cognisance of the person or thing and so we do not become conscious about this. So when asked about the passing of the person or thing we deny of having seen them. Obviously the person or thing does not have any effect on us. Our mind has no thought or feeling etc. about the person or thing. The draṣṭā puruṣa sees the dṛśya somewhat in this manner. In fact the perceiving is done by mind-citta with the help of indriyas. But on account of the delusory saṃyoga, we are led to believe that the draṣṭā puruṣa is perceiving and cognising the dṛśya. This delusion is caused, as said, by the misidentification of the citta, the factual cogniser, with puruṣa, which is a mere passive perceiver or rather a mere potentiality or perceiving, drsimatra, by which not only dṛśya, but the factual perceiver citta and its act of perceiving also is witnessed very unconcernedly.

When an object or phenomenon is presented to the sense organ e.g. eye or ear etc., as soon as the instigating energy viz. light or sound waves etc. reach and stimulate the respective sense organ, the object will be perceived by it in its specific way. Through it, it will be cognised by mind and citta and through this it will be witnessed by the puruṣa. This can be shown in the following chain : Object→Sense organ→Brain→Mind→Citta→Puruṣa (draṣṭā).

In this it may so happen that when the stimulating energy from the object reaches the sense organ and so it is perceived by the organ, it yet may not be cognised by the mind or citta or puruṣa. Therefore the chain will be broken and the reaction or effect on mind-citta level is prevented. For example, if we are sitting in a somewhat darkened room and there be a snake or scorpion near us, we may see it only as some vague object, but do not cognise it precisely as that which it really is. So no fear etc. is produced in our mind. On the contrary, if our mind cognises the object as a snake or scorpion, fear and the further chain of reactions e.g. sweating etc. would start in our body-mind-citta complex. The example given is for the mind-citta, which usually peceives and cognises simultaneously. But in the case of the draṣṭā-puruṣa, the perception is mere perception. There is no further chain of reactions. This is what is meant by dṛśimāra i.e. mere potentiality of perceiving.

However in our life, we are always misidentifying the citta (mind) with puruṣa and so always feel that the puruṣa is perceiving and also cognising, whereas the real cogniser, and in this sense perceiver, is citta. The puruṣa remains totally unaffected by the chain of reactions, even if it be started in the citta-body level, due to the cognitive perception. This is what is emphasized by the term 'śuddha' i.e. pure. The words draṣṭā, dṛśi are related to the sense and activity of vision but they are pertinent equally to the other four senses and varieties of perception.

SS. - **तदर्थ एव दृश्यस्यात्मा ।।२:२१।।**

TL. - tad-artha eva dṛśyasyātmā - II:21.

WM. - tat (→d) = it;
artha = for the purpose of;
eva = only;
dṛśya (sya) = dṛśya, seen (of);
ātmā = soul, here essence, essential purposes.

TR. - The essential purpose of dṛśya (the seen i. e., the manifest creation is to serve its (draṣṭā's) purpose.

CE. - This sūtra is almost paraphrasing the last part of the sūtra, II: 18, 'bhogāpavargārtham dṛśyam'. The statement about the relationship of dṛśya and draṣṭā is made here primarily from the angle of draṣṭā. From the viewpoint of the yoga and the individual, as per this sūtra, the (limited) purpose of dṛśya the creation, is that it is, as if, created solely to serve the objective of draṣṭā. This objective or purpose according to yoga is to remove the blemish, even if it be unreal, over the puruṣa of its draṣṭā-hood, in which it has, at least apparently, been sullied by kleśas and karmas-Karmāśya-Karmavipāka (see sūtra I:24 for this) and revert it to its pure-pristine state, its svarūpāvasthā, which is the attainment of kaivalya.

As repeatedly stressed, puruṣa is never tainted nor gets involved with dṛśya i.e. prakṛti. It ever remains totally alienated from prakṛti, which fact is indicated by the term 'śuddha' applied to it in sūtra II:20. Yet even the illusion of its involvement with prakṛti, which is designated as saṃyoga, must be done away with for having the puruṣa in an individual, back in its absoluteness i.e. kaivalya and this thing cannot be accomplished without the help i.e. the bhoga or utilisation of dṛśya, as pointed out in the sūtra II:18 and the present sūtras. From the standpoint of the yoga-sādhaka this is the essential purpose, which dṛśya serves for him.

SS. - **कृतार्थं प्रति नष्टमप्यनष्टं तदन्यसाधारणत्वात् ।।२:२२।।**

TL. - kṛtārthaṃ prati naṣṭam-apyanaṣṭaṃ tad-anya-sādhāraṇatvāt- II:22.

WM. - kṛtārtha (ṃ) = (kṛta = accomplished + artha +Purpose). One whose purpose has been accomplished;

prati = towards, for;

naṣṭa(ṃ)	=	destroyed, annihilated;
api (->y)	=	yet;
anaṣṭa (ṃ)	=	(a + naṣṭa) not destroyed;
tat (->d)	=	its;
anya	=	others;
sādhāraṇatva (at)	=	(sādhārana = universal + tva = ness) universality, universal or common availability; (on account of).

TR. - For the one (yogī) whose purpose has been accomplished (the dṛśya i.e. the creation) is annihilated, (= not now existing) yet (it is actually) not destroyed, (as is evident) on account of its universal availability for others.

CE. - This sūtra is trying to explain an important tenet of Sāṃkhya-Yoga, which however is very difficult to comprehend and explain.

The yogī, who attains the ultimate goal of yoga viz. kaivalya, reaches a state where only one tattva viz. puruṣa remains. Prakṛti is totally dissolved or destroyed or at least is as good as destroyed for the yogī. The designation kaivalya, which is used for this ultimate attainment, also has the same significance viz. aloneness, where only one single entity is absolutely pervading, without there being present anything else. This single entity is, according to Sāṃkhya-Yoga, only the pure puruṣa-tattva.

However, this disappearance of the second principle viz. prakṛti is limited only to that one accomplished yogī. His consciousness or citta is transformed in a peculiar manner, very difficult to comprehend. Its ability of becoming conscious, so to say, is resorbed into its source, which is puruṣa. In its basic composition citta is prākṛtika and so is merged into pradhāna or mūla-prakṛti. So now the citta of the yogī is no more functioning or we may even say that it is no more existing. The yogī can no more become aware of or cognise the dṛśya i.e. the manifestation of creation or prakṛti. So the dṛśya is as good as non-existent for him. And if existing means becoming conscious, this ability of his has returned to its original form=svarūpa and become one with citi or citiśakti (IV:34) i.e. the unmanifest potentiality of consciousness, which is that of puruṣa-tattva and so it can be said that the yogī is now again re-established and existing in pure purūṣa-hood. This is kaivalya.

But according to Sāṃkhya-Yoga prakṛti is eternal and so can never be destroyed. So prakṛti, creation or dṛśya is really not destroyed. For other persons, who will be taking the path of yoga, it will be needed to serve and does serve the purpose of bhoga and apavarga, as said in sūtras II:18 and 21. In fact the wording of the last portion of the present sūtra asserts the indestructibility of dṛśya i.e. prakṛti, for which the proof is the fact that prakṛti is always available universally to serve the purpose of every person, who may wish to become a yoga-sādhaka.

Very often a question arises as to whether there is only one or there are many puruṣas. Though the present sūtra has no explicit mention, but in the light of the explanation given above, it may be looked at as supporting the plurality of puruṣas, same as sūtra I:24.

SS. - **स्वस्वामिशक्त्योः स्वरूपोपलब्धिहेतुः संयोगः ।।२:२३।।**

TL. - sva-svāmi-śaktyoḥ sva-rūpopalabdhi-hetuḥ saṃyogaḥ - II:23

WM. -

sva	=	one's own, belongings;
sva-śakti	=	the potentiality or characteristic of belonging to one;
svāmi (n)	=	owner, possessor, master;
śakti (→yoḥ)	=	power, potentiality (of the two);
svarūpa	=	(sva=one's own i.e. original+rūpa = form, state) one's own original state;
upalabdhi	=	gaining, here regaining;
hetu (ḥ)	=	purpose, objective (is);
saṃyoga (ḥ)	=	saṃyoga, the illusion of linking of puruṣa with prakṛti (is).

TR. - (1) Saṃyoga has the objective of the regainment of their own original states of the two potentialities of being the possession and of being the possessor.

OR

(2) The purpose of saṃyoga is the regainment of the awareness (by puruṣa) of its nature and the unfoldment of powers in them both (i.e. puruṣa and prakṛti).

CE. - The rendering (1) of the sūtra is more literal, with the meaning of the word upalabdhi being taken as gaining or here better as regaining. But upalabdhi has another meaning as knowing, cognising. Some commentators prefer this sense and give a rendering some-what as in (2) above, which is worth consideration. Probably misled by the primary meaning of the word puruṣa viz. man, a male human, the term puruṣa even in the discussion of Yoga-darśana is used as though it represented a male person. This can be evident from the pronoun 'he' used for the puruṣa. But the puruṣa in Sāṃkhya is a technical term, which stands for an abstract and eternal principle. The best suited gender to be used in the English language for it would be neutral, so as to avoid confusion of its having a body and sex etc. Nevertheless according to the usage in Sanskrit and other Indian languages probably masculine pronouns are employed for puruṣa (tattva) even in English writings on Yoga and which may be excusable for this reason. But the trouble is that other traits of a (male) human being are also sometime misconceived as pertaining to this puruṣa-tattva. One most common misconcept seems about puruṣa being conscious. Many commentators even designate it as conscious or the consciousness-principle. But if puruṣa be able to become conscious, it could and would become conscious about also the dṛśya and the chain of reactions would start and it would get affected as explained in sūtra II:20. But puruṣa, as per fundamentals of Sāṃkhya-Yoga, is apariṇāmi = unchangeable, therefore unaffected. So it cannot be even conscious. In fact, as per our understanding, it is the background principle of consciousness and not itself consciousness or not even conscious. The consciousness is latent or unmanifest in it. It is however the source of consciousness and citta gets its consciousness from it. To indicate this unmanifest potentiality of consciousness, the term citi or citi-sakti is used for puruṣa (sūtra IV:22 and 34). In the rendering (2) above puruṣa is spoken of as becoming 'aware' and developing 'powers' and this is against apariṇāmitva of puruṣa. For this reason rendering (1) seems preferable.

Another fundamental and eternal querry arises in the Sāṃkhya-Yoga darśanas. This is : "Why puruṣa, which has no reason to get involved in prakṛti, seems apparently to get linked with it?". Since the question is eternal and therefore unanswerable, here it has been answered, again as before, from the limited view-point of Yoga and the individual sādhaka.

Why and how the saṃyoga i.e. the illusion of the linking of puruṣa and prakṛti has been produced can never be answered by anybody- at least in the usual manner i.e. in words and so there is no sense in seeking such an answer. But the fact that saṃyoga is there, as is evident from the suffering that we have to undergo (cf. sūtra II:17), is undeniable. So the purposeful querry for the sādhaka would be : "What does this saṃyoga mean to me and since it is an inevitably accomplished fact, how can I utilise it to my best advantage?" The answer to this question is implied in this sūtra. This saṃyoga is helpful to the sādhaka to achieve his ultimate objective viz. the goal of Yoga i.e. the attainment of kaivalya or the regainment of the original status of the potential entities present in him viz. svāmi-śakti- the possessor potentiality, invested in puruṣa and sva-śakti- the potentiality of being the possession, invested in dṛśya or prakṛti.

The saṃyoga, which is the cause of duḥkha (sūtra II:17), is here being looked upon most optimistically as a thing which can lead to kaivalya i.e. svarūpa-pratiṣṭhā, which will give absolute liberation from suffering. The positive and optimistic stand of Patañjali towards life and its sufferings is clearly and emphatically put forth by this sūtra.

SS. - **तस्य हेतुरविद्या ।।२:२४।।**

TL. - tasya hetur-avidyā - II:24

WM. - tasya = its;

hetu (ḥ->r) = cause (is);

avidyā = avidyā, non-vidyā.

TR. - Its (saṃyoga's) cause (is) avidyā.

CE. - Avidyā is the understanding or view-point which is basically wrong from the spiritual or yogīc standpoint. Avidyā, as defined in sūtra II : 5, in its deepest sense is nothing else but saṃyoga itself. Saṃyoga, which is the deluding misidentification of citta, a vikṛti, (evolute) of prakṛti, with puruṣa, takes up the various forms of the many erroneous viewpoints explained in the sūtra II:5. In other words though saṃyoga is avidyā, in the usual logical manner of speaking avidyā seems to be the cause or origin of saṃyoga as expressed in this sūtra.

SS. - **तदभावात्संयोगाभावो हानं तद्दृशेः कैवल्यम् ।।२:२५।।**

TL. - tad-abhāvāt-saṃyogābhāvo hānaṃ
tad-dṛśeḥ kaivalyam -II:25.

WM. - tad = its;

abhāva (āt)	=	absence, disappearance (Through);
saṃyoga	=	saṃyoga, the illusion of linking of puruṣa and prakṛti;
abhāva (ḥ->o)	=	absence, disappearance (is);
hāna (ṃ)	=	hāna, relinquishment, cessation, avoidance, annihilation;
tat(->d)	=	that, which;
dṛśi (->eḥ)	=	dṛśi, potentiality of perceiving (of);
kaivalya (m)	=	kaivalya (absoluteness).

TR. - Through its (of avidyā) disappearance (there is) disappearance of saṃyoga, which is (the same thing as) hāna, (and from the standpoint) of dṛśi (the perceiving potentiality) (it is) kaivalya.

CE. - Saṃyoga, which leads to duḥkha (sūtra II: 17) can be done away with , if avidyā is removed. From the achievement aspect it is called hāna, the achieving the cessation of suffering (duḥkha). This is the achieving the goal of Yoga (and in fact of all darśanas) as it is popularly looked at. Looked at from dṛśi's (perceiving potentiality i. e. puruṣa) angle it is kaivalya (Absolute pervasion of one principle viz. puruṣa). Thus this sūtra broadly explains the way of attaining kaivalya with total abolition of duḥkha and of gaining everlasting happiness or peace. This is the way of doing away of saṃyoga, the delusion, which leads to an identification of citta with puruṣa and this can be accomplished by the removal of its cause avidyā. In other words kaivalya is nothing else than doing away of saṃyoga or dissolution of avidyā. The word Yoga is most often said to mean union, which is explained to be that of soul (ātmā) with Super-soul (Paramātmā) or God. Strangely enough, as per this explanation of the nature of Yoga, doing away with union-saṃyoga is Yoga, that is to say viyoga is Yoga. Not only Patañjali, but Lord Śrī Kṛśna defines (Bhagvad Gītā VI:23) Yoga in exactly the same strange manner viz. 'tam vidyad duḥkha-saṃyoga-viyogaṃ yoga-saṃjñitam' 'Know that disunion (viyoga) of conjoinment (saṃyoga, affectation and affliction) of duḥkha (suffering) (is) named Yoga'.

SS. - **विवेकख्यातिरविप्लवा हानोपायः ।।२:२६।।**

TL. - viveka-khyātir-aviplavā hānopāyaḥ - II : 26

WM. -

viveka	=	discrimination;
khyāti (ḥ->r)	=	knowledge, realisation;
aviplavā	=	(ā = Not + viplavā = Break (fern)) not broken, uninterrupted;
hāna	=	hāna (Avoidance, dissolution, here of suffering);
upāya (ḥ)	=	remedy, measure for (is).

TR. - The remedy for (this) hāna (abolition of suffering) (is) uninterrupted vivekakhyāti (discriminating knowledge).

CE. - Viveka means discrimination and from the standpoint of Sāṃkhya-Yoga, this discrimination is only between dṛśi-puruṣa and dṛśya prakṛti, since the delusory misidentification of these two principles is the ultimate cause of duḥkha. Khyāti (from the root khya = to know) means knowing or knowledge. This is usually interpreted as understanding or comprehending intellectually. But here the word khyāti is not such mere intellectual understanding, but actual experiencing or realization of the distinction between these two principles. Such a realization may come to a learned person in a contemplative state. But as soon as he would be again engrossed in the daily worldly activities, that awareness may become clouded. Therefore obviously to do away with duḥkha for ever this discriminatory knowledge must become firmly and permanently established and should not be lost even for one instant. This is the only way for the permanent abolition of duḥkha, which the sūtra emphatically puts forth.

SS. - **तस्य सप्तधा प्रान्तभूमिः प्रज्ञा ।।२:२७।।**

TL. - tasya saptadhā prānta-bhūmiḥ prajñā - II:27

WM. -
tasya = its;
saptadhā = seven-fold;
prānta = boundary;
bhūmi(ḥ) = land, region;
prajñā = power of knowing, here supra-intellectual intuitional higher potentiality of knowing, ṛtambharā prajñā of sutra I:48.

TR. - Its (of vivekakhyāti) prajñā (has) sevenfold well - marked stages.

CE. - The vivekakhyāti is, said, not mere intellectual comprehension, but an actual experiencing or realization of the distinction between the puruṣa and prakṛti. To attain this the proper understanding about these two principles is a prerequisite and the starting stage. The complete 'Realization' of the distinction will be attained by the sādhaka gradually and in a definite number of stages as is clear from this and the next sūtra (II:28). These stages are distinctly separated from one another and are seven in all. This ultimate Realisation becomes possible through a new faculty which is developed during yoga-sādhanā, particularly during dhāraṇā, dhyāna and samādhi. This faculty of Realization is in some respects like intuition, that is, it gives knowledge directly without the intermediacy of senses etc. In this sūtra it is mentioned by the word prajñā merely. But the word prajñā here should not be understood in the sense of its common usage i.e. mere intellectual comrehension. In fact this special faculty for attaining knowledge directly has already been mentioned in the sūtra I:48 and there it has been qualified as ṛtaṃbharā prajñā. This prajñā, arises during the early stages of sabīja samādhi (I:48), which is able to give knowledge of the reality behind things and phenomena. It goes on becoming more and more penetrative as the practice of samādhi continues and during the further stages of samādhis, viz sabīja, nirbīja and dharmamegha, goes on giving the knowledge of subjects chosen for the process of dhāraṇā, dhyāna and samādhi, which is nearer and nearer to the Ultimate Reality. This gradual approach to the Ultimate Reality takes place in seven distinctly separated stages as per this sūtra. At each stage the sādhaka gets a knowledge or experience of the subject chosen for meditation, which is nearer to the Ultimate Reality behind it than in the preceding stage.

Patañjali has used the term prāntabhūmiḥ and not simply bhūmiḥ in this sūtra. The reason seems to be that according to him the development of prajñā is through stages, which are distinctly marked just like geographical political provinces and that their number is also very exact viz. seven. However there exists a possibility that some sādhakas may feel that these stages are less or more than seven. Patañjali merely mentions that these stages are exactly seven, yet he does not give any names of these. Some commentators have given the names and descriptions of the nature of these stages. But whether these names and explanations were acceptable to Patañjali is questionable. Since Patañjali does not clarify anything about these seven prāntabhūmis, it does not matter much for the practical sādhaka as to what be the names and particular characteristics of these prāntabhūmis. What, according to the present commentator, is the main purpose of this sūtra is that Patañjali wants to bring it to the notice of the sādhaka that the development of (ṛtaṃbharā) prajñā is gradual and that most probably the sādhaka will experience distinct stages in this development i.e. he will have the Realization of the Reality in seven stages, each of these approaching more and more near to the Ultimate Reality.

SS. - **योगाङ्गानुष्ठानादशुद्धिक्षये ज्ञानदीप्तिराविवेकख्यातेः ।।२:२८।।**

TL. - yogāṅgānuṣṭhānād-aśuddhi-kṣaye jñānadīptir-ā-viveka-khyāteḥ - II:28.

WM. - yogāṅga = (yoga + aṅga) limb or member of yoga (system or physique);

anuṣṭhāna (āt->ād)	=	(anu = successively + ṣṭhāna = placement) A repetition of a thing or process, precisely in the same manner successively and usually for a period, day after day (through);
aśuddhi	=	(a = not + śuddhi = purity) impurities;
kṣaya (e)	=	diminution and ultimate disappearance (in);
jñāna	=	knowledge;
dīpti (ḥ->r)	=	illumination (is);
ā	=	till, upto;
viveka	=	discrimination;
khyāti (eḥ)	=	knowledge realization (the state of).

TR. - Through repeated daily anuṣṭhāna (precisely same routine) of the limbs of the body-yogique (i.e. the members of the system of yoga) with diminution (and consequent) disappearance of impurities, (there arises) the illumination of knowledge (which develops) upto the stage of viveka-khyāti (the ultimate Realization of the discrimination between puruṣa and prakṛti).

CE. - After discussing the basic philosophico-metaphysical background of Sāṃkhya-Yoga, of which the understanding is necessary as pre-requisite for an efficient and successful practice of yogāṅgas, Patañjali in this sutra opens the discussion of the systematic practical path of aṣṭāṅgayoga.

The word anuṣṭhāna has a meaning that the practice of a particular technique or routine is to be repeated exactly in the same manner (indicated by the prefix 'anu') usually from day to day or even many times per day as may be convenient and feasible for the sādhaka. In this sutra Patañjali thus recommends the daily regular practice of all the necessary yogāṅgas.

The broad effect of the practice of yogāṅgas is the gradual diminution and ultimate disappearance of the impurities of all types. These impurities or deficiencies may be of any type and may be related to any part of the human body-mind-spirit complex. As the impurities go on reducing, the inner light of knowledge to be gained through the awakening of ṛtaṃbharā prajñā goes on getting brighter and brighter and more and more penetrating. Thus, as explained under sūtras I:44, II:27 etc., successively closer, clearer and more and more correct realization of the Reality behind the subject chosen for meditative practices is achieved by the yogasādhaka. This process continues till the viveka-khyāti stage is reached. This is the penultimate stage or the threshold of kaivalya.

SS. - यमनियमासनप्राणायामप्रत्याहारधारणाध्यानसमाधयोऽ-
ष्टावङ्गानि ।।२:२९।।

TL. - yama-niyamāsana-prāṇāyāma-pratyāhāra-dharaṇā dhyāna-samādhayo' ṣṭāvaṅgāni - II:29

WM. - yama = yama (rule of self-restraint);
niyama = niyama (rules of observation);
āsana = āsana (posture);

prāṇāyāma = prāṇāyāma (expansion i.e. control of prāṇa through control of breathing);

pratyāhāra = pratyāhāra (withdrawal and total subjugation of senses);

dhāraṇā = dhāraṇā (restraint of citta so as to have a constant contact of citta with the subject of meditation);

dhyāna = dhyāna (A totally uniform experience of the subject of meditation);

samādhi (...dhayaḥ->dhayo) = samādhi(s), (a state of citta where the subject of meditation is experienced devoid of its form and in its subtle essence) (are);

aṣṭa (ḥ->o = av) = eight;

aṅga (āni) = limb (s), member (s), part (s).

TR. - Yama, niyama, āsana, prāṇāyāma, pratyāhāra, dhāraṇā, dhyāna (and) samādhi (are) the eight members (of the systematic discipline of yoga, as presented here by Patañjali).

CE. - Patañjali's practical system is divided into eight sections called limbs (of the body yogique), which are enumerated here. Very often these are spoken of as eight steps or stages. This creates an impression that there is a rigid sequentiality in these eight angas, so that any particular aṅga can and should be practised only after the aṅga preceding it, in the enumeration in this sūtra, have been practised, or better still, have even been mastered. With such an understanding, many a times some critics raise an objection about the practising of a particular aṅga without having previously practised the preceding aṅgas.

This objection is particularly raised in connection with the fashion of practising yogāsanas and prāṇāyāmas without any obvious attempt of practising yamas and niyamas or even without knowing anything about these latter two aṅgas, which practice is very much in vogue at present in India as well as abroad. The objection is, however, not valid. Firstly it must be noted that the āsanas and prāṇāyāmas popularly practised at such centres belong to Haṭhayoga and not to Pātañjala-yoga. Whether the principle of sequentiality is applicable, if at all, as thought by these critics, to the Haṭhayogic āsanas and prāṇāyāmas is very moot question. According to the present commentator observance of yamas and niyamas does not seem to be obligatory prerequisite for the practice of āsanas and prāṇāyāmas in Haṭhayoga. Not only this, but Haṭhayoga does not seem to give much importance to yama-niyama and so does not give any instruction or commandment for their observance. Out of the three most authentic texts of Haṭhayoga viz. Haṭha-pradīpikā, Gheraṇḍa-saṃhitā and Śiva-saṃhitā, the latter two do not contain even the words yama or niyama, leave aside any description or instruction about them. Haṭhapradīpika (H.P.) also does not give any directive for observance of yamas or niyamas, not even any enumeration of description of these . In H.P. the word 'yama' occurs only once (I:38) and 'niyama' only twice (I:15 and 38) in their specific sense of rules of observances, but the mention is just incidental. In I:38

Svātmārāma, the author of Haṭhapradīpikā, eulogising Siddhāsana, says that just as mitāhāra is foremost among yamas and ahiṃsā among niyamas, so is this one (āsana), named Siddhāsana by the siddhas, topmost among all the āsanas. The second mention is of niyama only, but instead of advising about their observance, it is stated (I:15) that too rigid insistence (āgraha) about observance of niyama is detrimental to progress in Yoga.

[Note - Kaivalyadhāma, S.M.Y.M. Samiti, published a critical edition of Haṭha-Pradīpikā in 1970. More than 100 manuscripts and all the available printed editions were consulted for this. Only in one of these, the ślokas enumerating ten yamas and ten niyamas have been given numbers in continuing sequence, which gives an impression, as though, they are authentic part of the original text, which is not the case, as will be seen below. Only a few other of these, no doubt, include these ślokas of yama and niyama, but indicate a doubt about their authenticity in some way e.g. by giving separate serial numbers or not giving any number at all or using parentheses. Most of the others, almost over hundred manuscripts, do not contain these ślokas of yama-niyama at all. From this it can be said that these ślokas are interpolated by some copier, who had wrongly presumed that yama-niyama are essential and obligatory aṅgas of Haṭhayoga also. But H.P. clearly states : "The sequence of practices in Haṭha (yoga) is āsana, various types of kumbhaka (prāṇāyāma), techniques known as mudrā and nādānusandhāna" (I:56). It further affirms : Āsana, being the first aṅga of Haṭha, is described first' (I:17). From these statements it can be seen that according to H.P. yama-niyama are not the essential aṅgas of Haṭhayoga, nor they are prerequisite for Haṭhayogic āsana-prāṇāyāma. Further confirmation of the fact that the yama-niyama ślokas are interpolations is that they contradict the śloka I:38, which is genuinely of the original text of H.P., since it is found in all the versions without a single exception. There it is stated that mitāhāra is foremost in yamas and ahiṃsā foremost amongst niyamas, where the spurious ślokas of yama-niyama mention ahimsa as foremost in yamas and not at all as a component of niyama; and though mitāhāra is enumerated in yamas it is at very lower i.e. ninth position.

This does not mean that Haṭhayoga belittles yamas and niyamas. H.P. itself (not directly using these terms) frequently mentions that observance of some of these is helpful to the yogī for giving him rapid and good success in yoga (I:57; III:92, 117 etc.). But Haṭhayoga does not insist on nor recommends the practising of any yama or niyama as a compulsory part of its essential discipline. The reasons for this may be : (1) The things comprising yama and niyama are such that it is quite obvious that their observance is beneficial for everyone. For yogasādhaka therefore these become a discipline to be voluntarily adopted for one's own behaviour. So there should be no need that he be commanded to follow these good rules. Moreover each author enumerates only five or ten things under each of these two, which may again be varying from author to author. As said, while discussing vitarkas (I:17, 42 etc.) not only the things enumerated under yama and niyama by different authors, but all similar things, which even common sense tells that they are conducive for yoga and spiritual sādhanā, should be practised by a sādhaka voluntarily as his discipline. Therefore there is no sense in enumerating a few of these, nor there is any need to expressly give instruction for their observance. (2) To some extent it has been seen that even a little training of Haṭhayogic āsanas, mudrās, prāṇāyāma etc. brings down the bad habits e.g. of heavy smoking and in a few persons of drinking. Similar yoga training given to prisoners reduced the criminal tendencies in them and a number of hardened violent criminals were converted into docile persons, who began to co-operate with the jail authorities and willingly submit to the jail discipline, against which they were rebellious before. The reason for these changes was found to be that the internal urges, which made these persons behave in this evil (and irrational, because these persons were aware of disadvantages accruing from these bad things) manner diminished and disappeared by this Haṭhayogic training and practice. Ancient Haṭhayogis must have noticed such result and come to conclude that practices of āsanas, bandha-mudrās and prāṇāyāmas would make the observance of yama-niyamas spontaneous and so there was no need to give directive for their obligatory observance.]

Even in Patañjali's aṣṭāṅgas the sequentially of any one aṅga and the aṅga next to it or the aṅgas after it as enumerated in this sūtra is not essentially and always obligatory. Wherever Patañjali thinks that the sequentiality in successive aṅgas is essential, he has explicitly indicated it. Thus prāṇāyāma needs āsana as a pre-requisite, as is indicated by the wording 'tasminsati' in the sūtra II:49, defining prāṇāyāma. Again there is definitely a sequence in dhāraṇā→dhyāna→samādhi as is evident from the wording 'tatra' in the sūtra III:2 of dhyāna and 'tadeva' in III:3 of samādhi.

But there is no such obligatory sequentiality in each of these eight aṅgas and its succeeding aṅga. It would be absurd and impracticable to assert that the niyama should not be practised unless the yama is practised i.e. till a satisfactory mastery has been achieved over this first aṅga. Because if such a view is accepted, then the observance of śauca, which incorporates body cleanliness, could not be practised unless the sādhaka has satisfactorily obeyed the injunction about the observance of yama. That would mean that unless the sādhaka is a satisfactory ahiṃsaka, satyavādin, brahmacārin etc., he is not entitled to take a bath, which is a part of śauca, the first of the niyamas.

Thus, excepting where specifically mentioned by Patañjali, these aṅgas need not and should not be considered as consecutive stages. That means that a sādhaka may start practising all the eight aṅgas simultaneously, to the extent which may be possible and practicable for him according to his circumstances. This rule or principle is applicable even to those aṅgas for which Patañjali has indicated a sequentiality as obligatory. Thus a person may and can practise prāṇāyāma, even if he is not able to maintain an āsana for long or even if he is not able to adopt a yogāsana. No doubt, in this case his prāṇāyāma may and will not be as efficient and fruitful as when done in a suitable and mastered āsana. So also a sādhaka may try to go through dhāraṇā, dhyāna etc. even from the beginning, though, obviously he will not be much successful in progressing on this line.

No doubt, even when the obligatory sequentiality does not exist in the successive aṅgas, there is vague or loose linking in them. If a sādhaka has practised the aṅgas standing in this enumeration earlier, his practice of the later aṅgas will be better. But in the same way the proficiency in the earlier aṅgas will be more satisfactory, more the mastery he may have over the later aṅgas. However as a practical hint it may be mentioned that a sādhaka should not be too sensitive about this relationship amongst these aṅgas and the level of proficiency he may have achieved in various aṅgas. He should try sincerely and to the best of his capacity to do the maximum practice of all the aṅgas simultaneously from the beginning. Because if he has to wait for achieving mastery over each of the five upāṅgas (sub-members) themselves of the first aṅga of yama, he will never be able to start, at least to make any progress on the path of Yoga. For example the criteria of perfection in the practice of yamas indicated in sūtras II:35 to 39 are such, which probably nobody will ever attain or has attained these ever before. So waiting for perfection in these aṅgas is purposeless.

There strikes an obvious similarity of the eight aṅgas of Pātañjala Yoga and the path of Buddha. In some respects there is a broad parallelism in the nature of these aṣṭāṅgas of the two schools. On account of this many scholars have even suggested that Patañjali has copied this eightfold classification and even borrowed some things in his system from Buddhism (and also Jainism). But it seems more probable that no one of them borrowed anything from the other directly. Certain notions were becoming very popular in those times. The fashion of classifying a system in eight aṅgas seems to be one such. That is why both Patañjali and Buddha seem to propose an Aṣṭāṅga Mārga, the Eight-Member Path.

SS. - अहिंसासत्यास्तेयब्रह्मचर्यापरिग्रहा यमाः ।। २:३० ।।

TL. - ahiṃsā-satyāsteya-brahmacaryāparigrahā yamāḥ -II:30

WM. -
ahiṃsā = (a = not + hiṃsā = injuring etc.) non injuring, nonviolence;
satya = truthfulness;
asteya = (a = non + steya = stealing) non-stealing;
brahmacarya = (brahma = brahman + carya= conduct, behaviour) Basically a mode of life of discipline conducive for spiritual attainment, but usually understood and translated as continence or abstinence in respect of sex;
aparigraha (āḥ->a) (= non + pari = all +graha = taking, receiving or accepting things) non-accepting of things and nonhoarding of things (plural);
yama (āḥ) = yama, rules or injunctions of self-restraint (are).

TR. - Ahiṃsā (not injuring any thing), satya (truthfulness in every way in life), asteya (not stealing i.e. not having any thing which rightly does not belong to one), brahmacarya (disciplined life of self-restraint, specially in matters of sex) (and) aparigraha (non-receiving and possessing and not accumulating of things) are the yamas.

CE. - The designation 'yama' is derived from the root verb 'yam', which means to control or restrain. So these upāṅgas (sub-members) of yama are injunctions for self-restraint. Many commentators have differentiated yamas from niyamas with an explanation that the former are rules of social behaviour, while the latter are rules of personal behaviour. According to the present commentator this is only partially correct. The observance of yamas by a yoga sādhaka has not the primary objective to produce a good and well disciplined society. These observances are recommended to produce a comparatively peaceful condition of the mind, which is the first prerequisite for the practice of yoga. The breaking of any of the yamas is to be avoided mainly because it produces an adverse effect on the mind leading to its disturbance. From the point of view of yoga ahiṃsā is not practised so much for not causing injury to others, but to avoid the evil effect of hiṃsā that is produced on the mind and disturbs it. For this reason not only hiṃsā in act, i.e. actually causing injury to others, is to be avoided. Indeed thinking of injuring others is as bad as or even worse than actually injuring. Hiṃsā in thought is also hiṃsā, probably the worst part of hiṃsā. The same is true for the rest of the yamas also. The good result of ahiṃsā observance for the society is from the yoga point a by-product. Viewed in this way both yamas and niyamas are rules for one's own behaviour. If there be a difference, it is that the observance of yamas is for bettering the inner atmosphere while that of the niyamas for external behaviour.

The observance of yamas should be on all the three levels viz. kāyika i.e. by body, vācika i.e. by speech and mānasika i.e. by mind. Most of the yamas, but particularly ahiṃsā, satya, asteya and brahmacarya should be observed in all these aspects. Even if one does not cause by some physical action actually some injury or harm to others and yet mentally has an intention or idea to cause such injury or harm to others, one has, from the point of yoga, broken the yama of ahiṃsā on mental level. So also a speech, which may give mental pain to someone, is an act of hiṃsā on verbal plane. Thus a sādhaka has to be very cautious and keep a watch on his activity so as to avoid any such act of injury or harm in any manner caused by him consciously or even inadvertently.

In the case of satya the term is translated as truthfulness and so gives an impression that it would only mean always speaking truth. But an act of deceit or even an idea of deceiving is a breach of the yama of satya.

Asteya i.e. non-stealing is not limited to actual purloining of things from others which rightly do not belong to oneself. Even an intention or desire to possess things belonging to others is a mental steya i.e. stealing. Instances of verbal stealing are not unknown. The plagiarism often practised by writers and speakers is an example of this, considered as a punishable criminal act even by the present day laws.

Brahmacarya is usually translated as continence or abstinence from sex, celibacy, chastity etc. But the word brahmacarya is made up of two words : brahma (n) i.e. the highest Reality (the word brahman is the Vedāntic term for this Highest Reality or Principle. But this very specific meaning is not there behind the term when used in this compound word brahmacarya and when used specially by other Darśanas) + carya i.e. mode of behaviour. Thus the basic and broad meaning of brahmacarya is a mode of behaviour which will be conducive for reaching the highest goal for the spiritual sādhaka. So brahmacarya should be understood as a life correctly disciplined for spiritual progress and ultimate realization.

In this wider sense, brahmacarya would include not only all the other yamas and even niyamas mentioned by Patañjali but all the things mentioned under yama-niyama by every other text. In a way every self-restraint, which most often our common-sense tells us as being helpful for spiritual development, is implied and should be included in brahmacarya. As is obvious, a brahmacarin (follower of brahmacarya) should not be an asatyavādin (lier and deceiver), nor hiṃsaka (one who commits hiṃsā), nor an epicurean and glutton i.e. one breaking the yama or niyama of mitāhāra recommended by some other yogic texts. Sāṃkhya and Patañjali seem to be fond of enumerating things in groups of fives. But if one single all inclusive yama was to be mentioned it could be only brahmacarya, because it will imply obeying all the rules of behaviour essential to a spiritual sādhaka, which would incorporate all yama-niyamas, ordered by all texts.

In such a disciplined life the proper restraint of sex activity is obviously very important. Sex is a very powerful force in the life activity of living beings. It is also a very essential activity of life. Without it the continuance of species will be impossible. Therefore fundamentally sex is not a thing to be deprecated and to be totally proscribed. Hence explaining brahmacarya simply as continence or abstinence from sex is not proper. Moreover even for highest spiritual progress and attainment sex may not be always a bar. This is evident from the fact that in all the cultures of the world there are innumerable instances of persons, who have reached very high levels in spiritual progress and yet had enjoyed conjugal life, most probably with sex activity included. Even in the sphere of Yoga names of such persons come prominently and easily before our mind, viz. Yogeśvara śrīkṛṣṇa, Yogeśvara ādinātha or Mahādeva Śaṅkara, Yogī vaśiṣṭha, Yogī yājñavalkya and many others. Complete abstinence from sex may become essential for a yoga-sādhaka at certain stage during his spiritual development, but it may not be unavoidably necessary at all times, even in spiritual development. When the sādhaka will reach such a stage, most probably the urge for sex activity will inwardly disappear automatically or at least diminish, if he be following the path of yoga in a systematic way and on correct scientific principles. So the sex activity will be curbed to the required extent and may in suitable cases become completely extinct. On the other hand, if the inner urge is very strong and still the person forcefully abstains himself from sex enjoyment, only because he has been hearing that sex is undesirable and a hindrance for spiritual development, such a forced constraint may have a very harmful effect. There are instances that such a forced and compulsive abstinence from sex leads even to a total disruption of personality. It often leads to mental aberration and even to insanity. So the controlling of sex activity in brahmacarya should be done in a judicious manner, so as to avoid such harmful consequences. More important for brahmacarya is preparing the mind so that the impulse and desire for sex gets diminished, that mere avoiding physical sex acts forcibly, when the urge is still there. The following statement of Gītā made about enjoyment of things (viṣayas) by means of senses and organs (karmendriyas), though general, can be very aptly applicable to the enjoyment of sex-

'karmendriyāṇi saṃyamya ya āste manasāsmaran I
indriyārthān-vimūḍhātmā mithyācāra sa ucyate'II (B.G. III:6)

TR. - The deluded person, having no proper understanding ability, restrains the organs of action (karmendriyas) and yet goes on thinking of the objects of enjoyment for these organs and senses in his mind. This is said to be a false i.e. wrong mode of behaviour.

To what extent the sex activity is to be avoided by any one sādhaka can be guided by a good guru or still better by a sādhaka himself, who is sincerely trying to prepare his own mind for such restraint. The urge of sex is a very disturbing and devastating force, not only for a spiritual sādhaka, but for a person who is desirous of reaching a high level even in mundane affairs. So the need to curb this urge is universal, which is implicitly accepted by the whole human society. No doubt for a spiritual sādhaka controlling of this urge is of utmost importance. If this is thoroughly imbibed by the sādhaka and he tries earnestly to achieve the control over the sex-urge, the judicious sex control as is necessary for his own spiritual progress will be spontaneously and willingly practised by him. The present commentator has a firm opinion that most of such self-restraints necessary for real progress in Yoga become spontaneously and easily practicable for the sādhaka provided he understands the principle and purpose behind such restraining and sincerely strives for it, accompanied by a regular, sincere and intensive practice of the aṣṭāṅgas of yoga, as far as possible in his circumstances. It has been already pointed out under II:1 and 2 that the practice of yamas becomes more facilitated, the more reduced are the kleśas and the most effective method for this kleśa-tanukaraṇa is the practice of kriyā-yoga.

Yama and niyama are the first and second of the aṣṭāṅgas, while āsana and prāṇāyāma are the third and fourth in this series, so very often it is opined that the latter two should be practised only after having a fair proficiency in the former two. But a fact is very often overlooked that a sincere and intensive practice of asanas and prāṇāyāmas is also helpful to reduce the urges making a man break the rules of yamas. No doubt this is more markedly observable for āsanas and prāṇāyāmas of Haṭhayoga. But it is equally true for Patañjali's āsana and prāṇāyāmas. So also a regular practice of other aṅgas viz. pratyāhāra, dhāraṇā, dhyāna and samādhi will be helpful in the adherence to and observance of the practice of yama, even if in the early stage of abhyāsa these practices of the sādhaka may be very imperfect, so far so that they may not be even worthy of their names.

Mere outward i.e. physical abstinence from sex activity will not be at all an observance of brahmacarya. Besides being gravely harmful, this will not serve the purpose, because mentally thinking of and indulging in the ideas of sex is the real cause for disturbance of the inner atmosphere and is the worst breach of the yama of brahmacarya by a yogasādhaka. The yamas being the self-restraints, controlling one's own activity merely on body level is of secondary importance in their respect. The more important and the real observance is at the mind level. A prisoner may perforce have to forego sex activity, yet he may be indulging in thoughts of sex, in which case he cannot be considered as following brahmacarya. Brahmacarya is also, therefore, to be practised in all the three aspects viz physical, verbal and mental, the last being the most important.

The word aparigraha is made up of a = not + pari = indicative of all inclusiveness + graha = receiving and keeping. So parigraha would mean receiving and hoarding everything available. Aparigraha is opposite of this and means to receive and keep nothing. By this yama the yoga sādhaka is expected not even to accept anything which is not immediately needed for his life-maintenance and his essential duties. And still further, not to go on collecting things with a possibility of their becoming useful at some future time. This yama in this rigorous sense would be very hard to obey. It means that a sādhaka really keeps nothing as his possession. However even if such a literal and strict observance is not ordinarily feasible, the sādhaka should sincerely strive to reduce his needs to the bare minimum and should completely avoid the tendency to collect and hoard things, which he may feel would not be needed by him in quite near future. More the sādhaka can follow this principle better will he be obeying the injunction about aparigraha.

Many yogasādhakas interpret the word aparigraha to mean giving up attachment to things. They, therefore, feel and claim that even if they collect things, since mentally they are disattached or non-desirous for them, they are obeying the yama of aparigraha. But such an understanding is not correct. Non-attachment or mentally relinquishing the desire for things is saṃnyāsa. This can be on the mental plane. But aparigraha does not mean only this much. Out of the yamas mentioned by Patañjali, this is the only one, whose observance on physical plane (by body) is more important than that on mental level. Indeed aparigraha on mental level is saṃnyāsa and the practical aspect of saṃnysa in actual life is aparigraha. A person may be a true saṃnyāsi i.e. he has lost all attachment and desire for things i.e. has a total (Vaśīkāra, I:15) vairāgya. In that case making use of things with complete aloofness and without a feeling of pleasure and enjoyment may be a feasible and possible state. But in such a case, though the person may be rightly called a virāgī and saṃnyāsī, he is not an aparigrahī. Because a real aparigrahī has not to have things, which are not unavoidably necessary. In fact saṃnyāsa and aparigraha are two facets of the same coin and so should go together. Aparigraha without saṃnyāsa (desirelessness and disattachment) and vairāgya would not be easy to practise. So also, if saṃnyāsa is not accompanied by aparigraha, the danger lurks that the person may get habituated to the use of pleasure-giving things and attachment with desire for them may again raise their heads in the mind of the saṃnyāsī.

Patañjali mentions five yamas and five niyamas, but other spiritual, religious and yogic texts mention ten each of yamas and niyamas. Again the enumeration of these ten yamas and niyamas is also varying in different texts. It is also seen that the items mentioned under yama in one text are noted as niyama in another text (cf.CE. II:29, Note, p.234). Thus, if considered in a broad way, all these things enumerated under yamas and niyamas in different texts seem to be injunctions or rules of self-restraints and for one's conduct, which are generally called good rules of self-control and behaviour, which are conducive for spiritual advancement. Patañjali has mentioned five which he probably considers as cardinal and of utmost importance. It is evident that though Patañjali does not mention these other rules of self-restraint and good behaviour, they could not have been thought as unnecessary by him. In a way, as said, these all are automatically implied in brahmacarya.

SS. - **जातिदेशकालसमयानवच्छिन्नाः सार्वभौमा महाव्रतम् ।।२:३१।।**

TL. - jāti-deśa-kāla-samayānavacchinnāḥ
sārvabhaumā mahāvratam - II:31

WM. - jāti = birth in specific circumstances, caste;

deśa = country, region;

kāla = time;

samaya = occasion;

anavacchinna(āḥ) = (an = not+avacchinna= broken, separated for exception, limited, conditioned) not conditioned or made an exception (plu.);

sārvabhauma (āḥ→a) = (sārva = all + bhauma = pertaining to ground or layer or level) pertaining to or applicable to all levels, universal, supreme;

mahā = great;

vrata (ṃ) = vow (is).

TR. - (The observance of yama is to be practised as) the supreme (i.e. applicable and obligatory in all circumstances without a single exception) great vow, not conditioned by (either) birth (in a particular social status, caste) (or) region (of residence) (or) the times or occasion.

CE. - The sūtra tells that yama i.e. observance of these rules of self-restraint is a mahāvrata = great vow i.e. an obligatory observance of a very great rule. It further adds that it is sārvabhauma, which means obligatory in all circumstances and under all conditions. This itself implies that the observance of these for a yoga sādhaka is to be without any exception or excuse. But Patañjali is not satisfied with this implied injunction. He explicitly mentions all those things, which usually are put forth as an excuse for not being in a position to adhere to these rules. The life circumstances, specially the social status or in Hindu society, the caste can be and is very often made an excuse for breaking one or more of these yamas. The peculiar customs and laws prevalent in a region or a country or a particular period of time may sometimes appear as if they become hindrance in the way in following the yamas. Particular occasions may be felt as if not allowing the adherence to the yamas. Instances of one or more of these factors being put forward as an excuse for the breaking of a particular yama are quite common. For example a person telling a lie or behaving deceitfully i.e. breaking the yama of satya, often makes an excuse that the particular occasion (samaya) or place (deśa) made it impossible for him to behave truthfully. Nowadays people very often - and these include even yoga propagators, who take pride in saying that they teach and emphasize on the observance of yama--are seen to say that the present times are such that to behave honestly and truthfully is almost impossible. So also caste or social status is, some times superstitiously, made an excuse for untruthful behaviour e.g. superstitiously the castes of gold-smiths and tailors in India believe that to deceive their customers and purloin some of the precious metals or cloth entrusted to them is a birth-right or even a religious (?) duty of their caste. This is not limited to India or Hindu casteism only. Sometimes a profession becomes such an excuse for deceitful behaviour e.g. a policeman's profession. All such excuses are not permissible for a yogasādhaka, who really wants to have progress on the path of Yoga. At least, if he makes such excuses, even if occasionally, his progress will be retarded to that much extent.

It has already been mentioned that the really important aspect of yama is the mental aspect and not the related bodily action. Thus, it may sometimes be, that a person, who may apparently be troubling or even killing someone else, may still not be breaking the yama of ahiṃsā, provided the purpose at heart is not to cause harm to the other party and the act is not being done for his own interest or benefit. Specially, if such a breach of yama in the form of bodily act is being done with a true intention of giving benefit to the person or animal against whom apparently that act seems to be directed or at least because it is an unavoidable necessity for the benefit of the society or majority and in no way is for the selfish interest of the committer, then that act will still be in conformity with the obeying of the yama of ahiṃsā. Very obvious instances of this are that of a surgeon and a soldier fighting for a just and right cause.

Some old commentators interpret this sūtra as distinguishing between a mahāvrata and a (ordinary) vrata. They, therefore, explain that strictly obeying yamas without any kind of exception for any reason, as is indicated in the sūtra and clarified in the discussion above, is to be designated as a mahāvrata or great vow. According to them this type of rigid observance of yamas is for advanced yogis only, who want to reach perfection (i.e. kaivalya?). For an ordinary (?) yoga-sādhaka the observance of yama as only a 'vrata' would be sufficient. In this simple 'vrata' type observance sometimes exception could be made, when the breach of yama seems legitimate in specific circumstances and from a practical worldly point of view. But this interpretation does not seem to be valid. At least there is no clear ground to say that Patañjali wanted to put forth such a distinction. He does not seem to have thought of such two or more grades of intensiveness in yoga sādhana for various categories of yoga-sādhakas. On the contrary II:35 to 45 indicating the fruits or criteria of perfection in the observance of yamas and niyamas give an impression that Patañjali put an ideal of reaching perfection in every aspect of yoga and particularly observance of yama-niyama before every yoga-sādhaka. It would be absurd to think that Patañjali expected some yoga-sādhaka to have a mediocre development on the path of Yoga and so would suggest some laxity in the rigorous discipline in their case. According to this commentator's view Patañjali's injunction is for each and every yoga-sādhaka and so every yoga-sādhaka should try very sincerely to obey the yamas (and niyamas also) without trying to find any excuse for breaking these. No doubt, in practical life in the world, in spite of the most firm determination not to break the rules of yama, the sādhaka will perforce have to behave in such a way that he may seem to break the rule, at least on physical level. This however would not matter. In fact it will not at all be a real breach of yama, provided the intention of the sādhaka is not to that effect. As already stressed, the real obeying of yama is on mental level and not merely in the form of carrying out the physical action outwardly. Having this understanding clearly there is no reason to make a distinction as of mahavrata and vrata in respect to the abidance to the rules of yamas.

SS. - शौचसंतोषतपस्वाध्यायेश्वरप्रणिधानानि नियमाः ।।२:३२।।

TL. - śauca-santoṣa-tapa-svādhyāyeśvara - praṇidhānāni niyamāḥ - II : 32.

WM. -

śauca	=	cleanliness;
santoṣa	=	contentment;
tapas	=	austerities;
svādhyāya	=	(sva=one's own+adhyaya= section or chapter of a book) one's own regular study or reading;
iśvara-praṇidhāna	=	worship (i.e. pūjana) of iśvara with surrendering attitude;
āni	=	plural ending;
niyama (āḥ)	=	niyama, rule of behaviour (are).

TR. - The niyamas (rules of behaviour) are śauca (cleanliness), santoṣa (contentment), tapa (austerities), svādhyāya one's own study) (and) iśvara-praṇidhāna (pūjana with surrender).

CE. - Śauca which means cleanliness has been explained by most commentators as purification of body and mind both. But here it seems that the word should be understood primarily as the cleanliness of the body. Though the words 'śauca', 'sucitā' etc., derived from the verb-root 'śue', meaning to cleanse, to purify, can be used in relation to the purificatory processes pertaining to both the mind and body, the word śauca is usually used for cleansing processes more concerned with the body. In fact a usual special meaning of śauca is defecation or evacuation of excreta (bowels). And the word here is very probably used in the sense of body-cleansing procedures. The reasons for taking this sense of the word here : (1) There are many different techniques in yoga for the purification of mind. In fact the main aim of any yoga system is first to purify the mind, after which only its stabilization and tranquillisation could become possible. Most of the aṣṭāṅgas of Patañjali's system have purification of mind as the first objective. All five upāṅgas of yama, the remaining four upāṅgas of niyama, the techniques of Pranavajapa and of manasasthitinibandhana and cittaprasadana (I:28 to 39), the meditative processes of samāpatti, dhāranā, dhyāna and samādhi and even āsana and prāṇāyāma lead directly or indirectly to mental purification. Therefore, there is no reason for and purpose in mentioning this very thing again separately under niyama through a designation of śauca. (2) The word niyama has a general sense of things of practical conduct to be performed regularly, usually daily. Thus, the things coming under niyama are to be put into actual practice i.e. they are things to be performed by body. Except santoṣa all the remaining four angas of Patañjali's niyama are of such nature. That tapas, svādhyāya and iśvara-praṇidhāna are components of kriyā-yoga and so are activities predominantly to be done by the body has been clearly and emphatically brought out under II: 1. Taking this fact into consideration śauca also must be understood as bodily activity i.e. cleansing of the body. ,

Though Patañjali does not mention even indirectly about the special purificatory techniques for cleansing of internal organs of the body e.g. neti, basti, dhauti, which are purely

Haṭhayogic, these or any other (e.g. Āyurvedic) methods of cleansing the body from outside or inside can be included in śauca and adopted for having the body in most clean and efficient condition.

Santoṣa means contentment. Inclusion of this item under niyama seems a little anomalous, because it is a mental attitude, while the remaining four upāṅgas of niyama are, as already emphasized, primarily bodily actions. The present commentator feels that looking in this way, one item each from yama and niyama viz. aparigraha and santoṣa respectively could interchange their places. The only reason why Patañjali might have thought of putting them in their present arrangement might be that they were enumerated thus in the ancient tradition of Yoga, which Patañjali indicates to have adhered to (1:1). It can also be said that though santoṣa is primarily a mental attitude, by including it in niyama Patañjali wants to emphasize that a mere pretence of having a contented mind is not enough for a yoga sādhaka. He should regulate his actions in life to depict this contentment in actual practice. Often it is seen that people claim that they are contented and have no desire for any worldly acquisition. But in actual life their actions show that they are still hankering after things like wealth, power etc. This is to be avoided strictly and totally by the real aspirant of yoga.

About the remaining three angas viz. tapas, svādhyāya and iśvara praṇidhāna, enough has been explained under II:1, kriyāyoga, of which they form the components. As already indicated niyama means a thing or activity to be done regularly. By inclusion of these three angas of kriyāyoga again under niyama, Patañjali wants to stress that these things need be done as an obligatory duty every day. No doubt the suitable mental attitude should be accompanying the physical performance of each item of niyama. This has also been pointed out in the earlier discussion under II: 1. Mere mechanical performance of these rules on physical level would not serve the real purpose and would not be worthy of being called a part of Yoga.

It has been pointed out under II:1 in connection with iśvarapraṇidhāna that performance of worship in the form of pūjana or havana is to be done with an attitude or surrendering to iśvara. But in the beginning this attitude may not be developed easily. However if the sādhaka keeps the awareness that the attitude of total self surrender to iśvara is to be developed and that is the essential purpose of this physical activity, then the initial more or less mechanical performance would change into a real worship and the attitude of total surrender to iśvara would be gradually developed. It has been indicated that this is the reason why kriyāyoga is recommended as the starting point of the practical sādhanā according to Patañjali's plan.

It has been stressed that the term śauca in the enumeration of niyama means mainly cleansing of the body. But again it needs to be pointed out that ultimately the purpose of these body cleansings is not for the body merely, but for the purification and better evolution of the whole human organism and personality of the sādhaka. The purificatory procedures forming the preliminary performances in the Hindūistic rituals e.g. mantrācamana, aghamarsaṇa etc. are primarily cleansing procedures related to body, but when they are practised in the ritualistic manner they are supposed to produce purification on psycho-spiritual plane through these physical cleansing procedures.

Thus though both yama and niyama are rules for regulating oneās behaviour, the mental attitude and the effects on psychological plane are the essence in the observance of yama and the corresponding outward and physical activity is of minor or very little importance. On the other hand in obeying of niyamas the physical performance has greater importance, whereas the mental attitude is a desirable accessory accompaniment.

SS. - **वितर्कबाधने प्रतिपक्षभावनम् ।।२:३३।।**

TL. - vitarka-bādhane prati-pakṣa-bhāvanam - II:33.

WM. -

vitarka	= vitarka i.e. evil tendencies and actions;
bādhana (→e)	= (in case of) disturbance, trouble, hindrance;
pratipakṣabhāvana(m)	= (prati = opposite + pakṣa = side + bhavana = repeated treatment given (to the citta) for moulding in a particular manner,cultivating a tendency) Trying to mould the citta (here mind) in (a tendency of) opposite type (direction), trying to cultivate opposite tendency.

TR. - In case of the hindrance (in the proper observance of yamas) through vitarkas (try) cultivation of the opposite tendencies (to those of vitarkas).

CE. - Vitarkas are antiyamas as defined by Patañjali in the next sutra (11:34) and as explained before under sūtras I:17, 42, 43. This sūtra recommends that the sādhaka should try to cultivate the tendency opposite to the particular vitarka, when it disturbs the citta of the sādhaka and instigates him to break the rule of yama, which is opposite to that vitarka. Thus when a sādhaka will have thoughts of and impulses for hiṃsā or asatya (untruthfulness, deceit etc.), the sādhaka should deliberately try to curb these thoughts and impulses, by telling his own mind that these evil thoughts and impulses are not helpful for his purpose i.e. his proper progress on the path of Yoga and so try to force the mind to think in the opposite manner. Thus if the sādhaka has a hatred or despise against a person, thing or phenomenon, whenever he will encounter or even remember that person, thing or phenomenon, his mind will have the hateful or despising thoughts, which will create an impulse to harm or destroy that person thing or phenomenon. At such a time, consciously and deliberately the sādhaka should warn himself that this kind of thinking and action are things, which will retard his progress on the path of Yoga and he need develop a love and liking for that person, thing or phenomenon. It may seem that this is not a much practicable injunction, but if the sadhaka sincerely tries to follow this principle, he will come to realize that it works. Though bringing about such a change of attitude towards persons and things hated and disliked, would be very slow in the beginning, if the sādhaka determinedly persists, he will find that it is possible to bring about such a total change of tendency in the longer run ultimately.

It has been already explained that this injunction is meant to be and can be practised in our day to day worldly life. How the vitarkas dwindle and ultimately disappear by the cathartic process of samāpattis has already been explained under sūtras I:42 and 43.

SS. - **वितर्का हिंसादयः कृतकारितानुमोदिता लोभक्रोधमोह-पूर्वका मृदुमध्याधिमात्रा दुःखाज्ञानानन्तफला इति प्रतिपक्षभावनम् ॥२:३४॥**

TL. - vitarkā hiṃsādayaḥ kṛta-kāritānumoditā lobha - krodha moha-pūrvakā mṛdumadhyādhimātrā duḥkhājñānānantaphalā iti prati-pakṣa-bhāvanam - II:34.

WM. -

vitarkā	=	vitarkas;
hiṃsā-ādayaḥ	=	hiṃsā (causing injury to others) etc.;
kṛta	=	done by oneself;
kārita	=	got done through others;
anumodita (ā)	=	approved and sympathised, seconded and supported, abetted (plu);
lobha	=	greed;
krodha	=	anger;
moha	=	infatuation, delusion leading to confusion;

pūrvaka (ā)	=	preceded by, caused by (plu);
mṛdu	=	mild;
madhya	=	medium;
adhimātra (ā)	=	extreme degree (plu);
duḥkha	=	pain, misery;
ajñāna	=	ignorance;
ananta	=	endless, infinite;
phala(ā)	=	(leading to) Fruit, result (plu);
iti	=	so, therefore; Such is, thus;
prati	=	opposite;
pakṣa	=	side, type;
bhāvana (m)	=	cultivation of tendencies in the mind.

TR. - Vitarkas are hiṃsā and such other things, done by oneself (or) got done through others (or) approved and sympathised (when done by others), (which) may be caused through greed (or) anger (or) infatuation, (and which may exist in) mild, medium (or) extremely intense degree (and which) may lead to endless results of pain (misery and), ignorance. So (try to) cultivate tendencies (in mind), opposite (to the particular vitarkās).

CE. - The part statement of this sūtra, viz. 'Vitarkas are hiṃsā and such others', has been fully discussed under I:17,42 and 43. Patañjali further clarifies here that these evil thoughts and actions are equally harmful for a yogsādhaka, whether he does them himself or instigates others to do these or even when he is not directly and apparently involved in the thought or performance of the deed, but abets it even by having a sympathetic attitude.

The causes usually leading a man to such evil thoughts and actions are an individual's greed, and/or anger and/or infatuation. Again the degree of intensity of evilness of these thoughts and actions may be variable and can be roughly graded as of mild, medium or extreme degree. The evil thoughts and actions lead to the unwanted results of pain, misery and ignorance which again are never-ending.

The word 'iti' can be translated either as (1) 'so', 'therefore' or as (2) 'such is'. The significance of the complete statement of the sūtra would vary slightly according to the meaning chosen out of these two. However, the general purport and the directive to be obtained from the sūtra do not on the whole change with these two meanings of 'iti'.

With the meaning (1) the sūtra would mean that since the vitarkas are not conducive to the progress in Yoga, 'pratipakṣabhāvanam' i.e. cultivation of opposite thoughts and actions, should be attempted to counteract the ill effects of vitarkas. This is the meaning of the sutra given above under TR.

If the second meaning is accepted, the sutra would mean that cautioning the mind that 'the vitarkas are harmful even when not perpetrated by oneself, and caused by greed etc.' is itself the pratipakṣabhāvana. No doubt, this full understanding about the nature of virtarkās would itself make the sādhaka not to think or behave in this evil i.e. 'vaitārkika' and undesirable way and the cultivation of opposite kinds of thoughts and actions would be automatically practised.

This method of counteracting vitarkās can be practised only during the wakeful state of day-to-day life, since it is to be done deliberately. Obviously, therefore, it cannot be practised during sleep nor during meditational processes (e.g. dhāraṇā, dhyāna,), because a deliberately directed activity of mind would be a hindrance and an interruption to the smooth and continuous process of meditation, particularly dhāraṇā and dhyāna.

A doubt may arise whether such a simple directive for cultivating tendencies opposite to the undesirable evil tendencies, which are spontaneously arising and seem almost as the natural responses to particular circumstance causing them, would be practicable and so of any use. But experience will show the sādhaka that it works and produces to certain extent the expected result. Anyway the evil things are undesirable and so they must be counteracted even in the ordinary worldly life. It is , therefore, still more incumbent on a yoga-sādhaka and the method recommended in this sūtra seems to be the only possible and available one to achieve the desired objective. As mentioned so often, the other angas of Yoga e.g. āsana, prāṇāyāma, pratyāhāra and the meditational (i.e. inward going) processes also help directly or indirectly in this respect and with a sincere practice of these angas, the observing of yama-niyama becomes easier and the pratipakṣabhāvana is facilitated.

SS. - **अहिंसाप्रतिष्ठायां तत्संनिधौ वैरत्यागः ।।२:३५।।**

TL. - ahiṃsā-pratiṣṭhāyāṃ tat-sannidhau vaira-tyāgaḥ - II:35.

WM. - ahiṃsā = ahiṃsā, non-injury, non-violence;

pratiṣṭhā (yāṃ) = firm establishment (of);
tatsannidhau = (tat = his + sannidha = near, surrounding + au = In (suff. . 7th loc. case) in his vicinity;
vaira = hatred, enemity;
tyāga (ḥ) = renouncing, giving up.

TR. - (The result) of the firm establishment of ahiṃsa (nonviolence) is the giving up of enemity (even by others) in his (yogi's) vicinity.

CE. - Sūtras II:35 to 45 indicate the results of ideal observance of yamas and niyamas. They can be looked upon also as the criteria of such perfect observance of these good rules of conduct.

However the criteria mentioned in these sūtras are such as will be impossible or at least very improbable to achieve. This is more true about the criteria of perfection in the observances of the yamas. They may seem to be almost like siddhis or miraculous powers, except perhaps the result of ovbservance of brahmacarya, which is not difficult to achieve.

The criterion of perfection in ahiṃsā mentioned in this sūtra is that not only the yogī, but even those round about him lose the feeling of enemity or hatred. It is not clear whether this is only a temporary effect i.e. the disappearance of enemity is only seen while in presence of the yogī or whether the hatred and enemity are permanently done away with. Obviously, the yogī himself must have reached a stage, where all feeling of antipathy, hatred, enemity, which leads to a desire to cause harm to others, has completely disappeared in him. Only then the perfect observance of ahiṃsa would be possible for him on all three levels mentioned and which may lead to the defect noted here. But the sūtra stipulates that there is giving up of hatred or enemity in the vicinity of the yogī, which clearly means that all who may be round about the yogī i.e. the others than the yogī himself, should lose totally the feeling of enemity and hatred. And this may and should include even the animals. Indeed it is believed that even animals of prey lose their tendencies to kill their natural victims, when they are near such yogīs and saints. Pictures are seen where tigers and their natural prey-deers as well as cows and other such animals, which also may serve as their food, are seen staying and even playing together in a very friendly manner. Such a depiction of Mahāvīra, the last, 24th tīrthaṅkara of Jainas is popularly displayed and similar pictures of other saints, not only of Indian saints, but those of other countries and religions, are not uncommon. Even in the present times something similar can be seen in the case of some saintly persons.

The most well-known example of a staunch devotee or apostle of ahiṃsā in recent times has been that of Mahātmā Gandhi and it is a good proof that the result of the practice of ahiṃsā stated in this sūtra is actually achieved to a great extent in the practical life. There are a number of instances, where persons, who were most antipathic to Gāndhī himself or to other persons near him, lost or at least lessened their such antipathic feelings and even became very friendly when they were in presence of Gāndhījī and especially when he had talked with them to convert them to views, he wanted them to have.

The most remarkable example of such an effect of Gāndhījī's personality on antipathic person is of Mr. Jinnāh. The latter has been reported to have expressed his opinion about Gāndhījī in most disparaging manner, even going, it is said, to the extent of calling him a 'cunning fellow' and a 'rascal'. In fact these deprecating epithets were employed by Mr. Jinnāh for Gāndhījī, when he is said to have declined to have a meeting with Gāndhījī. The reason put forward by Mr. Jinnāh for refusing to meet Gāndhījī was that when in the presence of Gāndhī, Mr. Jinnāh used to find that he lost all the zeal for fighting out with and opposing Gāndhījī. Thus, in a way this was rather a hidden and unintended praise of Gāndhījīs virtue or power and shows the effect that a staunch follower of ahiṃsā and satya has on the antipathic feelings of his opponents. Thus we see that the statement in the sūtra is true in the sense that the vaira or enemity disappears or at least diminishes in the presence of a sincere practitioner of ahiṃsā.

But as said, to achieve the level of perfection indicated by the sūtra is very difficult-almost impossible-to reach. This also is depicted from the example of Gāndhījī. In modern times, perhaps he is the one person, who has tried to the maximum possible to adhere to the practice of ahiṃsā and that also most sincerely. Yet there were obviously persons, who had enemical feeling towards Gāndhījī himself and feeling of antipathy mutually amongst his own closest followers was not completely absent. From this we can only conclude that it is in our hands only to try to be sincere in practising yamas to the utmost that may be feasible for us, though the perfection indicated in the sūtras may be only ideal and so never or be reached.

Some explanation about why and how the enemity, even in ferocious, carnivorous animals against other animals, may disappear in the presence of a yogī, who has highly advanced in the practice of ahiṃsā may be seen in the article published by this commentator : 'The Position of Yoga as a Science Today'; Yoga Mīmāṃsā, VIII, No.l, pp. 15 to 19, 1965.

SS. - **सत्यप्रतिष्ठांया क्रियाफलाश्रयत्वम्** ।।२:३६।।

TL. - satya-pratiṣṭhāyāṃ kriyā-phalāśrayatvam - II:36

WM. - saty = satya, truthfulness;

pratiṣṭhā (yām)= firm establishment (of);

kriyā = action;

phala = fruit, result;

āśraya (tvam) = support (State of), state of being supported by something else, dependence.

TR. - (The result) of the firm establishment of satya (truthfulness) is the dependence of the fruit on (the commensurate with its corresponding, causal) action.

CE. - The sūtra, when understood in its simple straightforward word meaning, does not seem to indicate any special or remarkable result derived from the firm establishment in i.e. the perfect observance of the yama of truthfulness, because the fruit or result is always dependent upon i.e. certainly going to be the outcome of any action according to 'Karma-Siddhānta'. But according to this 'Law of Karma' itself, it is almost impossible to predict with hundred percent certainty what result would appear as the fruit of any action, because the exact outcome or happening at a particular moment, at which the fruit of that action is going to ripen, i.e. is being produced, is not dependent on i.e. not the result of that one single action alone. It is the sum-total of the fruits or results of innumerable actions, committed in a number of past lives, whose maturation i.e. fruit ripening or result-production is to take place at that very moment. And it would be beyond anybody's ability to compute precisely and thus definitely determine the exact nature of this result. Thus, though as per the Law of Karma, the fruit of each and every action is inevitably to follow, once the action is done and so is surely dependent on that action, yet nobody can foretell the exact nature nor the maturation time of the fruit of that particular action. What the sūtra, therefore, means is that the person, who observes the yama of satya to perfection, would be able to forecast the exact nature of the fruit of any particular action, done by himself or even by others.

It may be felt that such a follower of the yama of satya is able to overthrow the above-noted principle of unpredictability of 'karma-phala'. But such is not the case. The very rigorous and sincere attempt of practising truthfulness in all its aspects, conditions the citta and mind of the sādhaka in such a way that it cannot have any thought or idea or imagination, which would not correspond to the actuality, even when this may be related to a future time. It may be said that for the citta of such a sādhaka, the adherence to satya, so to say, becomes spontaneous and so whatever arises in his citta and mind in relation to any happening, even of future, there is an exact correspondence of this content of his mind with the actuality of the respective future happening. So whenever he expresses any speculation, it, as if miraculously, comes to be true. Instances of this ability to forecast future happenings, seem to be possessed by many persons even in ordinary life. In most of these cases it will be found that such persons are very honest and truthful in their behaviour.

SS. - **अस्तेयप्रतिष्ठायां सर्वरत्नोपस्थानम् ।।२:३७।।**

TL. - asteya-pratiṣṭhāyāṃ sarva-ratnopasthānam - II:37

WM. -

a-steya	=	non-stealing;
pratiṣṭhā (yāṃ)	=	the firm establishment (of);
sarva	=	all;
ratna	=	jewel, treasure;
upasthāna(m)	=	self-presentation before (somebody).

TR. - (The result) of the firm-establishment of asteya (non-stealing) (is) self-presentation by all jewels (treasures) before (the yogī).

CE. - If the literal meaning of the sūtra is taken, it does not seem to make any neat sense. It is absurd to believe that jewels i.e. valuable treasures will, in some magical way, come and gather before the yogī, who observes the yama of asteya very rigorously. Such a thing has never happened nor can be expected to happen. The explanation given by I.K.Taimni that the yogī gets the ability to know the treasures buried near about him, also does not seem to be very convincing nor any instances of such phenomena have been seen. Also the explanation given by other commentators (e.g. Kolhatkar) that if the yogī has a need of anything valuable for unselfishly benefitting others for some reason, then such valuables would be available to him instantly, does not seem to be very satisfactory. But a sādhaka, who will be very sincerely trying to adhere to the yama of asteya, would be recognised by all as a person of utmost honesty and when such occasions may arise everyone would want to entrust their valuables to the custody of such a person only. Thus such a yogasādhaka may become the custodian of many treasures. In this way metaphorically at least, all kinds of jewels i.e. valuables would be 'presenting themselves' before him. We see the truth of the statement of the sūtra in the actual life, all the world over, in the fact that only persons of high integrity, who would be believed as never to embezzle the funds entrusted to them, are only appointed trustees, custodians and treasurers of valuable possessions.

SS. - **ब्रह्मचर्यप्रतिष्ठायां वीर्यलाभः ।।२:३८।।**

TL. - brahma-carya-pratiṣṭhāyāṃ vīrya-lābhaḥ - II:38

WM. - brahma-carya = brahmacarya, usually translated as celibacy, continence, abstinence from sex but fundamentally a life of self-discipline conducive for spiritual development;

pratiṣṭhā (yām) = the firm establishment (of);

vīrya = vigour, vitality;

lābha (ḥ) = gain (is).

TR. - (The result) of firm establishment of brahmacarya (life disciplined for spiritual development incorporating judicious sex restraint) (is) the gain of vigour.

CE. - Brahmacarya, whether understood in its narrower sense of judicious sex-control or in the wider sense of a life of discipline in every respect, which is conducive to the spiritual progress and Ultimate Realization, leads to the gain of vigour, energy and virility, is a fact, which is well-recognised. Such a result is observable even in the life of persons, who lead a moderately disciplined life. It has been already pointed out that translation of brahmacarya as continence or abstinence from sex is rather misleading and may even lead to harm. A disciplined life itself means keeping everything in its proper and optimal limit. Evidently this would prevent the waste of energy in unnecessary and undesirable activities. This saving of energy automatically leads to an accumulation or gain of vigour. No doubt, even if brahmacarya is interpreted as a restriction of sex activity, if this be practised in a wise and judicious manner, it leads to a remarkable accumulation of vitality, since the sex activity is highly energy dissipating activity. The waste of physical energy in the sex activity is not the primary thing for which the restraint is advised. Rather it is the effect on the mental side, which is more harmful and sometimes even leads to the total wreckage of the personality of a man, if the sex becomes dominating beyond proper limits. Restraint of sex has been recognised as a factor helpful to both physical and mental vigour, practically in all the societies of the world. Even in the primitive people, the restraint of sex is temporarily advised and practised, when vigour is necessary for special tasks to be undertaken. The reflection of this belief can be seen in the restraint in respect to sex imposed on the armed forces of all the nations, when they are expected to engage themselves in the active warfare. Thus this sūtra of Patañjali, in a way, puts forth the effect of self-restraint, which has been observed and accepted universally.

SS. - **अपरिग्रहस्थैर्ये जन्मकथन्तासंबोधः ।।२:३९।।**

TL. - a-parigraha-sthairye-janma-kathantā sambodhaḥ -II:39

WM. -

a-parigraha	=	non -receiving, non-possessing, non-accumulating, non-hoarding;
sthairya (→e)	=	stabilization (in);
janma	=	birth i.e. life;
katha (ntā)	=	why and where fore (ness); purposeful (ness);
sambodha (ḥ)	=	full knowledge (is).

TR. - In the stabilization of aparigraha (non-possessiveness) (results) the full knowledge of the purposefulness of (one's own) life (or lives).

CE. - This sūtra cannot be easily explained in a reasonable way. Even assuming that a sādhaka has achieved the highest stage of aparigraha i.e. he has no feeling of possession of the smallest and most insignificant thing of this world and has kept nothing in store with himself for possible future use, why should this lead to a complete understanding of this or perhaps even of earlier lives, does not become clear. The word 'janma' has been interpreted by most of the commentators as being in plural i.e. indicating many lives and therefore 'janma-kathantā-saṃbodha' would mean' the full knowledge of the purpose of many (i.e. this and others past) lives. Most of the old commentators explain it in the following manner:-

"The attempt for perfect practical observance of the yama of aparigraha gradually leads to the diminution of the tendency of possessiveness i.e. the feeling of mine-ness. When this later leads to the diminution and finally the disappearance of the ego or I-ness (asmitā), the saṃskāras lying in the deeper and deeper layers of karmāśaya (part of citta) i.e. the older saṃskāras and still more older the ones of the past lives will get a free play and will rise up into the present consciousness level and thus there would be revival and recollection of the past lives, which will help to understand the purposefulness behind these lives".

But this explanation is not quite satisfactory. (1) This release of saṃskāras of the past lives is, according to their own explanation, not the result of the perfect observance of aparigraha alone. It additionally needs abolition of the tendency of 'my-ness' (possessiveness) and also the disappearance of the ego-sense i.e. asmitā (I-ness). So the release of the saṃskāras and through it the gaining of the knowledge of the past lives can not be claimed to be the result of aparigraha-sthairya alone.

The abolition of ego is not accomplished through aparigraha-sthairya, but would result through the meditative aṅgas, especially dhyāna and samādhi. But the sūtra says 'janmakathantā saṃbodha' as a result of mere aparigrahasthairya. (2) Even if the mechanism of the process given by them be accepted, the recollection of saṃskāras or memories of past and present lives would give the knowledge merely of the happenings of those lives. How and why it will reveal the purposefulness behind those lives is still not understandable.

According to us the rigorous and sincere practice of non-possessiveness would gradually bring the realization to the sādhaka that since he can do without most of the things, which he once used to think as unavoidably essential for maintenance of life, those were, after all, not really that much essential. This will, with the perfection in the yama of aparigraha, lead to the realization of the futility of all worldly possessions and the sādhaka will therefore begin to understand that possession of worldly goods, which all the humans are hankering after to amass, is not the real purpose of human existence; but that it is to get liberated from all such attachments, which really lead to bondage. Thus the firm establishment in the vow of aparigraha culminating into its perfection will lead to a very high state of vairāgya, which is one of the two most essential requirements for reaching the goal of citta-vṛtti-nirodha (I:12) and through this to the only purpose of life, in the view of Yoga, viz- Apavarga (liberation) and Kaivalya (Absoluteness).

It has been already pointed out (I:12,15,16) that observance of vairāgya, though it is a mental attitude, will not be perfect unless it is accompanied on the practice-side by aparigraha. Nay, even if vairāgya is developed in a yogī to a very high degree e.g. even upto Vaśīkāra stage (I:15), there still remains a great possibility that the yogī may again get entangled into the world through enticement by viṣayas (objects and subjects) enjoyable through indriyas (senses and mind), if he neglects to abide by the yama of aparigraha.

The words sthairya and pratiṣṭhā both are almost synonymous meaning firm establishment or stabilisation in a state. In sūtras II:35 to 38, stating the phalas (fruits) of the firm establishment in the first four yamas, Patañjali has used the term 'pratiṣṭhā', whereas almost for the same thing he uses the word sthairya in the present sūtra. Though the meaning of both words being almost the same the matter is not very important, yet a question seems pertinent. Why has Patañjali, who seems to be very meticulous about the use of very proper terms, used only in this sūtra of the yama-phalas a different word?

As is usual, even in the significance of two synonyms there is some shade of difference. Pratiṣṭhā has an association of respectfulness or even reference along with stabilisation, while sthairya is devoid of any such additional sense. It means simple steadiness or stabilisation. The persons, who are followers of any one of the yamas of ahiṃsā or satya or asteya or brahmacarya, receive respect-almost a reverence due to a saint-in the society, because the adherence to these yamas becomes easily noticeable in the society, since it affects the behaviour of the person in the society and at all times such persons are very rare. The stabilisation in these four yamas is thus a matter of pratiṣṭhā also. On the other hand a person, who may be trying to develop the tendency of aparigraha in himself and may cut down his needs and renounce possessing things, may not be noticed at all. And if, at all, noticed by society, may be wrongly branded as an unsuccessful man (in worldly way) and a pauper and looked upon disparagingly. So he may get no pratiṣṭhā with his stabilisation in his vow. The simple word sthairya would be quite suitable in this case.

SS. - **शौचात्स्वाङ्गजुगुप्सा परैरसंसर्गः ।।२:४०।।**

TL. - śaucāt-svāṅga-jugupsā parair-asaṃsargaḥ - II:40

WM. -

śauca (āt)	=	(observance of) śauca (cleanliness) (From);
svāṅga	=	(sva = one's own + āṅga + body-member) one's own body;
jugupsā	=	disgust, abhorance;
para (aiḥ→air)	=	others (by or from);
asaṃsarga (h)	=	(a + saṃsarga + ḥ) Non-contact, disinclination towards touching or physically contacting (is).

TR. - From (the observing the niyama i.e. rule of) śauca (results) disgust about one's own body (and) disinclination towards being touched by other.

CE. - As mentioned before, the term śauca here stands primarily for body-cleansing. If a sādhaka is very meticulous about thoroughly cleansing each and every part of his body, he will get more and more aware that most of the organs of the body are producers of disgusting waste products. As this awareness goes on becoming stronger, he will be realizing more and more, that body and its parts are not objects about which one should be enamoured, but on the contrary a thing only worthy of despise. Thus, this will lead to a feeling of detachment towards the body. This disappearance of 'mama-tva' (mine-ness) for the body is a primary and essential requirement for the progress on the path of Yoga. A common man has a deep rooted misidentification of the self with the body and unless this is done away with, the progress towards the realization of the Real-self will not start at all.

The physical contact with other persons is also a hindrance in the path of Yoga, especially during the meditational practices. Not only direct bodily contact, but nearness of another person may influence the sādhaka's state of meditation. No doubt, the presence in the close vicinity of a person may prove neither helpful or disturbing in the process of meditation. This will depend on the totality of saṃskāras, not only of the present life but even the past lives of that person, and it would be very difficult to predetermine whether the effect produced by that person's presence in the nearness would be facilitatory or hindering. Because even if a person be very virtuous and pious in the present life, some of his past lives may not be necessarily of the same type and if the sum-total of the saṃskāras of the past lives be more of evil nature, then such a person, no doubt pious and virtuous in the present life, may still create an environment around himself, that may be obstructive to the good meditation by others in it. Therefore it was an ancient rule of convention to avoid such nearness of any person during meditational practices.

Direct physical contact with other person's body leaves also some residual effect of his saṃskāras on the yoga-sādhaka, so that it can create interference in meditation even practised later, even when that other person may not be near about at that time. Therefore it is advisable also to avoid bodily contact with others as far as possible as a precautionary measure. This will be facilitated by a sincere and rigorous observance of śauca, because just as it leads to loss of attachment towards one's own body, it will lead to loss of enamourment towards other person's bodies also. This again will be helpful in observance of brahmacarya in its usual sense i.e. restraining sex activity.

SS. - सत्त्वशुद्धिसौमनस्यैकाग्र्येन्द्रियजयात्मदर्शनयोग्यत्वानि च ।।२:४१।।

TL. - sattva-śuddhi-saumanasyaikāgryendriya-jayātma-darśana-yogyatvāni ca-II:41.

WM. - sattva = (sat = to be + tva + ness) literally beingness basic personality or nature

śuddhi = purification;

saumanasya = (su→sau= good + manas + mind +ya = suffix indicating a state) Good condition of mind, cheerful and peaceful state of mind;

aikāgrya	=	(eka→aika = one + agra = point +ya = ness) one-pointed - ness;
indriyajay	=	(indriya = organs+jaya = conquest) mastery over organs, total subjugation of all organs;
ātma	=	self;
darśana	=	vision, here realization;
yogyatva	=	(yogya = Fit + tva = ness) fitness, eligibility;
āni	=	suffix of plurality;
ca	=	and.

TR. - And purification of sattva, cheerful calm state of mind, one-pointedness (of mind), total subjugation of all indriyas (sense and action organs including mind) and eligibility for self-realization (are also the further results of sauca).

CE. - The results of observance of the niyama of śauca mentioned in this sūtra are the ones which have led the commentators to interpret śauca as mental purification. As already explained these primarily mental results cannot be achieved without first having a body, which is thoroughly cleansed and purified. The well-known adage: 'Healthy mind in a healthy body', is a pointer in this direction, showing that the principle on which the statement in the present sūtra is based is known to a common man also.

Sattvaśuddhi is a purification of the basic personality or the deep nature of the individual. In the traditional language this can be expressed as greater and greater preponderance of sattva with corresponding diminution in the rajas and tamas. So the citta of the sādhaka loses its fickleness and dullness, which are caused respectively by rajas and tamas. The citta thus becomes more stabilized and attains a greater penetrative ability, so that the potentiality of understanding or enlightenment is enhanced. This result, though apparently purely mental is, as said, achieved by reduction of rajas and tamas. The rajas, which is the factor leading to turbulence and tamas, leading to dullness, will be reduced when the malas or toxins of the body will be reduced, which will be accomplished by thorough cleansing and purification of the body. Thus observance of śauca will lead to diminution of rajas and tamas and through this to sattva-śuddhi.

The results mentioned after this are in a way consequences or concomitants of sattvaśuddhi. Saumanasya, which literally means a 'good condition of the mind', would mean a somewhat pleasant and calm state of mind. It is, so to say, a precondition of cittaprasādana mentioned in sūtra I.33. When the preponderance of sattva will be there in the citta, it will have left very little rajas and tamas in it. These latter two are the factors leading to a disturbance and depressed state of mind and so when they are reduced the mind becomes calm and cheerful. Thus saumanasya is in fact not so much a consequence but rather an aspect and outward sign of sattvaśuddhi itself.

The next result of 'aikāgrya' is an intensification of saumanasya, because when the calmness is very well established in the mind, it can be easily channelised into any desired direction. This is what aikāgrya or ekāgrata means.

Since toxins are removed by body-cleansing and purifying, the organs of the body work in the most efficient manner and so much effort is not needed to control them and to get mastery over them. It becomes almost spontaneous and a natural result.

Śauca purifies the body and this results into sattvaśuddhi etc. So the whole of the body-mind complex of the yogasādhaka is in the fittest condition for taking up the further practices leading to the realization of the 'Real Self' (ātma-tattva) principle in himself.

SS. - **संतोषादनुत्तमः सुखलाभः ।।२:४२।।**

TL. - santoṣād-anuttamaḥ sukha-lābhaḥ - II:42.

WM. - santoṣa (āt→ād) = contentment (from);
anuttama = (an = not + uttama = best) unexcellable;
sukhalābha(ḥ) = (sukha = happiness + lābha = gain) gain of happiness (is).

TR. - From (practising of) contentment the highest happiness is gained.

CE. - It was already mentioned that contentment, which is a mental attitude should have been enumerated properly in the list of yamas. But perhaps by including it in niyamas, all the remaining four of which are the things to be practised (i.e. done by means of body), Patañjali wants to stress that this mental attitude of contentment should be reflected in the behaviour of the sādhaka in his day to day practical life. This means that he should not be satisfied merely by having no covetuousness for things, but he actually should try not to gain these things for his use. In other words the santoṣa on practical level will be evident only if the sādhaka at the same time observes the vow of aparigraha.

The cause of unhappiness and mental pain is always unfulfilment of some desire. Obviously, therefore, if the sādhaka is really totally contented and therefore has no desire for anything, he will have no cause for such unhappiness. In other words he will be the happiest man. Contentment is the real happiness and this evident truth is only reiterated in the present sūtra.

SS. - कायेन्द्रियसिद्धिरशुद्धिक्षयात्तपसः ।।२:४३।।

TL. - kāyendriya-siddhir-aśuddhi-kṣyāt-tapasaḥ - II:43.

WM. -
kāya = body;
indriya = organs;
siddhi (ḥ->r) = perfection, most efficient state;
aśuddhi = (a = non + śuddhi - purity) impurities;
kṣaya (āt) = diminution and disappearance (from);
tapas (aḥ) = tapas, austerities (from, through).

TR. - From diminution and disappearance of impurities through (practice of) tapas (austerities) (results) the most efficient (i.e. perfect) condition of the whole body system and its organs.

CE. - Every variety of tapas involves some performance related to the body. Usually this thing is expected to cause some constraint or discomfort for the body. The purpose, however, is not just to inconvenience the body, but to produce some kind of purification in it. Thus, most varieties of tapas will reduce malas i.e. toxins in the body. This 'aśuddhi-kṣaya', therefore, will lead to efficient working of the various systems and organs of the body, that is the whole of he body. This is what is meant by 'kāyendriya-siddhi'.

Mere adherence to that performance of tapas which is to be done by the body, would not, however, make it a 'tapas' in true sense. The sādhaka should have an understanding and expectation that this body-purification would lead also to the purification of mind and also an increase in its efficiency. If the tapas is practised with this outlook then only it is worthy of being called tapas. This point has been made clear, while discussing tapas as a component of kriyā-yoga under sūtra II: 1. Why Patañjali does not make explicit mention of this mental purification aspect of tapas is not clear. Perhaps it is implied in indriyasiddhi, because manas (mind) is counted as eleventh indriya, but distinct from the other ten, which are intrinsic components of body and so are included already in 'kāya'.

SS. - **स्वाध्यायादिष्टदेवतासंप्रयोगः ।।२:४४।।**

TL. - svādhyāyād-iṣṭa-devatā-saṃprayogaḥ - II:44.

WM. - svādhyāya(āt→ād) = (sva = one's own + adhyāya = chapter) one's own prayer-type reading portion (from or through);

iṣṭadevatā = (iṣṭa = desired + devatā = deity) desired deity;

samprayoga(ḥ) = (sam= wholly + pra = thoroughly +yoga = intimate meeting), meeting actually and closely (is).

TR. - From (practice of) svadhyaya (one's own daily specific prayerful literature -reading) (results) the actual meeting of the desired deity.

CE. - Full discussion of the meaning and scope of svādhyāya and its precise nature which leads to actually meeting the god or goddess to whom the sādhaka is specially devoted has been done under sūtra II:1.

SS. - **समाधिसिद्धिरीश्वरप्रणिधानात् ।।२:४५।।**

TL. - samādhi-siddhir-īśvara-praṇidhānāt - II:45

WM. - samādhi = samādhi;

siddhi (ḥ->r) = perfection, accomplishment (is)

īśvara-praṇidhāna (āt) = worship i.e. actual pūjana with attitude of total surrender to īśvara (From).

TR. - From (practice of) īśvarapraṇidhāna (pūjana with surrendering to īśvara) (results) perfection in samādhi.

CE. - The sūtra is almost a paraphrase of the sūtra I:23, as the word cittavṛtti-nirodha i.e. samādhi is implicit there. The only addition here is of the word siddhi i.e. perfection or accomplishment. Secondly the significance of īśvara praṇidhāna in sūtra I:23 is mainly of the mere mental attitude of surrender to īśvara, but here it being a niyama, it is a practical performance and an obligatory daily duty. No doubt the attitude of self-surrender to īśvara must also accompany the physical act of pūja or worship-offering. But in case this attitude of total self-surrender is not present in the sādhaka, this regularly repeated daily action of worship-offering would ultimately awaken and develop this mental attitude of self-surrender. This significance of īśvarapraṇidhāna should be clearly understood by the yoga-sādhaka and he should obey this niyama very sincerely and regularly even after the attitude of self-surrender has been developed in him, right upto the end of his practical path of Yoga. Patañjali obviously has this idea in including īśvarapraṇidhāna both in kriyāyoga (II:1) and also here in niyama.

As said above, though this sūtra is almost a paraphrase of sūtra I:23, the word implied there can be 'samādhi', while the wording here is 'samādhi-siddhi'. Thus in I:23 Patañjali indicated that a sādhaka with theistic inclination may attain the last stage of total cittavṛttinirodha and thus the highest state of samādhi by resorting to the process of surrender to īśvara i.e. any aspect of the Highest Divinity according to his own concept, but by the use of the conjunction 'or' (i.e.vā). Patañjali also seems to state in the Samādhi pāda that the cittavṛttinirodha and higher states of samādhi could be achieved without īśvara-praṇidhāna, through resorting to abhyāsa and vairāgya, in case the sādhaka is disinclined to accept any principle or element like īśvara. This 'vā' i.e. 'or' is absent in the present sūtra. Secondly īśvarapraṇidhāna is included in kriyāyoga as well in niyama by Patañjali, which both, as explained, are obligatory for a yoga-sādhaka. So here Patañjali has as good as retracted his earlier notion of the path of īśvarapraṇidhāna being alternative to that of abhyāsa-vairāgya and has stressed that īśvarapraṇidhāna is a must for a yoga sādhaka.

Again the word 'siddhi' i.e. perfection (of samādhi) also leads to similar conclusion. A yogī may reach a very high stages of samādhi through mere abhyāsa and vairāgya, yet these will be lacking in something important. This lacuna will be made up by resorting to īśvarapraṇidhāna and so the 'perfection' in samādhi will be achieved.

This lacuna is that even if the yogī reaches the highest state of samādhi by resorting to abhyāsa and vairāgya purely, there is a possibility that he can attain in this the state of prakṛtilaya (I:19) only. Some kind of obstruction may be there, which may prevent him from attaining kaivalya i.e. the separation of the pristine puruṣa principle. Since, as enunciated in sūtra I:24, īśvara is the only aspect or example of pure and pristine puruṣa-tattva īśvara-praṇidhāna creates a link or bridge with which the contact in between the sullied puruṣa tattva in the individual and the genuine, pristine, pure puruṣa tattva, which is īśvara, is established, the sādhaka, who takes recourse to īśvarapraṇidhāna, can easily reach kaivalya, without any mishap. The individual and apparently sullied puruṣa tattva in him, as if, sheds the shroud of saṃyoga and imitates the genuine pure puruṣa i.e. īśvara. In other words īśvara, as if, affects the individual puruṣa in the sādhaka just like a lode-stone and thus the īśvarapraṇidhāna helps to guide the individual puruṣa to revert back to its svarupāvasthā i.e. its pristine state. Such a help is not available to the yogasādhaka, who depends only on abhyāsa-vairāgya, devoid of īśvarapraṇidhāna and so the possibility and danger of his stagnation in the state of mere prakṛtilaya (or may be even videha) is very much present.

It may be again stressed here that though by the use of the conjunction 'vā in sūtra I:23 Patañjali seems to suggest īśvarapraṇidhāna as an alternative path to that of abhyāsa-vairāgya, in pāda II ultimately he almost affirms that īśvarpraṇidhāna must be combined with abhyāsa-vairāgya, since he includes it in kriyāyoga and niyama, which both are essential components of his Yogasystem.

Another importance of īśvara-praṇidhāna, not so much from spiritual angle, but more from social angle, is that the yogī who takes recourse to īśvarapraṇidhāna will have his citta's emotional potentiality alive at a proper level. He, therefore, will not turn into a dry, hard, callous person. This is desirable as the yogī has, to a great extent and during a greater part of life as yogī to live in the society and so, if the yogī is a totally emotionless i.e. almost an in-human person, he will be a trouble to the society. This is prevented by īśvarapraṇidhāna.

SS. - **स्थिरसुखमासनम् ।।२:४६।।**

TL. - sthira-sukham-āsanam - II:46

WM. - sthira = steady, stable;

sukha = pleasant, comfortable;

āsana (m) = āsana, yogic posture (is).

TR. - Āsana (yogic posture) (is) stable and comfortable

CE. - This is the simple and concise definition and characterization of āsana i.e. the posture helpful for Yoga. According to this characterization any posture of body, which will be comfortable and as a consequence of this, which could be maintained steadily for adequately long time, can be the āsana desirable for Patañjali's Yoga System.

The word āsana is derived from the verb-root 'ās', which means to sit, to remain sitting etc. Usually the articles used for sitting e.g. mat, wooden platform etc. are also called 'āsana', the word being derived from the same root-meaning. The articles meant to be used for lying down, sleeping, standing or walking upon are never called āsana. From this we get an indication that the posture referred to by the term āsana should be a sitting posture only. The use of this designation for supine or standing states of body, as is done for Haṭhayogīc postures, is rather a misnomer and as extrapolation. Anyway, the posture indicated by the term āsana in Patañjali's system must be only a sitting posture, looking to its purpose of being used for the practice of subsequent aṅgas i.e. prāṇāyāma, and meditational procedures. In the sūtras there is no clear mention that āsana is a sitting posture, nor of the other usual directives, which are traditionally so well known, as well so naturally adopted by the sādhaka himself that Patañjali might have felt them as not necessary to be pointed out explicitly. These are that the posture must be a sitting, squatting posture, the legs being folded over one another and rather fixed in some way, so as to preclude movement and the spine (neck and back) being kept erect, but without any strain. These directives, as is well-known, are clearly given in Bhagvadgītā (B.G.) and Upaniṣads. The firm position with legs folded and fixed, providing a stable support to the upper part of the body and the erect position of the back and neck is a posture of the body, which can be maintained in the most relaxed condition for some hours, but at the same time it helps the mind to remain alert and therefore the possibility of drowsiness and falling into slumber is avoided. The supine position e.g. that in Haṭhyogic Śavāsana would be probably even more stable and relaxed, but in that position there is a great tendency to go into sleep. Standing or other positions attained by the body in other Haṭhayogic āsanas would not be as relaxed and steady as would be desirable for further meditative practices. From this it can be concluded that Patañjali's āsanas can be only sitting posture, having the characteristics described above and by B.G. (VI: 11 - 13).

The duration of maintenance has not been mentioned by any text, but can be easily understood, because this āsana is to be maintained for further practices. As per sūtra II:49 āsana is an essential requisite for prāṇāyāma. But it can be easily seen that it will be necessary also for the practice of dhāraṇā, dhyāna and samādhi. Obviously, therefore, the duration of maintenance of a few minutes or of even an hour would not be enough. Naturally, for having such a stability for a fairly long time the posture must be quite comfortable. If there be any tension, pressure, pain or any other discomfort, the sādhaka would consciously or unconsciously make some movement. So sukha i.e. comfort is the first requisite, which only makes the second pre requisite of steadiness possible.

Many Yoga teachers and experts seem to believe that the Haṭhayogic āsanas are included in the aṅga āsana of Patañjali. Some have even expressed that Haṭhayoga or at least its āsana-prāṇāyāma parts are the extension and elaboration of Patañjali's aṅgas of āsana-prāṇāyāma. But it is very difficult to fit the definition and characterization of āsana noted in the present and the next II:47) sūtra by Patañjali to the Haṭhayogic āsanas, because the majority of the latter would be hardly comfortable and could not be maintained, and that also with no movement, for more than few minutes. Some yoga teachers, therefore, interpret the sūtra in a different way. They say that the present sūtra gives the effects of asana practice and render it as: 'Āsana is that which gives sthiratva (steadincss) and sukha (pleasure, comfort). But the word in the sūtra is sthira and not sthiratva or sthairya etc., which only can mean steadiness. Moreover if Patañjali werc indicating the effect of āsana in this sūtra he would have used the wording such as āsanāt (From āsana i.e. the 5th ablative case of āsanena (Through āsana i.e. the third instrumental case as has been done elsewhere by him (II:40 to 45, 52,55, I:12,23,29,33,39; III:16 to 50; I:34; II:15 etc.). In fact in sūtra II:48, where he is clearly mentioning a result of the practice of āsana, he has used the fifth ablative case : - tataḥ (From that).

Really Haṭhayogic āsanas are not at all the thing which Patañjali had in his mind, when he gave this characterization of āsana, because, excepting the so-called meditative āsanas viz. Padmāsana etc., the definition in the sūtra would hardly fit to the other āsanas of Haṭhayoga. It would be almost impossible to practise the balancing and even the other difficult and complicated āsanas e.g. Mayūra (Peacock), Vṛścika (scorpion), Dvipāda-kandhara (Both legs on neck), Garbha (Foetus) etc. in the way mentioned in the sūtras. It has been seen (in Kaivalyadhama Laboratories, of. Yoga Mīmāṃsā. XII. No. 1, pp. 1-13, 1959) that even some of the difficult āsanas of Haṭhayoga e.g. Paścimotāna (Back-stretch). Hala (Plough), Matsyendra and Ardha (Semi)-Matsyendra etc., in which balancing is not involved, can be maintained fully comfortably, without any muscle stain during maintenance phase. But this can be for a few minutes and not very long as is probably implied in this sūtra.

No doubt the Haṭhayogic āsanas helpful for meditation viz. Padma (Lotus), Siddha (Perfect), Svastika (Benevolent), Sama, (Equilibrated), Bhadra (Auspicious), Vajra (Adamantine) etc. can be maintained as per this sūtra for even some hours. This commentator had occasion to test one person, who sat in Padmāsana for a little more than nine hours without the slightest movement, just like a statue. This performance of his was checked by keeping a very strict watch upon him, by batches of two persons, who were having two hour shifts. Moreover a number of persons have been observed as being able to sit quite comfortably in Padmāsana or Siddhāsana for two hours or more, after which they could move about very easily and without any pain or discomfort, within a few minutes after the release of the āsana. So these Haṭha-āsanas, suitable for meditation, can very well fit into and be utilized according to the concept of āsana given by Patañjali in these sūtras. But it may be pointed out that Patañjali himself does not insist upon even any one of these āsanas as an obligatory one for his system. According to his description any erect sitting posture, which the sādhaka may be able to maintain without any voluntary movement, comfortably for sufficiently long period, as may be required for his one seance of prāṇāyāma and meditational practices, would be the satisfactory yogāsana for that sādhaka. Thus if a person is not able to sit in a squatting posture or an āsana e.g. Padmāsana on the ground, but is able to sit comfortably, steady for some hours, in a chair, perhaps legs hanging but resting on a pedestal, even this posture would be a yogāsana for that person. The main requirements are : (1) The posture should be a sitting one. (2) The back and neck should be erect without straining and stiffness. (3) The whole body is totally relaxed (sūtra II: 47), so that no pain, pressure or discomfort is felt in any part. (4) The posture, therefore, could be maintainable for a very long period and should be maintained with least possible movement, preferably not even a single voluntary movement for sufficient time to finish the daily practice of Prāṇāyāma and meditation. Nevertheless, it may be mentioned that the Haṭhayogic meditational āsanas have been discovered and recommended by the ancient Haṭhayogins, perhaps, because they have some advantages. It has been the personal experience of this commentator that by gradually increasing the practice of the maintenance of Padmāsana, he could sit for about two and a quarter hours in it without any strain or discomfort and so without any need of movement. On the other hand if he sat just in the ordinary folded legs squatting position, usually adopted by Indians in the old times and which to a great extent resembles the meditational āsanas, he could not maintain it motionless for more than 20 to 25 minutes, because the legs began to give a painful feeling. This in spite of the fact that he was habituated to sit in the pose from his childhood and every day for long periods, but with movements. It seems, therefore, that, the Haṭhayogins devised these postures specially to be used in meditation because they could be maintained for this purpose for long durations in the manner as indicated in this sūtra.

Another point to be noted is that though Haṭhayogic āsanas are not strictly in the purview of Patañjali's āsana nor Haṭhayogic texts give any instructions similar to that in the present sūtra about the general manner in which the āsanas be performed, if the Haṭhayogic āsanas are also maintained, for whatever maximum period they could be maintained comfortably i.e. without strain or pain and so as far as possible without any voluntary movement, they would give better results, particularly on the psychological and spiritual side. Only then they would be worthy of the designation 'yogāsana'. Even the unavoidable movement, involved in going into the final position of the Haṭhayogāsana and again while releasing the āsana, would be very slow and smooth without any jerk or undue force. These points are often overlooked when teaching and performing these Haṭhayogic āsanas. It has been seen that these āsanas are very often taught by very renowned yoga teachers with jerks, force and pressure. In such cases the āsanas no more remain 'yogāsanas' but become more or less calisthenic physical exercises. The Haṭhayogāsanas performed in this latter manner like calisthenics may give some physical benefits and may even be useful for alleviating and curing certain diseases, but they will not be able to produce the effects on mental and spiritual level to the same degree, as they would, if performed as far as possible, according to the way indicated by Patañjali (in these sūtras, II:46 and 47).

Though, as per the present commentator, the Haṭhayoga school is totally independent of and alien to Patañjali's Aṣṭāṅga school, there is no harm in adopting and combining judiciously the Haṭhayogic practices e.g. āsana, prāṇāyāma, mudrā and even nādānusandhāna along with the practice of Aṣṭāṅgas of Patañjali, if the sādhaka so desires, because there is no antagonism between the two. On the contrary the Haṭhayogic techniques may help to accelerate the progress of the sādhaka on the Aṣṭāṅga yoga path also.

SS. - **प्रयत्नशैथिल्यानन्तसमापत्तिभ्याम् ।।२:४७।।**

TL. - prayatna-śaithilyānanta-samāpattibhyām - II:47

WM. -
prayatna = effort, straining, forcing;
śaithilya = relaxing, giving up, releasing;
ananta = (an = not + nata = end) = endless, infinity;
samāpatti = samāpatti, merging into, identification;
bhyām = (dual, 3rd instrumental case suffix) with.

TR. - (The performance of āsana should be) with the two (namely) (total) relaxation of effort (and) anantasamāpatti (merger of mind with something ananta i.e. infinite).

CE. - This sūtra mentions two other essential requirements of the āsana. These two conditions are such as cannot be guaged by a person observing the performance of āsana as an onlooker. They can be felt and judged by the performer himself internally. During the maintenance phase the performer should be completely relaxed in each and every part of the body. There should be no effort i.e. straining at all anywhere. This is easily attainable in the āsanas usually adopted for meditation e.g. Siddha, Padma etc. But, as said, (cf. sūtra II:46, CE. and Y. M. XII, No. 1, pp. 1-13, 1969), this can also be achieved to a very great extent even in many other Haṭhayogic āsanas, probably excluding the balancing ones, which has been proved by the electromyographic (i.e. studying the electrical activity in the muscles) testing during such āsanas.

The word 'ananta' literally means 'endless'. It is also the designation of a mythalogical cobra in the Paurāṇika legends, who is depicted as supporting the earth on its hood. The old commentators have interpreted this word as indicating this snake. They therefore recommend to have samāpatti (meditation, here they call it dhyāna) on this snake.

But the basic sense of 'infinite' is also in this word. Indeed the mythic snake is given this name because it is supposed to be infinite in length. However the precise purpose of Patañjali in recommending samāpatti on ananta does not become clear, if the word be interpreted as this mythical serpent. The word may be better understood as infinity or some thing symbolic of this. The proper explanation of this process would be, therefore, to have samāpatti on an object of infinite dimensions e.g. the sky or the ocean etc. The meaning of samāpatti here also is the same as that in I:41. Thus the citta is to be directed to some object of infinite dimensions and an attempt is to be made to merge the mind into it and let it become one with it. The practical directives for the ananta samāpatti would be to think and visualize in the mind of anything like the sky or vast ocean, which has no finite dimensions and try to become one with it mentally. One can, therefore, visualize oneself to be like a log of wood lying in the vast ocean and imagine that one has become a part and parcel of that ocean just like a real floating log of wood would be or one can imagine oneself to be a kite which is suspended motionlessly in the vast sky, as often kites are seen just hanging in the air. Creating such imagery in the mind, in which one visualizes oneself to have become an integral part of such an infinite object, leads to a total forgetfulness of and even temporary detachment mentally from one's own body. No doubt, this requires a fairly long and serious practice. This is the true meaning and technique of ananta-samāpatti.

Prayatnaśaithilya and anantasamāpatti go hand in hand and in fact are closely related, so that one of these cannot go to perfection unless the other is also fairly attained to a very high degree. Though prayatnaśaithilya is more concerned with the body, it has some relation also to mental relaxation and vice versa ananta-samāpatti, which is more concerned with the mind, has a physical repercussion also. Only when both these are achieved to satisfactory high degree, the āsana will become an ideal āsana of yoga according of Patañjali's view point. In fact if a high degree of these two requirements is achieved, so to say, near to perfection, the further aṅgas of Aṣṭāṅgayoga viz. prāṇāyāma and to a great extent dhāraṇā and dhyāna are facilitated to a very great extent. It has been seen that a practice of sitting very relaxed in some of the standard āsanas used in meditation or even in a simple squatting with legs folded, for more than half an hour, leads to reduction of respiratory rate to about 50 % or in some cases with good relaxation even to 20 % of the normal rate in sitting rest. The pulse rate is also reduced to 60 to 50 % of the normal rate. The blood pressure also goes down by 5 to 15 counts, (i.e. systolic B.P. goes down by 5 to 15 mm. Hg.). These physiological changes and the statement about the internal state reached, made by the subject, point out clearly that the subject goes into a deep absorption state akin to meditation, sometimes perhaps almost reaching the dhyāna state of Patañjali (III:2). Therefore the āsana in Patañjali's system is not only a physical activity and even Haṭhayogic āsanas, when done according to these directives of Patañjali, become much more than simple physical exercises. They are then really very useful psycho-spiritual techniques.

SS. - **ततो द्वन्द्वानभिघातः ।।२:४८।।**

TL. - tato dvandvānabhighātaḥ - II:48

WM. - tataḥ (→o) = from or through that;

dvandva = literally two versus two i.e.conflict;

anabhighāta (ḥ) = (an = Not + abhi = Intense + ghāta = attack assailment), no assailment or attack (is).

TR. - From that (practice of āsana) (results the condition of) no assailment from the (various) conflicts.

CE. - The word 'tataḥ' (From that) means by a good and long 'practice of āsana'. The result of this is the immunity from the ill-effects, which are produced from conflicts i.e. two opposite factors trying to disturb and pull apart the organism. The ancient commentators give the instances of these dvandvas as heat versus cold, pleasure versus pain, humidity versus aridity, attraction versus hatred and such others. How the ill-effects of dvandvas, even those having ill-effects on the body e.g. heat vs. cold, pain vs. pleasure could be remedied by the āsana of Patañjali's description is not very clear. If at all such result may be shown by a long practice of the various complicated āsanas of Haṭhayoga, but here, as said, these are not intended by Patañjali. So these dvandvas be better understood as psychological conflicts. These certainly are counteracted and gradually made ineffective by the practice of even a meditational āsana, maintained for a long time and in a manner perfectly as described in sūtras II:46 and 47. This happens because psychological conflicts are always accompanied by tensions both physical as well as mental. The practice of maintaining a meditational āsana with complete physical relaxation (prayatnaśaithilya) as well as complete mental relaxation (anantasamāpatti) conditions the body-mind-complex to preserve this state of total relaxation, even when it is attacked by disturbing factors and faced by disturbing situations. It is also a well recognised fact that if the human organism does not produce tensions, which is a counteracting reaction to the adversity, then the ill-effect of that adverse condition is not augmented, but on the other hand it gradually dwindles and ultimately disappears. Thus the dvandvas or mental conflicts gradually lose their force and are overcome. Therefore, out of the dvandvas mentioned by the ancient commentators, the dvandvas of rāga-dveṣa, of pain-pleasure and such others can be counteracted by the (meditational) āsana practice. No doubt the Haṭhayogic āsanas performed in the ideal yogic way, as said above, will also lead to such an effect.

SS. - **तस्मिन्सति श्वासप्रश्वासयोर्गतिविच्छेदः प्राणायामः ।।२:४९।।**

TL. - tasmin-sati śvāsa-praśvāsa-yor-gati-vicchedaḥ prāṇāyāmaḥ - II:49

WM. -

tasmin	=	in that;
sati	=	while being;
śvāsa	=	inhalation;
praśvāsa	=	exhalation;
yoḥ (→r)	=	(6 th, possessive case suffix-dual) of the two.
gati	=	motion, here rhythmic regular movement;
viccheda (ḥ)	=	cut, interruption, break, (is);
prāṇāyāma (ḥ)	=	prāṇāyāma (is).

TR. - While being in that (āsana or dvandvānabhighāta) the break in the (regular rhythmic) movement of inhalation and (/or) exhalation (both) (is) prāṇāyāma.

CE. - Please see combined CE. under II:53.

SS. - **बाह्याभ्यन्तरस्तम्भवृत्तिर्देशकालसंख्याभिः परिदृष्टो-दीर्घसूक्ष्मः ।।२:५०।।**

TL. - bāhyābhyantara-stambha-vṛttir-deśa-kāla- saṅkhyā bhiḥ paridṛṣṭo dīrgha-sūkṣmaḥ - II:50

WM. -

bāhya	=	outward, external;
ābhyantara	=	inward, internal;
stambha	=	motionlessness, stoppage;
vṛtti (ḥ->r)	=	mode of behaviour (here of respiration);
deśa	=	region, extent, expanse;
kāla	=	time;
saṅkhyā	=	number (of rounds);
bhiḥ	=	(3rd, instrumental case suffix, plural) by means of;
paridṛṣṭa (o)	=	seen on the whole, measured, regulated;
dīrgha	=	prolonged;
sūkṣma (ḥ)	=	subtle, fine (is).

TR. - (Prāṇāyāma becomes of three varieties) (of) outward (modality), inward (modality) (and) standstill modality, (on account of being) measured (and regulated) by means of expanse, time (and) number (of rounds), (so that it becomes) prolonged (and simultaneously) subtle.

CE. - Please see combined CE under II:53.

SS. - **बाह्याभ्यन्तरविषयाक्षेपी चतुर्थः ।।२:५१।।**

TL. - bāhyābhyantara-viṣayākṣepī caturthaḥ -II:51

WM. - bāhya = outward;
ābhantara = inward;
viṣaya = concerned subject, concern;
ākṣepī = one excluding;
caturtha(ḥ) = fourth (is).

TR. - The fourth (variety of prāṇāyāma is) unconcerned with the external (or) internal (modality of respiration).

CE. - Please see combined CE. under II : 53.

SS. - **ततः क्षीयते प्रकाशावरणम् ।।२:५२।।**

TL. - tataḥ kṣīyate prakāśāvaraṇam - II : 52

WM. - tataḥ = from that;
kṣīyate = dwindles and finally disappears;
prakāśa = illumination;
āvaraṇa (m) = shroud, covering.

TR. - From it (Prāṇāyāma) disappears the covering on the (internal) illumination.

CE. - Please see combined CE. under II:53.

SS. - **धारणासु च योग्यता मनसः ।।२:५३।।**

TL. - dhāraṇāsu ca yogyatā manasaḥ -II:53

WM. - dhāraṇā (su) = dhāraṇā (in, plural);
ca = and;
yogyatā = fitness, preparedness, eligibility;
manas (aḥ) = mind (of).

TR. - And fitness of the mind (for entering) into dhāraṇās (also results from prāṇāyāma).

CE. - It has already been (sū.I:34) pointed out that though the word 'prāṇa' originally stands for a subtle, fundamental, ultimate life-force, in a practical way this force is most closely linked to and represented by respiration, which is the most essential activity characteristic of living organism. So very often the word prāṇa is used in yogic literature for the respiration or breath. The term prāṇāyāma is specifically used for certain respiratory practices which are the practices for controlling the respiration, which usually is of such a nature that it produces a slackening and consequent prolongation of the process of breathing.

Patañjali at the very start of the topic of prāṇāyāma seems to give an emphatic injunction that prāṇāyāma should be practised while sitting in āsana only. Thus there seems to be an obligatory sequentiality, āsana being a prerequisite for prāṇāyāma. Haṭhayoga does not seem to have this kind of obligatory relationship between its āsana, prāṇāyāma aṅgas, since at least one variety of prāṇāyāma viz. Ujjāyī has been said (H.P. II:53) as the one which could be practised while 'walking and standing' also. But Patañjali does not subscribe to such a view.

The word 'tasminsati' can be interpreted in two ways, tasmin (in that) may stand for (1) dvandvānabhighāta or for (2) āsana. If the first sense is accepted then the sūtra would mean that the prāṇāyāma should be practised only after dvandvānabhighāta (unaffectedness from conflicts) i.e. a mastery over the practice of āsana has been achieved. With the second sense the sūtra meaning would only be that the prāṇāyāma is to be done always sitting in āsana, mastery over it not being essential.

The main purpose of the sūtra, however, is not vitiated whether we accept the first or second of these meanings. In both one thing is common that prāṇāyāma is compulsorily to be done only after adopting the āsana. Since as already mentioned all the angas of Pātañjala Yoga are mutually facilitator, it is quite evident that the practice of prāṇāyāma will be as much more efficient as the higher the mastery over āsana has been acquired.

A third implication of the term 'tasminsati' is also possible. In this the sūtra meaning would be that simply being in āsana or may be better still, being in dvandvānabhighāta, which is the result of the mastery over āsana, will itself automatically and spontaneously lead to 'gativiccheda' i.e. disruption or cessation of the respiration. This implied meaning is worth notice, because as mentioned in sūtra II:47, the respiration gets very much slackened, so much so that the sādhaka sometimes feels that his breathing has stopped, simply when he sits relaxedly in the āsana without voluntarily trying to control his breathing. In other words a long practice of āsana and a fair mastery over it leads to spontaneous prāṇāyāma.

The meaning of both the words śvāsa and praśvāsa seem to be indefinite. Each of these words has been used both for inhalation as well as for exhalation. However most of the commentators have interpreted śvāsa as the act of inhalation or air inhaled and praśvāsa as the act of exhalation or the air exhaled. For the purpose of interpreting the sūtra II:49 however, it becomes immaterial as to what is the precise meaning of each of these words. Because the statement (without translating the main technical words) is 'prāṇāyāma' is gativiccheda of both the śvāsa and the praśvāsa. So whether the śvāsa stands for inhalation and praśvāsa stands for exhalation or vice-versa, gativiccheda of both of them (together or individually of each) is what is the characteristics of prāṇāyāma.

The interpretation of the pivotal word 'gati-viccheda' is the crucial thing in the interpretation of the sūtra II:49 and in a way the whole of Patañjali's prāṇāyāma topic. 'Viccheda' means a break. In a regular and rhythmic process any alteration in that regularity or rhythmicity would be disruption or break i.e. viccheda in that regularity or rhythmicity.

The first and simple meaning of the word 'gati' is movement or motion. But for a regular or rhythmic (in technical term of physics a simple harmonic) motion also the word 'gati' only is used e.g. gati of a vehicle, gati of a laṃbaka (pendulum), gati of hṛdaya (heart), gati of śvasana (respiration). Additional adjective e.g. 'niyamita' (regular), 'layabaddha' (rhythmic) etc. is prefixed to the word gati only when the aspect of regularity or rhythmicity is to be stressed. So when there is alteration in the regularity or rhythm of such a motion, it is a break or viccheda in that niyamitatā (regularness) or layabaddhatā (rhythmicity) or (niyamita i.e. regulated) 'gati'. If a car is moving at a regular speed or gati at 60 km. per hour and the speed is suddenly reduced to 50 km. per hour, we do say that there is a 'break' in the speed or the gati of the car. Any other activity taking place at regular intervals, say every Wednesday if it does not occur on any Wednesday or even if it takes place on some other week-day, it will be called a break (viccheda) in it. So also if the rhythmic movement i.e. rate of beating of heart or rate of respiration suddenly changes this will also be termed a break in the rate of heart-beats or rate of respiration. In Sanskrit the wording used would be actually 'hṛdayagativiccheda (or bhaṅga)' and 'śvasanagati viccheda (or bhaṅga)'.

So the compound word 'gativiccheda' has two meanings : - (1) A break i.e. a total pause or cessation in that gati i.e. movement and (2) a break in the regulated movement (gati) i.e. a change in the regularity or rhythmicity of the movement. In reference to respiration, which is a regular simple harmonic and rhythmic activity, a complete cessation i.e. a total or long pause will be one sort of gativiccheda and also a modification in the smooth normal breathing rhythm will be a second type of gativiccheda.

One thing is to be specially noted that in the sūtras Patañjali has no where used the technical terms pūraka, recaka, kuṃbhaka, which are usually used respectively for inhalation, exhalation (these being usually deliberate and prolonged) and retention or suspension of breath during prāṇāyāma. These are really technical terms introduced by Haṭhayoga for the three phases of prāṇāyāma, but which have become common to most of later yogic literature and are used even when prāṇāyāmas of any other school are being discussed. Occasionally the terms pūraka and recaka have been used even for normal inspiration and expiration, which, no doubt, is not precise.

Here it may again be mentioned that almost all commentators of Yoga Sūtras and writers on Yoga have assumed that Patañjali's Yoga and Haṭhayoga are one or at least intimately related. Many highly esteemed yoga teachers seem to believe as said, that Haṭhayogic āsanas and prāṇāyāma are an enlargement of Patañjali's āsana and prāṇāyāma, which is not acceptable to this commentator. Just as, excepting the few āsanas usable for meditation, majority of Haṭhayogic āsanas are not in the purview of Pātañjala Yoga, in the same way Hathayogic prāṇāyāmas are not necessarily belonging to Pātañjala Yoga. In Haṭhayoga kuṃbhaka, i.e. retention of air inhaled, in the lungs, after pūraka i.e. complete deep inspiration, is considered as the unavoidably essential part of prāṇāyāma. Indeed Haṭhapradīpikā (HP.) designates the eight types of prāṇāyāma, not as prāṇāyāmas but as kuṃbhakas, though the main factors which distinguish these various prāṇāyāmas from each other are the mode of either inspiration or expiation. Other texts of Haṭhayoga and other schools also very often use the term kuṃbhaka for prāṇāyāma. This has led many yoga experts to a conviction that prāṇāyāma is a breathing practice incorporating kuṃbhaka or breath-holding as an obligatory phase.

So according to their view gativiccheda has to be interpreted in the first manner i.e. cessation or total suspension of breathing. All the three sūtras (II:49 to 51) describing the techniques of prāṇāyāmas will have to be understood as per them, according to this characteristic concept of prāṇāyāma.

On the other hand, if the meaning of gati is accepted to be a regular rhythmic mode of movement (of respiration), gativiccheda would mean any alteration in the rhythmicity or regularity of breathing. In that case will not mean kuṃbhaka alone, but controlling and altering either the inspiration or expiration or both. No doubt kiṃbhaka or suspension of breathing will be one way of controlling breathing and so will get included in the varieties of prāṇāyāma with this second meaning of gativiccheda.

A number of ancient commentators of Yoga Sūtras viz. Vācaspatī Miśra, Vijñāna Bhikṣu, Nagojī, Bhojadeva, Bhāvāgaṇeśa etc. as well as some modern Yoga experts subscribe to this second view about the meaning of gativiccheda and the nature of prāṇāyāma (cf. The discussion on the Prāṇāyāma in Pātañjala Yoga Sūtras as well as its evolution in the articles by Svāmi Kuvalayānanda in Yoga Mīmāṃsā, vol .VI, (No.l), pp. 41 to 60; VI, (2), 129 to 153; VI, (3), 125 to 357). As said, the suspension or retention of breath is included as variety of prāṇāyāma in their this interpretation. Indeed all commentators and yoga adepts unequivocally accept that prāṇāyāma incorporating kuṃbhaka is superior to others involving modification of respiration, because it leads to better levels of spiritual attainment. In the perfection of prāṇāyāma suspension of breathing becomes spontaneous and that is the supermost variety of prāṇāyāma according to all, including Patañjali.

Accepting the alteration of the rhythmicness of breathing as also a gativiccheda of śvasana (breathing) has an advantage.

Kuṃbhaka, though no doubt the most powerful and valuable component of prāṇāyāma, is also liable to produce highly harmful results, if a sādhaka commits even inadvertently some error in its practice. Therefore it is to be handled with great caution, just as a highly potent drug or a very effective weapon can create great harm or even kill the user, if he does not know how to use these properly and does not observe all the precautions to be taken in their use, kuṃbhaka can produce very disastrous results. Instances are not unknown, where persons doing prāṇāyāma wrongly have turned incurably insane or contracted some very grave diseases, leading even sometimes to early death. Looking to this it is wise and very necessary to advise a sādhaka to resort to kuṃbhaka only when the possibility of such adverse effects will be absolutely avoided. When a sādhaka is constantly hammered with the teaching that praṇāyāma essentially means kuṃbhaka and that there can not be any prāṇāyāma without kuṃbhaka and so on, he is led to a belief that he must practise kuṃbhaka right from the beginning of his practice of prāṇāyāma. Again since he is told that kuṃbhaka is the most valuable part of prāṇāyāma, he tries even from the beginning to do it to the maximum extent possible. In such attempts, very often he is not conversant with all the prerequirements and precautions or sometimes he transgresses some of these restraining conditions and unnecessarily invites troubles. As said the disastrous effects are so deep-seated and advanced that nothing can be done to counteract them. Therefore it is advisable that the kuṃbhaka be introduced at fairly late stage, after the sādhaka has practised various modes of prāṇāyāmic breathing without kuṃbhaka for a long time, which would train his inspiratory and other related organs, so that they are fit to meet the stresses and gaseous pressures produced by the practice of kuṃbhaka. Even after this the kuṃbhaka should be introduced at first for a very short duration of a few (5 to 10) seconds and this duration should be very cautiously and gradually increased by small steps of two seconds or so every week.

If an overall consideration of the nature of prāṇāyāma is made, its objective in a general way seems to slacken and so prolong the whole process of respiration. The suspension of breathing and kuṃbhaka, no doubt, produce this slackening and prolongation to the maximum possible extent. But the same type of effect is produced to a lesser extent by slow inspiration and slow expiration. So if the inspiration or expiration or both are slowed down and prolonged, the effect of a little kuṃbhaka is produced (and is added to the effect of kuṃbhaka, if the prāṇāyāma involves also kuṃbhaka). Indeed the key-principle of prāṇāyāma seems to be to have the whole respiratory process as slow as possible, which automatically means making it prolonged to the maximum. In sūtra II:50 Patañjali mentions a general characteristic of all varieties of prāṇāyāma as 'dīrgha-sūkṣma (ḥ) i.e. prolonged and subtle (fine), which term clearly indicates this very key-principle for prāṇāyāma.

As said, kuṃbhaka is esteemed as the essence and most valuable part of prāṇāyāma. This kuṃbhaka is usually holding in of breath after a full inspiration. The name 'kuṃbhaka' derived from the word kuṃbha i.e. a pitcher, really therefore, should be applied to filling lungs with air and retaining it just like the filling up and retaining water in the pitcher i.e. kuṃbha, whose purpose or use is only this. So the literal meaning of kuṃbhaka in relation to prāṇāyāma is this filling of lungs fully with air and retaining that inspired air in the lungs. In such a kuṃbhaka, after the air is filled to the maximum capacity, it is not allowed to go out. When the air is thus held up in the lungs there is an exchange of gases in between it and the blood flowing in the capillary blood vessels in the lungs. The oxygen from the air goes into the blood through the intervening layers of the walls of the lung alveoli (infinitesimally small pockets or cells) and the blood capillaries and the carbon-di-oxide (CO_2) from the blood comes into the gas in the lung alveoli. In normal breathing after a very short time (few seconds) and as soon as a certain level of CO_2 is reached in the gas contained in the lung alveoli, there arises an impulse for breathing out (this is governed by certain controlling centres in the head and neck) and then in response to it we exhale.

When the breath is held in during Kuṃbhaka, resisting the impulse and desire to breathe out, the gases get a much longer time for their exchange than the normal time and there is a greater amount of exchange in the gases i.e. more oxygen from lung-air goes into blood and reversely more CO_2 from blood comes into the lungs. Thus there is great depletion of oxygen and great increase in CO_2 concentration in the air or gas that is held in the lung alveoli. However this cannot go on indefinitely. After either a certain low level of oxygen concentration or a certain increased level of CO_2 concentration is reached, the governing centres will send such a strong impulse that there will be compulsorily an exhalation. Neither in the normal breathing nor even in prāṇāyāmic breathing does the oxygen level become so low as to create an impulse strong enough to make it compulsory to exhale immediately. On the other hand the level of CO_2 is so high as to make exhalation unavoidable. Thus during the training and practice of prāṇāyāma what the sādhaka would be trying to achieve (no doubt most often unknowingly) is to habituate the respiration-controlling centres to withstand gradually higher and higher concentrations of CO_2. In the beginning when a certain threshold-concentration of CO_2 is reached, it becomes unbearable and the person, receiving an impulse from the respiration-control centre, breathes out. But when he begins the attempt of breath-holding (kuṃbhaka), even when the impulse comes, the person can voluntarily resist it and delay the exhalation. A regular practice of this thing, continued over days, gradually conditions the respiration-control centres to tolerate higher and higher concentrations of CO_2 and the threshold causing the compulsive impulse goes on rising. This fact is clearly mentioned in Haṭhayogic writings, where it has been indicated that the sādhaka should try to resist the impulses (udghāta) for exhaling out up to the third udghāta, when it would become almost impossible to hold in the breath any further and the exhalation would become unavoidable. It has been also indicated that the time after which the first and subsequent udghātas would come up would go on increasing, longer is the practice of kuṃbhaka. No doubt this process of conditioning the respiratory-control centres to higher and higher concentration of CO_2 has a limit and when this limit, which is variable from individual to individual, is reached, then there would not be any possibility of further increasing the time of kuṃbhaka. This threshold limit is near about 7.5% concentration of CO_2 in the air inside the lung alveoli. Again since there is a proportionality in time durations of inhalation (pūraka), retention (kuṃbhaka) and exhalation (recaka) of 1:4:2, usually recommended as the best to be achieved in the Haṭhayogic tradition, when the kuṃbhaka will increase, the durations of pūraka and recaka will also increase, i.e. the processes of inhalation and exhalation will be slackened. Such a slackening will lead to better exchange of gases between the blood and the lung alveolar air.

Thus the consideration of the principle and the whole process of prāṇāyāma, as recommended and practised in Haṭhayoga tradition, clearly shows that one aim of the whole training of prāṇāyāma is to condition the respiratory control centre to bear comfortably the highest possible concentrations of CO_2. If this principle is recognised, then it can be clearly understood that even when any one of the phases of breathing i.e. either inhalation or exhalation or both are made slow, there will be increased exchange of gases between the blood and lungs and the CO_2 concentration in the lungs would be higher than in the normal breathing. Obviously this concentration will be higher, the slower are the respiratory phases. The respiratory control centres will, therefore, be conditioned to tolerate concentrations higher than in normal breathing. Thus the slow inspiration and still better, slow expiration would serve the same purpose as a kuṃbhaka, though to a lesser degree. Late Dr. S.L.Vinekar, former Joint Director of Research, K.S.M.Y.M.Samiti, himself an advanced yoga sādhaka, a medical man well-versed in the practices of a number of yoga schools and a scientific researcher in the field of yoga, characterized slow inhalation and slow exhalation as 'Kuṃbhakas with safety valve open'. What he meant by this is that all the possibilities of harm caused by kuṃbhaka noted above, are completely avoided in this type of slow breathing and yet the benefits of kuṃbhaka to a moderate degree are obtained and so they also can be rightly designated as prāṇāyāmic breathing. Taking all this into consideration it seems proper to include even slow breathing i.e. slow inspiration or/and slow expiration without any breath-holding in the term prāṇāyāma. In view of this, the term gativiccheda should be interpreted, not merely as the total suspension of breathing i.e. kuṃbhaka, but also as alteration of the normal rhythm of breathing.

No doubt this alteration of the normal breathing should not be of any type. Because with such a loose and wide significance given to the term gativiccheda even the altered breathing in disease or abnormal conditions e.g. asthma, coughing, singing, etc. would get included in prāṇāyāma. Again rapid breathing during exertion, deep breathing would also be included in prāṇāyāma, against which the term dīrgha-sūkṣma (II:50) is Patañjali's injunction. Though Haṭhayoga texts do not affirm this last principle explicitly, it is to be noted that kapālabhāti, a technique of rapid breathing is not enumerated under prāṇāyāma, but is one of the ṣaṭkarmas i.e. six (cleansing) actions. Bhastrikā prāṇāyāma has in the first part of it a rapid breathing, but this in combination with the second part results ultimately in an overall slackening and prolongation of respiration.

Therefore, though gaticcheda is to be interpreted as a modification of normal breathing, this modification will have to be restricted to finer and slow breathing only. Any sort of rapid and violent breathing would not be prāṇāyāmic, at least according to Patañjali and also in view of above discussion. This is clearly indicated, as said, by the phrase 'dīrgha-sūkṣma' used by Patañjali in sutra II : 50. The word prāṇāyāma itself, in a way, indicates this. Āyāma means expanse and the process of expanding. So the word prāṇāyāma literally means expanding or elongating prāṇa. Since prāṇa on practical level means breath, prāṇāyāma would mean elongating breath i.e. in Sanskrit making it dīrgha. This prolongation of breath simultaneously results into the breath becoming finer and finer, which is indicated by the term 'sūkṣma' in sūtra II:50.

There are some indirect additional indications also pointing to the fact that a rapid and so a violent breathing is not to be classed as prāṇāyāma. In Yoga Sūtra itself Patañjali mentions a technique of forceful breathing, specially involving a rapid forced exhalation (in Sūtra I:34), helpful for cittaprasādana, which evidently is not a technique of prāṇāyāma, as has been misunderstood by some commentators. From this it seems that a rapid and violent mode of controlling breathing does not come under prāṇāyāma.

The similar rapid forceful breathing technique of Kapālabhāti of Haṭhayoga, as already noted, is not categorised as prāṇāyāma, but is enumerated in purificatory techniques, yet it is seen that a number of yoga teachers bracket it with prāṇāyāma and even often refer to it as prāṇāyāma. On account of such confusion and poor understanding about prāṇāyāma, it was felt necessary by this commentator to deal in such details and often with reiteration, of not only Pātañjala, but also of Haṭhayogic prāṇāyāma, the latter being confused with the former.

In respect of Kapālabhāti it need be mentioned that the results of gas exchange studies on kapālabhāti are quite different than those on (even Haṭhayogic) prāṇāyāmas. The researches in Kaivalyadhāma (Lonavla) laboratories have shown that prāṇāyāmas (at least the two varieties which are very commonly practised and which were, therefore, studied, viz.. Ujjāyī and Bhastrikā) do not lead to any significant increase in the oxygen absorption or in CO_2 elimination, above those in the normal resting state. In fact, if at all, both these are very slightly lower than those in the normal state. On the contrary, it has been seen that during kapālabhāti there is roughly 10% more oxygen absorption and so also almost 10% more CO_2 elimination than that in the normal resting breathing. Thus from blood purification aspect kapālabhāti does enrich and purify the blood with respect to oxygen and CO_2 respectively. As said, prāṇāyāmas do not show such effects, which however, are often claimed about them, this being based on mere conjecture. (Miles W.R., J. Applied Physiol. XIX, (1), 75-82,1964; Rao, S. Indian J. Med. Res; LVI, (5), 701-705, 1968; etc. have reported increased oxygen absorption in prāṇāyāmic breathing than in normal breathing. This may be due (1) to their subjects not being as adept and as practised in prāṇāyāma as ours and (2) to the testing technique, which was graph-recording type, which may not be as precise as the chemical analysis method used in Kaivalyadhāma Laboratories). Moreover as is apparent and also inwardly experienced by every sādhaka, prāṇāyāma is not only restful for body, but gives a very peaceful feeling to the mind. In that case there is no reason that oxygen absorption or CO_2 elimination should increase in prāṇāyāma above the normal and this is exactly the result of our studies on prāṇāyāma carried out in Kaivalyadhāma laboratories.

The ancient yogins, nevertheless, had recognised the distinction between these effects of Kapālabhāti and prāṇāyāmas, may be through their intuitional and experiential methods. They had differentiated quite correctly the purificatory effects of the respiratory practice of Kapālabhāti from absence of these in prāṇāyāmas and so excluded the former from the prāṇāyāmic practices and put it in the ṣaṭkarmas (i.e. six practices for purification). Even in Haṭhayoga, Bhastrikā seems to be the only variety of prāṇāyāma, which includes a rapid breathing. But as pointed out the chemical analysis of the respiratory gases shows that the whole process ultimately produces the same results as a slow breathing prāṇāyāma. Moreover the time-duration of one complete cycle of Bhastrikā, performed by a Haṭhayogic sādhaka with a moderately satisfactory progress, is many more times than that required for his one smooth normal breathing cycle. This itself is a clear indication that even with rapid breathing as a part of it, Bhastrikā is a slow-breathing process. So it can be definitely affirmed that both Patañjali's as well as Haṭhayogic systems do not recommend any rapid-breathing process as prāṇāyāma and that all the prāṇāyāmic techniques are those where the result is ultimate slackening of respiration.

Indeed, the key-principle of prāṇāyāma, according to the present commentator and in view of the above discussion, seems to be to make the whole process of respiratory slow and consequently prolonged. In this either only one, two or all the three phases of the respiratory cycle, viz. inspiration, expiration and cessation can be made slow and prolonged. With various types of permutations and combinations of these, there can be innumerable varieties of prāṇāyāma. Haṭhayoga, whose starting point seems to be the body and the manipulation of various processes taking place in it, has developed a number of peculiar practices of prāṇāyāma, which may have as their objectives varying effects on the physical and mental planes. As already pointed out, Patañjali's aṣṭāṅga system does not recommend and most probably does not accept all these varieties of prāṇāyāma, as of any special significance for its purpose. Patañjali's prāṇāyāma seems to be very straight-forward and probably has only four simple variations as indicated by the sūtras II:50 and 51. Some scholars, e.g. Dr. K.S. Joshi (in Y.M., XX (12),pp.38-43, 1981) etc. think that there are only one or two varieties of Patañjali's prāṇāyāma. In passing it may be mentioned that though Patañjali does not specifically name any Haṭhayogic type of prāṇāyāma, nor can it be said that he considers these as of importance, yet a yoga-sādhaka may, if he so likes, practise any one or more varieties of these Haṭhayogic prāṇāyāmas as there seems to be no apparent and definite contraindication to preclude this.

The most feasible interpretation from sūtras II:50 and 51 seems to be that Patañjali considers that there can be four possible modifications (gativiccheda) of normal restful respiratory activity, which will, therefore, result into four varieties of prāṇāyāma. Obviously these are : (1) bāhya (2) ābhyantara, (3) stambha and (4) caturtha. The term vṛtti of the sūtra II:50 can be advantageously applied to all the first three of these words, so that the full names of these three varieties of prāṇāyāma would be (1) bāhyavṛtti, (2) ābhyantara-vṛtti and (3) stambha-vṛtti prāṇāyāmas. This term vṛtti is absent in sūtra II:51 and the phrase bāhyabhyantara-viṣayākṣepī itself negates the sense of vṛtti, because viṣaya (topic, concern) here stands for vṛtti and ākṣepī means that which excludes. Therefore viṣyākṣepī here is as good as vṛttivihīna (= devoid of vṛtti i.e. devoid of modality of action). In fact a very precise word to be used as the designation or qualification of the fourth variety does not clearly come up in the sūtra and so the best way to designate this variety seems to be to call it simply the 'Fourth' = caturtha, as has been done by Patañjali. The meanings of the words bāhya, ābhyantara and stambha are quite clear, as given in the WM. above. The word vṛtti has been rendered as 'mode of behaviour' which here is of breathing. So (1) bāhya vṛtti (2) ābhyantara vṛtti and (3) stambha vṛtti would mean respectively breathing which has (1) an external modality i.e. breathing out or exhalation, (2) an internal modality i.e.

breathing in or inhalation and (3) stand-still modality i.e. suspension.

The main difficulty is to decide the exact meaning of these terms depending on whether we understand gativiccheda as : (1) alteration in the rhythmic breathing or (2) total suspension of breathing. In the first case the bāhyavṛtti prāṇāyāma would be the breathing in which only exhalation is modified and that also made necessarily fine (faint) and prolonged. Ābhyantara vṛtti prāṇāyāma will have only the inhalation phase prolonged and faint. In stambha vṛtti the breathing is suspended i.e. completely stopped for some time. From the wording of the sūtra II:50 this much can be clearly stipulated. It is not explicit as to what would be the nature of the remaining phases in each of these prāṇāyāmas viz. of the inhalation in the bāhya vṛtti prāṇāyāma and whether there would be any suspension of breathing included in this bāhya variety : the same is true for the other, viz ābhyantara vṛtti about which no clear indication about its exhalation and suspension phase is there. In stambha vṛtti it is still more confusing, since there is no explicit indication about the inhalation and exhalation, yet there cannot be a cessation of breath totally independent of these two phases. Then again a difficulty arises about distinguishing the stambha vṛtti from the caturtha. This latter is described as bāhyābhyantara-viṣayākṣepi = excluding the correlation with the externality or internality of the mode of breathing i.e. without any dependence on exhalation and inhalation. Therefore this is also a suspension or cessation of breathing and simply from the wordings of the two sūtras II:50 and 51 it does not become clear how these two varieties viz. stambha vṛtti and caturtha are different from each other.

Merely going as per the meanings of the words actually present in the sūtra II:50 and accepting gativiccheda as mere alteration in the rhythmicity of breathing, the three varieties of sutra II : 50 would be : (1) bāhyavṛtti, where exhalation alone is made prolonged and finer (fainter) the inhalation remaining normal and there being no wilful attempt for any suspension of breath. (2) ābhyantara vṛtti, correspondingly would be where the inhalation is prolonged and finer, exhalation remaining normal and no attempt at stopping the breathing. Thus in both these varieties the breath cessation is not at all to be resorted to. (3) stambha vṛtti where breathing is brought to a standstill. Whether after inhalation or exhalation being not stipulated, the option is open to the practicant. So, the suspension can be introduced either after inhalation or after exhalation or even after both in one single round of prāṇāyāma. It does not seem to be obligatory to have the inhalation or exhalation prolonged and faint, but considering the overall discussion above, it seems desirable to have both these phases also prolonged and faint in stambha vṛtti prāṇāyāma.

Many yoga adepts may object to the above explanation of the techniques of the three varieties of Pātañjala prāṇāyāma. The main reason for this objection would be that most of the yoga adepts are trained mainly or at least at the start in Haṭhayogic techniques of prāṇāyāma, since these are very popular and are the ones which are in vogue and are only the ones taught as prāṇāyāma. These yoga adepts have, therefore, a very staunch idea, very deeply ingrained in their mind that prāṇāyāma must have kuṃbhaka (breath holding in) as an essential part and that inhalation and exhalation in prāṇāyāma are only of pūraka and recaka type i.e. full and deep. Indeed it can be noticed that all these experts freely use the terms pūraka, kuṃbhaka and recaka while discussing Patañjali's prāṇāyāmas also, without any discrimination. This we feel is quite wrong as Patañjali himself seems to have totally avoided these terms, though it seems quite probable that Haṭhayoga was well established before his time and so these technical terms of Haṭhayoga might be known to him. Anyway we feel that it is necessary to keep in mind this discrimination and so avoid the use of Haṭhayogic technical terms in discussing the things in Pātañjala Yoga Sūtras. Because this can lead to a wrong or at least Haṭhayogically biased interpretation of Patañjali's techniques, as, we feel, has happened in the case of Pātañjala prāṇāyāma.

Thus the sūtras of Patañjali need not and should not be interpreted on the lines of synonymous and parallel techniques and processes of Haṭhayoga. Patañjali's sūtras should really be interpreted merely on the basis of the words they contain and independently of the views and principles of any other system. But this seems not to have been done by most of the commentators, inclusive of the first and the most revered one, Vyāsa, who very often has given explanation of Haṭhayogic and other lines as is very obvious from his comments on the sūtra II:46 of āsana. If, therefore, the sūtras on prāṇāyāma of Patañjali are interpreted in this independent manner, then the above interpretation and explanation only is valid.

Though, as said above, even either a prolonged fine inhalation or exhalation can make the respiratory process a prāṇāyāma as per Patañjali's sūtra II:50, an ardent sādhaka can have both these advantageously combined in one single cycle of prāṇāyāma, since there is nothing in the sūtras against doing such a thing. To eliminate unnecessary risk, he should at first avoid suspension of breathing, but later on (preferably after about an year's prāṇāyāma practice without breath-suspension and when his slow exhalation gets prolonged to 30 seconds or more) he can add even the suspension phase in his prāṇāyāma practice. Even in this it would be better to introduce first the suspension of breath after, exhalation i.e. the so called bāhyakuṃbhaka. After a few days (3 to 6 months) the holding-in of breath after inhalation i.e. the so-said (ābhyantara) kuṃbhaka be attempted. As a safety precaution it would be desirable to have both these types of breath suspensions introduced very gradually and in very small measures or stages. In the beginning they should be 5 to 7 seconds and then they be increased by 2 to 5 seconds per week or so. With such cautions and gradual progress, all possibilities of harm will be completely avoided.

Accepting the meaning of gativiccheda as suspension or complete cessation of breathing for a time being, the three varieties of prāṇāyāma in sūtra II:50 would be : (1) bāhya vṛtti i.e. suspension of breath after prolonged exhalation, otherwise called bāhyakuṃbhaka. (2) ābhyantaravṛtti i.e. suspension of breathing after prolonged inhalation or the usual (socalled ābhyantara) kuṃbhaka, (3) stambha vṛtti would be then a variety in which suspension of breath should be the dominant feature. So it could be a respiratory cycle in which the suspension will be there, after both inhalation as well as exhalation and this would be prolonged to the maximum possible. This is the only feasible way in which this sūtra, if at all, can be explained, when gativiccheda is equated with suspension of breathing. In reality when this meaning of gativiccheda is accepted, it becomes very difficult to interpret properly the sūtra II: 50, so as to clearly distinguish the varieties of prāṇāyāma, each from the others, because even both the (1) and (2) above are really stambha vṛtti prāṇāyāmas and so really a distinct third variety, which could be differentiated from these two by this specific characteristic does not at all exist. This is the reason why the sūtra need be interpreted as here above, when gativiccheda is assumed to be suspension of breath.

This difficulty could have been avoided in the interpretation of the sūtra II:50, even when gativiccheda was equated to suspension, by breaking the compound word bāhyābhyantara stambha vṛtti as (1) bāhyastambha vṛtti and (2) ābhyantara stamhavṛtti only i.e. the mode of suspension after exhalation and the mode of suspension after inhalation. In that case there need not have to be read and postulated a third separate variety viz. of stamvbha vṛtti i.e. of mere suspension modality. But such an easy solution and explanation of sūtra II:50 is precluded by the word 'caturtha' in the next sūtra II:51. By this it is definite that there are four varieties of Pātañjala prāṇāyāmas and as that in sūtra II:51 is 'fourth', the remaining three must have been indicated before it i.e. in sūtra II:50. But with the break up of the compound word suggested here the varieties in sūtra II:50 could be only two and in total only three and so this break up of the compound word is untenable.

These three varieties of prāṇāyāma mentioned in sūtra II:50 are regulated in three ways viz. by means of deśa, kāla and saṃkhyā. Deśa, which means region or expanse, stands for the distance up to which the movement of air (or prāṇa) is felt in the breathing activity. In exhalation, this distance can be easily and directly measured by feeling the touch of the exhaled breath by holding the fingers in front of the nose or can be adjudged by holding some suitably light material e.g. a wisp of cotton, or a thread or a paper-strip in the same manner in front of the nose. In inhalation it is adjudged by a sensation, initially of coolness, and late with training in minute observation, of throbbing or pressure, up to different deep inner parts of the body. In this inner feeling, the sensation is produced more mentally i.e. by the movement of prāṇa than is caused by the actual contact of inhaled air. That is why very often practitioners of prāṇāyāma report that they feel that the air (prāṇa) going up to navel (nābhī) or even toe nails, which anatomically is not possible. In this way the deśa is a measure of the force of breathing. More the force of breathing, the greater will be the deśa i.e. the extent to which the movement of air or prāṇa away from the opening of nose, is felt.

Kāla means time and so it would be the time required for each and every phase of breathing and in this way that for one complete cycle of breathing or prāṇāyāma. This kāla will become elongated, slower is the breathing i.e. inhalation or exhalation and in the case of suspension by mere effort of will. Thus the two measuring parameters of prāṇāyāma viz. deśa and kāla are interrelated and are inverse of one another. In respect of inhalation and exhalation, therefore, one would be enough for regulating these, since for inhalation and exhalation, if deśa be reduced, kāla would increase and vice versa. But there is a purpose in mentioning kāla as a separate parameter from deśa, because in suspension, since there is no movement of air or prāṇa, deśa cannot be adjudged. For this phase therefore kāla is the only available measure through which the suspensions can be prolonged or shortened.

Thus though Patañjali mentions time as an important parameter for regulation of prāṇāyāmic breathing, which will be influencing the degree of effects produced by prāṇāyāma on the physical, mental and spiritual planes in the human being, he has not mentioned any precise units or measures of this nor any relative proportion, as beneficial, in between the time durations of the different phases of prāṇāyāma, as has been done by Haṭhayoga. According to Haṭhayoga tradition a time ratio of 1:4:2 respectively for Pūraka, Kuṃbhaka and Recaka is the best and so most desirable to achieve. However if this ratio can not be practised by a sādhaka, then he should resort to other ratios e.g. 1:2:2 or 1:2:1 etc. Usually the suspension phase (ābhyantara kuṃbhaka) is to be kept longest and the exhalation should be preferably longer than inhalation or at least equal to it, but never shorter than inhalation. Any similar stipulation or directive is not given by Patañjali, nor can it be easily assumed as implied in the parameter kāla. So Patañjali's prāṇāyāma may probably have an inhalation longer than the exhalation, as would necessarily happen in the variety having prolonged inhalation as the sole modification of breathing in the second variety. As stressed before, the key principle of prāṇāyāma, both from Patañjali's as well as Haṭhayogic stand, is the slackening of breathing. So for Patañjali's purpose any mode of prāṇāyāma would be satisfactory, where even one phase is made slow. Obviously if all the phases viz. inhalation, retention, exhalation and suspension (after exhalation) are prolonged, to the maximum no doubt very judiciously, cautiously and gradually and so wherever feasible also finer, it would be the best variety of prāṇāyāma. Still if a sādhaka wants to adopt the recommendations of Haṭhayoga regarding the ratio of durations of the phases, there is no bar for him in Patañjala Yoga Sūtra against doing so.

One thing must be made clear. This is that, whatever the kāla i.e. duration of time, for different phases a sādhaka chooses, must be kept constant for his prāṇāyāma practice for all the cycles and for a number of days, till he is well accustomed to these and they become quite easy-almost natural for him. He should not change the durations of the phases in any haphazard manner in successive cycles of prāṇāyāma during a single seance or even from day to day quite frequently.

Saṃkhyā means number and in connection with prāṇāyāma here it can signify only the number of repetitions of the prāṇāyāma cycles. The more the number of repetitions, the more intensive and effective will be the prāṇāyāma. It has been observed that when a number of cycles of prāṇāyāma are successively practised, there is a mutually facilitatory and amplificatory effect.

As already said, the term dīrgha-sūkṣma, which means prolongated (and) fine (subtle, faint) does not indicate two independent qualities or, as has probably been done by some commentators, as two categories or varieties of prāṇāyāma, (1) dīrgha and another distinguished from this (2) sūkṣma. The term in sūtra II:50 is to be looked upon as a single qualificative of the word prāṇāyāma in the sūtra II:51. When any of the three types of prāṇāyāma, mentioned in sūtra : 50, is prolonged by prolongating one or more phases of the respiratory cycle, this automatically results into making that phase fine (or faint) i.e. either inhalation or exhalation or both these, which consequently results in making the whole respiratory process fine or subtle (sūkṣma). Since the breath suspension has no relation with deśa i.e. the speed or force of movement, as it is a stand-still state, the qualificative sūkṣma is not relevant in its case. It can only be dīrgha by prolongation of the time-duration i.e. kāla of the breath suspension. But as explained even the stambhavṛtti has to have inhalation and exhalation associated with it. These phases, therefore, can be also made slow and fine in this third variety. In brief Patañjali seems to stress in the sūtra II:50 that all the three varieties of prāṇāyāma mentioned there result by a deliberate controlling of the three phases of respiration, existing even in normal resting breathing, by means of deśa (indicative of force of breathing). Kāla (time) and saṃkhyā (number of rounds) and which could give better results if they are made dīrgha-sūkṣma (prolonged as well as finer).

Also by this phrase any rapid breathing is excluded from Pātañjala prāṇāyāma.

The 'caturtha' i.e. 'fourth' variety is described in the sūtra II:51 as 'bāhyābhyantara viṣayākṣepī' i.e. excluding or not correlated with external or internal modality of breathing. This qualifying phrase clearly indicates that the (modes of) inhalation and exhalation are not at all of any significance in this variety. Obviously, therefore, this gativiccheda is not through a modification i.e. controlling of the inhalation and exhalation and must therefore be a suspension of breath or stambhavṛtti. The question then arises : In what way this stambhavṛtti differs from that in II:50 ? This difference lies in the spontaneity of the process. In the third i.e. the stambhavṛtti, there is a willful suspension of breathing usually and preferably either at the end of a controlled inhalation or a controlled exhalation. But in this fourth variety the suspension may not be after such a willfully controlled inhalation or exhalation, as these are 'excluded', as indicated by term 'bāhyābhyantara viṣayākṣepī'. That means that this gativiccheda or suspension takes place spontaneously at any stage of any phase of breathing. That is the breathing may stop any time after a partial exhalation. This phenomenon is very well recognised in Yoga. Even in Haṭhayoga this type of spontaneous suspension of breathing or kuṃbhaka is recognised and called kevala-kuṃbhaka. This completely uncontrolled and spontaneous suspension of breathing is a natural and inevitable result of a very long and intensive practice of various types of prāṇāyāmic breathing with phases controlled.

The caturtha prāṇāyāma being a suspension spontaneously occurring anywhere in breathing and the inhalation and exhalation therein also being uncontrolled, this variety of prāṇāyāma cannot be wilfully made prolonged and fine, as suggested for prāṇāyāma in sūtra II:50. But since it comes only after a very long-perhaps some years'- practice of the other voluntarily regulated prāṇāyāmas, which are always performed in the dīrgha-sūkṣma manner, the sādhaka becomes conditioned to this type of respiration even when breathing normally in day to day life all the 24 hours and so the breathing in the caturtha prāṇāyāma automatically remains dīrgha-sūkṣma.

The results of prāṇāyāma are mentioned in the sūtras II:52 and 53. The first of it is the removal of the shroud on the inner illuminating potentiality. The illustration of a lamp-chimney covered with a number of translucent or opaque covers or thick layers of smoke and dirt is quite apt for understanding the parallelism with this phenomenon. As successively the covers are removed or the dirt is wiped off the light of the lamp becomes clearer and brighter. A similar kind of change is experienced after a long practice of prāṇāyāma, when continued over a number of days. The potentiality for getting the Ultimate Knowledge or Realization and experiencing the Final Reality is present in every individual. But the saṃskāras of innumerable lives lying in the karmāśaya part of citta distort this ability and serve as shrouds or screens interfering in correctly perceiving and comprehending the reality behind the objects and phenomena. This hindrance is reduced in a large proportion by the practice of prāṇāyāma. Just as a person, around whom there are a number of loud noises going on, cannot hear a feeble sound or a person surrounded by dazzling lights cannot see feebly glowing objects, these deviations of the saṃskāras do not allow citta to grasp the reality completely, independently and without these distortions. The first effect of prāṇāyāma, which is invariably noticed by the sādhaka very easily and with even a short practice of a few days, is a tranquillization of the mind. Here in these sūtras on prāṇāyāma Patañjali does not explicitly mention this result. But it is implied in sūtra II:53, as will be seen below. However in sūtra I:34 he has recommended a respiratory technique for cittaprasādana (a pleasant peaceful condition of citta). Strictly speaking that technique is not a prāṇāyāma, because it involves a rather forcible and so rapid exhalation. Yet even such a controlled respiratory activity leads to the tranquillization of citta as stated by Patañjali and confirmed by many yoga-sādhakas. On account of the main physiological characteristic of prāṇāyāma viz. slowing of breathing, leading to the conditioning of the respiration-regulating centres in the central nervous system to the higher concentrations of CO_2 the tranquillisation is much more marked and quickly achieved. This effect is experienced and reported by every practitioner of prāṇāyāma, not only of Pātañjala varieties, but even the Haṭhayogic ones. The citta then becomes fit for turning its activity in any desired direction. In other words the citta can penetrate very deeply and thoroughly into the knowledge of any desired subject i.e. can go into the meditational processes of dhāraṇā→dhyāna→samādhi upon that subject. This capacity to have clear perception or comprehension of the knowledge about any chosen subject is what is indicated by the phrase 'prakāśāvaraṇa kṣaya (removal of shroud or obstacle in the way of illumination).

The other effect mentioned in sūtra II:53 indicates that prāṇāyāma is a necessary prerequisite for entering into dhāraṇā i.e. the first stage of meditation i.e. the inward going journey of the citta. How this happens has been explained just above. The tranquillization of citta, producing in it an ability to penetrate into the reality behind any subject chosen for meditation, is the 'yogyatā' (fitness) enter into the first stage of the meditational process viz. dhāraṇā. This is what is stated in sūtra II:53. The plural form of the term dhāraṇā used therein has probably led to the interpretation of dhāraṇā, as has usually been given by most of the commentators. They explain that dhāraṇā means directing the mind on a region i.e. a limited area or spot, which they say is to be chosen preferably in one's own body e.g. the hṛdaya (heart) or bhrū-madhya (space between two eyebrows) etc. But this explanation is quite unsatisfactory and even impracticable, as can be seen in CE. on sūtras III:1 to 4 related to dhāraṇā etc. The explanations of these earlier commentators are based on the techniques of dhāraṇā as recommended and followed in the Tāntrika, particularly Haṭhayogic tradition. In this tradition a number of points and specially certain organs and parts of the body have been recommended as the subjects or rather as the objects for dhāraṇā on which the concentration of the mind is to be attempted. Naturally many mystical explanations are associated with these body points, on account of which there are possible a variety of dhāraṇās. Since in the sūtra II:53 Patañjali has used the plural form 'dhāraṇāsu' (in dhāraṇās), the commentators have been misled into thinking that this plurality is referring to these varieties of dhāraṇās. According to the present commentator, during the stage of dhāraṇā in the process of meditation the pratyaya (experience by citta) of the one single chosen viṣaya (subject), which the citta gets during the progress of dhāraṇā, goes on varying continually. This happens because of the innumerable different associations that the citta has with the notion of that subject chosen for meditation. It would be impossible to have the awareness of these associated notions in the citta for all the innumerable notions at one and the same moment. Some of them may become dominant at a moment when others will dwindle. In this way the precise nature of the pratyaya (experience of the subject in the citta at a particular moment) will be going on varying substantially from time to time. We may even express this in other words, that during dhāraṇā the citta is getting varying pratyayas of one and the same subject (for complete explanation see CE on sūtras III:1 ff.). This is what is indicated by the plural usage 'dhāraṇāsu'.

It would be desirable to resume briefly the main points of this whole long discussion of prāṇāyāma.

1. Prāṇāyāma must be done in a comfortable posture, better in some standard yogāsana e.g. Padma, Sidhha etc. preferably after getting a fair mastery over the āsana.

2. Prāṇāyāma is a gativiccheda i.e. interruption of śvāsa-praśvāsa i.e. normal rhythmic inhalation-exhalation. Thus it is

a modification or alteration of the normal mode of breathing. However this modification should result in slackening i.e. prolongation of the breathing and this makes the breathing finer (feeble, subtle or fainter). Violent breathing is not to be incorporated in Pātañjala prāṇāyāma.

3. Consequently a cessation of breathing (i.e. kuṃbhaka of Haṭhayogic terminology) can be and is the most important phase and characteristic of prāṇāyāma. So varieties of prāṇāyāma involving cessation would be producing better results, specially for psycho-spiritual purpose, but this kuṃbhaka (cessation or suspension) being a hazardous phase should be undertaken only after the sādhaka is able to have a prolonged exhalation, preferably lasting for 30 seconds or at least the maximum possible for that sādhaka.

4. Even in this, the suspension at the end of a deep slow exhalation is safer and be attempted first. Only after adequate practice of this type of suspension and when it is longest and yet comfortably easy, the attempt for the suspension at the end of inhalation (antara-kuṃbhaka) be started. Either type of these suspensions should be of about 5 seconds in the beginning and the duration be increased gradually and in small measures e.g. 2 to 5 seconds per week.

5. Nevertheless, enfeebling and prolonging either the exhalation or inhalation or both can also give similar benefits as that from suspension, but to a lesser degree. However this is safer and as said, should be practised first. So, all these types of respiratory modifications can be prāṇāyāma as per sūtra II:50.

6. The key-principle of prāṇāyāma seems to be prolongation and consequent subtlization (refining, enfeebling) of the respiratory phases. So as per sūtra II:50 a prolonged and finer exhalation or a prolonged and finer inhalation or a mere (deliberate) suspension of breathing can be a Pātañjala prāṇāyāma.

7. Although Patañjali's wording in sūtra II:50 mentions three types of prāṇāyāma involving a deliberate modification of only one phase of breathing and in sūtra II:51 a fourth variety of prāṇāyāma, which is spontaneous, a sādhaka can advantageously adopt a technique of prāṇāyāma in which all the three phases are controlled and simultaneously made slow and faint. Thus after an adequate preparation i.e. practice of safer prāṇāyāmas without breath-suspension, he can practise the technique where the inhalation and exhalation both are prolonged to the maximum and there are fine both bāhya (external i.e. after full exhalation) and ābhyantara (internal i.e. after inhalation) stambhas (suspensions or so called kuṃbhakas) are also as prolonged as he can safely and comfortably incorporate, keeping in mind the directives in para 4 above.

8. After a very long (may be years') practice of this type of prāṇāyāma the sādhaka may start getting the spontaneous suspension viz. the caturtha prāṇāyāma of Patañjali at some time when his respiratory system gets adequately conditioned. This is the sign of a real mastery over or the perfection in prāṇāyāma.

SS. - **स्वविषयासंप्रयोगे चित्तस्वरूपानुकार इवेन्द्रियाणां प्रत्याहारः ।।२:५४।।**

TL. - sva-viṣayāsaṃprayoge citta - svarūpānukāra ivendriyāṇām pratyāhāraḥ - II:54.

WM. -

sva	=	one's own specific;
viṣaya	=	subject or object;
asaṃprayoga (e)	=	(a = not + sam = complete + pra = thorough+yoga = meeting, uniting) state of not having any contact at all (in);
citta	=	citta;
sva-rūpa	=	one's own form or state or nature;
anu-kāra	=	following, imitating;
iva	=	as if;
indriya (āṇām)	=	indriyas, senses, organs (of, plural);
pratyāhāra (ḥ)	=	Pratyāhāra (prati = towards oneself + āhāra = Pulling, drawing in) i.e. drawing in (of indriyas by citta) towards itself (is).

TR. - Pratyāhāra (is) that condition (of the body and its senses) in which the senses, having no (ability of) contact with the subjects (or objects) of their (specific enjoyment) (they) as if, follow the nature of citta.

CE. - Pratyāhāra is the fifth aṅga (limb or member) of the corpus of Patañjali's eightlimbed (aṣṭāṅga) yoga system. As per sūtra III:7 it is the last aṅga of the bahiraṅga (exoteric) Yoga. In this way it is the borderline between the bahiraṅga and antaraṅga (esoteric) yogas. It can very well be included in antaraṅga yoga also, as it is like a 'No-man's land'. In WM, the break-up of the name is given. Pratyāhāra is thus, related to the citta, its part the mind and its appendages the sense organs. So the specific meaning of the term Pratyāhāra in aṣṭāṅga yoga becomes "Withdrawal of the senses inward towards their source viz. the mind and ultimately the citta" and this is what is explained in the sūtra. When the sādhaka has become adept in Pratyāhāra, the senses, as if, lose the ability to make contact i.e. experience and enjoy the objects and subjects, which are the normal targets or spheres of experiencing and enjoying for them. In this way the senses appear to have been drawn in towards the source of their power of experiencing i.e. getting aware and comprehending viz. the mind and still further in the citta. In a way, they, therefore, take up the form of citta i.e. are merged into it and so have no separate activity or existence outside of citta. As these openings to the external world are not functioning, the mind and citta do not receive any message or communication from any subject or object outside. Evidently this is an essential prerequisite for the further stages of meditation viz. dhāraṇā, dhyāna and samādhi. If the citta goes on receiving distracting messages from the outer world through the agency of senses, there would not be any citta prasādana (pleasant peaceful state of citta) and the citta will never be able to go deep into its own inner recesses,which is what broadly happens during dhāraṇā→dhyāna→samādhi. Therefore for an efficient citttaprasādana achieving of Pratyāhāra to a satisfactory degree is desirable. Considered in this light Pratyāhāra becomes the first step or at least the threshold i.e. almost a part and parcel of meditational process itself.

Patañjali does nowhere clearly state how to achieve Pratyāhāra. The reason is that it, in a way, comes spontaneously as a result of long and sincere practice of the first four aṅgas and particularly of a very long and intensive practice of prāṇāyāma. An indication of this is obtained by the fact that a complete novice, who may not have even heard the name of Yoga or prāṇāyāma, when is taught a technique of prāṇāyāma of any type - may be even Haṭhayogic-and he practises it correctly for some days, it can be observed that his eyelids will have a tendency to droop and the eyes may be closed completely or at least will remain in the usually so called 'ardhonmīlita (half open) or nasāgra (directed to the tip of the nose) dṛṣṭi (gaze). This will happen even when the novice does not know about this effect nor is he told about it, because this is a natural result of prāṇāyāmic breathing. This happens as a preliminary change on the way to Pratyāhāra, because the eye being the most dominant of the five senses and naturally having a shutter like appendage of the eyelid, by closing of which, its activity can be curbed to a great extent, such a closure automatically happens, as it is an essential step for the Pratyāhāra of the sense of vision. Nature has not provided similar shutters or damping devices to the other four senses. But a long and intensive prāṇāyāma practice gradually cuts down the acuity of all the five senses and finally they are so enfeebled that they are not able to receive and respond to outside vibratory or other type of impacts or impulses, which usually stimulate them and so they, do not communicate anything from outside to their master, the mānasendriya (mind-sense). This process of Pratyāhāra is to a very great extent selfactuated and so not much can be deliberately attempted to achieve it, except, as said, a long and intense practice of prāṇāyāma. Nevertheless a wilful effort and a forceful and determined command given by the mind to the senses for not going in search of and indulging in the subjects and objects of their enjoyment and frequent reiterations of these warnings help in curbing to some extent such tendencies of the senses, at least in the initial stages. No doubt, a significant progress and final perfection of Pratyāhāra is accomplished only through intensive practice of prāṇāyāma carried on for some years and really occurs only spontaneously. This is suggested also from the sūtra II:53, as the mind would be fit to enter into dhāraṇā, only if Pratyāhāra of the senses has been achieved to a satisfactory extent.

SS. - **ततः परमा वश्यतेन्द्रियाणाम् ।।२:५५।।**

TL. - tataḥ paramā vaśyatendriyāṇām - II:55.

WM. - tataḥ = from that;

paramā = extreme, highest, complete (Fem. form);

vaśyatā = subjugation, mastery, control;

indriya (āṇām) = indriya, sense (of, plural).

TR. - From that (Pratyāhāra) (results)the complete subjugation of the indriyas (senses).

CE. - The sūtra tells of the practical result of Pratyāhāra and is clear in itself. The total curbing and abolition of the tendency of the senses to have contact and experience of the subjects or objects respectively amenable for perception through them, will be possible only when the senses will be subjugated and obey their controller, the mind (manas) and their ultimate master, the citta. In this state of total mastery, even when the subjects available for their enjoyment are presented respectively to the pertinent senses and may even have a direct contact with them, where it be necessary for perception they lose the ability to perceive and experience those subjects, since the citta of the sādhaka, wanting to have Pratyāhāra, would then not permit them to do so.

That the phenomenon of the senses becoming incapable of perception is feasible even in non-yogic conditions is evident in the insensibility produced in almost all senses by the anaesthetic drugs like ether and chloroform etc. and in tactile sense in the skin-patches in leprosy. The non perception by senses even without such artificial means or abnormal condition of disease, is also a common occurrence, when a person, whose mind is intensely engrossed in a concentrative activity elsewhere, does not see things which take place before his open eyes or does not hear a sound audible to others present in the room and denies to have seen or heard those things, though the pertinent stimuli viz. light or sound waves must have obviously reached and locally influenced his open eyes or ears. From this common experience also it can be understood that the attempts to withdraw the senses deliberately in the initial development of Pratyāhāra would be of help, as suggested above. Probably the Ṣaṇmukhī mudrā recommended in Haṭhayoga is also a deliberate attempt and technique helpful for Pratyāhāra, although Haṭhayogic texts do not clearly mention any such thing.

* * * *

३ विभूति पादः

3 VIBHŪTI PĀDAḤ

(Section of Vibhūtis i. e. Special Developments)

SS. - **देशबन्धश्चित्तस्य धारणा ।।३:१।।**

TL. - deśa-bandhaś-cittasya dhāraṇā - III:1.

WM. -

deśa	=	(1) place, spot, (2) (conceptual) region or sphere;
bandha (ś)	=	binding, fixing, confining;
citta (sya)	=	citta (of);
dhāraṇā	=	dhāraṇā.

TR. - Dhāraṇā (is) confining of citta (1) on a spot; (2) within a limited (conceptual) sphere.

CE. - Please see combined CE. under III:4

SS. - **तत्र प्रत्ययैकतानता ध्यानम् ।।३:२।।**

TL. - tatra pratyayaika-tānatā dhyānam - III:2

WM. -

tatra	=	there, therein;
pratyaya	=	experience or content of citta;
eka-tānatā	=	(eka = one + tānatā + stretchedness) literally a condition of one thing (here the experience or content of citta) stretched long, one-subjectedness or one-pointedness (of citta);
dhyāna (m)	=	dhyāna (is).

TR. - (1)There (on that spot), (2) therein (in the process of dhāraṇā), (to have) a continuous attachment on the experience of one (single subject) (is) dhyāna.

CE. - Please see combined CE. under III:4

SS. - **तदेवार्थमात्रनिर्भासं स्वरूपशून्यमिव समाधिः ।।३:३।।**

TL. - tad-evārtha-mātra-nirbhāsaṃ sva-rūpa-śūnyam-iva samādhiḥ - III:3.

WM. -

tat(d)	=	that;
eva	=	itself;
artha	=	essence, reality;
mātra	=	mere, only;
nirbhāsa (ṃ)	=	(niḥ (r) = deep+bhāsa=view, vision) clear vision or perception (is);
svarūpa	=	(sva = one's own+rupa = form) one's own i.e. original form or appearance;
śūnya (m)	=	void, devoid (is);
iva	=	as if, almost;
samādhi (ḥ)	=	samādhi (is).

TR. - That (dhyāna) itself (is transformed into) samādhi (when the subject) is devoid of its original form (and yet) is clearly perceived (experienced) in its mere essence.

CE. - Please see combined CE . under III:4.

SS. - **त्रयमेकत्र संयमः ।।३:४।।**

TL. - trayam-ekatra saṃyamaḥ - III:4

WM. - traya (m) = the three, triad (is);
ekatra = (1) at one spot;
(2) together, simultaneous;
saṃyama (ḥ) = saṃyama (is).

TR. - The three (i.e. dhāraṇā, dhyāna and samādhi), (1) at one spot (i.e. on one subject); (2) together (become) saṃyama.

CE. - Though the second pāda is named Sādhana-pāda, strangely the most important of the Sādhanas, which here are aṣṭāṅgas, are enumerated in the first three sūtras of Vibhūti-pāda. Looking in this way the discussion of all the eight aṅgas ends at the eighth sūtra of this pāda and so the Sādhana-pāda should end at this eighth sūtra and the Vibhūti-pāda should begin from the ninth sūtra onwards. It is not very clear why Patañjali has ended the Sādhana pāda, as it is found at present in all the versions of Yoga Sūtra. This anomaly has led many scholars to opine that the original arrangement and division into pādas of Pātañjala Yoga Sūtras might have been different, when they were compiled by Patañjali and probably later some editors might have altered the arrangement in various ways. This might have probably occurred more than once, leading to the present, somewhat irregular, arrangement. The only explanation for such irregularities seems to be that the word 'pāda' used for these sections means a 'leg' or 'foot' and the idea behind this is a 'stable stand or foundation'. Then the four legs should be of similar length just like the four legs of an animal. To have such equalization, some sūtras of the Sādhana pāda might have been taken into the next pāda describing Vibhūtis. However, this is also not a very satisfactory explanation, since the fourth i.e. Kaivalyapāda is of much shorter length than the others and even the first i.e. Samādhipāda contains four sūtras less than the fifty five each in the Second and the Third pādas.

The three last aṅgas, out of the aṣṭāṅgas, consisting of the different stages of the meditational i.e. inward going process of the citta viz. dhāraṇā, dhyāna and samādhi, are essentially consecutive. This is clearly indicated by the first word in each of the sūtras of dhyāna and samādhi (III:2 and 3), which also show that the earlier one of these three is transformed and culminated into the next stage. This is further supported by the statement of the fourth sūtra :- 'The three (processes), when together, result into saṃyama'. In other words saṃyama is a composite of these three processes and so they must come one after another in the order mentioned in the sūtras. Vedāntic people often enumerate this trio as dhyāna-dhāraṇā-samādhi, but according to Patañjali's description dhāraṇā leads to dhyāna i.e. dhyāna is a state of greater concentration and penetration than dhāraṇā. Very probably the precise notions behind these two terms in Vedānta are quite different than those in Pātañjala Yoga and other Yoga Schools.

Dhāraṇā is defined as deśabandha-cittasya i.e. binding or fixing the deśa i.e. a region of the citta. The older commentators have interpreted deśa as a (physical) spot or place. But deśa gives an idea of a rather wide sprawling expanse or region, while the words spot or place have a notion of comparatively a narrower expanse. Therefore to interpret deśa as a spot or place is not very precise. Moreover the earlier commentators have stipulated that this spot is a physical spot, such as an object, particularly and preferably a suitable part or organ of the body e.g. hṛdaya (heart), bhrū-madhya (midbrow), mūrdhnā (apex of the cranium) etc. This interpretation again seems erroneous, because further it has been suggested by them that after choosing such a spot for directing the citta i.e. attention or awareness, on such a spot in dhāraṇā, the sādhaka may choose another subject for dhyāna, which should plreferably be a deity i.e. an image of a god or goddess of one's own devotion. But the processes of dhāraṇā, dhyāna and samādhi are the ones, in which the citta or awareness is to go on becoming more and more concentrated and ultimately one-pointed and further even to transcend this one pointedness. The state of dhyāna has been described as of pratyayaikatānatā. Now if such a continuously prolonged uniform consciousness of one single content (i.e. subject) in citta is to be achieved in dhyāna, when it will be successfully achieved, obviously the citta can have in it only one subject. When this is the aim to be achieved, then there is no sense in having one subject e.g. a body part for dhāraṇā and having another subject e.g. the image of the deity for dhyāna. It is, in fact, an absurd directive, contrary to the purpose. It will be impossible to have awareness of a single subject, if the citta is made to be aware of two different subjects simultaneously viz. one i.e. the spot, for dhāraṇā and another i.e. the deity, for dhyāna. Indeed, even if the sādhaka tries to do this, when and if at all he goes into a state of real dhyāna, as defined in the sūtra III:2, only one pratyaya (i.e. content or subject in the citta) will persist in his consciousness, may be either the subject (i.e. spot) chosen for dhāraṇā or that (deity) for dhyāna. For this reason deśa cannot be a spot on which the citta is to be directed. It then is to be interpreted in some different manner. Looking at the whole purpose and the nature of these 'inward going processes' the proper meaning of deśa seems to be an internal conceptual region or sphere.

Patañjali's sūtras do not stipulate anything about the nature of the subjects to be chosen for these meditational processes. From the above discussion, the only conclusion about the choice of the subject seems to be that it should be essentially and always one and the same for all the three aṅgas. Nevertheless it is naturally to be expected and is also advisable that the subject chosen is one which will help the sādhaka in attaching and concentrating his citta on it without effort. So a subject for which the sādhaka has a natural liking or rather a deep devotion e.g. a god or goddess for which he has the highest devotion or his guru or some such other saint would be facilitatory for the objective of the meditation.

Now when the sādhaka chooses such a subject, say for example Rāma, the natural thing that he is expected to do in the first stage of meditation i.e. dhāraṇā (which literally means 'the process of holding' here, in the citta) and savitarkā samāpatti, as explained under sūtras I:42 and 43, (See also the articles by this commentator (1) "Saṃyama" and (2)"Meditational Processes in Pātañjala Yoga Sūtras (P.Y.S.)", in Yoga Mīmāṃsā Journal, respectively in Vol. XV, No. 2, pp. 1-16, 1972 and Vol. XX, Nos. 1 and 2, pp. 81-99, 1981 and Chart I after p. 124 in this commentary) will be a process of thinking in some manner in the usual way about this subject

Rāma. The ideas or thoughts, that will appear in his mind on account of the habitual usage by the mind of words (śabda → artha → pratyaya → jñāna vikalpaiḥ saṃkīrṇā, I:42 and III:17), will be tainted by vitarkaful (evil) saṃskāras coming up from the karmāśaya part of citta on account of these getting falsely linked to the subject Rāma, due to the preconceptions and associations about Rāma, already existing in the sādhaka's mind. In the beginning, when he will try to keep his mind and citta attached to the subject in such a thinking manner, on account of the natural fickleness of the mind, it will very soon leave the subject and very probably will be thinking of something else, not at all connected with Rāma in the least manner. This is the most usual experience of any novice, who starts an attempt at meditation.

After a few days of such attempts of concentrating the mind, the wandering of the citta lessens. It may so happen that now, though the citta still wanders, yet the thoughts and ideas that arise in the citta have always some connection with the subject Rāma. Thus, though the mind is wandering the awareness about Rāma is always present in the background, uninterrupted even for a moment. When such a state is reached, then only it can properly be called dhāraṇā. The simile of a vagrant animal tied to a post by a chain or rope can very aptly be given to this happening. Now that animal can thereafter move only in a limited region and is always bound with the post and can never get disconnected from the post and go away anywhere or any distance from it. A definite circle, whose radius is the length of the chain and centre is the post, becomes the region fixed for the movement of the animal. The circumference of this circle would be the boundary of this sphere of movement. A similar thing occurs in the process of dhāraṇā also. And this is what is meant by deśa-bandha i.e. binding or confining the region of the movement of citta i.e. limiting the conceptual sphere of citta's movement. Thus, if Rāma is the subject chosen by the sādhaka for his meditation and if this Rāma is the well-known Rāma, as usually understood to be the son of Daśaratha, the king of Ayodhyā etc., during the earliest stages of meditation the sādhaka will and may think of this Rāma in any number of possible ways, depending upon the preconceptions, which he may have in his mind about this Rāma. At first, probably even within a few seconds, his mind may wander away into thinking of some other thing, totally alien to Rāma, e.g. he may begin thinking of a bazaar, a railway platform or some such other things. But later, as the wandering of citta is curbed to some extent, his mind may have different thoughts, but such thought will be in someway or other connected with Rāma. He may thus be thinking of Sītā, Hanumāna, Lakṣmaṇa, Vanavāsa (forest-residing), father's extreme love for son, son's highest devotion and unquestioned obedience to the parents, brotherly affection and attachment etc., all these ideas constantly related to Rāma. Nay, his mind may even be thinking of bazaar, but even in that he may be thinking of a temple of Rāma, where the idol of Rāma is very beautiful and very much to his liking. Thus each and every idea that arises in his mind has always to do something with Rāma and so Rāma is the central or background point of his mind's activity. Then the duration for which such unbroken awareness of Rāma is present in the mind for that much duration dhāraṇā persists.

It may and most often does happen that the ideas, which may arise in the mind in this first part of dhāraṇā, involving savitarkā samāpatti, are associated with undesirable or evil things, as already explained under the sūtras of samāpatti and elsewhere (cf. I. 42 ,43 and above). This trend of evil thoughts appearing in meditation from the past evil saṃskāras (or in modern terminology, from evil preassociations) has been seen even with sādhakas, whose current life is very good, virtuous and pious, even when they were meditating with very pure and sacred subjects like the deities or very holy saints. The explanation of this phenomenon is also given (ibid) to which also the reader may again refer. A number of such well-meaning sādhakas have mentioned of such a disturbance or hindrance occurring in their meditation, which perplexed and depressed them and they wanted a clarification and guidance. The explanation given here and elsewhere (cf. as above) about the whole process of meditation satisfied them and removed their discouragement and they were able to proceed successfully to further stages of meditation, even to a real state of 'dhyāna' as per Patañjali's definition (III:2). When this appearance of evil thoughts (vitarkas) is overcome by the process of meditation itself, as already explained, the sādhaka enters the next part of dhāraṇā, which is the nirvitarkā samāpatti, where the evil or 'vaitarkika' aspect of the thoughts and ideas is almost and ultimately totally removed. This nirvitarkā samāpatti is the dividing region, or the so-called 'No-man's land', in between the savitarkā and savicārā samāpatti sub-stages or portions of dhāraṇā. After the citta (i.e. its saṃskāra or smṛti storehouse = Karmāśaya part) is totally voided of evil-saṃskāras i.e. is purified from virtarkas or has transcended the sphere of virtarkas, begins now the sphere of vicāras i.e. only good thoughts (N.B. vicāra itself implies goodness of thought; the prefix 'su' or 'ku' is joined to it only when emphasis on respectively goodness is to be given in contradistinction to evilness) desirable for a yogasādhaka appear in the mind. This is the savicārā samāpatti part or substage of dhāraṇā. As the citta goes further inwards in its journey, the vicāras also dwindle and finally become extinct. This is the nirvicārā samāpatti which forms the last portion or substage of dhāraṇā.

As already explained the thinking activity of the mind comes to an end here. Thereafter the citta has only an awareness of a feeling of joy or bliss and further that of one's pure being-ness (or existing), which are indicated by the words ānanda and asmitā respectively in sūtra I:17.

As per sūtra I:46 the four samāpatti-s lead to and culminate into samādhi, while as per the present sūtras III: 1,2,3 in between dhāraṇā and samādhi intervenes the state of dhyāna. From this we have to infer that the state of dhyāna, as defined in III:2, is reached somewhere at the later part of the nirvicārā samāpatti process (cf. Chart after p. 124).

The definition of dhyāna is 'pratyaya-ekatānatā' i.e. 'an unbroken continuously stretched awareness of a very precisely uniform experience of the subject', chosen for these meditational processes. The consciousness about the subject should be so uniformly exactly the same throughout the process of dhyāna that there should not be even a minutest variation in this awareness or cognition of the subject. Evidently, therefore, this will be a pure consciousness of the pleasant existing or 'blissful beingness' of the subject will be thus untenable with the notion of pratyayaikatānatā i.e. with the state of dhyāna. That means, there will be no thinking activity at all about the subject during dhyāna, since any thinking or ideation will at once lead to the possibility of an alteration, at least in some slight manner of this ideation. If the alteration occurs it will mean the breaking of the pratyayaikatānatā, which will mean interruption of dhyāna, which will be then again a regression back to dhāraṇā state. From this, we can conclude that the dhyāna is achieved when nirvicāra samāpatti is near to its perfection. This state of thoughtless i.e. idealess consciousness of pure pleasure-giving existence (in the citta) of the subject of meditation however persists for fairly long time. Ultimately it is transformed into a samādhi, which is sabīja, as is clearly indicated by sūtras III:3 and 8.

In the above discussion, it is implied that the process of dhāraṇā culminates and is transformed into dhyāna. This is also indicated by the first word 'tatra' in sūtra III:2 of dhyāna. The meaning of this word has also been wrongly understood by the former commentators on account of misunderstanding about the meaning of the word deśa. They interpret this word tatra (= there) to mean 'in that spot', on which the citta is to be fixed in dhāraṇā. But it has already been shown above, how directing citta on a given spot, which is thus the subject for dhāraṇā, and also on another subject to be chosen for dhyāna cannot lead to pratyaya-ekatānatā, or if and when the latter be attained, either the spot for dhāraṇā or the subject for dhyāna can alone remain in consciousness i.e. be the pratyaya (content) of citta. So 'tatra' here means 'in that dhāraṇā.' So then, the sūtra III:2 means that 'there i.e. in that dhāraṇā, when pratyaikatānatā i.e. uninterrupted experience of one subject (exactly same all through) is extended over a long duration, it is dhyāna. Thus dhyāna is clearly a culmination and transformation of dhāraṇā.

Continuing the simile of the vagrant animal bound to a post, the state of dhyāna can be equated to the state of the animal when the tying rope is made so short that the animal is tightly bound directly to the post itself. There is no slack in the rope and the animal cannot move away from the post even slightly. The same is the case of citta in relation to the subject of dhyāna. This process of transformation of dhāraṇā into dhyāna is slow and prolonged and the progression can be compared to a gradual shortening of the length of the rope till it becomes zero. Thus during the transformation of dhāraṇā into dhyāna gradually the extent of deśa i.e. the sphere of movement of the citta round about the subject of meditation, goes on becoming lesser and lesser and ultimately one pointedness is reached, when the citta is fixed upon the central core of the subject i.e. the first glimpse of the reality of the blissfulness lying behind the subject is achieved, the process culminates into dhyāna.

A very apt example of the mental state akin to dhyāna is the state of concentration in Arjuna's mind in the well-known story in the Mahābhārata epic. The guru Droṇācārya had fixed a wooden parrot on a tree and was asking each of his pupils in archery to take an aim on the eye of the bird for shooting his arrow exactly in it. After the student was ready to shoot, Droṇācārya asked him what he could see. Some said they were seeing the bird affixed on the tree, others were seeing the bird only and so on. But Arjuna could see the centre of the bird's eye only, not the tree, nor the bird nor even its whole eye. This is what should happen in dhyāna. Arjuna's reply shows that most probably he was not even conscious that what he was seeing was an eye of a wooden bird and that the bird was resting on a tree. He was not thinking in any way either of the eye, the bird, the surroundings, the circumstances etc. He was conscious only of the presence of a point, the centre of the bird's eye. Surely 'svarūpa' i.e. the form of the thing as a point was present in his consciousness. The 'svarūpa-śunyatā' i.e. dissolution of form, the characteristic of the start of sabīja samādhi (sūtra III:3) was not yet reached, but pratyayaikatānatā was certainly achieved.

From this, it can be seen that this dhyāna according to Patañjali is a very precise state about the experience (pratyaya) and comprehension or knowledge (jñāna) of the chosen subject. It is not any state where some kind of contemplation or deep thinking about the subject is going on in the mind, which activity is often loosely and popularly called dhyāna and is often translated by such words as concentration, contemplation and more often meditation etc. This contemplative activity is involving the śabda (word)-artha (meaning)-jñāna (knowledge) vikalpas, as mentioned in the sūtra I:42 and is a process, which according to Patañjali's descriptions belongs to the category of samāpattis viz. savitarkā and savicārā samāpattis. But in dhyāna the vikalpas of words etc., which become hindrances into the state of dhyāna, disappear and the state of dhyāna is not of thinking in the usual manner (as is implicit in the English words meditation etc. used to translate the word dhyāna), but of experiencing a subtle essence or reality behind the subject. Therefore, as has been stressed, Patañjali's dhāraṇā, dhyāna and samādhi are sharply defined states and these designations, therefore, are to be treated as technical terms of the discipline of Yoga having precise meaning and should not be translated loosely by such English words.

The word 'tadeva' meaning 'that also' or 'that itself', in the sūtra III:3, shows that 'that dhyāna itself becomes i.e. is transformed into samādhi', defined by that sūtra. The description of this samādhi is practically the same as that of nirvitarkā samāpatti, given in sūtra I:43 and as per sūtra I:44, also applicable to nirvicārā samāpatti, with the only difference that the two phrases in the description interchange their position in this sūtra and are in neuter gender in this sūtra as against those in the sūtra I:43, in which they are in feminine gender. The difference in the gender form is because in sūtra I:43 the phrases qualify the feminine gendered subject (nirvitarkā) samāpatti, while here (sūtra III:3) they are used to describe samādhi, a masculine noun.

The description here of the samādhi, which is the transformation and culmination of dhyāna, is arthamātra nirbhāsam and svarūpa-śūnyam-iva. 'Arthamātra nirbhāsa' means clear perception of mere essence behind the form having qualities of the subject, chosen for meditation. The second phrase 'svarūpa-śūnyam-iva' amplifies further this meaning of the first phrase by saying that the svarūpa i.e. the original form and appearance of the subject becomes almost extinct. Therefore, the subject is now perceived or experienced in its usual way that it is experienced in our empirical life, but is experienced or comprehended or better still 'realized' in its subtle essence or reality, which is lying behind it.

As said, this description is almost identical to that of nirvitarkā and nirvicārā samāpattis. As explained there, the perfection and culmination of nirvicārā samāpatti is the state of sabīja samādhi and in fact the description is not so much of samāpatti, but rather of this samādhi variety. This is quite confirmed by this sūtra, III:3 which is explicitly of samādhi. Again from sūtra III:7 and 8, it is clear that this samādhi is sabīja samādhi. From this it can be concluded that the states of dhāraṇā and dhyāna are coexistent with the processes of the four samāpattis. Dhāraṇā comprises of the two vitrarkā related samāpattis, savicārā samāpatti and the earlier portion of nirvicārā samāpatti. Dhyāna comprises of the later part of nirvicārā samāpatti. When the thinking comes to an end, at the endpoint of nirvicārā samāpatti, begins the sabīja samādhi. In this way as per sūtra I:46, the four samāpattis end into sabīja samādhi, which is the same as to say that dhāraṇā and dhyāna culminate into sabīja samādhi and so there is no disconsonance in the two statements of sūtra I:46 and III:3, 7 and 8. (cf. Chart after p. 124).

The sūtra III:4 defines a technique and a process called 'saṃyama', which as per the sūtra "is made up of the three together". These three are evidently the preceding three meditative states of dhāraṇā, dhyāna and (sabīja) samādhi. Now, as per the sūtras and the discussion above, these three states are consecutive, the earlier one transforming into the next. What is therefore, meant by the word 'ekatra' i.e. together ? Any three distinctly different and consecutive states cannot become together i.e. simultaneous. The older commentators have tried to explain the word ekatra in a completely different way. The words like ekatra (in one place), anyatra (in another place), ending in the suffix 'tra' usually are related to a spot or place. As explained, they have opined that two different subjects viz. a place for dhāraṇā and a god etc. for dhyāna (and samādhi) can be chosen by the sādhaka for meditation. (No one has suggested that two different subjects, one for dhyāna and another for samādhi could be chosen. All agree that for these two the subject must be one and the same). Consequently they interpret the word ekatra to mean that in saṃyama the dhāraṇā, dhyāna and samādhi should be in one place i.e. the subject of the three should be one and the same. Naturally it becomes a question- why this simple modification of having one and the same subject for the whole process of meditation instead of different subjects for its components dhāraṇā, dhyāna (and samādhi) should need a different technical designation for modified process ? Does the process become so drastically different? This is not the case. They, therefore, explain the need for this new designation 'saṃyama' on the ground that this phenomenon has to be mentioned again and again in the further discussion of vibhūtis and to avoid the difficulty of mentioning the combination of these three each time, Patañjali has introduced the new brief word for the three states. But this is not a satisfactory explanation. Instead of coining a new technical term Patañjali could and would have used the nontechnical common word 'antaraṅga' (= internal part, core etc.) which he has also mentioned for the three in sūtra III:7.

When a sādhaka practises dhāraṇā, dhyāna and samādhi, as clarified before, the subject chosen for all three of them must always be necessarily one and the same. Even when the sādhaka has become quite adept at these, so as to have good dhāraṇā and have it transformed into dhyāna and this latter into samādhi, at first he will require a long time to accomplish these transformations. But as this abhyāsa will be continued day after day, he will become more and more efficient in his meditation and the three processes become smooth and easy for him. Consequently the time duration required for transforming these meditational stages successively into the following stages would become smaller and smaller. When the sādhaka will have perfection or real mastery over the complete process, the time for each stage will be shortened to such an extent that the dhāraṇā will be instantly changed into dhyāna and so also dhyāna will be instantly transformed into samādhi. Thus, though actually the whole process of meditation will proceed through all these three inevitably essential stages of dhāraṇā→ dhyāna→samādhi, the sādhaka will have a feeling and experience that his citta has at once attained the samādhi state, as if without passing through the stages of dhāraṇā and dhyāna.

In other words the dhāraṇā and dhyāna, as it were, get merged into and become one with samādhi, that is they become almost simultaneous i.e. 'together'. This togetherness or apparent merger of the three actually different processes into virtually one happens, as said, only when the sādhaka has a complete mastery over the whole process. This mastery is such that the sādhaka can go into samādhi in one instant. That means the whole process is fully under his control and therefore it is quite apt to designate such a mastery over the process by the term 'saṃyama' = complete control.

In this third, Vibhūti-pāda Patañjali states that application of saṃyama, choosing different subjects for this process, leads to the production of a number of Vibhūtis. These Vibhūtis are some sort of knowledges or powers which appear to be miraculous. Another word commonly used for such miraculous powers is siddhi. Patañjali has himself used this word in this sense in the sūtras III:37 and IV: 1. There is a difference between the word vibhūti and the word siddhi. At least Patañjali seems to make a distinction between the two. In this vibhūti-pāda he has mentioned about thirty different subjects to which the application of saṃyama can produce about fifty five vibhūtis. These vibhūtis are, thus, produced only through Yoga and by a definite rule i.e. by a scientific law of application of the process of saṃyama. In other words these vibhūtis are definite results of a law known to the science of Yoga, albeit they appear like some astounding supernormal powers. On the other hand siddhis are results produced also by some processes other than Yoga (IV: 1) not understood by the science (of yoga) and so mysterious or as if magical. Other distinguishing features are that vibhūtis are a definite happening in the progress of Yoga. Since they appear at a fairly advanced stage in the progress in Yoga, the yogī has a high level of vairāgya developed in himself and he, therefore, will not exploit the power of these vibhūtis for any selfish worldly gain. They, therefore, do not become hindrances in the path of his yogīc development. On the contrary, some of these (III: 38 to 55) are positively helpful in this development. In fact Patañjali seems to think some to be essential prerequisite (III:44, 48, 49, 50, 52, 55) for attaining Kaivalya. Siddhis, on the contrary, are always exploited for some worldly and most often selfish benefit. They, for this reason, become hindrances or retarders in the progress in Yoga, which fact is very popularly known and also stressed by Patañjali (III:37). it need be clarified here that the earlier commentators have not fully recognised the great cautiousness of Patañjali in using the technical words with utmost exactitude and so have not given much importance to the fact that Patañjali has used the word vibhūti as quite different in sense from siddhi. They have on the contrary understood these as totally synonymous and so used them quite interchangeably without any discrimination. So almost all of them have said that vibhūtis, being siddhis, are hindrances in the Yoga path, which again is their interpretation of sūtra III:37. But this is erroneous as will be seen in the explanations of that sūtra below. If what they say is true then it is a question as to : - 'Why has Patañjali gone to so much trouble in recommending as many as thirty or so subjects (alambanas) for practising saṃyama upon them and giving the description, in details, of the vibhūtis resulting from them, if these latter are really hindrances to the progress in yoga ?' This point has struck some of these commentators such as Taimni and others. They try to reply to this objection by stating that these vibhūtis, if at all, serve the only purpose of adjudging the rate and magnitude of the progress on the path of Yoga, just as the milestones on a road. They need not and better should not be attempted to be achieved. It is best for a yogī, really interested only in attaining Kaivalya, to avoid them totally. We feel that if the gaining of vibhūtis were so harmful, Patañjali would have totally omitted their mention or if at all, he would have, as a good śāstrakāra (scientific expounder), thought it obligatory not to omit the mention of such a remarkable phenomenon and important technique for it, he would have done it comparatively briefly. Certainly then, he would not have spoken in such almost a commendatory manner about these, giving so many ālambanas (topics) for performing saṃyama and stating all the harmful (?) resultant vibhūtis in details. In our opinion, already expressed, vibhūtis are not detrimental to Yoga as siddhis can be. They are, some at least, helpful for yogī's progress and a few almost essential, as said by Patañjali himself, for attainment of Kaivalya.

The word vibhūti, made up as :- vi = viśeṣeṇa = Particularly, in a special manner + bhūti, from root bhū = to become, with suffix 'ti', indicative of a process, thus literally means a state of special development, which also means that it is a development, which is possible to have by any man, who makes necessary proper efforts for the same in the prescribed manner. The word vibhūti has been used by Bhagvadgītā also practically in the same sense in the tenth adhyāya.

A question is often raised as to whether these vibhūtis can be really produced and that also through application of saṃyama. It should be noted that out of the fifty five or so vibhūtis mentioned by Patañjali in this pāda, the larger number are those, which are some sort of knowledge. The remaining ones, which seem like some miraculous powers, are also abilities, which a person gains, because he has acquired the knowledge of a nature's law not known to the most of humanity, by application of which he can achieve some results, which cannot be rationally understood by others, who are ignorant of that law working behind them and for this reason they are only magic or miracle for them. Just as any modern inventions like electric gadgets, radio, television, aeroplane etc. may and even do appear as miracles to an aboriginal, who might have lived all his life in a forest or desert, completely untouched by any thing of modern civilization, but are quite well understood and so quite ordinary for a man living in the modern civilized society, these vibhūtis are miraculous for a non-yogī, but are quite natural for a yogī, who has mastery over the technique of saṃyama. It may also be noted that a yogī, who might have a mastery over saṃyama and so can experience a vibhūti, when he performs saṃyama on the subject proper for the appearance of that vibhūti, even when he has no desire for having that vibhūti or who may operate that vibhūti by deliberately performing saṃyama on the proper subject, may still not be able himself to explain the whole mechanism of the phenomenon fully, just as a man operating a T.V. set or radio may not himself be able to explain the complete working and principles of these gadgets. Yet both of them are getting results, which seem miraculous to a person totally unacquainted with these phenomena, which are happening or working quite according to definite natural laws, well known to the adepts of the respective science, but of which the other person has no inkling at all.

Saṃyama produces the respective vibhūtis, when applied to various subjects (ālambanas) as recommended in the subsequent sūtras of this Vibhūti-pāda. The list of vibhūtis given here is not exhaustive. Other similar type of vibhūtis can result by applying saṃyama in a similar manner to other kinds of subjects, which a yogasādhaka may choose for the application of saṃyama and so the number of possible vibhūtis is infinitely large. Patañjali has only mentioned some important ones. Some of them, though to a very great extent of mundane importance and use, may still be of some use even to a sādhaka having merely spiritual interest and ideal. Some few, as said, are definitely helpful and two or so (sūtras III:49, 50 and 52 to 55) at least essential prerequisites for kaivalya, as shown above.

Since the vibhūtis are the results of the working of a definite natural law of the science of Yoga, when the sādhaka chooses a particular subject for the meditation and if the sādhaka is already an adept at saṃyama, his meditation will be automatically of the saṃyama grade and then the pertinent vibhūtis will necessarily appear as per this law, whether the yoga-sādhaka wants these or not. For example : the sādhaka, interested solely in spiritual development and Realization, also often chooses the Sun as the subject for his meditation, as it is an ālambana (= viṣaya, subject) which is highly revered as one of the best symbol of Divinity and so looked upon as a very valued help for spiritual development. If the sādhaka is adept at saṃyama, as soon as he starts to meditate i.e. begins dhāraṇā on the Sun, it at once is transformed into dhyāna and sabīja samādhi, accomplishing the saṃyama on the Sun. Then as per sūtra III:26 the vibhūti of bhuvanajñāna (knowledge of all the worlds) will come to him definitely, but this sādhaka will ignore the vibhūti and will try to proceed further into nirbīja and dharmamegha samādhis and through these finally to kaivalya. On the other hand, if the sādhaka has not a very advanced vairāgya (i.e. Vaśīkāra) and so gets involved in exploiting the vibhūti of bhuvanajñāna for some worldly benefit, there is a very great chance, nay almost a certainty, that the enticements of worldly gains of pleasure, power etc., which usually accrue in such uses of the vibhūtis, will entangle him into mundane affairs forever and he may totally forget the real goal of Yoga i.e. of attaining kaivalya. The vibhūti then becomes a siddhi. The sūtra III:37 indicates this and cautions against this possibility.

The second question as to whether saṃyama can yield the claimed resultant vibhūtis, which appear almost to be unbelievable, the reply can be in most of the cases in the affirmative and the phenomena can easily be understood by some parallel examples from the mundane spheres. Very probably the highest achievements in various spheres of activities of the humanity, which are, often and quite aptly, called divine, are a result of a process, which is, if not actually saṃyama, very much akin to it. All the works of divinely sublime poetry, painting, sculpture and, may be even science, have been accomplished by the respective individual authors of these, when the individual had knowingly or unknowingly gone into a state very similar to saṃyama. In this respect, some well-known examples of discovery in the sphere of physical sciences are very remarkable, where the known facts clearly show that the process was, as it were, of saṃyama, though the concerned person might not have been at all conversant with the meditative processes of dhāraṇā, dhyāna and samādhi, at least may not be deliberately following these techniques with a proper understanding about these. Those examples are of Archemedes, Newton and Kekule, who have discovered laws or principles, which have been recognised after them. If we take into consideration the fact and sequences of the happenings, one commonness is found in all of these cases. The discoverer of the scientific law or principle had devoted a lot of time and energy to find out the solution to a tough problem in the science that was facing before him. After a long time and mental efforts, he had come to feel that the solution was beyond him, at least under the then existing limiting circumstances. He, therefore, gave up the attempt and was in a relaxed condition of mind, when he was not giving least attention to the problem. At such a moment of complete effortlessness, the solution, as if, exploded in his mind.

Archemedes was told by his patron king to find out the proportion of dross in the gold of the royal crown, without damaging the crown in the slightest degree. If he could not give the answer, dire consequences would have resulted for him. For this reason, he had been very intensively concentrating on finding a method to do what the king wanted him to do. For a long time, probably for some months, he could not find any way to get the answer. Then, as the story goes, he was taking a bath, a thing which a person does very often to overcome tiredness and at least when he is not doing any serious thinking, when the answer, as if, flashed into his mind very clearly. The happening was so stunning for him that completely forgetting the circumstances, he ran on the street, shouting 'Eureka eureka' (I have found it.) in a totally naked state. This whole description shows that the famous Principle of Archemedes was inspired to its author in some mysterious and perhaps divine manner, rather than it having been thought out by him in active deliberation and not being a result of his conscious effort.

Details of the story about Newton are not known as extensively. But it can be safely assumed that he was perplexed about the forces regulating the movements of stars and planets and was trying to find out the laws governing these movements for a long time. He is said to have got the answer, while he was sitting in his garden, when he saw an apple falling from a tree. He must have been taking rest and relaxing in the garden, when, obviously he was, for the time being, not deliberating about the problem and merely saw the falling of that apple quite unconcernedly, i.e. with sākṣībhāva (= mere witness-attitude) according to Yoga terminology. This we can conclude from the fact that this was not the first time that he was seeing a fruit falling to the ground. This was a simple occurrence, which might be one out of thousands of similar observations, which he must have made upto then. But the story is told in such a way, as though this single observation led him suddenly to visualize a very important scientific principle. This description again shows that the phenomenon was a case of inspiration, which suddenly flashed in his mind, when he was not at all thinking about the matter and was more or less in a relaxed mood.

The above two stories, though probably historically true, are somewhat like legends. But the story about Kekule's discovery of the structural molecular formula of benzene is a very precisely recorded historical fact. Benzene is the foundation stone or the parent material of a whole class of chemically synthesized substances. The branch of chemistry, which deals with these substances is that of aromatic organic chemistry, which has given us many valuable drugs and other synthetic or natural products used in almost all industries and useful in many ways to man. In fact the modern civilization would have been very much poorer without these substances. The need of the knowledge about the exact arrangement of the atoms of carbon and hydrogen in the molecule of benzene was, therefore, very essential for the progress of this particular branch of chemistry. Particularly Kekule, who was a German, and other German chemists had a most pressing urgency in this respect, because political leaders of Germany were expecting that they will have to go to war with Britain for some world power situation of the time. They were also aware that the war would not remain an affair limited to these two adversaries, but that many or most of the other prominent nations would be implicated, getting allied to either side. In such a situation Germany would be at a great disadvantage. It had to import many things - commodities most essential for life as well as for carrying out a long war-from other distant countries. Many of these were under British rule or under the rule of other nations, who were expected to enter the war as allies of Britain. For this reason and as Germany had no free access to the sea nor a navy as powerful as Britain, Germany would have found it almost impossible to continue the war even for a few months, as the supplies of many commodities essential for this would be completely stopped and stocks of these could not last beyond those few months. So the German Government had issued a secret directive to all chemists that they should discover methods by which all such products could be synthesised from raw sources which could be easily available to Germany even after the start of war with Britain and its probable would-be allies. As said benzene held a very crucial (strategic ?) position in this respect and so the knowledge about its structure became a dire urgency for Germany. Because with this only it would become possible to synthesize those essential commodities. Kekule, being among the topmost chemists, felt a great responsibility and obligation to find out benzene's structure. He, along with other chemists all the world over, was trying for a long time to determine this structure of benzene. But all his endeavours were of no avail. Ultimately he reached such a point of despondence that he began to feel that the problem could not be solved by him during his life time. He, therefore, decided to give up the quest totally. On the very night that he came to this conclusion, he got a dream in his sleep, which was repeated exactly in the same manner several times during that night. In this dream he saw six snakes, each one holding the tail of the other, in front of it, in its mouth, the whole forming a closed hexagon. Since this was a strange vision and the dream was repeated several times, Kekule, after waking up in the morning, was perplexed by the queerness of the dream and was uneasily and very vaguely puzzling as to whether the dream had some meaning. It is a recorded and authentic fact that while he was taking his breakfast and at that time was completely unconcerned with even the deciphering of the dream, suddenly it became quite clear like a flash of inspiration in his mind that what was revealed to him in that strange vision of the dream, was the solution of the problem, which he had given up as insoluble in a frustration. Thus he had, so to say, a revelation of the hexagonal ring formula of benzene molecule. Here again we see the same chain of events repeated as in the other two legends. The person is very actively and seriously deliberating for a long time to find the answer to a problem. He is exhausted and gives up the problem as insoluble. Since the efforts have been given up, he is relaxed and now is not at all thinking of the problem. In this state intuitionally the knowledge, he was seeking, is revealed to him in a flash of inspiration.

These stories explain to some extent the mechanism or chain of happenings, through which even the knowledges mentioned in the vibhūtis of this third pāda as well as other similar ones become intuitionally revealed to the yoga sādhaka on account of the arise of the ṛtaṃbharāprajñā at the start of sabīja samādhi (as per sūtra I:48). As explained, the stages of dhāraṇā and dhyāna each last for a long period before attainment of the stage of sabīja samādhi, in the earlier days of this abhyāsa. But these time durations go on shortening with progress and facilitation in these techniques and ultimately disappear almost completely, when the whole process becomes instantaneous and the stage of saṃyama is reached. The long time-durations during the early days of abhyāsa are an indication of a deliberate effort of the citta to concentrate and focus its grasping power on the subject chosen for meditation and the disappearance of the time durations is consequently a clear indication of the total absence of effort during saṃyama. In this effortless state the citta is able to transcend the barriers which are keeping it away from the reality behind that subject and then the citta is able to comprehend that reality gradually in stages. In penetrating upto this reality the citta inevitably grasps every aspect of the knowledge of that subject, a part of which is more of an empirical nature and the vibhūti that is gained is of this category. As already said the spiritual sādhaka is conscious of the secondary nature of this empirical knowledge and so he relinquishes it and tries to grasp only that which is of prime value to him. We had to use the words like comprehending, grasping, knowledge, experience etc., because these are the only words, which are nearabout in the sense, which we want to communicate. But indeed we have no words to express the occurings in the whole phenomenon of samādhi and saṃyama. The comprehension etc. therein is of a totally different order than our usual intellectual and empirical comprehension and the knowledge in samādhi-saṃyama is also of different category than what we understand by knowledge in the worldly way. If at all we can say that it is a realization where the citta becomes one with the reality behind the subject chosen for meditation.

SS. - तज्जयात्प्रज्ञालोकः ॥३:५॥

TL. - taj -jayāt-prajñālokaḥ - III:5.

WM. - tat (→j) = (of) that;
jaya (āt) = victory, mastery (from, through);
prajñā = special intuitional power, here ṛtaṃbharā prajñā;
āloka (ḥ) = light, illumination, flashing forth (is).

TR. - Through the mastery of that (saṃyama) flashes forth the light of prajñā (i.e. ṛtaṃbharā prajñā, the special intuition like power produced in sabīja samādhi)

CE. - By this sūtra it is indicated that even the process of saṃyama is a progressive thing. The saṃyama has been explained as a process in which the sādhaka feels as if his citta is going into sabīja samādhi directly, as it were, without passing through the prior stages of dhāraṇā and dhyāna. So the saṃyama is for him instantaneous sabīja samādhi. This sūtra uses a phrase-'tajjayāt' = 'Victory over it (i.e. saṃyama)', which means that even after the sādhaka is able to attain in this manner the sabīja samādhi instantaneously, as soon as he starts meditation on a chosen subject, there still is a continuous trend of intensification going on in this also. As this saṃyama-process becomes more and more intensified, the light of the ṛtaṃbharā prajñā, which has arisen in at the start of sabīja samādhi (sūtra I:48) will become more and more penetrating.

Another simpler interpretation may be that having mastery may simply mean to have merely the ability to enter into saṃyama which is instantaneous sabīja samādhi in which the penetrative potentiality of prajñā (ṛtaṃbharā) awakens in the sādhaka. This then would be a paraphrasing and reiteration of the statements in sūtras I:46 to 48. There it was said that ṛtaṃbharā (Reality-bearing) prajñā arises in the perfection of nirvicārā (devoid of thinking process) state, which is technically called nirvicārā samāpatti (I:43, 44). But it has also been explained that the perfection of nirvicārā samāpatti, where the process of thinking is totally abolished, is also the start of sabīja samādhi. The reason of the reiteration is that the ṛtaṃbharā prajñā becomes really purpose-serving, when the ability to have sabīja samādhi in the mode of saṃyama is developed in the sādhaka. The sādhaka then can make use of it deliberately, if he has such desire, to avail of the vibhūtis, when, no doubt, they are on par with siddhis.

SS. - **तस्य भूमिषु विनियोगः ।।३:६।।**

TL. - tasya bhūmiṣu viniyogaḥ - III:6

WM. - tasya = its;
bhūmi (ṣu) = stages, levels (in, plural);
viniyoga(ḥ) = application, utilisation (is).

TR. - Its (i.e. of the light of prajñā) application is to be made in the stages.

CE. - This light i.e. penetrative power of ṛtaṃbharā prajñā is developed gradually and so the knowledge or realization of the reality lying behind the subject chosen for meditation is also revealed through it gradually in varying stages. In each stage of the development of the light of prajñā, the knowledge is more and more approaching the total and final knowledge of the Ultimate Reality, which later is revealed to the sādhaka only at the perfection of nirbīja samādhi i.e. in dharamamegha samādhi, when he attains Kaivalya-hood. Patañjali has mentioned this fact previously also in sūtra II : 27, where he pointed out that this progression and intensification of the penetrative power of (ṛtaṃbharā) prajñā takes place through seven bhumis (= stages or levels). Patañjali has not thought it necessary to describe the characteristics of these seven stages of prajñā nor the distinction in between the various stages. He has not mentioned even the designations of these seven stages, as has been given by some commentators. Probably he did not feel this as of any purpose, as said under sūtra II:27, because he might have thought it enough that the sādhaka be made aware of gradual progression through seven levels, as the essential and the most purposeful realization is the Ultimate Realization, which only is the true and complete knowledge of the Final Reality. The reiteration of this prajñā-development in the present sūtra again is intended for reminding the sādhaka that though he will have an impression at every new stage as if he is experiencing (seeing) the Reality, this impression will not be true. The knowledge he will thus be getting successively in these stages, when saṃyama is applied to a subject, will, therefore, not be the true knowledge all at once. It also serves as a reminder that thus the sādhaka may not get perplexed by the fact as to why the aspect of the Reality being revealed to him through the continuous process of meditation is varying successively from stage to stage.

SS. - **त्रयमन्तरङ्गं पूर्वेभ्यः ।।३:७।।**

TL. - trayam-antaraṅgaṃ pūrvebhyaḥ - III:7

WM. - traya (m) = the triad (is);
antaraṅga (m) = internal, core, esoteric part (is);
pūrva (ebhyaḥ) = earlier or preceding ones (of).

TR. - The triad (dhāraṇā, dhyāna, samādhi) is the core (esoteric part) of the preceding ones.

CE. - The 'preceding ones' are the five former angas out of the aṣṭāṅgas of Yoga viz. yama, niyama, āsana, prāṇāyāma and pratyāhāra. Therefore Patañjali here points out that the more essential and important part, which is the core of the eight-membered system of Yoga is the process of meditation comprising of dhāraṇā, dhyāna and samādhi. The first five members in their comparison are to some extent preparatory ones and secondary in importance. They serve to make the sādhaka fit for undertaking meditation by removing various malas (= impurities) and doṣas (lacunae), so that meditation becomes easy and almost natural. The most purposeful part of Patañjali's aṣṭāṅgayoga is this triad of the meditational stages, because it reveals the knowledge-or the better word is experience (anubhūti)- to the sādhaka, which is what the Yoga is meant to do.

SS. - **तदपि बहिरङ्ग निर्बीजस्य ।।३:८।।**

TL. - tad-api bahir-aṅgaṃ nirbījasya -III:8.

WM. - tadapi = (tat (→d)= that + api = even) but even that;

bahiraṅga (ṃ) = (bahir = external + aṅga = member) external or exoteric member or part (is);

nirbīja (sya) = (nir = not + bīja + seed) seedless (of).

TR. - But even that (i. e. triad of dhāraṇā, dhyāna and samādhi) is (merely) the exoteric part of nirbīja (samādhi).

CE. - Very often persons interested in Yoga feel and even speak as though the goal of Yoga is the ability to go into samādhi. Many sādhakas seem to believe that if they are able to enter into deep absorption states, which they rightly or wrongly call dhyāna, they have reached the highest achievement in yoga-sādhanā. Patañjali has clearly pointed out that there are various distinct stages of development in meditation. Even the last of the eight aṅgas of sādhanās i.e. aṣṭāṅgas, viz. samādhi is not a uniformly same one single stage. Patañjali has mentioned three definite levels or stage or types of samādhi viz. sabīja, nirbīja and dharmamegha. As nirbīja, (I:51) follows sabīja (I:46) it is obvious that even sabīja samādhi, which is what usually meant when the word samādhi is used without any further epithet (as in sūtra III:3), even in its advanced stage of saṃyama, is not the last stage of the practical sādhanā. In this sūtra this fact is affirmed in a clear statement. In a way the sūtra gives a hint to the sādhaka that he should not feel smugly satisfied with the attainment of sabīja samādhi, or even saṃyama. There is scope for further development, which is more esoteric and important and that is nirbīja samādhi. But it need be borne in mind that even this nirbīja samādhi is not a uniformly constant state. Most probably there is gradual progression in the intensity of penetration and the ability to grasp the reality behind the subject even during this nirbīja samādhi. But as the whole of the further progress is taking place in the 'anya' (= other, than samprajñāta) region of the inward journey of citta, it is totally beyond description (cf. sūtra I:18) and that is why nothing about its stages etc. can be said. Nevertheless, we get a hint of this progressiveness of nirbīja samādhi from the mention of dharmamegha samādhi, which is the culmination of it.

Another hint that we get from this and subsequent sūtras is that the knowledge which is gained in the sabīja samādhi and its advanced stage of saṃyama has an aspect of more of worldliness and if so desired, of a possibility of utilisation for mundane purpose. But once the citta has transcended this and entered into the nirbīja samādhi state, there is no more worldliness associated with the knowledge (?) or rather realization. Whatever the sādhaka acquires after this is only significant from spiritual angle.

SS. - **व्युत्थाननिरोधसंस्कारयोरभिभवप्रादुर्भावौ निरोधक्षण चित्तान्वयो निरोधपरिणामः ।।३:९।।**

TL. - Vyutthāna-nirodha-saṃskāra-yor-abhibhavaprādur bhāvau nirodha-kṣaṇa-cittānvayo nirodha -pariṇāmaḥ - III:9

WM. - Vyutthāna = (1) outgoing ; (2) distraction or engrossment in worldliness;

nirodha = restraint and ultimate cessation

		of vṛttis i.e. functional modifications, of citta;
saṃskāra (yoḥ->yor)	=	saṃskāra, impression, influence (of dual number);
abhibhava	=	subjugation, here dwindling and ultimately disappearance;
prādurbhāva (au)	=	arising, appearance (dual no);
nirodhakṣaṇa	=	(nirodha = cessation + kṣaṇa = instant, moment) the instant of nirodha i.e. cessation;
cittānaya (ḥ->o)	=	(anvaya = contact) contact of citta;
nirodha-pariṇāma(ḥ)	=	nirodha (= cessation) transformation.

TR. - Nirodha- transformation is when the citta makes a contact with the moment of nirodha (vṛtti-less condition, may be even happening naturally) while - (1)The outgoing saṃskāra (impression or influence of vṛtti) is dwindling and disappearing and the incoming saṃskāra (impression or influence of cessation of vṛtti) has arisen;- (2) the saṃskāra (impression) of engrossment in the worldliness is dwindling and the saṃskāra (impression) nirodha (= cessation of the vṛtti) has arisen.

CE. - Patañjali in this and subsequent four sūtras is stating very broadly the nature of three pariṇāmas (= transformations) that are taking place continuously even normally and specially in Yoga during meditational practices in the inner world i.e. citta and also three parallel transformations taking place in external physical world. The transformations taking place in the citta are described in sūtras III:9 to 12. In sūtra III:13 Patañjali merely mentions that the similar three transformations in the things of the physical world are described by the previous sūtra (III:12), no doubt, with substitutions of proper words etc. The main purpose of mentioning here these transformations seems to be that for getting the vibhūti of atīta-anāgata-jñāna (Past and future knowledge), mentioned in sūtra III:16, the saṃyama on the triads of these pariṇāmas is recommended. It becomes obligatory, therefore, that the triads of pariṇāmas be explained to the sādhaka, as he may not be knowing about these pariṇāmas. Indeed the sūtras III:9 to 15 are thus merely introductory to the presentation of the pariṇāma-trayasaṃyama yielding atīta-anāgata-jñāna and do not explain really any important things either for spiritual or practical purpose of Yoga.

The sūtra III:9 has been rendered slightly differently in its translations (l) and (2) above. But these two are not much different in the overall purport of the sūtra. The main difference in the two renderings is of the meaning given to the word vyutthāna. In (1) it means outgoing or dwindling vṛtti. In (2) it means the usual state of citta of being engrossed in the worldly distractions. Consequently the meanings of nirodha becomes in (1) restraining and stoppage of vṛttis and in (2) the state of the cessation of vṛttis i.e. vṛttiless state. The translation (1), which is on the lines of those or most of the earlier commentators, indicates that in nirodha-pariṇāma (transformation) i.e. in the process of the citta transforming from its normal state or worldly engrossment into the niruddha state, vṛttis go out and the condition of vṛttilessness arises in the citta.

But this translation does not throw much light on the process of this transformation.

In the translation (2) what is implied is that even normally citta goes into a vṛttiless state for an instant i.e. for an infinitesimally small duration of time (almost a point or an atom or quantum of time, if such measurements be valid for time). But this naturally occurring nirodha i.e. vṛttiless condition is for such a short duration and is so filling that the citta cannot become, so to say, conscious of it. At least it does not recognise or catch this occurrence of cessation of vṛttis. As is the case with any continuous activity having alternately directionalities opposite to one another, as for example to and from (Simple Harmonic, in the terminology of physics) motion of the pendulum or the inward and outward movement of air in breathing etc., it becomes necessary to assume that whenever the movement or activity in one direction ends and the movement or activity in the opposite direction is going to begin, there is an instant or very minute interval of time when there must not be any movement or activity in the thing or phenomenon viz. the pendulum or the breathing. Similarly when one vṛtti (=activity of citta) diminishes and then disappears and after it a new vṛtti comes up in the citta, hypothetically it is to be assumed that there must be an instant or a very minute time-interval when there would be no vṛtti in the citta i.e. the citta is then in vṛttiless state. This is, therefore, a normally occurring vṛtti-nirodha, of which, however the citta does not become conscious. (At least it has no active saṃskāra i.e. effective impression on the citta). As citta is not even aware of this happening it is of no purpose, just as the naturally occurring breaks in breathing in the normal respiratory cycle are not called kuṃbhakas or prāṇāyāmas. So Patañjali adds that the nirodha pariṇāma (= transformation) becomes purposeful and would produce its effect, only when the citta contacts or catches the kṣaṇa (= small time, moment) of nirodha (= vṛttilessness) and thus becomes actively aware of the occurrence of this nirodha and only then would it be meaningful to give it this name.

The word kṣaṇa is used for a very small duration of time just like the English words moment and second. But the magnitude of time-duration indicated by all these words is so small that they are used in the sense of an instant or a point of time. Some commentators have opined that kṣaṇa is a definite measure or unit of time. Anyway, whether a point or a very minute duration of time, the kṣaṇa is so small that, as said, the happening taking place in it is normally almost impossible for the citta to notice or grasp it. The word kṣaṇa has such a notion in this sūtra.

SS. - **तस्य प्रशान्तवाहिता संस्कारात् ।।३:१०।।**

TL. - tasya praśāntavāhitā saṃskārāt - III:10

WM. - tasya = its;
praśānta = peaceful, undisturbed;
vāhitā = (condition of) flow (-ing);
saṃskāra (āt) = influence, impression (through).

TR. - Its (of nirodha-pariṇāma) undisturbed flow through saṃskāra (deepening of impression)

CE. - The effect of nirodha (condition of citta in which vṛttis are reduced and later are totally extinct) starts as soon as nirodha-pariṇāma is there i.e. as soon as citta catches the kṣaṇa (instant) of nirodha and so grasps or gets aware of the latter. But the effect would be transitory. So this effect of this nirodha-pariṇāma (transformation) needs to be stabilized. This stabilization is achieved by deepening the influence or impress (saṃskāra) by repetition of the things through which the transformation was accomplished. In sūtra I:12 abhyāsa and vairāgya are said to be the means for achieving this nirodha. Out of these vairāgya, being a mental attitude, which is developed gradually, there is nothing of repetition pertinent in its case. Therefore the repetition can only be in abhyāsa. This, as per the present commentator, means abhyāsa of aṣṭāṅgas. But in this context, more pertinently it is of the last three meditational aṅgas, which are chiefly the aṅgas, which directly bring about nirodha. The term saṃskāra usually means the residual impression or influence left over by every action or incidence that the citta has to go through. This is stored, as said, in that part of citta designated as karmāśaya, whose exact location and nature are not definitely identified. Nevertheless according to the generally accepted belief of this phenomenon, every karma (action) does leave such impression in the karmāśaya and so if a particular action is repeated many times, this impression is supposed to get deepened. Thus each repetition of the action facilitates the further repetition of the same action. This is what is called the habituation or 'conditioning'. Therefore, for having an easy and smooth continuous activity of any sort, this conditioning is necessary. With it that particular level of activity can be maintained effortlessly and smoothly for a long time. Such a facilitating effect is a very common experience for everyone, who has tried to develop a skill in any particular type of activity, for which he has to repeat the activity very often, which is termed as having practice (abhyāsa) of that thing. According to this general principle, when the citta goes into vṛttiless state by the abhyāsa, particularly of the last three meditational aṅgas, and this abhyāsa is repeated day after day, the state of nirodha is maintained longer and longer and becomes smoothly established. This is what is explained in the sūtra.

Under sūtra I:13 it has been pointed out that some commentators have explained the term abhyāsa as practising some such technique as they think is described in this sūtra. They say that the naturally occurring nirodha, during the small interval in between the disappearance of one vṛtti and rising up of the next vṛtti could be deliberately caught (i.e. the citta becomes aware of it and grasps it) and then a practice or attempt be made (obviously deliberately) to prolong this vṛttiless interval. But as explained there, this deliberate action of citta would itself be a citta vṛtti and so the vṛttiless state would be disrupted. Therefore this is not a feasible technique for the establishment of nirodha. That is why, though Patañjali mentions this phenomenon here incidentally, merely as a necessary introduction to statement of the vibhūti of the knowledge of the past and the future, he does not seem to present it as a recommended technique for abhyāsa i.e. practising.

SS. - **सर्वार्थतैकाग्रतयोः क्षयोदयौ चित्तस्यसमाधिपरिणामः ।।३:११।।**

TL. - sarvārthataikāgratayoḥ kṣayodayau cittasya samādhi-pariṇāmaḥ -III:11.

WM. -	sarva	=	all, many;
	arthatā	=	subject-ness (purposive-ness);
	ekāgratā (-tayoḥ)	=	(eka=one+agra=point, end + tā = ness) one-pointedness (= one-subjectness). (dual, of two);
	kṣaya	=	dwindling or diminishing and disappearing;
	udaya (→au)	=	arising, uprising (dual form);
	citta (sya)	=	citta (of);
	samādhi-pariṇāma(ḥ)	=	samādhi-transformation (is).

TR. - The samādhi-pariṇāma (= transformation) (of citta) (takes place) when multi-subject-ness of the citta diminishes and ultimately disappears (and) one-pointed-ness (one-subject-ness) of the citta arises.

CE. - These three pariṇāmas are enumerated in an order which may seem just the inverse of what a modern writer would adopt. But this seems to be the usual way of presentation in the ancient Indian way of writing and particularly the one adopted by Patañjali in these Yoga-Sūtras. The final or more important thing is mentioned first and then to clarify the doubts or questions that may possibly be raised in the mind, the secondary things are explained later. Thus ekāgratā (one pointed-ness) which is the prerequisite for samādhi, would have been explained first, according to the modern method, then samādhi and thereafter nirodha, which are sequentially later, being results of the preceding one of these three pariṇāmas.

When the state of samādhi is established in the citta, the transformation which takes place in the citta is described in this sūtra. Sarvārthatā (= multi-subjectness) i.e. the activity of the citta of grasping a number of subjects simultaneously or very rapidly one after the other, which is the normal tendency of the citta, which is often referred to as the fickleness of citta, goes down and ekāgratā (one-pointedness, or still better, one-subjectness) arises in the citta.

As said, the sūtra merely states the occurrence taking place in this transformation, without much further elucidation.

The reading in all available versions of the Pātañjala Yoga Sūtras of the first pāda (part or phrase) of the sūtra is without exception 'sarvārthatāikāgratayoḥ'. That means the second word in this compound-word is invariably 'ekāgratā' in all the versions. Swāmi Kuvalayānanda (cf Y. M., VI, (4), 323-331, 1957) has proposed that the better reading in place of this word would be 'ekārthatā'. Though this is not found in any version, the suggestion, however seems to be quite pertinent, as in contrast to Sarvārthatā of citta, it has ekārthatā in samādhi. The difference in the meanings is quite clear. Artha is, as discussed by him, the subject or object from the world outside of citta (N.B. .The body is also 'outside' in this context), which is comprehended by the citta with the help of 'śabda (word i.e. a combination of sounds), which is conventionally used for that subject or object in the language of the thinking person. In meditational practices and particularly in the samādhi pariṇāma (transformation) one subject or object is chosen for directing the citta upon it. Normally the citta is in the habit of grasping a number of subjects or objects in its usual way of thinking. But in samādhi, which is preceded by dhāraṇā and dhyāna, the sādhaka selects a single subject (or object) and tries to think and know about it in the first stages. The ekāgratā results at a much later stage of samādhi, when the subjectedness i.e. the form with attributes, disappears from the citta and svarūpaśūnyatā is attained. Thus both the readings of the word are correct, as they describe quite clearly the transformation that is taking place in the citta in samādhi pariṇāma. The only difference is that with 'ekārthatā', the earlier part of this transformation is described while with 'ekāgratā' the later stage of the transformation gets described. However, the reading 'ekārthatā' is preferable as it goes better with 'sarvārthatā' on account of rhyming and as it mentions the nature of change as soon as the pariṇāma begins .

SS. - शान्तोदितौ तुल्यप्रत्ययौ चित्तस्यैकाग्रतापरिणामः ।।३:१२।।

TL. - śāntoditau tulya-pratyayau cittasyaikāgratā-pariṇāmaḥ - III:12.

WM. -

śānta	=	pacified, subsided;
udita (au)	=	rising, coming-up (dual no);
tulya	=	equivalent, same, identical;
pratyaya (au)	=	experience or content of citta, (dual no.);
citta (sya)	=	citta (of);
ekāgratā	=	(eka=one+ agra=point+tā= ness) one-pointedness, one-subject-ness;
pariṇāma (ḥ)	=	transformation (is).

TR. - The ekāgratā-pariṇāma (transformation into one-pointedness) of the citta is (that in which the experience (of the citta), which has subsided (and) the experience, which is arising (in the citta) are both identical.

CE. - This is a statement explaining the achievement of one-pointedness by the citta from its usual fickleness i.e. continuous running from one subject to another. Even in one-pointedness the citta, as it were, does not give up its usual tendency. So, it is explained, that even in the ekāgratā the citta is still changing the subject from instant to instant. The only peculiarity is that the subject or vṛtti about it which is subsiding and the subject or vṛtti which is coming up in the next instant in the citta are both identical in every respect, without there being the slightest difference in experience (pratyaya) that the citta is having about the subject. This creates the feeling of having the exactly same continuous experience of a subject i.e. maintenance of ekāgratā over a long period.

SS. - **एतेन भूतेन्द्रियेषु धर्मलक्षणावस्थापरिणामा व्याख्याताः ।।३:१३।।**

TL. - etena bhūtendriyeṣu dharma-lakṣaṇāvasthā-pariṇāmā vyākhyātāḥ - III:13

WM. -
etena = by this;
bhūta = (1) living beings; (2) mahābhūtas (five elements);
indriya (eṣu) = organs, body-parts (here the word is standing for organisms or living things) (in, plural suffix);
dharma = dharma, essential or basic properties;

lakṣaṇa	=	(1) time-variation; (2) secondary characteristics, external signs and symptoms;
avasthā	=	conditions, states;
pariṇāma (āḥ->ā)	=	transformation (s);
vyākhyāta (āḥ)	=	stated, explained (plural).

TR. - By this (i.e. preceding sūtra) are (also) explained the dharma (= basic properties), lakṣaṇa (1. time variations or, 2. secondary characteristics) (and) avasthā (state) pariṇāmas (transformations) (taking place) in (1) living beings, or (2) Mahābhūtas (primary elements) (and) organs (i.e. living things).

CE. - The word 'etena' is in singular and so ordinarily it should be interpreted as 'by this i.e. the preceding sūtra III:12'. But most of the commentators have said that the sūtras III:9, 11 and 12 respectively expound also the dharma-pariṇāma, lakṣaṇa-pariṇāma and avasthā pariṇāma taking place in bhūtas and indriyas. Some of them even go so far as to say that though Patañjali has not used these words expressly in sūtras III:9 to 12, nor has explicitly indicated thus, the sūtra III:9 explains the dharma pariṇāma, III:11 lakṣaṇa-pariṇāma and III:12 avasthā pariṇāma taking place in the citta, just as they take place in the bhūtendriyas. In other words, though Patañjali designates the pariṇāmas of the citta, noted in sūtras III:9, 11 and 12, respectively as 'nirodha', 'samādhi', and 'ekāgratā' pariṇāmas, according to the interpretations of these commentators their correct designations should be in that order 'dharma', 'lakṣaṇa' and 'avasthā' pariṇāmas of the citta. Obviously therefore, by the word 'etena' they must be understanding as -'by the above statement exposition of description etc. 'This interpretation of theirs does not much appeal to us, particularly because (1) Patañjali would not give misleading designations. (2) If nirodha, samādhi and ekāgratā were respectively dharma, lakṣaṇa and avasthā of the citta, he would have mentioned it at least in another sūtra. Moreover this does not seem to be really the case, at least with the normal citta. In view of this we feel that the word 'etena' means by the preceding III:12 sūtra', as would be the meaning, as said, normally also.

The word 'bhūta', literally meaning, 'that which has become', can be applied to both the living as well as non-living things. Most commentators understood by it 'living beings'. But we feel that here this word stands for 'non-living things' which are made up of the five (mahā) bhūtas only and have no indriyas (organs) nor organisation anywhere or of any sort in their structure. The word 'indriya', on the other hand, stands, according to us for living beings or organisms which have organs i.e. indriyas. Thus the term 'bhūtendriyāṇi' includes, as per our view, all things living as well as non-living of the external material world. If, as the other commentators say, 'bhūta' means 'living beings' and 'indriya', 'their organs or senses', it would have to be understood that the three pariṇāmas mentioned in this sūtra happen in living beings and their indriyas and not in the nonliving matter. This would mean that non-living things do not undergo transformations. But surely this is not true. In fact the dharma, lakṣaṇa and avasthā pariṇāmas are the transformations taking place in all the matter in the external world, whether living or non-living.

Dharma means a fundamental property or the essential nature of a thing, which, so to say, characterizes that thing as of a specific type or species. If a dharma be changed, the thing will very probably be changed so markedly that it may not even be recognized as its former self and may be looked upon as a completely new thing. The transformation of a caterpillar into a butterfly is a good example of dharma-pariṇāma, in which a number of dharma are transformed, giving the net result as a butterfly.

The earlier commentators, following the first one Vyāsa, interpret lakṣaṇa as the time sequence of appearance of dharmas. This interpretation being based, according to them, on the technical terminology, can be accepted. But lakṣaṇa usually means signs or symptoms. When dharmas are altered some secondary signs and symptoms also are usually altered. Again in the caterpillar to butterfly example, a number of secondary signs e.g. colour, form etc. are changed. The time sequence is included in this, as time i.e. past, present or future is also a sign or secondary factor of the dharma. Obviously these lakṣaṇas being of a secondary nature do not change the thing to such an extent that its basic type or species may not be recognizable. For example moustaches and beards are secondary characteristics, which make it easy to distinguish a male human from a female human. Yet they are not really basic signs in the human. Therefore we find some men without even a vestige of a beard or moustaches and on the other hand some women having a good growth of hair on the upper lip and chin. However, by these, never a confusion is caused in recognising the person as a male or a female nor such an anomaly really changes the sex of the person.

Avasthā means a state. The word has an implied meaning that this state is stable over a sufficient length of time. The avasthā transformation is mentioned last, because whenever there is a transformation in either dharma or lakṣaṇa the state is inevitably changed i.e. avasthā-pariṇāma is an essential consequence of dharma and lakṣaṇa pariṇāmas. Every object, person or incidence in the world is undergoing these transformations continuously, since these are all the products of prakṛti and this has an intrinsic trend of ever changing.

For preparing three sūtras of the dharma, lakṣaṇa and avasthā pariṇāmas in bhutendriyas on the pattern of the sūtra III:12, in the latter the words 'pratyaya' and 'ekāgratā' will be replaced by the word 'dharma', lakṣaṇa' or 'avasthā' in this order, in the three respective sūtras successively in each; 'tulya' will be substituted by 'bhinna' (= different) and in place of 'cittasya' will now come 'bhūtendriyeṣu' (or even may be 'bhūtendri-yāṇām i.e. possessive case, just parallel to cittasya), with end-suffixes as proper to the gender and number of the concerned words. These sūtras will be as : -

1) śāntoditau bhinnadharmau bhūtendriyeṣu dharmapari-ṇāmaḥ.

2) śāntoditau bhinnalakṣaṇau bhūtendriyeṣu lakṣaṇaparinā-maḥ

3) śāntodite bhinnāvasthe bhūtendriyeṣvavasthāpariṇāmaḥ

SS. - शान्तोदिताव्यपदेश्यधर्मानुपाती धर्मी ।।३:१४।।

TL. - śāntoditāvyapadeśya-dharmānupātī dharmī - III:14.

WM. -

śānta	=	pacified, quietened, subsided;
udita	=	arisen, come-up, manifest;
avyapadeśya	=	undesignated, unmanifest;
dharma	=	dharma, basic property;
anupātī	=	common to one existing in something consistantlly, inhering;
dharmī	=	dharmī, bearer or carrier of dharmas.

TR. - Dharmī (= carrier or supporter of dharmas) inheres in itself, dharmas (basic properties) (which have) subsided, (are) manifest (and as yet) unmanifested.

CE. - This sūtra seems to have been introduced to counteract the view put forth by some spiritual schools e.g. Vijñānavāda of Bauddhas etc., about the unsubstantiality of the external world. Sāṃkhya and Yoga both consider prakṛti to be continuously changing. Therefore all prākṛtika things suffer change as an inevitable continuous process. But from this one may be misled to the belief that there is no permanent principle or reality behind the phenomenal world, which theory is propounded by the above-mentioned schools e.g. Vijñānavādins and probably much popular at the period these sūtras were compiled. To do away with such a mistake Patañjali clearly states in the present sūtra that the prākṛtika things are continually undergoing transformations, broadly described in the preceding sūtra and particularly in the dharma-transformation, in which the thing may be so much changed that it may not be recognised as its former self, yet there is a background support of a steady substantial principle or reality upon which these transformations are taking place and this principle he designates by the simple term 'dharmī', which means 'one having or bearing the dharmas'.

The practical importance for yoga-sādhanā of the sūtra is, as said, that Patañjali recommends choosing of a definite subject for meditation and in its higher and higher stages the reality behind the subject is gradually revealed in stages (seven as per sūtra II:27), the ultimate realization of the reality being obtained in the culmination of nirbīja samādhi i.e. dharmamegha samādhi. This realization of the reality will only be possible, if there be any such reality at all, behind the subject chosen for meditation, which will unavoidably always be from the realm of prakṛti, whether from inner world or from outer phenomenal world. So the process of meditation as described in Pātañjala Yoga Sūtras would be valid only if such an unchanging principle is accepted as lying behind the apparent and outward changes. For this reason it is necessary that the sādhaka has this understanding clearly. One point needs clarification here. The dharmī is not the final Reality, because it is the puruṣa-tattva. But this latter cannot have any attributes i.e. dharmas etc. However this Reality is revealed only at the last moment. Till then this reality is always encrusted with, so to say, garbs or layers, due to saṃyoga or avidyā, which are prākṛtika in their nature and this secondary reality becomes the dharmī persisting as a constant in all these transformations.

SS. - क्रमान्यत्वं परिणामान्यत्वे हेतुः ।।३:१५।।

TL. - kramānyatvaṃ pariṇāmānyatve hetuḥ - III:15

WM. -

krama	=	sequence, here specially, succession of events taking place according to a law of nature governing that process;
anyatva (ṃ)	=	(anya = other + tva = ness) differentness, variation;
pariṇāma	=	change, transformation;
anyatva (→e)	=	otherness, differentness (in);
hetu (ḥ)	=	cause, (is).

TR - The cause underlying (in) the differentness of a transformation (is) the differentness in the sequence (krama).

CE. - Hereafter, from sūtra III:16 begins the description of vibhūtis. As said, Patañjali does not seem to consider these special developments occurring on the path of Yoga as anything miraculous i.e. siddhis. But generally commentators speak of these developments as miraculous and even use the epithet 'siddhi' for them. Very probably to remove the erroneous view, Patañjali at the start explains the broad principle of these developments and transformations taking place in the psychic potentialities of the sādhaka. The statement made in this sūtra is what a modern scientific view will give for any process, which may at first seem miraculous or astoundindy strange, which would really only mean that we are ignorant of the law governing that process. One expects a particular kind of result of a transformation, according to the understanding current at that time about that process. But it may so happen that at some occasion the result may be completely different from the expected one. In such a case the person may become puzzled and may be even led to believe that something miraculous has happened. But Patañjali by this sūtra explains that there is really no miracle. This strangeness of the result also is produced by a law of nature. Certain factors, which may either be as yet unknown or uncontrollable, have interfered with the process, which is indicated by kramānyatva, giving rise to completely different result (= pariṇāmānyatva). If these factors and their action becomes known and understood, the process becomes quite rationally explainable and all miraculousness about it disappears. The vibhūtis, even though they may at first appear as miraculous, are taking place in accordance with a law of nature. Thus the technique of saṃyama applied to topics will produce the various vibhūtis according to a certain rule. That is why indications of getting such transformations or results could be broadly enumerated by Patañjali in the following sūtras.

SS. - **परिणामत्रयसंयमादतीतानागतज्ञानम्** ।।३:१६।।

TL. - pariṇāma-traya-saṃyamād-atītānāgata-jñānam - III:16

WM. -
pariṇāma = transformation, change;
traya = triad;
saṃyama (→āt→ād) = saṃyama (through, from);
atīta = past;
anāgata = (an = not+āgata=come) not yet come, future;

jñāna (m) = knowledge (is).

TR. - Through the saṃyama of the triad of pariṇāmas (results) the knowledge of the past and the future.

CE. - It is not always easy to explain the vibhūtis mentioned by Patañjali in this pāda, in a way as would make it possible to understand reasonably as to how they are produced.

In this sūtra Patañjali indicates a saṃyama which will enable the yoga-sādhaka to have the knowledge about things and incidents of the past and the future. For this the subject for saṃyama recommended is the triad of pariṇāmas. The triads are the ones noted in sūtras III:9, 11 to 13. As said, the triad noted in sūtras III:9, 11 and 12 is of the internal or mental tansformations, while the triad for objects in the external world has been indicated in sūtra III:13. Thus, the saṃyama on these two triads will show the sādhaka all the steps of transformations through which respectively the inner psychic world i.e. citta-mind with their contents and the things in the external world pass. Even in the dhāraṇā and dhyāna the concentration is of such a high order that the so-called 'concentration' of an ordinary thinking man can stand nowhere in comparison to the former. The penetrative power of mind-citta in these yogīc states is very great. The further stage of (sabīja) samādhi has a further intensification of this penetrative capacity and when it is developed to the grade of saṃyama this power increases to a degree beyond imagination. So when an object or phenomenon is chosen as the subject and saṃyama is directed to the triad of pariṇāmas, pertinently concerned with it, on account of extraordinary penetrative ability, which is active in the saṃyama, the whole course of transformations taking place in that object or phenomenon will become clearly perceptible to the sādhaka in every minute detail.

As already explained under sūtras III:1 to 4, the vibhūti, which is a natural result of the saṃyama applied to a particular subject, will inevitably appear as soon that particular saṃyama happens or is deliberately performed by the yogī. If the yogī is not interested in the knowledge or power accruing from that saṃyama, he will ignore it totally. He will be paying attention to that part, which is, if at all, helpful for his purely spiritual sādhanā and objective. The remaining part of that knowledge (or power), which has more a mundane value, will remain in his citta as merely a back-drop, which is of no concern to him.

Indeed, amongst the vibhūtis and the subjects of saṃyamas recommended for their appearance, there are some which are more or less of spiritual value. Mention of a few of these, which are almost essential or of very high value for the attainment of kaivalya has been made under sūtras III:1-4. Others e.g. saṃyama on sūrya giving rise to bhūvanajñāna and such others, where the vibhūti is such as can be used for mundane purpose, but where potentiality for spiritual advancement is also present, are also incorporated in this enumeration of the III pāda. While there are still others e.g. pariṇāma-traya saṃyama giving rise to the knowledge of past and future, mentioned in this III:16 sūtra and others in the next few sūtras seem to be knowledges or powers, which seem to have merely mundane value. The yogī, really interested only in attainment of Kaivalya, will choose subjects for saṃyamas only of the first type and if some reason necessiates him of the second type, where spiritual benefit is possible to avail. Normally he will never choose the subjects for saṃyama of the third type resulting into mere mundane vibhūtis. However, if on some occasion, he feels that gaining of a mundane vibhūti is desirable for him with a view to universal good, he may deliberately choose the pertinent subject for this vibhūti to avail and utilize that knowledge or power for only universal welfare. No doubt, a yoga-sādhaka, who is interested in the worldly advantages from these vibhūtis, would be intentionally choosing the subjects for saṃyama, which will give rise to such vibhūtis usable for worldly gain.

When a yogī or sādhaka performs saṃyama on the proper subject with a definite desire to gain a vibhūti for utilizing it for a certain worldly objective, he can then direct or restrict the knowledge or power rising in that vibhūti in such a manner as will best suit his objective. Thus in the present case, if the yogī wants to know about the past history of a thing, he will direct the saṃyama of triad of pariṇāmas pertinent to that thing in such a way that the knowledge in a backward sequence on the time scale of the transformations that had occurred in that thing will be revealed to him. When the yogī wants to have the knowledge about the future of that thing, he will extrapolate the saṃyama to the triad of transformations, going forward (i.e. in future) on the time scale, starting from the present state of the thing. (N.B.. For accepting the feasibility of gaining the knowledge of past and future and specially the future, some basic notions about time as a definite entity need be revised. Patañjali himself had to refer to this point in connection with some philosophical and practical aspects of higher Yoga. For discussion of these, see sūtras III:52 and IV: 12).

Since according to Patañjali the transformations that take place in all things are comprised in the respective triad of pariṇāmas as pertinent to the thing depending upon whether it is subjective i.e. of the inner (mental) world or objective i.e. of the external (material) world, the application of the saṃyama to the proper triad of pariṇāmas in relation to the nature of the thing will enable the yogī's citta to see, so to say, like a cinema film, the whole sequence of transformations that the thing had passed through and also the sequence of transformations that it will have to go through hereafter. This is how the knowledge of the past and future of anything whatsoever would become possible for the yogī through saṃyama on the pariṇāma-traya.

SS. - **शब्दार्थप्रत्ययानामितरेतराध्यासात्संकरस्तत्प्रविभाग-संयमात्सर्वभूतरुतज्ञानम् ।।३:१७।।**

TL. - śabdārtha-pratyayānām-itaretarādhyāsāt-saṃkarastat- pravibhāga-saṃyamāt-sarvabhūta-ruta-jñānam - III: 1 7

WM. -

śabda	=	word;
artha	=	meaning;
pratyaya (→ānām)	=	experience or understanding of, the mind (which is also content of mind), (of, plural);
itaretara	=	(itara + itara = other + other) upon one another;
adhyāsa (āt)	=	false super-imposition, (from, through);

saṅkara	=	haphazard grouping or mixing, leading to confusion;
tat	=	(of) that, here those;
pravibhāga	=	complete separation, distinction;
saṃyama (āt)	=	saṃyama, (from, through);
sarva	=	all;
bhūta	=	living creatures;
ruta	=	sound or language of creatures;
jñāna(m)	=	knowledge, comprehension.

TR. - Due to false superimposition (misidentification) of words (here sounds), (their) meanings (and their) comprehension (in the mind) over one another, there is produced a haphazard mixture (of these), (causing confusion). Through saṃyama on the (condition of) their complete separation (from each other) (is gained) the knowledge (i.e. comprehension) of the language (sounds) of all creatures.

CE. - Adhyāsa is a wrongly made superimposition of a thing upon another. This naturally produces a distortion in the understanding about these things. In human language we use words (= śabda) to which arbitrarily some meaning (= artha) is attributed and when such a word is used in speaking (or writing), an image (= pratyaya) is produced in the mind of the listener, through which he gets an understanding or knowledge (jñāna) about the thing being spoken of. By convention it is presumed that these three viz. word, its meaning and the knowledge produced in the mind through them are intrinsically interrelated, but while discussing this matter under sūtra I:42 it has been shown that this is vikalpa i.e., an unreal imagination only.

However, man has been conditioned for millenniums to treat these three as essentially related, as if they be almost one and he behaves in the world, while using the language, with a dependence on this wrong assumption. Because the speaker and the listener both usually know the convention, there is no occasion normally for confusion. But there are occasions also when it is seen that working on this assumption (which fundamentally is not true) causes confusion, when the listener misunderstands about the talk of a speaker. This fact is stated in the first part of the sūtra.

According to the latter part of the sūtra, if a man would recondition himself, so that he does not work on this wrong assumption of intrinsic inter-relationship of the three, that is he does not attach the conventional meaning (= artha to the combination of certain sounds (which we designate as 'word' = śabda and so an arbitrary image (= pratyaya), conventionally linked with that 'śabda-artha', would not be created in his mind and if instead of this he would direct the process of saṃyama on the sound-combination produced by a living creature, with, no doubt, a desire to know what is the reality it is meant to communicate and tries, to grasp this without intervention of any conventional artha-pratyaya, then he will be able to understand whatever, a living creature is trying to communicate through those sounds.

This may at first seem quite unbelievable and not very feasible. But if we try to see how two human beings, who do not know each other's language, would communicate with each other, we can realize that communication can be had without the aid of the trio of the śabda-artha-pratyaya, which are the basic factors in the use of verbal language. Sounds or words, which do not mean anything to the hearer, in such a communication are often accompanied by suitable gesturs. This whole complex way of expression is able to communicate the thought of one person to the other, without there being any use of 'formal words'. This mechanism of 'word-less' communication through mere sound can be still more strikingly seen and understood, if we see how the animals communicate with one another. And sometimes even a human being can comprehend what an animal is trying to communicate by mere sound, without trying to imagine a word with a meaning, through those sounds. We know very easily merely from the wailing, moaning, cooing, whining etc. of an animal, whether the animal is in pain, misery or in a joyful state. Readers must have such experiences with domestic animals like cows, buffaloes and pet animals like dogs, cats, parrots etc. The author had on many occasions an intimation of the presence of a dangerous animal in the vicinity, very often a snake, by the peculiar cries of birds, specially of the common myna birds. Thus it can be seen that even in ordinary life the thoughts, ideas and feelings are communicated very well without words bearing conventionally any meanings and not only between two humans, but also between man and animals. In fact when the mental content is communicated through sounds only, so to say, in this direct manner, the understanding of the recipient is very clear and there is no possibility of any confusion or misunderstanding, as happens in wordy communication. A baby -child uses no words, but the mother and child communicate very often through meaningless sounds, may be some times supplemented by gestures, and yet the communication is perfect.

Thus what Patañjali states in the latter part of the sūtra is very true. If a man develops this ability to catch the experience of others communicated through the sound (no doubt this immediately would be converted and interpreted by his mind into meaningful words, since that mind is habituated to think etc. with the aid of formal words only from the language the man knows and usually used) without there being any need that these sounds be formal words in any verbal language of his acquaintance, then he would be able to understand the natural pure sound-language and will not have to depend on the conventional and artificial wordy languages of man. He will thus become able to understand what a languageless creature expresses through its sounds. Of course, for being able to understand fully the sound language of a particular species of animal, he will have to remain in close association with the members of that species for a fairly long time and get himself thoroughly acquainted with this sound-language of that particular species. In support of this, instances can be mentioned of naturalists, who have lived with apes and a few other species of animals and have, so to say, decoded or deciphered their sound languages and even prepared (sound-record) dictionaries of such animal sound-languages.

In all this what is achieved first is to separate the śabda (in Sanskṛta = sound) as a group of sounds from śabda (in Sanskṛt also = word) as a formal word and then develop the capacity to get the experience or content of the mind of the other party, the speaker, who may be a human or animal, directly from that 'śabda' (= sound). If therewith, the yoga-sādhaka also applies the technique of saṃyama on this separation of śabda as mere sound from śabda as the word linked with conventional meaning etc. and desires to gain directly the knowledge of what is in the mind of that other party then, on account of the high penetrative power developed in the saṃyama, the yoga-sādhaka will have that knowledge perfectly. This is what is affirmed in this sūtra by Patañjali.

SS. - **संस्कारसाक्षात्करणात्पूर्वजातिज्ञानम् ।।३:१८।।**

TL. - saṃskāra sākṣātkaraṇāt-pūrva-jāti-jñānam - III:18

WM. -		
saṃskāra	=	impressions (of past actions)
sākṣātkaraṇa (āt)	=	(sa=with + akṣa = eye, karana = production) literally production with i.e. before the eye, therefore presentation before (the inner or mental) eye i.e. bringing back or rejuvenating to the awareness in mind (by or through);
pūrva	=	earlier, previous;
jāti	=	births or lives;
jñāna (m)	=	knowledge (is).

TR. - By bringing back the saṃskāras (latent impressions of past karmas saying in the karmāśaya) to the awareness in the mind, (by performing saṃyama on them), (is gained) the knowledge of previous lives.

CE. - According to the ancient Indian understanding, every action and experience of life leaves an impression or record in the karmāśaya part of citta. What is the exact nature of this recording and where the location of this karmāśaya is not clearly explained anywhere. This notion of karmāśaya, being the storehouse of saṃskāras i.e. residual impressions of karmas, is easily understandable, if one takes into consideration the potentiality of remembering i.e. memory. Everyone knows that we can remember the incidents from our past. Even modern science has not been able to locate precisely the place where this impression is made and retained. Yet, since it is possible to remember i.e. revive the past experience, it logically becomes unavoidable to accept that its record must have been made and retained somewhere. Modern science accepted uptill recent times the storage of such impressions of experiences only of the current life, that is experiences undergone only after the man was born. During last few decades the notion is altered and widened. It is now accepted that even in prenatal period such impressions are made and retained by an individual. This is based on the observations that the origin of many troubles arising in the life of an individual can be rationally explained only with the assumption of such prenatal impressions. The well known stories of Prahlāda and Abhimanyu having heard and learnt well some things taught to their mothers, while they were still in the wombs, show that this phenomenon was well-recognised and known to even layman for ages in India. Proceeding on the same lines, many problems about the troubles and difficulties in an individual's life can be more rationally understood, if it be assumed that the individual had existed in a number of previous lives and the impressions of the happenings in those past lives have been retained and are in some way brought forward in the further lives of that individual. Particularly in higher meditational states of Yoga there are many experiences, which can be rationally explained in a more satisfying way by assumption of such a retention and carriage forward of the saṃskāras of the past lives. That is why ancient Indian thinkers postulated a theory and it has been accepted popularly.

The present sūtra tells the method of reviving and remembering the past lives. The process is almost the same as the revival of memory. In this latter, usually some outside stimulus causes the reactivation and revival of the saṃskāra and thus comes up the remembrance of a past happening. Many a time such external stimulus is not perceptible, it may not be there and yet one remembers a past happening. Then the feeling is that the memory of a particular incident has come up without any pertinent reason. In the same way the saṃskāras of past lives also come up into the present consciousness, sometimes without any apparent stimulation. This has already been explained while discussing the meditational processes of samāpattis and dhyāna etc. (I:17, 42, 43, III:2). However, if and when an advanced yoga-sādhaka wants to remember any of his past he can deliberately stimulate the saṃskāras lying in the karmāśaya, by means of the very penetrating and searching process of saṃyama on the karmāśaya. In this way it is quite understandable and possible that a yogī, who has a mastery over the process of saṃyama, can very easily know about his past lives.

SS. - **प्रत्ययस्य परचित्तज्ञानम् ।।३:१९।।**

TL. - pratyayasya para-citta-jñānam - III:19

WM. - pratyaya (sya) = content of citta (of);

para = others;

citta = citta (here may be interpreted as mind);

jñāna (m) = knowledge.

TR. - (By performing saṃyama) on the content of citta (or mind) is gained the knowledge about other's citta (or mind).

CE. - The sūtra indicates the saṃyama which needs to be performed to gain the knowledge of other's citta i.e. of the content at the moment in the other's citta.

As explained (sūtra I:2) citta is a vast thing and the mind is only a part of it, with which the common man is usually acquainted and which he employs during his normal conscious activity. The word used in the sūtra is citta but at least for this sūtra it can be understood primarily as the mind part of the citta. For this reason in the rendering of the sūtra, the word has been interpreted as mind.

According to the wording of the sūtra, if the yogī wants to gain the knowledge of the citta of another person, he has merely to apply or direct the saṃyama (which is implied, as is indicated by the parentheses in the rendering and has to be understood from the context) on the content of his own mind or citta.

Though it is not explicitly stated, evidently the application of this saṃyama on the content of his own citta would be practised by the yogī only with a desire to know the content of the mind of a particular person. In doing this the yogī's citta will work like a reflector or mirror and automatically produce the exact image of whatever may be present at that moment in the mind of that particular individual. Because when this saṃyama will be practised by the yogī with an intention to know the content of the other's mind, the activity and the space (?) for the content in the yogī's mind will respectively be directed and kept reserved only for this purpose. Thus the mind of the yogī will be emptied of all other content and will be filled with the reproduction of the content of that other person's mind. This is the way in which the mechanism of this type of saṃyama can obtain the knowledge of other's mind.

SS. - **न च तत्सालम्बनं तस्याविषयीभूतत्वात् ।।३:२०।।**

TL. - na ca tat-sālambanaṃ tasyāviṣayībhūtatvāt - III:20

WM. -

na	=	not;
ca	=	and;
tat	=	that;
sālambana (ṃ)	=	(sa = with + ālambana = support) with the supporting subject or basis;
tasya	=	of that;
aviṣayī-bhūtatva (āt)	=	(a = not +viṣayī + subject-oriented + bhūtatva = state) of being + āt = from, on

account of) not being oriented to that subject (on account of).

TR. - And not (the knowledge along) with the basis (i.e. the knowledge does not encompass and pertain to the external subject or object, which is the basis of the content in the mind of that an other person) on account of that (the external subject or object) having been not made the subject (for knowing i.e. being the aim or objective of knowledge).

CE. - This sūtra is a continuation of the preceding one and clarifies an important aspect about the knowledge to be gained of another person's mental content by the application of the saṃyama recommended in the preceding sūtra. The yogī will have an exact replica in his own mind of whatever may be the content at that particular moment in the mind of that other person, whose mind the yogī wants to read. The present sūtra clarifies that knowledge, when looked at from the aspect of the subject or object, which is the basis of that other person's mental content i.e. the subject or object about which he may be thinking at that moment, may be even wrong. Because it is merely a reflection of the contents i.e. thoughts in that other person's mind. So, if that other person has wrongly understood about that subject or object in his thought, then obviously the reflection in the yogī's mind, being an exact replication of that other man's thought, will also be wrong to the same degree. The reason for this wrongness is that, that particular subject or object is not the direct objective aimed at for comprehending by the yogī. The yogī's desire is to know only what the other person is thinking and accordingly whatever that person is thinking about that subject is only reproduced in the mind of the yogī, irrespective of whether that thought or understanding of the other person, is right or wrong in relation to that subject, which is the basis or support (ālambana) of his thought. So the sūtra wants to attract attention to and stress the fact that the knowledge through this type of saṃyama will be only of the thoughts in the other person's mind and not really of the subject of which the other person be thinking of. Therefore, there is a great possibility that the knowledge could be a wrong knowledge i.e. viparyaya in relation to the subject proper, in case that person's thinking about the subject be on wrong lines. So the yogī should be aware of this possibility and be cautious in making use of this knowledge.

SS. - **कायरूपसंयमात्तद्ग्राह्यशक्तिस्तम्भे चक्षुःप्रकाशा-संप्रयोगेऽन्तर्धानम् ।।३:२१।।**

TL. - kāya-rūpa-saṃyamāt-tad-grāhya-śaktistambhe cak ṣuḥ-prakāśāsaṃprayoge' ntardhānam - III:21

WM. -

kāya	=	body;
rūpa	=	rūpa tanmātrā, the subtle aspect of teja (= light) element (mahābhuta);
saṃyama (āt)	=	saṃyama (from practising);
tat(→d)	=	its;
grāhya-śakti	=	absorption - power;
stambha (→e)	=	stoppage, suppression (in);
cakṣuḥ	=	eye;

prakāṣa	=	light;
asaṃprayoga (→e)	=	(a = not + saṃ = total + pra = thorough + yoga = joining) no contact at all (in);
antardhāna (m)	=	disappearance, becoming invisible (is).

TR. - From saṃyama on the rūpa-tanmātrā of physical body (either of the yogī himself or of another person or object) (results) the suspension of the potentiality of absorption (and so also reflection, of light) on account of which (there is) no contact of the light (reflected from the surface of that body) with the eye, due to which (The yogī, or that other person or object) becomes invisible.

CE. - Often there are reports or stories about the ability of yogīs and saints to make themselves or any other object invisible. Though this power seems to be very strange and therefore, very hard to accept, such reports seem very often as though they are trustworthy occurrences. Such stories are current not about Indian Hindū yogīs only, but of saints of other regions and religions. Patañjali explains the principle on which this phenomenon very probably works.

It is well-known that objects are visible on account of the light, which is coming from those objects, either because they themselves are emitting the light or partly reflecting the light falling on them and this light reaching the eye. According to the ancient view, particularly expounded by Saṃkhya, it is presumed that the particular tanmātrā i.e. the subtle and unmanifest principle behind an element or mahābhūta, is the origin for the activity and effect of the corresponding mahābhūta. Thus the taijas (light or visibility element) mahābhūta is able to exist and act on account of its background tanmātrā 'rūpa'. Everything having a physical existence e.g. a body, becomes visible, because of the 'taijas' mahābhūta component in it, which is deriving its power from the rūpa tanmātrā in it indicated here by the term 'kāya-rūpa'. When saṃyama is directed upon this tanmātrā, it can be controlled and made inactive or ineffective. So the taijas element in the body will also not be able to do its work and so, if the body is self-luminous it will not emit any light or if the body is non-luminous it will neither absorb nor partially reflect the light falling upon it. So no light will go out from that body. Obviously no light from that body will reach the eye of the onlooker and so will not make contact with and effect on his eye. This is what is stated in the latter part of the sūtra :- 'On account of the rūpa-tanmātrā of the kāya (body) being curbed through saṃyama, the kāya (body) loses the ability of absorbing (and therefore differentially and partially reflecting) the light (and also emitting its own light, which again is dependent on the light-absorbing power) and so that particular body automatically becomes invisible. When the yogī wishes himself to become invisible, he applies the saṃyama on the rūpa-tanmātrā of his own body. When he wants some person or object to disappear, he has to direct the saṃyama on the rūpa-tanmātrā in that particular body.

[N.B.. Some versions of Yoga Sūtras contain one Sūtra following the present one as :- **एतेन शब्दाद्यन्तर्धानमुक्तम्** etena śabdādyantardhānamuktam', which means : - 'By this (same Sūtra) the disappearance of sound and others (i.e. touch, taste and odour) is also explained'.]

It seems to be an interpolation by some later commentator or transcriber, who thought that the disappearances with respect to other tanmātrās remain unexplained and therefore, this omission should be set right. Since majority of the Yoga Sūtra versions do not contain this extra Sūtra and since the disappearances with respect to the other tanmātrās viz. śabda etc. are implied, because if a thing becomes invisible to the eye and yet its presence can be sensed through either its sound or odour or touch or taste, the purpose itself of becoming invisible will be meaningless and so the other disappearances can be easily understood and explained on the same line, without having the explicit statement in such an additional Sūtra and so according to the brevity-principle of Sūtra-composition, this Sūtra becomes redundant. In Sūtras I:44 and III: 13, it may seem that a similar situation exists, i.e. a Sūtra merely saying that the Sūtra preceding to it also expounds some other parallel things. But it is not so. There is a difference that the names of the two samāpattis of I:44 and of the three pariṇāmas of III:13 are even not known to a (new) reader, leave aside other information about these. While it is expected that a student of Yoga Sūtra must be knowing the Sāṃkhya principles quite well and so he could easily deduce from Sūtra III:21 itself, the thing stated in the present extra Sūtra, as he also knows very well the remaining four tanmātrās and about their functioning exactly parallel to the rupa-tanmātrā.

Even when this extra Sūtra is added, it does not actually give any additional further useful clarification. Because, as said, it merely states that the previous Sūtra III:21 explains the disappearances with respect to śabda (sound) etc. It is obvious that if the saṃyama is applied to a particular tanmātrā in any body, the respective special quality indicated by the name itself of the tanmātrā viz. making sound, giving smell, touch and taste will become ineffective and so disappear (= nonexistent). Thus the person or object has to become simultaneously imperceptible to not only the sight, but in all other ways for all the senses, so that he or it can not be experienced and his or its presence not become known either by sound, touch, smell and taste also. The adept yogī as soon as he practices saṃyama on the rupa tanmātrā in a particular body to make it invisible, automatically simultaneously practises saṃyama on the remaining four tanmātrās also, as otherwise, as already noted, the invisibility would be purposeless.

SS. - **सोपक्रमं निरुपक्रमं च कर्म तत्संयमादपरान्तज्ञानमरिष्टेभ्यो वा ।।३.२२।।**

TL. - sopakramamṃ nirupakramamṃ ca karma tat-saṃyamāḍ aparānta-jñānam-ariṣṭebhyo vā - III:22

WM. - sopakrama (ṃ) = (sa = with + upakrama = approach, nearness) that having early maturity or fructification (is);

nirupakrama (ṃ) = (niḥ--nir = without + upakrama = nearness), that

		without early maturity i.e. that having maturation or fructification after long time (is);
ca	=	and;
karma	=	karma, act, deed;
tat	=	it;
saṃyama (→āt-ād)	=	saṃyama (from, through);
aparānta	=	(apara = ultimate + anta = end) death;
jñāna (m)	=	knowledge;
ariṣṭa (→ebhyaḥ→ebhyo)	=	evil omens (by, through);
vā	=	or.

TR. - Karma (is of two categories) with early maturation (and) with late maturation. Through saṃyama on it (i.e. rapidly maturing karmas and late maturing karmas) (is obtained) the knowledge of death or through evil omens (also)

CE. - Karma has a primary meaning of act or deed, but in the technical sense it means an act or experience, whose residual effect is stored in karmāśaya in the form of saṃskāra, of which there is a process of fructification giving rise to fruit i.e. result. This process of fructification i.e. maturation or ripening of the fruit naturally takes some time. One particular karma may give fruit i.e. the final result in a short while, for another a very long time may be needed to give the fruit. The terms for these two categories of karmas are sopakrama and nirupakrama.

But the words early and late both are relative. The same

thing may be said to have taken place early in one frame of reference as to time, while the same thing happening in same time may be judged as very late i.e. taking a very long time, in another frame of reference. The Sūtra does not explicitly give any such frame of reference by which the karma can be adjudged as sopakrama or nirupakrama.

But from the vibhuti viz. (fore) knowledge of (one's own) death, which results through the saṃyama on this aspect of karmas, it is clearly seen that the sopakrama is to be interpreted here as those maturing in the present life and the nirupakrama as those maturing after this life and may be after many lives.

The yogī directs the saṃyama on this characteristic of karmas, i.e. actually he directs the saṃyama on the total number of karmas (i.e. their saṃskāras) accumulated in his karmāśaya, with a desire to know the possibility of the maturation of each karma in his current life. By getting this knowledge of all the karmas that are going to be matured and exhausted in the current life-span, the yogī gets automatically at the same time the knowledge of what is going to happen in his whole current life and thus also the knowledge of when this life of his is going to end. If the yogī for some reason so desires, he may direct the saṃyama on the karmāśaya of any other person and in the same way get the knowledge of the happenings in the whole life and the time of death of that of other person also.

The last part of the Sūtra tells of another way in which also this portent of death can be got. However this is not gotten through any saṃyama nor even by some technique specific to Yoga. Many ill-omens are known as forewarning signs of death of a person. Some of these are merely conventions widely accepted or probably are only superstitions. But there surely are some, known to be certainly indicating death after a definite period. Some such are even mentioned in Āyurvedic texts. When these are observed to be happening, the time of death can be predicted, not only by a yogī, but even by any other man, who knows the meaning of these ill-omens. Patañjali mentions this thing here incidentally, even when it has no direct relation to saṃyama or Yoga, only because this is an easy and routine method of fore-telling the time of death, probably quite in vogue in ancient India. The knowledge of the time of death, otherwise, that of the life span at a sādhaka's disposal, has a significance for spiritual and yogīc sādhanā, because that will serve as a stimulus for maximum effort and greatest earnestness in the sādhaka, specially if and when he becomes aware that the period is rather limited. Perhaps a question may be raised : - 'would not an indication of a short life-time be a depressant and so a retarder ?'. Yes, it will be so ordinarily. But a yogī, who has reached the stage of mastery in saṃyama, will have his abhiniveśa i.e. desire to cling to life, almost curbed to nought. He will be having a high degree of vairāgya also. So he will readily adjust himself to the inevitable. So for him, as said, this will be only a warning to increase and speed up the sādhanā.

SS. - **मैत्र्यादिषु बलानि ।।३:२३।।**

TL. - maitryādiṣu balāni - III:23

WM. - maitryādiṣu = (maitri = friendliness+ādi=etc.+ṣu in, plu.) in friendliness etc., bala (→āni) = strength (s), power (s)

TR. - (By performing saṃyama) In friendliness etc. (result different) powers.

CE. - The Sūtra tells about the application of saṃyama to various good qualities like friendliness i.e. feeling of love towards every living creature and such others basically present in the human nature, which produces different powers for the yogī. Every human being has a feeling of friendliness or love for someone. If saṃyama is directed on this the friendliness can be developed to such a highpitch that the other person, if he were not responding in the same manner, will now develop the same intense feeling of friendliness towards the performer of saṃyama. He will then be very prone to do whatever the latter may wish him to do. Thus the yogī or sādhaka has, so to say, a power over the other person. Again with such a desire and applying saṃyama for it the intense friendliness or love can be developed for a large group of persons or even universally with a similar return response from the other side. This then becomes a great power and can be utilized for any purpose. No doubt imperfect sādhakas may be tempted to exploit it for some mundane gain. But a real yogī would use it, if need be, for selfless universal welfare. Well known examples of this are Christ, Buddha and in recent past, Mahātmā Gāndhi.

The word 'ādi', meaning etcetera, indicates similar other good human traits like sympathy, courage and such others. These also can be developed by application of the process of saṃyama on each of them so as to transform them into useful power sources.

Some commentators following Vyāsa, have interpreted the word 'ādi', by referring to the Sūtra I:33 (maitrikaruṇā---), as indicating karuṇā, muditā and upekṣā. In this the list is restricted to only these four traits, which curtails the utility of this good technique. Secondly even in I:33 upekṣā i.e. indifference being a negative trait cannot be developed into a positive and beneficial power and so the commentators have to add that it should be omitted from this list. But then the word 'ādi' becomes improper. So we think that here by this 'ādi' should be understood all good human traits like 'maitrī'.

SS. - **बलेषु हस्तिबलादीनि ।।३:२४।।**

TL. - baleṣu hasti-balādīni - III : 24

WM. - bala(→eṣu) = power, might (in, plural);
hasti = elephant (-ine);
balādīni = (bala = power + ādi = etcetera + ini = plural suffix) power etceteras.

TR. - (By applying saṃyama) in mights (of elephant and such others) (are gained) elephantine and such other mights.

CE. - In the preceding III:23 Sūtra the powers gained are more abstract and mental. Patañjali, in this Sūtra, affirms that in the same manner even physical powers or mights of various types and degrees can be acquired by applying saṃyama on the desired type of power or force, no doubt with a desire to acquire oneself of that power. Thus directing the saṃyama on the strength of an elephant with a desire to have it in his own body, the yogī can develop in himself a might or force equal to an elephant. The same will hold good in the case of other living creatures. It can even be postulated, on similar lines, that forces of inanimate power-sources, such as machines etc. can also be acquired by the yogī with he application of saṃyama on those respective forces. In Patañjali's time use of machines etc., producing tremendous powers as those of modern times, was practically unknown. So he had no occasion to mention about such things.

The claim in this Sūtra may look as too much exaggerated, but there are actual instances, where a keen desire to develop such unbelievably astounding great strength, no doubt, with proper accessory measures like exercise, proper food etc., are often seen and some of these may be fairly widely known. In India, a few decades ago, two well-known circus men, Professor Rāmamūrti (also known as Indian Sandow) and his disciple Ekanāthamūrti had shown such feats of strength. The present commentator himself had a chance to see the latter, stopping a Buick motor - car, attempted to be driven with its full force by the chauffeur of then Mahārājāḥ of Dewas senior, a princely state in Madhya Pradesh and also keeping an elephant of the same Mahārājāḥ immobile for over ten to fifteen minutes, by pressing with his hands against the elephant's trunk, even when the Mahout was personally instructed by the Mahārājāḥ to try to make the elephant move forward with all its might. This particular instance has been mentioned purposefully, because in this case of demonstration of actual possession of strength equal to or even more than that of the elephant, there was no possibility of a trick or fraud, due to the car-driver or the mahout having been in league with Ekanāthamūrti and so the demonstration was an unquestionable proof of a human being possessing actual hasti-bala (elephantine power). There is also a special significance from the point of view of Yoga. Ekanāthamūrti told the Mahārājah at the end of the circus-programme that both he and his guru Prof. Rāmamūrti had developed such strength, not by mere gymnastic exercises, but through Yoga, specially prāṇāyamic practices.

SS. - **प्रवृत्त्यालोकन्यासात्सूक्ष्मव्यवहितविपकृष्टज्ञानम् ।।३:२५।।**

TL. - pravṛttyāloka-nyāsāt-sūkṣma-vyavahita-viprakṛṣṭa jñānam - III:25

WM. -

pravṛttyāloka	=	(pravṛtti = higher sensual faculty + āloka = illumination); illumination of the higher sensual faculty;
nyāsa (→āt)	=	placing upon, directing to (from, by);
sūkṣma	=	fine, subtle, minute; vyavahita = hidden, unmanifest;
viprakṛṣṭa	=	far distant;
jñāna (m)	=	knowledge (is).

TR. - By directing the illuminative power of the supersensual faculties (of different senses) by means of practising saṃyama on them) the knowledge about subtle (or minute) hidden or far-distant (things is obtained).

CE. - In sūtras I:35 and 36 the pravṛttis (of indriyas i.e. senses) have been mentioned. There they have been qualified and specified as 'visayavati', because the object to be experienced is to be created by the mind itself, through imagination. But the same faculties of different senses can be developed to the highest intensity by saṃyama on them. If then they are directed, again with the technique of saṃyama, to an outside object or subject, its knowledge can be gained by the mind, even if the object is so fine that it is not perceptible ordinarily through the senses or is totally hidden (i.e. cut off by some suitable means) from all the senses and so cannot be perceived in any manner or even if it is far distant and so cannot be contacted and perceived by the senses at all. Again it should be understood that these faculties can give knowledge of such things, only if they are applied to the object with this purpose and through the process of saṃyama.

SS. - भुवनज्ञानं सूर्ये संयमात् ।।३:२६।।

TL. - bhuvana-jñānam sūrye saṃyamāt - III:26

WM. - bhuvana = world or universe;

jñāna (m) = knowledge (is);

sūrya (→e) = sun (in or on);

saṃyama (→āt) = saṃyama (from, through).

TR. - Through performing saṃyama on the Sun (is obtained) the knowledge of the world.

CE. - The term 'bhuvana' in the compound word 'bhuvana-jñāna' can be treated as singular or plural in grammatical number. In the former case the purport of the sūtra would be that the knowledge of our universe would be obtained through saṃyama on sūrya i.e. Sun, which is looked upon as the centre of the universe by popular belief and also in older concept of the universe in India and also elsewhere.

In Indian mythology there are referred a number of worlds (universes ?) besides our own world, though these can be different in some respects than ours. Yogīs and mystics seem to be able to develop the faculty in themselves, by which they can enter into and return from these other worlds. Indeed the affirmation of existence of such worlds is based on such experiences. Even modern science speculates the possibility of existence of one or more universes, which may be even an exact replica of universe and yet having complete inversion in the nature of some of the forces which sustain it. If the term bhuvana be interpreted as being indicative of plural number, then this sūtra would seem to state that knowledge about all these different universes can be gained by the yogī, if he desires for it, by directing the saṃyama on the Sun, which for us is the centre, not only of our universe, but the whole creation, though what is exactly the centre of our universe and of whole creation is a mute point. Our Sun, according to current knowledge is definitely not that. It is not even the centre of our own galaxy, in which it holds comparatively a minor position. But as said, for a person living on our planet earth, the Sun seems like the central point of the universe. Even in the view point of modern science, where the theory of our Expanding Universe is getting preponderance, our solar system seems to be the point from which different regions of the universe viz. other galaxies are, as if, scattering away. On account of this core position of the Sun, given mainly by our conception, when the saṃyama is directed upon the Sun, the knowledge of all the other words, which, from our point of view are distributed around this centre, becomes attainable.

SS. - **चन्द्रे ताराव्यूहज्ञानम् ।।३:२७।।**

TL. - candre tārā-vyūha-jñānam - III:27

WM. -	candra (→e)	=	moon (in);
	tārā	=	star (s);
	vyūha	=	orderly arrangement, plan;
	jñāna(m)	=	knowledge (is).

TR. - (Through saṃyama) on moon (is attained) the knowledge of stellar constellations.

CE. - The moon is the heavenly body which, though a satellite of our earth and a very minor heavenly object, forms an important entity for us in the whole assemblage of the stars and planets, on account of its brilliance and visible size, in relation to all the other heavenly bodies, except the Sun. In the night, when the Sun is absent, it is the brightest and the biggest luminous body in the sky. For this reason it has been even called Tārānātha (Master of stars) Nakṣatrādhipati (Lord of constellations) etc. Therefore, when saṃyama is directed upon it, with an idea that it is the key-member among the stars and planets and with a desire to have the knowledge of other stars and planets surrounding it, the knowledge about their orderly arrangement around this prominent member amongst them becomes clearly understandable for the yogī.

SS. - ध्रुवे तद्गतिज्ञानम् ।।३:२८।।

TL. - dhruve tad-gati-jñānam - III:28

WM. - dhruva (e) = polar star (in);
tat(→d) = their;
gati = movement;
jñāna (m) = knowledge (is).

TR. - (Through saṃyama) on (the Northern) polar star (is attained) the knowledge about their (stars and planets) movements.

CE. - This sūtra is on the same lines as the two just preceding it. Every heavenly body seems to move. According to a popular belief, based on a mythological story, the North polar star is the only exception. The story is about a child devotee of god Viṣṇu-Dhruva, the son of a king Uttānapāda was kicked down from the lap of his father by his jealous step-mother. He took the insult so deeply that he went into the forest and practised tapas (austerities) so long and seriously that Lord Viṣṅu appeared before him and offered to fulfil any desire of his. The child said that he wanted to have such a seat that no power in the world should be able to displace him even slightly from there. Lord Viṣṅu made him the immovable North-pole-star, which is, therefore, called Dhruva. For us the star of Dhruva is practically immovable (though it actually moves a little in a circle, for us of a few centimetre circumference, i.e. it moves less than 2 cms. in 1000 years-almost no movement noticeable in one life-time of man). On account of this immoveability of this Dhruva-star the word dhruva in Indian languages means perfectly immovable or steady.

We can measure and in fact become aware of a movement in relation to some standard reference point, which is relatively steady. In this way the pivotal point of movement of all the heavenly bodies, as seen from the earth, is the Dhruva-star, around which they all seem to move in circles. Thus this steady star of Dhruva is the point of reference by which we gauge the movement of the all other heavenly bodies, inclusive of the Sun and the Moon. Obviously therefore, neither of these latter two can help in getting the knowledge of the heavenly bodies. That is why the saṃyama on Dhruva-star is recommended as the only one which can give the knowledge about the stellar movements.

SS. - **नाभिचक्रे कायव्यूहज्ञानम् ।।३:२९।।**

TL. - nābhi-cakre kāya-vyūha-jñānam - :III29

WM. -
nābhi = navel;
cakra (→e) = circle or region roundabout (on);
kāya = body;
vyūha = orderly arrangements or systems or organisations;
jñāna (m) = knowledge (is).

TR. - (Through performing saṃyama) on the region round about the navel (is obtained) the knowledge of the organisations (or systems) in the body.

CE. - Most of the commentators have confused the term nābhicakra with the mystical Tāntrika Maṇīpura cakra. Though the words nāḍi and cakra have been used by Patañjali respectively in the next-but-one and the present sūtra, these do not seem to have the specific significance of the mystic cakras and nāḍis of the Tāntrika-yogas. If Patañjali were mentioning the regular Maṇīpura cakra here, there was no reason for him to use this out-of-the -way strange name in place of the proper term Maṇīpura cakra. On the contrary his use of the name nābhicakra, instead of that proper technical name, seems to us to show his clear intention to avoid any possibility of misidentification with those Tāntrika nāḍis and cakras, causing a confusion. As is shown by us cakra is used by Patañjali to indicate a roughly circular region, in which sense the word is very commonly used. The term nāḍi, which is a word formed by substitution of letter 'ḍ' in place of the similarly sounding letter 'l' of the word nali, which means a channel or gutter, is also used here in this very sense, as a nontechnical term. Even the Tāntrika technical term nāḍi has this same sense i.e. that of channel or passage; in the technical sense it is a channel or definite route for mystic energy like prāṇa.

Nābhi-chakra here, thus, means simply the region round about the navel. Any person, who has some knowledge of the development of an embryo or who has witnessed the delivery of an offspring from the mother's womb, knows that the offspring's whole organism is connected, controlled and nourished by the umbilical cord and that after impregnation of the ovule by the sperm, when the development of the embryo starts, the first group of cells produced is the point or region where later the umbilicus (i.e. navel) is formed, from which the umbilical cord starts and is connected to the mother's placenta. Around this, all the other organ-structures gradually develop. In this way the navel is the centre around which all other organs and systems of the body develop in the embryo. Looked at in this way navel is the origin or starting centre of the mammalian and that means of also the man's body.

In parallelism to the sūtras III:26 to 28, when the saṃyama is directed to this circle or region of the origin of the body, the organisation in the whole of the body becomes known to the yogī. The different organs and the systems in the animal, including the human, body have developed in its embryonic stage from this cakra i.e. from the circle or region around the navel and so the saṃyama on this cakra can give a very clear knowledge, not only of how the different organs and systems in the body are organised at that time, but, if the yogī so desires, of how this whole organisation was evolved right from its inception stage. Primarily the kāya-vyūha-jñāna in the sūtra is meant to be the knowledge of the yogī's own body and so the nābhicakra also his own. But if the yogī on some occasion wants to know about the organisation (which can be a little different in some respects) of another persons and animal's body, he can in the same way have saṃyama on the respective navel.

It will be seen that in the light of the above discussion about the navel-region being the starting point in the organised development of the body, the resulting of the knowledge of the organisation in the body through the saṃyama on the navel-region seems quite logical. On the other hand, why saṃyama on Maṇīpura cakra should give this same result does not become clear in any reasonable manner. Moreover, if saṃyama on one of the cakras and so also one of the nāḍis (and that also not any prominent one; at least its name does not occur in the enumeration of the ten or twenty four chief nāḍis enumerated in the Tāntrika texts) gives such vibhūtis, the saṃyama on other of the satcakras and on the other nāḍis, still more important from the viewpoint of Tāntras and of spiritual evolution, should be expected to give rise to similar vibhūtis. Naturally it is also to be expected that Patañjali would have mentioned certainly some of those saṃyamas and vibhūtis at least. His complete omission of the names of the well-recognised cakras and nāḍis of Tāntra -yogas and no recommendation of any vibhūti accruing from saṃyama on any one of them, is a clear indication that Patañjali in these sūtras is not talking about the cakras and nāḍis in the Tāntras, but using the words cakra and nāḍi in their ordinary sense of circular region and channel or tubule respectively and here in the sūtra III:29, by cakra he is simply mentioning the navel- region and as explained there, in 111:31, a specific anatomical hollow structure in the ear, respectively.

SS. - **कण्ठकूपे क्षुत्पिपासानिवृत्तिः ।।३:३०।।**

TL. - kaṇṭha-kūpe kṣut-pipāsā-nivṛttiḥ - III:30

WM. - kaṇṭha	=	throat, gullet;
kūpa (→e)	=	well, hollow shaft (in, on);
kṣut	=	hunger;
pipāsā	=	thirst;

nivṛtti (ḥ) = niḥ - ni = no + vṛtti = inclination disinclination, termination, cessation, disappearance (is).

TR. - (Through performance of saṃyama) On the throat-well (results) the disappearance of hunger and thirst.

CE. - For the common man the feeling of thirst is in upper part of the throat at the beginning of the gullet i.e. in the pharynx. That is why a thirsty person says that his throat is dried up and needs a wetting. This pharynx has a resemblance to the opening of a well .When very hungry the sensation of hunger may be located in the stomach, but most often it also is felt in the pharynx. At least first quenching and feeling of satisfaction is produced in the pharynx. So directing saṃyama in this region, which is the seat of the sense of hunger and thirst for a common man, the feelings of hunger and thirst can be made to disappear.

SS. - कूर्मनाड्यां स्थैर्यम् ।।३:३१।।

TL. - kūrma-nāḍyāṃ sthairyam - III:31

WM. - kūrma = tortoise, here a proper name;
nāḍi (→yāṃ) = channel, hollow tubular way (on);
sthairya (m) = steadiness (is achieved).

TR. - (By performing saṃyama) on kurmanāḍi (results) steadiness.

CE. - As said in sūtra III:29, this is not any 'prāṇavahā (channelizing prāṇa) nāḍi' of Tāntrika concept, as thought by some commentators. Indeed, 'kūrmai' does not occur as the name of any nāḍi in the enumeration of Tāntrika nāḍis. The word nāḍi is derived from the word nali = channel, by substitution of 'ḍi' for 'li' and carries the same meaning. It thus is used for any passage in the shape of a gutter, channel tubular structure or any other hollow roundish long structure. The word kūrma means a tortoise. So this word can be used for a hollow longish elliptical structure which has a resemblance to the tortoise.

If kūrma-nāḍi, though not enumerated among the main nāḍis of Tantra texts, be still presumed to be a nāḍi of minor importance only. The locations and functions of even the chief Tāntrika nāḍis are not precisely and clearly described, leave aside those of any minor nāḍis. In Tāntrika texts kūrma is the name of a secondary prāṇa or vāyu. The location of this prāṇa is given very vaguely as skin, bone etc. and function as winking etc.. There is no mention of any special channel for this prāṇa, which at least could be called as kūrmanāḍi after it. Even if it be presumed that there is a kūrma nāḍi, in which this kūrma vāyu or prāṇa flows, neither its location nor its functions are known, nor these can be guessed from those of the vāyu passing through it. Again it is difficult to see why samyama on a thing, whose function is winking and such others, should result in sthairya, whether of body or of mind.

Some orthodox commentators have tried to connect the word kūrma with the second incarnation, that of tortoise, of god Viṣṇu. They think that kūrma kept the Meru mountain up when the gods and demons were churning the milk-sea with it, to bring up the amṛta (Ambrosia); so also this kūrma nāḍi would be a steady support for the body and make the whole of it steady. But this explanation is only based on a mythological belief and even with that the exact position and nature of this kūrma nāḍi do not become clear, nay even its existence remains doubtful. They, therefore suggest rather a vague procedure that the sadhaka should presume that the kūrmanāḍi has its place some where in the body and that it has the same attributes as Kūrma-avatāra of Viṣṇu and practise saṃyama on this. In other words they suggest meditation or samyama upon Kūrmavatara of Viṣṇu, which, they say, will give steadiness. But this whole explanation is not very rational and is too far-fetched. Moreover it is almost a samyama on Kūrmāvatāra and not on kūrma-nāḍi. If this was the saṃyama for gaining steadiness, Patañjali would have stated thus directly and clearly.

Some commentators have suggested that the organ of heart is the kūrma-nāḍi. This is because (1) the oval shape of heart with the arteries and veins attached to it resembles some what a tortoise, (2) the hollow vascularity of the organ, (3) when emotion etc. cause instability of the body (i.e. shaking, tremoring etc.) the impact is felt in the heart and (4) when heart is smoothly working, usually body is steady. The first two points are favourable for accepting heart as kūrmanāḍī. But the behaviour of heart mentioned in (3) and (4) does not lead to steadiness of the body or mind, but is itself the result of the latter.

It is a well recognised fact in physiology that the stability of the body is regulated by the cochlea in the inner ear. This very small organ very much resembles the elliptical shape of the back of the tortoise with its four limbs extended. The resemblance of tortoise with cochlea is much closer than that with the oval shape of heart. The ellipse in the cochlea is formed by the spiralling of fine tubules. On account of this shape and hollow tubulous structure the name kūrma-nāḍi i.e. tortoise (-like) channel very properly fits to this organ. But a more significant reason is that this organ gives the awareness of our positioning in space e.g. whether we are standing, lying horizontally or sitting erect or inclined etc. Through this awareness only we are able to maintain our body in any particular position steady upto a desired period. If there is caused some defect or disorder in this organ, we cannot know in what position our body is and so no position can be maintained for any length of time at all. We lose the control on our positioning ability totally. We get dizzy, swoon and may fall down, if we try to stand. We cannot even sit erect. So from this functional aspect also this surely must be the kūrmanāḍi of this sūtra. According to the very old and popular belief Patañjali was an authority in Āyurveda, the traditional Indian science of life and health, equivalent to modern science of medicine. He is supposed to be the author of the most revered treatise of Āyurveda named Caraka Saṃhitā, Caraka being supposed to be a pseudonym of his. There are very well known panegyrical verses mentioning this fact. Whatever it may be, it seems that he had a good and minute knowledge about human organism. So he must be knowing well the structure and function of this organ. Therefore, no wonder, he suggested samyama on it to gain steadiness. So also a yogī, who has gained a precise and detailed knowledge of the organisation in the body through the saṃyama on nābhicakra as per sūtra III:29, will have a clear understanding of the structure and function of cochlea. Directing saṃyama on this organ of stability, with a wish to have steadiness of the body, the yogī can surely have it. Some commentators include steadiness of mind also in the sthairya of this sūtra. But that will be attained only after the steadiness of body and so for it also saṃyama on kūrma-nāḍi is necessary.

SS. - **मूर्धज्योतिषि सिद्धदर्शनम् ।।३:३२।।**

TL. - mūrdha-jyotiṣi siddha-darśanam - III:32

WM. -

mūrdha	=	situated in or at the apex the cranium or head, the spot usually known as brahmarandhra;
jyotiṣa (→ṣi)	=	light, luminescence (in, on);
siddha	=	siddha, accomplished yogī ;
darśana (m)	=	vision (is).

TR. - (By performing samyama) on the luminescence situated in the apex of the cranium (results) the vision of siddhas.

CE. - It is common and very well-known experience in almost all mystic schools that the sadhaka begins to see a light in some region of his body. This experience is well recognised in yogic circles. Patañjali twice makes a specific mention of this phenomenon, here and in sūtra I:36 where he mentions it as a useful technique for achieving steadiness of mind: The places in body where this light usually is seen are the apex of head, the midbrow region in the forehead, the heart and occasionally the navel region. As per the sūtra, directing samyama on this light at the top point of the head gives the vision of any desired siddha yogī or saint. The light is seen spontaneously by many sādhakas. It can also be wilfully produced as in sūtra I:36 or through saṃyama for this cranial apex called brahmarandhra (=opening leading to brahman, the final Reality or goal as per Vedānta, but used in this sense in common parlance also) is well known as a centre of manifestation of the spiritual force or light. This is also the point where the mystic Kuṇḍalinī merges with Śiva. This is also the 'Tenth door,' through which only the prāṇa of the Siddhayogīs leaves the body at the time of their relinquishing the body. It is affirmed that the prāṇa of the person who attains mokṣa, the final liberation, leaves the body at its fall, only through this 'door', which is found cracked and opened in such cases. All these beliefs show the importance of the apex of cranium for occurrence of spiritual phenomena. That is why when saṃyama is practised there-specially on the light ever glowing there, the self-principle of the desired Siddha manifests itself there, assuming a subtle prāṇic body.

SS. - **प्रातिभाद्वा सर्वम् ।।३:३३।।**

TL. - prātibhād-vā sarvam - III:33

WM. - Pratibhā (→āt→ād) = pertaining to Pratibhā i.e. the inspirational power (from, through);

vā = or;

sarva (m) = all (is).

TR. - Or, through (performing saṃyama) directed to Pratibhā (= the intuitional inspirational potentiality) (is achieved the knowledge of) all.

CE. - The full import of the word vā = 'or', here is : 'Or how long can I go on enumerating the saṃyamas of similar nature and the vibhūtis accruing from them. Thus shall summarize them in one sūtra here'.

In this sūtra Patañjali is therefore indicating a saṃyama, which will give knowledge of all subjects what so ever. Considering the position of the sūtra, this 'all' should be taken to mean 'all subjects similar in nature to those dealt with so far'. Pratibhā is the intuitional inspirational potentiality. All the lofty feats of art, literature and even science, in fact all supreme human achievements in all fields, have been possible through this potentiality of the geniuses, who were the authors of these superlative creations. All great poets, writers, dramatists, sculptors, painters, even scientists (cf. CE on sūtras III:1 to 4) have accomplished their supreme work though their Pratibhā. Such astounding, inspired almost divine creations would have not been at all possible without the agency of the divine gift of Pratibhā.

The difficulty about this Pratibhā is that it is not under the voluntary control of the genius. That is why the same poet or artist can not produce to order the creation of the same high value again. When the yogī directs the saṃyama on his faculty of Pratibhā, which is latent in every human, with a desire to develop it to its highest degree, it will become a means for the yogī, by which he can get the knowledge or potentiality of the types mentioned in the foregoing sūtras of vibhūtis. If, for example, the yogī wants to gain the knowledge of bhuvanas (sūtra III:26), he need not direct the saṃyama necessarily on the Sun, but through the highly developed Pratibhā he can get the same knowledge directly and easily. In this way instead of having to resort to different types of saṃyamas, he can have the power of Pratibhā developed to the maximum and with its use he can have any type of knowledge, specially useful for practical purposes, by simply directing the Pratibhā to that particular subject. Thus to conclude, if the yogī has once practised saṃyama on Pratibhā, it can be so developed that the yogī can get any type of knowledge of anything instantly by just desiring for it, by simply the use of this acute Pratibhā, (For understanding the mechanism of the rise of such inspirational knowledge, as though exploding or flashing in the consciousness, see explanations under sūtras III:1 to 4. CE, pp. 338 ff). He then has not to search and decide about the ālambana i.e. the support or subject on which to perform saṃyama, to get the desired knowledge (i.e. resulting vibhūti) and go on performing all these saṃyamas recommended so far and in a similar way saṃyamas, again and again, on other ālambanas or subjects for other such vibhūtis. But just as soon as a desire for any such knowledge arises in his mind, that knowledge at once flashes up in his mind. He becomes a 'sarvajña' in the usual sense.

It may be mentioned here that the word sarvaṃ basically means all. So the possibility that it may mean literally all the vibhūtis of the nature of knowledge, even those mentioned hereafter, may be included in this term. However, as said, from the positioning of the sūtra, the logical interpretation seems to be, 'all the preceding ones'. It is noteworthy that most of these vibhūtis mentioned prior to this are more of the nature of knowledge, which however could be used as powers. Vibhūtis stated hereafter are either more of the nature of a power, which can be used directly for some worldly gain or more significant for a spiritually inclined person.

As pointed out Pratibhā, an inspirational intuitional faculty, is inherent in every man. From the instances of Archemedes, Newton and Kekule described before (under sūtras III:1 to 4, CE) it can be seen that this faculty produces sometimes a knowledge in man spontaneously just like a flash. In the appearance of such knowledge, therefore, there is no use of the senses, nor there is any active thinking nor reasoning. In fact, very often the knowledge at first is not acceptable to reason. But by later experience, it is often proved to be correct. In this sense Pratibhā is a spontaneously flashing prajñā. As said the only defect with it is that it cannot be always available for use, when we need it. Moreover it may prove sometimes wrong also. When it is developed and sharpened by the process of saṃyama applied to it, it comes under complete control of a yogī and always gives correct knowledge. Indeed it is the Ṛtambharā-prajñā which is working here. In other words the ordinary Pratibhā is transformed into fully developed Ṛtambharāprajñā.

SS. - **हृदये चित्तसंवित् ।।३:३४।।**

TL. - hṛdaye citta-saṃvit - III:34.

TL. - hṛdaya (→e) = heart (in, on);

citta = citta;

saṃvit = consciousness, awareness, knowledge;

TR. - (Through saṃyama) on the heart (arises) the knowledge about the citta.

CE. - The dictionary meaning of the word saṃvit is consciousness, awareness etc. The word can be broken as saṃ = Complete + vit = to Know and thus would indicate knowledge or understanding. But knowledge is gained by the citta itself. Thus the statement of the sūtra is somewhat like, 'The saṃyama on heart gives the knowledge of citta to the citta itself' and so seems a little absurd. Because knowledge is gained by a knower (jñātā) separate from the thing becoming known. Awareness is not that much clear and crystallized and can be had to oneself. Knowledge can be usually neatly set in words. Awareness is rather comparatively vague and so usually cannot be properly put forth in words. But beyond this, there is not much difference in these two words. They can be interchanged, if context indicates such necessity. That is why the word saṃvit, usually translated as awareness or consciousness, has been rendered as knowledge by us in this sūtra. This is also in accord with the meaning derived from its break-up as shown above. In fact, the saṃyama on the heart gives complete knowledge of the citta (obviously to citta itself).

The region of the functioning of citta-mind in the body, according to modern understanding, would be the head or more precisely the brain and the nervous system linked with it, provided it be assumed and accepted that a region is there in the body, where mind-citta function. Actually it becomes incumbent to think of mind and citta as entities separate from body. Even then their closest linkage obviously is with brain and nervous system out of all the body systems. But this was not clearly recognised in the ancient times. The association of the citta-mind and the brain etc. cannot be easily seen without the help of suitable instruments. At least the relationship of these cannot be easily perceived through direct observation of the normal functions of the body in a normal healthy condition. On the other hand, if there is any emotional disturbance, there is felt a noticeable palpitation or thumping of the heart. (In a sudden terrifying shock there is a feeling of lumpiness in the stomach. But there is no sensation in the stomach in any other emotion. Even in moderate fear, there is no feeling in the stomach. Moreover stomach is looked upon as mainly an organ of digestion. So it is not connected with citta as its seat or field of function as is done with the heart). The quickening of the heart action and its palpitation take place in all kinds of emotional disturbances, e.g. in fear, joy, love, expectation etc. the beatings of the heart increase and this happens to some extent even in a moderate disturbance though emotional. This palpitating is clearly felt also. For these reasons the ancients (not in India, but elsewhere also) thought the heart as the seat of citta, at least its easily recognisable region of functioning. This is clearly seen from such idioms e.g. 'His heart has no pity', 'cruel of heart' etc., which are common to most languages. That is the reason the saṃyama on heart is recommended for gaining the knowledge of citta.

One point need be explained here in respect of saṃyamas and vibhūtis. Even if the relation between the ālambana (=support i.e. subject) chosen for the saṃyama and the thing of which the knowledge results from that saṃyama may not be really existing, as is presumed by the yogī, yet if the yogī has a firm belief about that kind of relation existing between the two, then the yogī will obtain that desired and expected knowledge through the saṃyama on that ālambana. Thus, for example, the heart may not really be the seat of citta, yet as the yogī has a firm conviction that the heart is the abode of citta, then as per this sūtra he will get the complete knowledge of citta through the saṃyama on the heart.

SS. - **सत्त्वपुरुषयोरत्यन्तासंकीर्णयोः प्रत्ययाविशेषो भोगः परार्थत्वात् स्वार्थसंयमात्पुरुषज्ञानम् ।।३:३५।।**

TL. - sattva-puruṣayor-atyantāsaṃkīrṇayoḥ pratyayāviś-eṣo bhogaḥ parārthatvāt svārtha-saṃyamāt-puruṣa-jñānam - III:35

WM. - sattva = (sat = to be + tva = ness) literally beingness, so the mere existence, a vague awareness of which can there be in citta, thus it may be said to be the mere existence of citta, almost devoid of active consciousness i.e. the state prior to its becoming citta (i.e. the means of consciousness);

puruṣa (→yoḥ→yor) = puruṣa - principle (of, dual)

atyanta = extremely;

asaṃkīrṇa (yoḥ)	=	(a = not+saṃkīrṇa = mixed, here miscible) im - miscible, having quite different natures, heterogeneous (dual 6 th possessive case suffix);
pratyaya	=	experience (of the citta), understanding;
aviśeṣa (ḥ->o)	=	(a = non + viśeṣa = distinction) nondistinction;
bhoga (ḥ)	=	life-experience (of enjoyments and sufferings) (is);
parārthatva (->āt)	=	(para = other's + artha = purpose +tva = ness) purposefulness or utility for other (from);
svārtha	=	(sva=self, one's own+artha= purpose) purposefulness for (one's own) self;
saṃyama (->āt)	=	saṃyama (from, through, by);
puruṣa	=	puruṣa principle;
jñāna (m)	=	knowledge (is, results).

TR. - The (erroneous) understanding of (total) non-distinction (i.e. total identity) of the two extremely heterogeneous (to such an extent that they, like two poles of a magnet, can never come even near to one another), (principles viz.) sattva and puruṣa is (resulting into) the life-experience (of enjoyments and sufferings). Through (performing) saṃyama on (the correct understanding of) what is for the purpose of (puruṣa, the really significant principle in) one-self (as differentiated) from what is for the purpose of the other (principle, namely sattva i.e. pristine formative state of citta, out of mūla prakṛti) (results) the knowledge about puruṣa.

CE. - Bhoga basically means experience, but, the word is usually used for good and pleasant experience, though occasionally for painful experience also. But as per sūtra II:15 all experience-even the pleasant one-is ultimately painful. So the proper meaning of bhoga should be pain, misery, sufferings etc. The first portion of the sūtra thus states a very general philosophical truth, pointing out the ultimate cause giving rise to this suffering experience. This is the phenomenon of having a confusion between and misidentiflcation of the citta with puruṣa, called saṃyoga and accepted by both Sāṃkhya and Yoga. The term used for citta here is sattva, indicating the stage of its emergence from the mūla -prakṛti, where it is yet to get its potentiality of consciousness. In other words it is prakṛti, which is yet to become cit-ta-'incit-ed'.

The statement lays a great stress on the fact that sattva i.e. (pristine) citta is extremely distinct from puruṣa. By this it means that they can really never come together or get even related in any manner.

In the latter portion of the sūtra is indicated the application of saṃyama, which would give rise to a very clear understanding of the exact and real nature of puruṣa. This will, therefore, also lead to the knowledge of its complete distinctness from the other principle prakṛti and its product citta. The common man usually has an impression that citta or rather its more active part, the mind, is the ultimate consciousness principle and so the source of the feeling of "I" or self. All the experiences that a man undergoes throughout his life are, therefore, looked upon by him as serving i.e. giving pleasure to this 'I'. But the real source of consciousness according to Sāṃkhya and Yoga is the puruṣa-tattva. So every experience in the ultimate sense is meant for serving the purpose of this puruṣa, the real principle behind the self. But, as said, this distinction is never clearly present in man, even when he may have merely intellectually understood it, by being acquainted with Sāṃkhya-Yoga theories. When saṃyama is directed to the distinction between the real purpose viz. serving the real self i.e. puruṣa and the apparent purpose viz. serving citta, with a desire to have a clear perception and conviction about this, the knowledge of the utter immiscibility of these two becomes firmly ingrained in the yogasādhaka.

This knowledge and further its actual realization comes up to the yogasādhaka in the progress of samādhi, particularly in the nirbīja samādhi. But Patañjali here gives a saṃyama by which the process is somewhat accelerated.

SS. - **ततः प्रातिभश्रावणवेदनादर्शास्वादवार्ता जायन्ते ।।३:३६।।**

TL. - tataḥ prātibha-śrāvaṇa-vedanādarśāsvāda-vārtā jāyante - III:36

WM. - tataḥ = thence, from that;
prātibha = related to pratibhā, inspired, intuitional;
śrāvaṇa = concerned with hearing, auditory;
vedana = (concerned with) touch, tactile sense, tactile;

ādarśa	=	concerned with vision, visual;
āsvāda	=	(concerned with) taste, gustatory;
vārtā	=	(concerned with) smell, olfactory;
jāyante	=	are produced.

TR.- From that (puruṣa-jñāna) are produced the inspirational (development of the faculties of) audition, tactility, vision, taste (and) smell.

CE.- The saṃyama mentioned in the preceding III:35 sūtra produces some secondary effects besides puruṣa-jñāna. These are enumerated in the present sūtra. These are the faculties of the sense which are inspirational and intuitional i.e. spontaneous and supremely efficacious. Due to them, experiences of objects can be obtained, which otherwise would not be ordinarily possible. This is indicated by the adjective prātibha. Vyāsa and following him many commentators think prātibha as indicating an independent faculty viz. prātibha. They, therefore, interpret that through its development can be perceived and experienced things which are subtle, hidden, far distant or even in the past or future. How far this is correct is uncertain. If prātibha is understood as indicating the independent sixth faculty viz. pratibhā, then it means that prātibha is not qualifying the further five words śrāvaṇa etc.. which indicate the functions of the five senses. That would mean that the five sense faculties of audition etc. are without any qualification i.e. just ordinary or normal functioning of the senses. But then the sūtra statement loses its whole purpose or significance. Therefore, we have understood prātibha as qualifying all the five words of sense-faculties following it and have translated the sūtra accordingly.

The word 'Vārtā' has been interpreted as olfactory i.e. concerned with the faculty of smelling by all commentators and so also by us in the translation of the sūtra above. But this meaning of the word is not found in the dictionaries, nor is it easily derivable or explainable. The reason seems to be that the remaining four senses of hearing, touch, vision and taste have been clearly mentioned, while the mention of the sense of smell is missing and so Vyāsa the first commentator presumed, rightly or wrongly, the word Vārtā to be standing for it. All the latter commentators followed suit. As there seem some plausibility, we have also given the same meaning. But other interpretation can be equally plausible, as will be seen below.

What seems more probable is that Patañjali actually does not want to mention the sense of smell in this sūtra. The reason may be that when these extra-ordinary sense-function-developments are produced by the said samyama they seem just like miraculous i.e. highly astounding developments, which is indicated also by the adjective prātibha. This is true for the four other senses excluding smell. In the case of the sense of smell, this development may not seem miraculous. As explained under sūtra 1:35, the similar development of faculty of all the first four senses named in this sūtra is produced by a strong desire for such development accompanied with an acute attention on the pertinent sense-organ. The effect in the case of the sense other than smell is not so much of an astonishing kind, while in the case of smell even there (results of the technique of sūtra 1:35) the effect is as good as miraculous. So this inspirational (prātibha) development in the cases of smell will not be anyway distinguishable from that produced by the method of sūtra 1:35. On account of this previous acquaintance with this phenomenon of (outer) causeless odour, its novelty or miraculousness will be lost. Thus it will no more be worthy of being qualified as prātibha i.e. inspirational., divine etc. and hence Patañjali might have thought it proper not to mention it among these divya (= divine) experiences.

If 'Vārtā' does not refer to olfactory sense, then what does it mean in the sūtra ? This word as such is not found in dictionaries and śabdakośas. (The nearest word is 'Vārttā' = News, but its spelling is different). It seems to be Patañjali's own coining. It could be derived from the root 'vṛt', meaning either (1) to behave, act, function or (2) to occur. It would thus mean either (1) the function or (2) occurrence, phenomenon etc. The translation of the sūtra then would be as : -

From that (puruṣa-jñāna) are produced the inspirational (or divine) (1) developments of functions ,...., (2) phenomena ..., of audition, tactility, vision (and) taste.

How far this is correct i.e. acceptable could be decided by the reader himself.

A question remains still unanswered as to why these supernormal or divine developments of the faculties of senses should arise by the said saṃyama or its result, the purusa-jnana itself. The explanation seems to be as follows : -

The indriyas (= senses) are the instruments for the mind, which therefore, in its ordinary course perceives the worldly objects, no doubt, through the intermediacy of the senses.

According to the Sāṃkhya - Yoga view, even mind and so also the senses are governed by the ultimate consciousness faculty or agency viz. the citta. But again the citta gets the potentiality to become conscious due to the mere presence of puruṣa. Simultaneously the 'Saṃyoga' i.e. misidentification of the citta with puruṣa comes into existence. The puruṣa-jñāna is the clear and firm understanding of the total distinctness of the citta from the puruṣa. With this firmly ingrained puruṣa-jñāna, the citta, though still conscious, becomes, as if, autonomous. Its limitations are gone and its power is enhanced astoundingly, so that it can now get the knowledge of things without the intermediacy of senses. In this way, the category of the knowledge becomes 'Direct' in real sense, i.e. inspirational or divine. The instruments of he citta viz. the mind and the senses become superfluous i.e. now unneeded by the citta. The external object or subject is experienced or enjoyed by citta directly in itself. This experience is of a different nature than a similar experience obtained through the technique of the viṣayavatī-pravṛtti of sūtra 1:35, where, the object is produced or imagined inside itself by the mind and so the mind as well as the senses are involved. That is in viṣayavatī-pravṛtti the particular experience is about an object or subject existing merely in the imagination in the mind and yet the experience about it is got by the mind only through proper sensation felt in the particular sense. But in this prātibha-jñāna the experience gained is of an external object or subject, actually present in the world and the citta gets its experience not on the sense level or mind level, but directly in itself and that is why it is felt as 'divine'.

SS. - ते समाधावुपसर्गा व्युत्थाने सिद्धयः ।।३:३७।।

TL. - te samādhāvupasargā vyutthāne siddhayaḥ -III:37

WM. - te = they, those;
samādhi (→au→av) = samādhi (in);
upasarga (→āḥ→ā) = interferences, obstacles (are);
vyutthāna (→e) = extrovertness, worldliness (in);
siddhi (→ayaḥ) = siddhi (s), miraculous accomplishment (s) (are).

TR.- They are obstacles in (the path of) samādhi, (but) siddhis in (the life of) worldliness

CE.- The word 'they' in the sūtra can be interpreted in three ways:-

1. The special developments, which at first seem to be the faculties of the senses, mentioned in the preceding 111:36 sūtra.
2. The vibhūtis mentioned so far prior to this i.e. in sūtras HI: 16 to 36.
3. All the vibhūtis noted in this third Vibhūti pāda and so also others similar ones not noted here.

From the position of the sūtra and the usual conventions of sūtra interpretation it is logical to accept preferably the first or at the most the second interpretation. But as is popularly understood, all siddhis i.e. miraculous accomplishments or powers are looked upon as hindrances for spiritual sādhanā, because they enable the yogī to do some miraculous feats and if he uses these for some worldly benefits, not even for himself but for the welfare of masses, this makes him very popular and attracts a large following. Again from this, other worldly advantages e.g. fame, wealth, power etc. accrue. Thus if the vibhūtis are exploited for worldly gains they, at least in this respect, become on par with the siddhis and prove an enticement for a yogasādhaka which entangles him more and more into worldliness. It may ultimately even lead to complete obliteration of the urge in him for spiritual awakening and attaining the goal. In this light the sūtra can be interpreted in the third way also and may be looked upon as a statement applicable to all kinds of siddhis and vibhūtis exploited like siddhis, whatsoever they may be.

As already mentioned under the sūtra III:4, Patañjali makes a distinction between a vibhūti and a siddhi. Therefore only in case the sādhaka exploits for mundane advantages a vibhūti, which might have appeared in him even spontaneously during practice of meditation, particularly when he has become efficient in the stages of dhāranā, dhyāna and sabīja samādhi i.e. achieved proficiency in saṃyama, then, as said, these vibhūtis no longer remain vibhūtis, but become, so to say, siddhis i.e. powers usable for advantages in the worldly life. In that case they would prove an obstacle for the spiritual development as explained above. That is the general purport of the sūtra.

The popular belief about siddhis, that they become hindrances in the spiritual progress of yoga sādhaka is true only in respect of siddhis, because, as said, they are always used for some mundane advantage. The belief does not hold true in respect of vibhūtis. The reason for this is that the siddhis are not necessarily a result of practice of some yoga technique. As Patañjali indicates in sūtra IV: 1, they are produced by other means also and may even be just congenital and so fortuitous. In such cases the persons getting the siddhi and even a person practising yoga with a desire to get some siddhi, will have no vairāgya and so they will naturally be inclined to derive worldly benefits and will use the siddhis for such advantages and that also for only selfish ends. Vibhūtis are not fortuitous. They are being produced as explained under sūtra III:4, through a scientific principle and are the result of application of the technique of saṃyama in a well thought-out manner. The yogī, who has reached a stage of good proficiency in saṃyama, will be having a high degree of vairāgya also. So the chance of his exploiting the vibhūti for selfish mundane gains would be very little. Nevertheless if he uses it that way, it, as said, no longer remains a vibhūti, but becomes on par to siddhi. Though the vibhūtis enumerated in sūtras III: 16 to 34 and 36 and also some mentioned hereafter are such as have no clear and prime significance for spiritual progress, but seem rather more useful for worldliness and so can be used, if so desired, like siddhis, those mentioned in the sūtras III:35, 43, 44, 47, 48, 49, 52 are the ones which are primarily helpful in spiritual progress and the probability of using them in worldly manner is very little or nil. Even out of these the vibhūtis of sūtras 35, 43, 47, 48, 52 are those from which no worldly benefit could possibly be derived, not only this but the sūtras I:50, 54, 55 very clearly state that some of these vibhūtis directly e.g. of sūtra III:52 or indirectly e.g. of sūtras III:35,49 are leading to kaivalya. Indeed from the way the statements in the sūtras III:49 to 51 and 52 to

55 are made, we think that when a yogī reaches kaivalya, he has already had essentially puruṣa-jñāna, the vibhūti of sūtra III:35 and sattva-puruṣānyatākhyāti of sūtra III:42 and also the vivekajajñāna, the vibhūti of sūtra III:52. From this it is clear that the vibhūtis as such are no hindrance to spiritual progress and therefore also to samādhi. They are also not of secondary importance, like milestones on a road, just useful for judging the progress in the path of yoga, as has been concluded by some commentators. At least a few are definitely very valuable for even a purely spiritually interested sādhaka and about these, Patañjali clearly states that they lead to kaivalya. Considering all this we feel that the warning in sūtra III:37 is only about the prātibha experiences of śrāvaṇa etc. These almost divine experiences are themselves even much more tempting than those other similar ones noted in sūtras I:35 and 36. There is, therefore, a still greater probability than in the case of those of sūtras I:35 and 36, that the yoga-sādhaka may be enticed to go on enjoying the pleasures of these divine experiences and this surely would be a hindrance for his progress. In the case of the sensual experiences to be got through the viṣayavatī-pravṛttis, Patañjali only hinted the caution by the use of the word 'Viśokā' in sūtra I:36, as has been explained there. But most probably, as the divine, apparently sensual-like experiences of sūtra III:36, are much more alluring, Patañjali thought it wise to give clear-cut and emphatic warning about their allurement. This again shows that the warning is only about these enticing divine experiences.

SS. - **बन्धकारणशैथिल्यात्प्रचारसंवेदनाच्च चित्तस्य परशरीरावेशः ।।३:३८।।**

TL. - bandha-kāraṇa-śaithilyāt-pracāra-saṃvedanācca cittasya para-śarīrāveśaḥ -III:38

WM. -

bandha	= binding, bond;
kāraṇa	= cause;
śaithilya (→āt)	= loosening, relaxation (from);
pracāra	= movement in all directions;
saṃvedana (→āt→āc)	= feeling, understanding, knowledge (from);
ca	= and;
citta (sya)	= citta (of);
para	= of the other;
śarīrāveśa (ḥ)	= (śarira=body+āveśa = entry) entry into a body (is).

TR. - From the loosening of the cause of the binding (of citta) and from the understanding (of its ways) of movements in all directions, the entry of the citta (of the yogī) into the body of another (living being) (becomes possible)

CE. - Citta abides in a particular body, because of the feeling of 'mineness' about it, which thus becomes a binding cause, When puruṣa-jñāna is arisen through the saṃyama of the sūtra III:35, the citta becomes, as if, independent from its rigid bondage to puruṣsa-tattva. With this awakens the realization that it is distinct from the body also and need not stick to this one body in which it has been so long abiding due to the fortuitous circumstance of birth in it. Thus it becomes, so to say, independent of the body also. The cause of binding it to that particular body is removed and so it is now free to leave that body and go out. Through vibhūtis of sūtras III:29 and 34 the yogasādhaka is able to understand thoroughly the ways in which it can move and work in the body and also its own nature and potentialities, from which it can also understand how in a parallel manner it can move outside that body to any desired place. The yogasādhaka, if he so desires, can transfer the citta into any other body as indicated in this sūtra.

A question becomes pertinent as to : Why would the yogī want his citta to enter into another body and where would he avail of the necessary body ? There can be various reasons for a person to want to enter another body, both non-spiritual and spiritual. If the yogasādhaka has not the required balancedness of mind, that is to say not adequate maturity, he may just want to test this vibhūti, which then would be a siddhi, as soon as he becomes conscious that such a miraculous power has awakened in him, like that well-known story of George Washington trying to test the axe presented to him in his boyhood by his father, by cutting the trees in the garden. But even a fairly mature yogasādhaka may wish to do this for enjoying some worldly pleasures, if he has not high level of vairāgya. The pauraṇic legend of king Yayāti entering a youthful body is an example of this. In another very famous legend of the Ādi (First) Śaṅkarācārya entering the body of a king, who had very recently died, the objective was not just pleasure seeking, but nobler and to some extent spiritual, of giving answer based on actual personal experience to certain objections raised in religious-spiritual philosophical discussion. Yet in all the three cases the intention is of getting some experience of mundane nature. But even an advanced yogī may do this for a solely spiritual purpose. He may enter by means of the (created) citta into the body of another person or even of any other living being, just to quickly exhaust all his past karma-saṃskaras. These bodies, prima facie, appear as if created by the yogī for this specific purpose and so even technically are named nirmāṇa (= created) kāya (= body) but as will be explained later (cf. sūtra IV:2 CE.), are requisitioned by the yogī from the regular production by the prakṛti and a citta is made to enter there.

The later portion of the question has been answered to some extent in this answer to the first part given above. The yogī uses a body of a person or living being, who has died recently, in whose body there is yet no decomposition and the body is suitable to fulfil the purpose of the yogī. But such a body may not be available, when it is needed. So some commentators have suggested that in such a circumstance the yogī will use the body of a disciple, who gives his consent for such a cooperation. But this will be feasible only if that disciple's body is suitable to serve the specific purpose of the yogī. The very highly advanced yogī, however, will use, as said, the suitable bodies, human or others, from those in the process of creation and always reādily available in the abundance of prakṛti.

A second series of questions arises as to what would happen to the citta in that other body. Whether the two cittas remain in one body or the yogī's citta would drive out the citta already present in that other body and then where ? And how can it be possible for the citta in that body to leave it, since it has not acquired the ability to go out of the body?

If the yogī avails of a freshly dead body, this question does not apply, because the citta has already gone out of the body at death. When the advanced yogī uses a body being newly created in the natural process of prakṛti, again the question is not pertinent. Because there is no citta in it and so yogī has in fact to create and supply it. When the yogī uses the body of the cooperative disciple, the disciple may himself be an advanced yogī or the guru may train the disciple in the technique of saṃyama by which he can take his citta out of his body and keep it in temporary suspension, without any body-support, for the time being. When the other person is not a yogī at all or is not a human, the citta in the other body is so subjugated by the powerful and domineering citta of the yogī that it is as good as a non-entity.

During the time the yogī takes his citta out of his own body, he surely makes a perfectly trustworthy arrangement for its preservation from animals, insects etc. and its safekeeping. As the body has not died, there is no decomposition, as it takes place in normal course after death.

SS. - उदानजयाज्जलपङ्ककण्टकादिष्वसङ्ग उत्क्रान्तिश्च ।।३:३९।।

TL. - udāna-jayāj-jala-paṅka-kaṇṭakādiṣvasaṅga utkrāntiś-ca - III:39

WM. -
udāna = udāna, a vāyu, a variety of prāṇa, which has an upward-pushing action;
jaya (→āt→āj) = mastery (from, through);
jala = water;
paṅka = mud, marsh;

kaṇṭaka	=	thorn (s);
ādi (su-sv)	=	etcetera (in);
asaṅga	=	(a=no+saṅga=contact) non-contact;
utkranti (ḥ->s)	=	(1) levitation, (2) death (at will);
ca	=	and, also.

TR. - Through mastery over udāna(acquired through saṃyama upon it) there is non-contact with water, marsh mud, thorns and such others (when the yogī has to move in or over these) and also the ...(1) levitation....(2) death at will.

CE. - In a way this sūtra indicates a special technique for attaining the lightness of the body to varying degrees. This ability called laghimā is one of the famous aṣṭasiddhis. The ability of making one's own body light to any desired degree is attained, according to this sūtra, by practising saṃyama on udāna vāyu and thus bringing it under complete control. Udāna, as its name indicates (ut->ud = upwards + āna = conductor, one who leads), is the aspect or function of the prāṇa, that mystic force or energy, which, according to yoga and other mystic schools of India, is the divine force responsible for each and every activity of a living being. This udāna aspect of prāṇa (the stem āṅa is a consonantal modification of the stem ana in the word prāṇa and is present in the names of all the four variants of prāṇa and stands for prāṇa) is the one, which brings about all kinds of activities in the body whose direction is upwards towards the head. There is no unity of views among different texts about the exact regions and also the functions of these various aspect of prāṇa. Generally the region of udana-activity is supposed to be from the chest upwards. And at least in this case there is an agreement about its function i.e. of directing movements of things upwards. Therefore, when the function of this mysterious force is brought under the control of the yogī's will by the performance of saṃyama on it, he can manipulate this force in anyway he may like. Then controlling it to the desired degree, he can counteract the downward pull of the earth and can make his body as light as it may be necessary for a particular purpose. In this way he can make his body just enough light, so that he can walk over a bog or a marsh, or even on the surface of water or on a ground surface covered with thorns or other pain-causing things.

There are given two interpretations of the word utkrānti, as indicated in the translation of the sūtra above. The degrees of lightness indicated by the first portion of the sūtra do not necessarily mean that the body of the yogī can become even lighter than air. So some commentators interpret in utkranti such lightness that the yogī can remain suspended in air, i.e. levitate. Other commentators interpret utkrānti as death, no doubt, that means at yogī's will. It is a widely held belief, already mentioned under sūtra III:32, and which is even explicitly expressed in some yoga texts, that a person, whose prāṇa goes out of his body at the time of death through the Daśamadvāra (= the Tenth opening) viz. the Brahma-randhra (Brahma-randhra is the anterios cannot be reborn and is liberated for ever = the anterior fontanel i.e. the membranous gap in between the frontal and parietal bones in an infant, which is completely closed in the child at about two years of age, by these bones growing and joining with one another. In an adult the point of this junction of these bone is called 'bregma'. The close similarity of the two words 'brahma' and 'bregma' tempts one to the idea that may be the latter is a distortion of the former and might have been even derived from the former), it is also believed that for this reason, when the accomplished Yogīs and saints leave the mortal coil of the body, their prāṇa goes out of the body from here, opening the 'door', which remains shut during the life-time. It has been reported by very trustworthy persons that in the case of some such saints the skull is cracked at this spot of brahma-randhra, producing an explosive sound of cracking, at the time of the passing away of the prāṇa of such an accomplished (= siddha) person. If the skull does not crack in this manner at the death of such a holy personage e.g. a paramahaṃsa, a sannyāsin, it is deliberately broken open at the apex later by striking with the pointed end of a conch, so that, if the prāṇa is still lingering in the body, it may escape through this passage only.

Thus if a Yogī wants to woo the death, then he will naturally have it in a way which will not lead to rebirth and so to suffering again (as per Sūtras II:13 to 15). This he will assure, therefore, by using the power of udāna, by which he will forcefully open this gate of brahmarandhra for the exit of the prāṇa from the body. This he will be able to do, only if he has acquired enough mastery over udāna, which he can only get through such a saṃyama. The reason why these commentators interpret utkrānti as death is, because, if the Yogī achieves the potentiality of controlling the force and activity of udāna to any degree desired, as is indicated by the first portion of the Sūtra, his ability to control it so as to make his body suspendable in air is also already implied in it. Moreover in Sūtra III:42 the saṃyama for the same vibhūti viz. levitation, in its superlative development viz. flying through the air, has been independently mentioned, so if here utkrānti also means levitational ability, then the statement of the Sūtra becomes a superfluous repetition. The separate mention of the word utkrānti, therefore, according to them, should have some different meaning, which is given by them as death; because this is the other possible meaning of this word suitable here and the death in the manner desirable for a Yogī, as explained, is possible only through the application of the force of udāna controlled by means of saṃyama.

Indians also believe that death is solely in the hands of destiny. None, except a highly advanced Yogī, can have death in the way and at the time he may wish. Only a Yogī can have it at will and this he can do only through application of such an udāna-saṃyama. This is also a reason to accept the meaning of utkrānti as death.

SS. - **समानजयाज्ज्वलनम् ॥३:४०॥**

TL. - samāna-jayāj-jvalanam - III:40

WM. - samāna = samāna vāyu, a variety of prāṇa;

jaya (→āt→āj) = mastery (from, through, by);

jvalana (m) = (1) burning, effulgence; (2) gastric or body fire (is).

TR. - (Through the saṃyama on samāna results) The mastery over samāna from which (is produced)..., (1)....effulgence; .... (2).. body fire.

CE. - Here is described a technique of saṃyama on another aspect or function of prāṇa viz. samāna. This is said to work either in the whole body or in the lower abdominal region, according to different texts. One of its function is digestion, absorption of the ingested nourishment and transportation of this to all the parts of the body. The result of the mastery over this variety of prāṇa or vayu attained through saṃyama on it is mentioned as jvalana, which literally means burning. Obviously this refers to the body of the Yogī, but therefore does not mean actual burning of his body in the usual sense. Two meanings are therefore imparted to this term, as indicated above.

It is believed that saints and divine persons have a glow or effulgence roundabout their body, particularly round about their heads like a corona. The belief about the existence and even vision of such effulgence seems to be Universal, since pictures depicting such coronal effulgence round the head of the saints and deities are found in all countries and peoples. The science of parapsychology has even devised instruments, which make it possible to see this effulgence, called aura, and to record it. As said, according to some texts, the region of the samāna is lower abdominal region, below the navel, called 'kanda'. This also is the abode of bodily fire, Vaiśvānara Agni, the digesting fire or force. It is also the Sūrya maṇḍala, the region of Sun, named Solar plexus in modern language. All this is indicative of the region as the origin of heat, governed by samāna. Since, this samāna vayu seems to regulate the body-heat production, its mastery may lead the production of such light radiation from the body of the Yogī, which may become visible to the naked eyes of some sensitive and devotional persons. According to parapsychological findings this aura or radiation-emanation is not restricted to the bodies of Yogīs and saints, but is a universal phenomenon, shown even by animal bodies. The colour and brightness of the aura varies according to every individual's nature or personality as well as the state of the mind at the particular time. In the case of saints the colour are pale yellow or white and the glow very brilliant.

A more feasible and so easily acceptable and also utilitarian interpretation seems to be the 2nd one, that the body or gastric fire i.e. the digestive power is enhanced by the control and manipulation of samāna, since this is the prāṇa or vāyu which govern the digestive function.

Patañjali makes no mention of any saṃyamas for the mastery over prāṇa and apāna, because this mastery is achieved by prāṇayāma, not only over prāṇa, but also over apāna as is explicitly said in Bhagvad-Gītā (IV:29 and V:27) and implied in the theories of the Hathayoga. So also no saṃyama on vyāna vāyu is recommended. This is because its exact location or region of function is not definite. It is vaguely said that it is everywhere in the body (vyānaḥ sarva sarīragaḥ = Vyāna goes all over in the body). No clear mention of its precise function is found in the texts. Due to this to gain mastery over it by saṃyama is neither practical nor of much use.

SS. - **श्रोत्राकाशयोः सम्बन्धसंयमाद्दिव्यं श्रोत्रम् ।।३:४१।।**

TL. - śrotrākāśayoḥ saṃbandha-saṃyamād-divyaṃ śrotram - III:41.

WM. - śrotra = ear, hearing;
ākāśa (→yoḥ) = space, ether (of, dual);
saṃbandha = relation;
saṃyama (→āt→ād) = saṃyama (through);
divya (ṃ) = divine, with miraculous potentiality;
śrotra (m) = hearing, ear (is).

TR. - Through saṃyama on the relationship between hearing the and the space (results) miraculous power of hearing.

CE. - The close relationship between space and the ability of hearing is very easily understood even by a common man. It was, therefore, well-recognised by the ancients. This is clearly seen from the statements of this relationship in a number of places in ancient writings e.g. the hymns in Puruṣa-sūkta etc. In the Sāṃkhya-Yoga metaphysical theories this relationship is clearly indicated in the statement of the origin of ākāśa (=space) mahābhūta (= elements) from the śabda-tanmātrā (=sound subtle element) and the relationship between the sound and the sense organ of hearing is an everyday experience. Providing hollow space as an aid for magnifying the sound is a principle, which has been widely used from ancient times in the musical instruments like drums, horns, pipes and stringed instruments. Some English commentators have translated ākāśa by 'ether', which means the vacuous space containing no perceptible material. But it is now well-known that the vacuous space neither conducts nor can magnify sound. Air-or matter-filled space can only conduct soundwaves. Therefore the correct word is space, which, for a common man, is generally always filled with matter or at least air. There is a very essential relationship between such space and the production of the sound.

In fact sound will be inaudible, if matter containing space is not there to carry the sound-waves from their origin to the eardrum. Indeed it is normally impossible even to produce sound in total absence of matter as well as space. Even the hearing by the ear is possible on account of such space inside the ear, both in front and behind the ear-drum. All this shows the intimate relationship amongst the space, sound and hearing. If, therefore, saṃyama is directed upon this relationship and with keeping special attention on the spaces in the ear (= śrotra) noted above, the ability of the ear to discern sound becomes highly enhanced. The Yogī can then hear very low (normally inaudible) or far distant sounds. This type of development of the auditory faculty can be had by the saṃyama noted in III:36. But the difference is that there the experienced sound is of an actually existent outside source and experience by the citta literally directly i.e. without the intermediacy and participation of the ear; while in the vibhūti of this Sūtra the use of the term 'śrotra' indicates actual participation of the ear in the act of hearing and the use of the term 'divine' (= divya) for qualifying it indicates that just as actually physically produced but normally inaudible sounds could be heard, so also mystic sounds, i.e. caused without any physical source, that of striking of two material things against one another, could also be heard by the Yogī, who gains the divyaṃ śrotram (= Divine ear) through this saṃyama.

SS. - **कायाकाशयोः सम्बन्धसंयमाल्लघुतूलसमापत्तेश्चाकाश-गमनम् ।।३:४२।।**

TL. - kāyākāśayoḥ saṃbandha-saṃyamāl-laghu-tūla samāpatteś-cākāśa-gamanam -III:42

WM. -	kāya	=	body;
	ākāśa (yoḥ)	=	space (of the two, dual no);
	saṃbandha	=	relationship;
	saṃyama (→āt→āl)	=	saṃyama (from, through);
	laghu	=	light in weight, small;
	tūla	=	(a tuft of) cotton;
	samāpatti (→eh→eś)	=	samāpatti (by, through);
	ca	=	and;
	ākāśa	=	space;
	gamana (m)	=	movement, travelling, flying (is).

TR. - Through the saṃyama on the relationship between the body and the space and (accompanied) by samāpatti with a small light tuft of cotton, (the yogī gets an ability of) moving through the space.

CE. - This is one of the vibhūtis which seem rather difficult to believe as really achievable. Nevertheless stories are often heard, not only in India, but in other countries also, about yogīs and saints, about whom it is claimed that they possessed or possess this ability. Even present day people report of sādhus and yogīs, who are said as possessing such a power of moving or flying through air. No doubt, even in these cases these persons are not actually seen while in the act of flying, but it is reported that they are seen at two different places far removed from each other at almost the same instant or with a very short time difference and so it is surmised that they have rapidly travelled through the space physically from one place to the other. It is difficult to decide about the veracity of these reports, but often they are corroborated by a number of persons.

Nevertheless, if this vibhūti is at all possible to have, the mode in which it can be had is indicated in the present sūtra.

Any concrete object and therefore also the human body occupies space and so, in a way, can be looked upon as contained in and supported by the space. Indeed if space were not there, things could not have come into existence (cf. Nāsadīya Sūkta,1). Space gives the support or the 'container' for existence. This is true for the body also, since it is also material and has to have space. If saṃyama be directed on this relationship between the body and space, the mental power directed in this, towards the space that is supporting the body, may have enough force to activate and move that space with its content viz. the body, in the manner and direction the yogī may want to shift it.

This is further facilitated by having samāpatti, a variety or stage in meditation (cf. sūtra I:41 ff.) on a wishp of cotton, fundamentally an object denser than air, but which is easily blown here and there by the air, as though it were lighter than air. It is often seen that a deeply ingrained prejudice or preconception, leading to diffidence, proves a hindrance in the proper utilization of a person's force or ability. Instances are well-known (e.g. Karṇa, berated and derided by his charioteer king Śalya and thus intentionally made diffident by the latter, with this very purpose) and very common, when a very hefty and strong man, who has, due to some reason, ingrained in his mind the idea that his opponent is stronger or more skilful than himself, becomes diffident and so is usually defeated, even when the opponent may be even inferior to him. This is true about not only physical might, but is equally applicable to mental ability. A person, who has developed a diffidence about his own capacities, is not able to achieve his best in those spheres also. Therefore for full and proper utilization of one's capacities and potentialities, removal of such preconceptions causing diffidence is necessary. The samāpatti on the cotton-tuft might have been suggested for this purpose. Because the mind and citta are not able to produce their maximum possible force or power, if they be hindered by such stubborn preconceptions. Such a deeply ingrained preconception always exists in the mind about an object denser than air never being able to float and fly in the air. Cotton is really much denser than air and so, normally it should not float over air and fly through space. But the artificially caused lightness (due to trapping of a lot of air in its interstices) of the cotton-tuft makes it possible that even such a denser-than-air object flies over air and moves in the space, apparently overcoming the earth's gravitational pull. The samāpatti directed on this cotton-tuft, which is imagined in the samāpatti as flying through air, makes it possible to remove the strong hold of the preconception from the mind, that denser-than-air things cannot fly over the air through the space. The power of the citta-mind is thus developed to its full force in the recommended saṃyama and with it the body can be made to fly in the space over the air.

SS. - **बहिरकल्पिता वृत्तिर्महाविदेहा ततः प्रकाशावरणक्षयः ।।३:४३।।**

TL. - bahir-ākalpitā vṛttir-mahā-videhā tataḥ prakāśa-āvaraṇa-kṣayaḥ -III:43

WM.- bahi (ḥ→r) = outward, external;
akalpitā = (a = not + kalpitā = imaginable, femin.) unimaginable;

vṛtti (ḥ→r)	=	modality of functioning of the mind and citta;
mahā	=	great, here supreme or all-time;
videhā (feminine)	=	body-less;
tataḥ	=	from that;
prakāśa	=	(inner) illumination;
āvaraṇa	=	covering;
kṣaya (ḥ)	=	diminution and disappearance (is).

TR. - (From that saṃyama also results) the vṛtti (i.e. of the mind or of the citta) (designated as) the Mahāvidehā (i.e. the Great-bodiless) (vṛtti with an) external (directionality) (and) unimaginable. From that (further results) diminution and disappearance of the covering (on the inner) illumination.

CE. - As said in the preceding III:42 sūtra, when it is claimed that the yogī had flown through the air, usually nobody claims to have seen actually his body in this act. Some commentators, therefore, explain that he makes it invisible by the saṃyama in sūtra III:21. What is more probable that he (i.e. his citta) leaves the body and moves in a body-less (= videha) state. With this type of understanding of the vibhūti of sūtra III:42 the objection of improbability is also set aside. The ability to go out of one's body and even look at it like an object observed by an onlooker is a very common and very primary development in yoga and is experienced by many yogasādhakas very early in their yoga-sādhanā, specially when they are well-versed in meditation. But in such bodiless state, the citta of the sādhaka maintains a liaison with the body and keeps a recognition awake that it is its permanent abode. (Para-psychology and perhaps also Theosophy postulate that in such extro-physique state, a plasmic fiberlike link is actually maintained between the body and the outer entity, may it be the spirit or mind etc.) This is the ordinary videha state (according to the yoga and mysticism. The term videhā in Vedānta has a different notion in it). Very probably, on account of the necessity of having a liaison with the body, the citta cannot move far away from the body. The movement in the space is possible to a limited extent, depending on the extensibility of the link. But to have a completely free movement through space to any external point, such a link causing a constraint is a hindrance. Through the saṃyama of sūtra III:42 this restraining link is also done away with. The citta of the yogī, thus, develops an ability of functioning in a bodiless state moving externally to any length. This potentiality or vibhūti is therefore designated here as Mahā-videhā. The other adjectives bahir and akalpitā amplify that the citta of the yogī can go to any external point even removed far beyond imaginable limits.

By the development of the power to move to any point of the Universe without any restraint, the citta is now able to get the knowledge of anything anywhere through direct perception. In this manner the limitation on getting knowledge is totally removed. The citta becomes almost omniscient, which is what is indicated by the phrase prākāśāvaraṇakṣaya, i.e. removal of covering or obstruction in the path of illumination i.e. knowledge.

The removal of the covering over the light is also mentioned as a result of the practice of prāṇāyāma in sūtra II:52. That is a potentiality of the citta developed on account of the tranquillization of the citta, due to which the citta is able to probe deeply into the subject, towards which it be directed in the meditation, which is to follow prāṇāyāma (at least in Pātañjala-yoga-system). The citta in that process gets knowledge in a manner which is akin to thinking. With the mahā-videhā vṛtti the citta actually goes out of the body to the subject about which it wants to know and so to say, directly observes it. The difference in the two prakāśāvaraṇakṣayas is somewhat of the type as that in between anumāna (= inference) and pratyakṣa (= direct perception by means of the senses).

SS. - स्थूलस्वरूपसूक्ष्मान्वयार्थवत्त्वसंयमाद्भूतजयः ।।३:४४।।

TL. - sthūla-svarūpa-sūkṣmānvayārthavattva- saṃyamād bhūta-jayaḥ - III:44

WM. - sthūla (tva) = gross (ness);
svarūpa (tva) = one's own natural form (ness i.e. state);
sukṣma (tva) = subtle (ness);
anvaya (tva) = conjoint (ness), related (ness);
arthavatva = purposefulness
saṃyama (→āt→ād) = saṃyama (through);
bhūta = elements viz. pañca mahā-bhūtas;
jaya (ḥ) = mastery, conquest, subjugation (is).

TR. - Through the performance of the saṃyama on the grossness, the naturalness, the subtleness, the relatedness and the purposefulness (of the pañca-mahābhūtas) (is attained) the mastery over the elements (i.e. the pañca-mahābhūtas)

CE. - All concrete or material objects are formed, according to the ancient traditional view, of five mahābhūtas or elements. In these objects none of these five elements is all alone in its pure condition. Thus in the grossest state of these elements, they are all five combined with each other in varying proportions to form the gross object in the world, with their different individual qualities of colour, shape, solidity, fluidity and so on. This is the grossness or gross state of these elements. Thus, though these mahābhūta elements are seen only in combination as objects or matter in the world and never in their own pure elemental state, it can be understood that there must be such simple elemental-state of theirs. This is their own natural state i.e. svarūpa-avasthā. The tanmātrā is the subtle state of these bhūtas. The subtlest tanmātrā 'śabda' is present (in a mysterious latent manner) in all the four tanmātrās comparatively grosser than it. The next grosser tanmātrā 'sparśa' is similarly latent in the remaining three grosser to it. In this manner each tanmātrā is latent in all the others grosser than itself. Then again, these tanmātrās and mahābhūtas combine with one another in different proportions. All these mutual relationships and combining capacities are their anvayatva (= relatedness). Each thing serves some purpose in the world. It is already explained under sūtras II: 18 and 2 1 that from the viewpoint of a yogī the purpose of the whole of the creation in the ultimate analysis is 'for his bhoga (= experiencing) and apavarga (= salvation)'. This is the arthavattva (= purposefulness) of the bhūtas.

These five are the steps in the development of the five mahābhūtas, through which the manifested world and the objects it contains are created. By directing saṃyama on these, the yogī can control the functioning of the mahābhūtas in the world and thus get mastery over them. Obviously, since he can control the functioning of the elements, he can make them do as he may wish and design.

SS. -	ततोऽणिमादिप्रादुर्भावः कायसंपत्तद्धर्मानभिघातश्च ।।३:४५।।		
TL. -	tato'ṇimādi-prādurbhāvaḥ kāya-saṃpat-tad-dhar - mānabhighātaś-ca - III:45.		
WM. -	tataḥ(->o)	=	from that;
	aṇimādi	=	(aṇimā = aṇimā+ādi = etcetera) aṇimā, the power to become small, one of the famous aṣṭa-siddhis (= the eight miraculous powers) and such others;
	prādurbhāva (ḥ)	=	appearance, arising (is);
	kāya	=	body;
	saṃpat	=	perfection, excellence;
	taddharma (+ āḥ->ā)	=	(tad=its+dharma = natural= characteristics or properties) its natural characteristics or tendencies;
	anabhighāta (ḥ->ś)	=	(an = non + abhighāta = attack)non-attacking, prevention (of ill-effects), non-affliction;
	ca	=	and.

TR. - From that (saṃyama or bhūta-jaya) there is the appearance of Aṇimā and the others of the eight siddhis and excellence in physique and nonaffliction by its (body's) natural tendencies.

CE. - Since the yogī has achieved the mastery over the five ṃahābhūtas, through the saṃyama prescribed in the preceding III:44 sūtra, he can do practically anything he may wish with material objects, in which, of course, his own body is also included. Therefore, the aṣṭa (eight) siddhis are, so to say, a natural consequence of this vibhūti. These aṣṭa-siddhis are : - (1) Aṇimā (= ability to be as small as one may want), (2) Mahimā (= ability to become as big as one may desire), (3) Laghimā (= ability to become light to any extent), (4) Garimā (= ability to be as heavy as needed), (5) Prāpti (= easy grasping by hand of any object however distant it be), (6) Prākāmya (= to have anything as soon as one has desire for it), (7) Īśitva (= power to create and control things) and (8), Vaśitva (subjugation of everyone and everything in his surrounding). (N.B.. There is some difference of opinions about the names and exact nature of particularly the latter four of siddhis. But for our purpose here that is not of much significance.)

The yogī's own body is also made of the five mahābhūtas and so controlling these as desirable, he can make its condition and working excellent. The qualities developed in this excellence are indicated in the next III:46 sūtra. Since the body functions at an optimum level, it will not be afflicted by the changes that occur in the natural course in the body and which being debilitating and painful nobody likes to have e.g. aging, diseases, death etc.

SS. - **रूपलावण्य बलवज्रसंहननत्वानि काय संपत् ।।३:४६।।**

TL. - rūpa-lāvaṇya-bala-vajra-saṃhananatvāni kāya-saṃpat - III:46

WM. -

rūpa	=	graceful form;
lāvaṇya	=	beauty;
bala	=	strength;
vajrsaṃhananatva (→āni)	=	(vajra = the god Indra's weapon, made from the bones of sage Dadhīci, supposed to be the most unbreakable thing, so the hardest + saṃhananatva = compactness, firmness, hardness, robustness) maximum sturdiness, adamantine robustness (plu-suffix = are):
kāya	=	body;
saṃpat	=	perfection, excellence.

TR. - Graceful form, beauty, strength and supermost sturdiness (enduring capacity) comprise the qualities of the perfection of the body.

CE. - The sūtra enumerates different qualities which go to make body perfect. Grace and beauty, which are the outward aspects of this, are mentioned first. But if a beautiful body has no strength, it cannot be called a perfect body. But again, if a strong person has (physical) softness, he may not be able to endure the attack of harmful things. So these inner components viz. strength accompanied by toughness of the body are also necessary.

The ancient meaning of Vajra is the weapon of Indra, specially prepared from the bones of ṛṣi Dadhīci to kill an invincible demon. This was said to be the hardest thing ever created, unbreakable by any other thing. So vajra comes to signify the most tough thing. The usual meaning of the word 'saṃhanana' is given as firmness, toughness etc. (derived from root saṃhan = to unite compactly), but it can mean also destruction by striking (from root han= to strike and kill, with prefix sam = completely). With the latter, the compound vajra-saṃhanana-tva would mean such hardness as would not be broken even by a vajra i.e. greater hardness than even vajra. This meaning is even better than the first.

SS. - **ग्रहणस्वरूपास्मितान्वयार्थवत्त्वसंयमादिन्द्रियजयः ।।३:४७।।**

TL. - grahaṇa-svarūpāsmitānvayārthavattva-saṃyamād-indriya-jayaḥ -III:47

WM. -

grahaṇa (tva)	=	grasping (ness), tendency or ability to grasp i.e. apprehend and perceive;
svarūpa (tva)	=	one's own natural form (ness i.e. state);
asmitā	=	(asmi = (I) am + ta = ness) am-ness, consciousness of one's existing;
anvaya (tva)	=	related (ness);
artha-vat-tva	=	purpose-full-ness;

samyama (→āt→ād) = saṃyama (through, from);
indriya = senses;
jaya (ḥ) = mastery (is).

TR. - Through performance of saṃyama on (the power of) apprehension, (their) own natural state, asmitā (awareness of I), relatedness (and) purposefulness (of the senses), (is achieved) the mastery over the senses.

CE. - Generally it is the understanding that the power of perception and apprehension by the senses resides in the outer-end-organs of these viz. the eye, the ear, the nose, the skin and the tongue, because the direct contact of these with the object or with the pertinent emanations e.g. light waves, sound waves, volatile odorous molecules, coming from the object produces the particular sensation in us. These outer sensations are connected by nerves to the centres in the brain, where the sensation is interpreted into the particular variety of experience. This whole organisation forms the complete sense organ and it, in the case of each individual sense, as a whole receives the stimulation and comprehends its meaning i.e. totally grasps the knowledge of the object. This is the grahaṇatva (= grasping ability) of the indriya (= sense).

But the indriyas being body-organs are also made up of five mahābhūtas and the five tanmātrās. Even there, each indriya (i.e. jñānendriya = sense) has a special closer relationship with one of the tanmātrās e.g. of the ear or hearing organ with śabda tanmātrā, of eye or vision with rūpa, of nose or olfaction with gandha etc. This is svarūpatva of the senses.

The five senses have been developed out of ahaṃkāra (literally maker or creator of I - ness) according to the Sāṃkhya view of evolution, which is generally accepted by Yoga. (But Patañjali seems to prefer and so substitutes the designation asmitā in place of ahaṃkāra. The latter term occurs no where in Pātañjala Yoga Sūtras). In Yoga the term asmitā is used for ahaṃkara. This asmitā or ahaṃkara aspect (or stage of evolution) of citta is the principle which factually becomes aware of the perception made by the sense or indriya. This asṃitātva is the subtle aspect (corresponding to sūkṣma in respect of bhūtas in sūtra III:44) in the development of indriyas.

As said the sense organs are closely related with tanmātrās and the tanmātrās are interlinked mutually (cf. sūtra III:44, CE). Again these are related to mind, asmitā and citta. These relationships amongst the various principles involved in the perception and its interpretation by cooperative functioning of all these principles is indicated by the term anvayatva (= relatedness).

The purposefulness (= artha- vattva) of the sense organs, from the viewpoint of the common man is quite obvious as they serve the citta and through it the individual as a whole, therefore this is their purposefulness in a general way. The common man gives value to happenings on this measuring-scale. If the happening either benefits or harms him, then only he takes it into account, otherwise it usually is ignored by him. The yogī has transcended this self-centred outlook. He does not evaluate the sense-experiences (got through happenings) on the scale of narrow self-interest. He looks at things on a scale of the whole cosmos. He can see the purpose of the providence behind things and phenomena and that is the arthavattva from his point of view. By practising saṃyama on these steps of the evolution of indriyas the yogī acquires the mastery over indriyas.

SS. - **ततो मनोजवित्वं विकरणभावः प्रधानजयश्च ।।३:४८।।**

TL. - tato manojavitvaṃ vikaraṇa-bhāvaḥ pradhāna-jayaś-ca - III:48

WM. -

tataḥ(→o)	=	from that;
manojavitva (ṃ)	=	fleetness or ability to move with the speed of mind (is);
vikaraṇabhāva (ḥ)	=	(vi = vinā = without + karaṇa = physical means, instruments + bhāva = condition) instrumentless condition (is);
pradhāna	=	pradhāna i.e. mūla prakṛti;
jaya (ḥ→ś)	=	mastery (is);
ca	=	and.

TR. - From that (indriyajaya) (the yogī achieves an) independence from the instrumentality (of the senses), and so the ability to move with the speed of mind and the mastery over pradhāna i.e. mūla prakṛti.

CE. - There are three results arising as consequent to indriyajaya. The yogī can now take himself bodily anywhere with the speed of mind i.e. within one instant. It is stated in sūtra III:45 that the difficulties and harmful changes caused by the limitations of the natural characteristics of the body (kāya-dharmas) are removed and the eight siddhis are achieved due to the bhūtajaya (mastery over the five mahābhūtas or elements). Also the yogī can fly through the space with saṃyama stated in sūtra III:42. Thus the restraining factors limiting the speed of movement of the body are already removed through these vibhūtis. Now due to the mastery over indriyas, these fully co-operate with the citta and so the yogī can give any speed to the body as he may desire. The maximum speed, which any material thing can have is, as per modern concept (of science), the speed of light. But for the common man mind seems able to go any where literally in no time and this is, therefore, the conceivable maximum possible speed and the speed of mind (manojava; mana (ḥ→o) = mind+Java = speed) is the term used to indicate the maximum conceivable speed, because for us mind is the only thing which can have, if at all, such a limitless speed.

Bhāva = the condition of citta. The ordinary citta takes cognisance of the outer world by the agency of the senses. - Through the saṃyamas of sūtras III:38 and 42 the citta can move out of the body without any restraint anywhere and it has been seen that, therefore, it can itself directly gain the knowledge of any desired external object or happening. Yet senses, as per their routine, still transmit on their part the information from the external world to the citta. Therefore, even when undesired, the stimulating information reaches the citta and produces therein disturbance, even when it is not wanted. But now with the indriyajaya achieved, the senses are obeying the yogī (i.e. his citta) in a totally submissive manner. But citta has now no need to depend on them. So the citta does not utilise their services at all. It accomplishes the task of getting knowledge of the external things without their help. This is its vi-karaṇa-bhāva (= independence from the instrumentality, of the senses) and this is the hundred percent perfect pratyāhāra (sense-withdrawal).

The yogī, who has experienced the vibhūtis described so far, is almost on the threshold of the mansion of kaivalya. This is also clear from the next III:49, 50, 55 and other sūtras. But if unexpectedly some difficulty arises, instead of reaching the terminal station of kaivalya, the danger of getting trapped indefinitely on the siding of the penultimate station of pradhāna or mūla-prakṛti, in other words of becoming a prakṛtilayī yogī, is always present in the path of the yogī. To avoid this danger the pradhāna (= mūla prakṛti) -jaya becomes necessary. The final development and expanse of prakrti is on the one hand non-living things made of the (five mahā-) bhūtas and on the other of living beings with indriyas. So the mastery over bhūtas (bhūta-jaya) and over indriyas (indriya-jaya) means also the pradhāna (i.e. prakṛti) jaya. Īśvarapraṇidhāna, as said elsewhere (cf. sūtra II:45), is also very helpful in avoiding the danger of getting trapped in prakṛti-laya state.

SS. - **सत्त्वपुरुषान्यताख्यातिमात्रस्य सर्वभावाधिष्ठातृत्वं सर्व-ज्ञातृत्वं च ।।३:४९।।**

TL. - sattva-puruṣānyatā-khyāti-mātrasya sarvabhāvādhi-ṣṭhātṛtvaṃ sarva-jñātṛtvaṃ ca - III:49

WM. - sattva = (sat = To be + tva = ness) sattva, the pure pristine state of the citta, just as soon as it came into being;

puruṣa = puruṣa principle;

anyatā = otherness, distinction;

khyāti = knowledge, there realization or experience;

mātra = only;

sya = of;

sarva = all;

bhāva = state (of existing);

adhiṣṭhatṛtva (ṃ) = superintendentship, presidentship, controllership, governing or regulating authority (is);

jñātṛtva = potentiality or power of knowing;

ca = and.

TR. - The potentiality to have the supreme control on all states of existing (= omnipotence) and the potentiality of having all knowledge (= omni-science) are the possessions of the yogī, who has attained the realization of the distinction between the sattva (= pure citta) and the puruṣa principle.

CE, - Some commentators think that Patañjali is recommending in this sūtra a saṃyama on the distinction between the two principles viz. the sattva-citta and the purusa. But in fact there is not even the least indication about performing of any such saṃyama here.

The word 'bhāva' is derived from the root bhū = to become. So bhāva in Yoga Sūtras usually means the (becoming and being i.e.) state of the citta. But it can be applicable in this same sense for the process of becoming and its durable result i.e. maintenance of state of any other object or phenomenon in the world. Thus sarva-bhāva-adhiṣṭhātṛtva here means that the yogī has full control over all the states of his citta as well over those of all the living and non-living things in the world and all the phenomena that occur anywhere in the world. Both these meanings are possible and also pertinently applicable here. The latter sense is more significant here and in other words it means that the yogī acquires omnipotence.

Sarva-jñātṛtva = ability to have all and any knowledge (no doubt, when the yogī has that need). This is different than sarvajñatva = the power of possessing all the knowledge (i.e. having at all the time the knowledge of everything, not only of the present time but of past and future also), attributed to īśvara by Patañjali (sūtra I:25). This is impossible to have for a human being, probably even if he be a yogī. On the other hand, this sarvajñātṛtva is quite feasible for a yogī approaching the highest development in the yoga. This is the practical omniscience.

These two vibhūtis, viz. the potentiality of controlling all states of existing i.e. omnipotence and the potentiality of having any desired knowledge i.e. omniscience, are the natural consequences of the realization (not mere intellectual comprehension) of the clear distinction of the puruṣa from the sattva-citta. This realization i.e. actual experiencing of the distinctness of these two principles, of which, in worldly life, there is a super-imposition of one upon the other, arises in the yogī not by any specific saṃyama, (the saṃyama III:35 to be practised for puruṣa-jñāna, though it makes the yogī firmly convinced of the total distinctness of the puruṣa from the sattvacitta, it is still on an intellectual comprehension level. It is not a realization i.e. actual experiencing), but gradually through all the various saṃyamas mentioned heretofore, particularly those in sūtras III:35, 38, 43, 44, 48 etc. This realization that puruṣa is totally alien and distinct from citta even in its pristine pure sattva state is an essential prerequisite for attaining kaivalya and indeed is the seminal stage of development in the progress on the yogīc path.

It need be specially clarified that the word 'sattva' has been explained by some commentators as 'sattva-guṇa'. But this usual meaning of these words is not adequate here and does not clarify the purport of the sūtra. The word, as said above, means sāttvika i.e. pristine pure state of citta as soon as it emerges out of prakṛti, even prior to its 'mahat' (on cosmic scale and buddhi in relation to the individual) development. Particularly at this stage it is so much misidentified with the puruṣa, that even for an advanced yogī its distinctness from the puruṣa, though intellectually comprehended, is very difficult to actually experience. This realization (without any special practice of saṃyamas) normally comes only in advancement of nirbīja samādhi, with intensive practice of this carried for a long period. The ultimate perfection of this realization and its culmination into kaivalya takes place in Dharmamegha samādhi, which again is the perfection and culmination, on its part of the nirbīja samādhi, which , therefore, takes place once only, just prior to the attainment of kaivalya. The practice of the various saṃyamas, no doubt, is helpful in accelerating and facilitating that whole process.

SS. - तव्दैराग्यादपि दोषबीजक्षये कैवल्यम् ।।३:५०।।

TL - tad-vairagyād-api doṣa-bīja-kṣaye kaivalyam - III:50

WM -

tat (→d)	=	about that or here those;
vairāgya (→āt→ād)	=	disattachment, renunciation (from, through);
api	=	even;
doṣa	=	defect, deficiency;
bīja	=	seed;
kṣaya (→e)	=	disappearance, elimination; destruction (in)
kaivalya (m)	=	kaivalya (is achieved).

TR. - Through disattachment for (and renunciation of) even those (the powers of omnipotence and omniscience, the fruit of sattva-puruṣānyatā-khyāti) results the elimination of (even) the seed of defects, (in which condition appears) kaivalya.

CE. - All vibhūtis appear like miracles to the common man and are very great powers, if used for worldly benefits. Therefore, as often has been indicated, there is high probability and great danger of the yogasādhaka getting enticed into using these powers for gaining some selfish material advantage. Surely this temptation would be the greatest with the powers of omnipotence and omniscience, just mentioned in the previous III:49 sūtra. If the yogī falls into this snare, he will become either a prakṛtilayī yogī or a videhī (minor god) (cf, sūtras I:19 and the next, III:51), since he has attained the realization of the distinction of the puruṣa from the sattva-citta, but he would not be able to reach kaivalya. He will be ensnared into this trap, if the ṣaḍripus (literally six enemies, the well-known weaknesses or faults i.e. doṣas in human nature, viz . (1) kāma = desire, passion; (2) krodha = anger; (3) lobha = greed; (4) moha = deluding and confusing infatuation; (5) mada = an excessively overbearing conceit and (6) matsara = jealousy, envy), their causal factors viz. the kleśas and the seed, i.e. the ultimate source, of all these doṣa viz. avidyā (sūtra II:4) are still present in him. The more powerful these doṣas i.e. faults in the yogasādhaka, greater is the chance of his ensnarement. If the yogasādhaka has highly developed vairāgya, these doṣas viz. ṣaḍripus i.e. six evil tendencies and also the kleśas will be feeble or even almost non-active in him. But to do away with them completely, their root cause or seed viz. avidyā should disappear. This seed of faults i.e. doṣabija, when removed, causes all faults also to disappear and perfection i.e. absoluteness, otherwise said, kaivalya is established, as said in this sūtra. But this root of all trouble i.e. seed of doṣas viz avidyā is the most difficult to remove. (In fact as expressed in sūtra II:25 disappearance of avidyā is the appearance or establishment of kaivalya.). But if the yogasādhaka has developed the utmost vairāgya (that means almost near to the guṇa-vaitṛṣṇya stage, mentioned in sūtra I:16) then only he will be able to remain disattached about the powers of omnipotence and omniscience mentioned in sūtra III:49 and renounce them. If he is able to do this, that is a clear indication that even the last trace of avidyā has also been eliminated in his case, because a yogī with any lesser degree of vairagya will find it difficult to discard these powers, which make him almost an almighty Bhagavāna or Semi-God. Thus when the bīja of doṣas viz. avidyā disappears, as said in the sūtra, kaivalya is established for him.

As already said, this sūtra indicates the role of vibhūtis in attainment of the ultimate spiritual goal of yoga. Even though the yogī does not make any direct use of the vibhūtis of omnipotence and omniscience, in fact he has to discard them-yet even this he could do, only if they have at all first arisen in him. And only when he relinquishes even these, his guṇavaitṛṣṇya vairāgya gets firmly established, and then only appears kaivalya for him.

SS. - **स्थान्युपनिमन्त्रणे सङ्गस्मयाकरणं पुनरनिष्ट-प्रसङ्गात् ।।३:५१।।**

TL. - sthāny-upanimantraṇe saṅga-smayā-karaṇaṃ punar-aniṣṭa -prasaṅgāt - III:51

WM. - sthāni (n) = someone appointed in a place of authority, local office-bearer, here various minor gods, who are like local office-bearers, carrying out specific functions or offices for the supreme divine power (sthāni→ sthāny);

upa-nimantrana (→e) = special invitation for accepting some honour or gift (in);

saṅga = contact or association leading to pleasure and consequent attachment, here attachment;

smaya = conceit, self-aggrandizement;

akaraṇa (m̩)	=	(a = not + karaṇa = doing) doing away (with), elimination, discarding;
punaḥ (→r)	=	again;
aniṣṭa	=	(an = not + iṣṭa = desired) undesirable, harmful, dangerous;
prasaṅga (→āt)	=	occurrence, eventuality (on account of).

TR. - With invitations from minor gods and other celestial beings (to receive honours and accept pleasure-giving gifts from them) (there will be a great probability of) attachment (towards these) and (an inclination towards) self-aggrandizement; (so the yogī must) discard these (invitations) on account of the possibility of the danger (of falling again into the ensnarement of temptation leading to worldly entanglement).

CE. - When the yogī becomes almost a Semi-God, on account of the gaining of the powers of omnipotence and omniscience, the minor gods and other celestial beings give invitations to him to accept godhood and to enjoy the (sensual) pleasures accompanying it. Instances of such a happening are quite numerous and well known, not only in Hindū mythology and religious circles, but are equally true in relation to Buddha, Jesus Christ, the prophet Mohammed, Zarathruṣṭra etc. In Hindū mythology the reason, as to why the celestial beings approach the yogī with such an offer, is made out to be their jealousy and fear that the yogī may become even superior to them, The well-known legends are of the supreme god Indra sending Apsarās (celestial damsels) to entice ṛṣis like

Viśvāmitra away from their austerities. These stories were really meant for the spiritual sādhaka to warn him that even such advanced yogīs like Viśvāmitra may be entrapped into these temptations and suffer a downfall. This sūtra also gives the same warning to the yogī of this danger lurking in the path of yoga, when he may feel that he has almost reached the goal and so now feeling sure of reaching it and overjoyed, may become lax and thus may unwittingly fall into the snares of temptation and conceit. The sūtra gives a clear and emphatic injunction that keeping in mind this last and sure-to-occur danger, he should be on the alert and determinedly refuse to accede to the request of these heavenly creatures and thus avoid the ensnarement. If he would not remain cautious and does not obey the injunction, he may himself become only a god i.e. videha, referred to in sūtra I:19, but his attainment of kaivalya will be delayed for an indefinitely long time.

This phenomenon of the divine beings trying to tempt the spiritual aspirant and thus device him from his goal, specially when he is almost on the verge of the final realization and illumination, seems, as said, a definite and regular occurrence in the case of all great souls, who have attained such realization. It is also not a mere myth or unfounded belief, because in the case of Gautama Buddha, Jesus Christ, Mohammada Paigambara and Zarathruṣṭra, their such experiences are authentically stated and almost well documented facts. All of them had to totally discard and overcome the allurements offered by the divine beings. Only then they could enter into the final beatitude of the Illumination, Realization, Mokṣa, God-consciousness, Kaivalya, Nirvāṇa or any other term one may like to use for that final goal, according to one's understanding about 'It'. Thus we see that the yogī or spiritual seeker has to pass this final test of having the Parama- Vairāgya by being totally disinterested in and discarding completely the Semi-Almighty -hood and the god-hood, when only he becomes eligible to enter that Final State. It seems thus that without actually passing the test i.e. giving proof of his supermost vairāgya, he cannot attain kaivalya, even if he has that degree of vairāgya (but which is not proved by such actual testing). This may also be one reason why the celestial beings offer these enticements at the last moment before attainment of the goal by the spiritual seeker.

SS. - **क्षणतत्क्रमयोः संयमाद्विवेकजं ज्ञानम् ।।३:५२।।**

TL. - kṣaṇa-tat-kramayoḥ saṃyamād-vivekajaṃ-jñānam - III: 52

WM. -

kṣaṇa	=	an instant, a point of time;
tat	=	it, its or their;
krama (yoḥ)	=	sequence (of the two, dual possessive);
saṃyama (→āt→ād)	=	saṃyama (from, through);
vivekaja (ṃ)	=	(viveka = discriminative ability + ja = born of) born of discriminative ability;
jñāna (m)	=	knowledge, realization (is).

TR. - The realization born out of the discriminative ability (is produced) through saṃyama on both the kṣaṇa and its (i.e. their, of many kṣaṇas) sequence.

CE. - The word kṣaṇa has two meanings - (1) a very small unit for measuring small periods or intervals of time and (2) an instant or moment, something akin to a point or an atom or a quantum of time (if it be permissible to use the latter three terms in respect of time). In this sūtra kṣaṇa has the meaning (2).

Amongst the various standards or dimensions, which we use to distinguish between two different things, the time is one, which is very helpful to determine the distinction. The other three dimensions usually used for this purpose are noted in the next III:53 sūtra. But philosophically time is not a separate entity and has normal existence. It is a mere conceptual creation i.e. a result only of the mind's working and in this way an illusion. Even modern physics is approaching a similar conclusion. What is real is an instant or kṣaṇa. Each kṣaṇa is discrete, independent from and unrelated to another kṣaṇa. The feeling of an unbroken continuity of these kṣaṇas i.e. of their sequentiality giving an impression of an unbroken flow of time is an illusion. This is explained by such examples as those of a flame or of a river. The continuously burning flame is the result of the heating and consequent glowing of carbon particles or atoms each of which, as soon as it burns out, is changed into a molecule of carbon di-oxide (CO_2), a gas which does not glow at that temperature. Thus the light of the flame at any particular moment is the total effect of all such burning atoms of carbon, which lose their ability to give out light in an instant, as soon as they are turned into CO_2 . Some other new atoms are burning at the next instant and giving out newly their light. The flame is the result of such different and discrete instantaneous flashes of burning carbon atoms. Thus though these flashes are really discontinuous, yet an illusion of the unbroken continuity of the flame is created. In the case of a river, the drops or particles of water at any particular spot are similarly changing from instant to instant and yet an impression of constancy and continuity of the river is produced. The same is the case with the kṣaṇas and the time. The impression that the time is an unbroken continuous thing is produced on the same lines. Patañjali further clarifies and amplifies this notion of illusoriness of the time in sūtra IV: 12. The feeling that the time is moving and that its future aspect is approaching and the past is going away can be considered an illusory impression, just like that which a passenger in a moving railway train gets about the trees and other outside things moving in the direction opposite to that of the train.

A corollary of this impression of this continuity of time is the conviction that every created thing is continuously changed and ultimately destroyed in the coercive flow of time.

Both these notions about the nature and the effect of time are so deeply ingrained in the mind of man, that it is very difficult, almost improbable to remove them. But unless the stronghold of these notions over the mind is removed, the real understanding and actual realization of the eternality would not be at all possible.

Every Darśana (School of philosophical thinking) explains the real 'viveka' (= discrimination) in its own special way and words. Yet the basic notion behind all these various expositions is the same or at least very similar. According to Vedānta 'viveka' is the distinction between nitya (= Eternal) and anitya (=Transient). While Sāṃkhya Yoga says that it is the distinction between the puruṣa and the prakṛti, Out of these, puruṣa is apariṇāmī (= Changeless), a principle which remains ever the same and so is nitya (= Eternal) and prakṛti, though everlasting, yet continually changing (= pariṇāmī) in its evolutes and so in this way is transient (anitya). Thus even this again means a discrimination between nitya and anitya. But as stated above the 'nityānitya-viveka-jñāna' would not be realized in its fullness unless the very deep-rooted preconcepts about the time, noted above, are totally removed from one's mind. For this, therefore, the yogī has to have a firm realization that time is not a continuously proceeding entity and so impermanence and change are not the results of its coercive force caused through its continuity. Change is the nature of prakṛti and so its evolutes are ever changing. It is not an effect of 'the course of time'. In everything manifested ever undergoing change, puruṣa is like a beacon, uninfluenced by time and never changing in the slightest degree. The yogī should not only understand these things, but they should become a reality, so to say, a real experience in him. But for this to happen, the primary prerequisite is, as said, total abolition of the concepts of an unbroken course or flow of time and its inevitably destroying every manifested thing. This the yogī can accomplish, as the sūtra says, by practising saṃyama on the fact that kṣaṇa is the only real thing, while time is only an illusion. Its concept is a fantasy created by the citta-mind complex, due only to innumerable discrete kṣaṇas parading before it in a compact sequence. This realization will give rise to the discrimination between nitya (= Eternal) and anitya (= Temporal i.e. affected by time) which will gradually change into a reality, as though a truth being ever present in the life. This is here indicated by the expression 'vivekajaṃ-jñānam',

For the Yogī who has mastered this saṃyama and acquired the vivekaja-jñāna, the time is, as though, vanquished and so no more is a limitation. Since time is the one factor, which is the most limiting and crucial one in being able to discriminate between two things (as will be seen in next III:53 sūtra), the yogī's power of discrimination becomes limitless, when its limitation is overcome with this saṃyama. This limitless discriminating power enables him to distinguish between even such similar objects and phenomena, which are otherwise impossible to distinguish from one another. He can, therefore, very easily realize the distinction between puruṣa and citta-sattva, which is most difficult to realize. Thus the saṃyama on the kṣaṇas and their closely knit orderly passage before the yogī (i.e. his before citta) leads to vivekajajñāna.

SS. - **जातिलक्षणदेशैरन्यतानवच्छेदात्तुल्ययोस्ततः प्रतिपत्तिः ।।३:५३।।**

TL. - jāti-lakṣaṇa-deśair-anyatānavacchedāt-tulyayos tataḥ pratipattiḥ - III:53

WM. -
jāti = species, class;
lakṣaṇa = outward signs or chartacteristics;
desa (aiḥ->air) = spot, placed (by, plural);
anyatā = otherness, differentness, distinction.

anavaccheda (→āt)	=	(an = not + avaccheda = separation) non-separation, non-distinction (from, due to, because);
tulya (yoḥ→yos)	=	equal, similar (of the two, dual);
tataḥ	=	from that;
pratipatti (ḥ)	=	knowledge, cognition (is).

TR. - From that (the saṃyama recommended in the preceding III:52 sūtra or the vivekaja-jñāna arising out of it) (becomes feasible) the cognition of the distinction of the two very similar things, which seem identical because they cannot be differentiated by (the usual means of) their species, (special) characteristics and places.

CE. - We usually use the three dimensions or criteria standards mentioned in this sūtra for differentiating things from one another. If the two things are of different species or classes e.g. a cow and a horse or a cap and a hat, they are easily distinguished and so jāti is the first criterion for distinction. If the two are of the same jāti, the outward signs or characteristics is the second helpful standard for distinguishing between the two e.g. a black cow from a brown cow. If the two things are of the same class and have very similar lakṣaṇas i.e. characteristics, they are usually recognised as two distinct individuals by their being in two places e.g. two copies of the same edition of a book and so identical in all respects, e.g. size, colour etc., are recognised as two distinct things, because they will be occupying two different places.

But differentiating between two things which are identical in these three aspects will be difficult, may be even impossible, For example if we see a book on a table and later, in our absence, some one takes it away, but keeps in its exact place another copy of the same edition of that book, which will be identical in every respect with the first copy, it will be not possible for us to recognise that the one book was substituted by another. In such a case the only thing that is different is the time factor. In the given example of the two books, the time, when the first copy was occupying the given spot and space, was different from the time, the second copy was occupying the identical spot and space. But the common man has not the capacity to take advantage of this fourth criterion for differentiating between the things, because he is not always able to judge this factor. In the given example of the two copies of the book, since we were not in a position to know that at some time one book took the place of the other one and so are not able to distinguish the second book from the first one. But the yogī who has totally transcended the limitation of the time by means of the mastery of the saṃyama of the preceding III:52 sūtra will be able to know, even in such a case, that the two books were different. Because, even if he was not present when the substituion was effected, as soon as he desires to know about the book, every instant of the existence of both those books stands before him as if it were the present moment and he easily perceives the substitution. Thus this accomplished yogī, who has transcended the limitation of time is able to use the fourth dimension of time with the same ease, as with the other three criteria and thus distinguish things, which for other men are exactly identical and so impossible to separate and distinguish.

The yogī, who has advanced to a stage of mastery over the technique of saṃyama (sūtra III:5) would have in its very early practice an experience of atīt-anāgata jñāna (= knowledge of past and future) through the practice of the saṃyama stated in sūtra III:16. The potentiality of omniscience (sūtra III:49) enables him to know about anything, any where and of any time, whenever he wishes for such a knowledge. Further with the overcoming the barrier and limitation of time through the saṃyama in this sūtra, he sees all things and phenomena, as though time does not exist, nor influences them. Every thing is for him in the present moment. He sees anything and any happening, which he may desire, as if it is before him at that very instant. Indeed he could, if he so desires, see every thing and every occurrence in the creation, of both past and future also, all at once, just as one sees different area far removed from one another all in one perspective, when one goes high up in the sky in an aeroplane. The whole time (past-present-future) is, so to say, spread before an omniscient and time-transcended yogī all at once just like a map.

SS. - **तारकं सर्वविषयं सर्वथाविषयक्रमं चेति विवेकजं ज्ञानम् ।।३:५४।।**

TL. - tārakaṃ sarva-viṣayaṃ sarvathā-viṣayam-akramaṃ ceti-vivekajaṃ-jñānam - III:54

WM. -

tāraka (ṃ)	=	delivering, saviour, liberating (is);
sarva	=	all;
viṣaya (ṃ)	=	subject;
sarvathā	=	in all ways, in all aspects;

viṣayamakrama (m)	=	(viṣaya = subject+a = not + krama = sequence) without sequentiality of the subjects;
ca	=	and;
iti	=	thus, of this type;
vivekaja (m)	=	born of discrimination;
jñāna (m)	=	knowledge (is).

TR. - And delivering (saving, protecting from dangers, and also salvation-giving), encompassing (comprehending) all subjects, in all their aspects and non-sequentially (i.e. not limited by their time correlation with other subjects), such is the vivekaja -jñāna (= Knowledge born of discrimination of purusa from citta-sattva).

CE. - The sūtra explains the nature and scope of vivekaja-jñāna.

Tāraka means that which saves or protects. This saving can be from worldly dangers and harms or in transcendental sense it can mean a Saviour - knowledge leading to Salvation. Both these meanings are implied in tāraka in this sūtra.

Vivekaja-jñāna enables the yogī to have the knowledge of any subject, whatsoever it be and that also of any and all aspects of it, which the yogī would like to know. Further this knowledge he can have without limitation or constraint imposed by the order or sequence with respect to time or placement (geographic or spatial positioning) or inter-subject correlationships. In short, the vivekaja-jñāna makes the yogī omniscient in its total sense. He can know of anything in the total creation (prākṛtika) of any time and from anywhere; but besides this he can have ultimate discrimination of puruṣa and prakṛti and through realization of this Transcendental Truth he achieves Absolute Freedom or Salvation.

SS. - **सत्त्वपुरुषयोः शुद्धिसाम्ये कैवल्यम्** ।।३:५५।।

TL. - sattva-puruṣayoḥ śuddhi-sāmye kaivalyam - III:55

WM. -

sattva	=	sattva i.e. here the pure primordial state of citta;
puruṣa (yoḥ)	=	puruṣa principle (dual possessive = of the two);
śuddhi	=	purity;
sāmya (→e)	=	similarity, equality (in);
kaivalya (m)	=	kaivalya (is).

TR. - In equality of purity of both the sattva (citta) and puruṣa (is established) kaivalya.

CE. - Some commentators think that Patañjali is recommending a saṃyama in this sūtra for achieving kaivalya. But the sūtra is only a clarification of the essential nature of kaivalya. Sattva = The primordial pure state of citta, as soon as it appears from mūla-prakṛti, this latter being incited (cit = incite + ta = past-participle suffix = ed) by the mere vicinage of the puruṣa-tattva (principle). It is purely sattva i.e. mere existence, rajas and tamas having as yet no distinct manifestations of their own and so not yet associated with sattva in this stage. This is a stage even prior to the mahat stage. In this latter rajas and tamas become manifest. The citta in this primordial state, though incited by the presence of puruṣa, is yet to develop its potentiality of consciousness i.e. the ability to become aware and perceive.

When kaivalya is established, the process of counter-evolution through practice of aṣṭāngas of Patañjali's system of yoga is completed. Citta which is an evolute (= vikṛti as per Sāṃkhya-yoga terminology. This term has a sense of a deteriorating change) of prakṛti, during the process of yoga i.e. the counter-evolution, goes backwards through all the stages through which it had evolved and ultimately reverts to its original state of pure mūlaprakṛti, completely unrelated and alienated from the puruṣa principle. Puruṣa, being apariṇāmi (= Immutable), is really ever pure i.e. always remained totally in its own natural state. But due to the production of citta, which becomes sentient due to its mere presence, an illusion is produced of its getting associated with prakṛti, which phenomenon is technically termed saṃyoga by Sāṃkhyayoga, even though in actuality there is nothing at all of this nature. But the whole of human life is going on under the influence of this illusion. The situation is somewhat like that of a good and righteous person falling under a false blemish of having committed a criminal immoral act and suffering through this for the time being, as long as he is not completely exonerated and proved totally innocent of that act. This apparent union i.e. saṃyoga is abolished with the arising of vivekaja-jñāna and sattva-puruṣānyatākhyāti and the puruṣa-principle abides, so to say, again completely unrelated to anything, in its totally blemishless and absolute state, at the time of kaivalya-siddhi i.e. establishment of Kaivalya. Prakṛti had become conscious, when it was affected by the puruṣa's nearness and so began its evolution towards the citta→buddhi→asmitāmātra→manas and so forth. But by itself it is non-sentient. Giving up this sentiency and thus getting free from consequences of this, it i.e. citta reverts to its primordial pure state of mere sattva and subsequently back to pradhāna or mūla-prakṛti state. At the time of appearance or establishment of kaivalya it also remains purely in its own nature, absolutely separated from and unconcerned with the puruṣa principle. This way only the state of kaivalya can be described or explained.

The sūtras III:49, 50 and the present one could be mistaken as prescribing a saṃyama or at the least a method for attaining kaivalya. Some commentators have, as said, fallen also in to such an error. But, in fact no saṃyama has been recommended for attaining kaivalya in the above mentioned sūtras, nor in any other sūtras. Though some of the recommended saṃyamas no doubt are directly helpful and others are indirectly helpful in facilitating and accelerating the attainment of kaivalya, not only this but some are almost like essential prerequisites for the kaivalya there cannot be one or even many saṃyamas, through the practice of which only, kaivalya could appear. Because according to the sūtra III:4 saṃyama is only an advanced stage, say almost a mastery over the practice of sabīja samādhi to such an extent that the essential prior stages of dhāraṇā and dhyāna are accomplished instantly i.e. without requiring any time by the citta for going through them. But sabīja samādhi is not the last and highest samādhi and so kaivalya cannot be reached through its practice alone, even if it be carried over any long period whatsoever. Kaivalya will make its appearance i.e. will become established after the practice of nirbīja samādhi carried over a very long period (may be even some years or if the saṃskaras cannot be done away with easily and quickly, even some lives) and only after it is perfected and culminates into the ultimate and highest samādhi viz. The Dharmamegha samādhi. By means of the saṃyamas, specially mentioned in the sūtras III:35,47,53 etc. and vibhūtis mentioned in the sūtras III:48,49,53 etc., the yogī approaches only very close to kaivalya. As per the sūtra I:51, the nirodha (= cessation) of all vṛttis (= functional modifications) of the citta is the characteristic or definition of nirbīja samādhi, and as per sūtra I:12 practice (abhyāsa, and here it means, of the aṣṭāṅgas) accompanied by high detachment (parama vairāgya) is the only and sure means for achieving cessation (=nirodha) of the citta-vṛttis. Even out of the eight aṅgas (= members of body-yogique) the first five are preliminary and exoteric. The last three viz. dhāraṇā, dhyāna and samādhi (which includes sabīja and nirbīja both) are the esoteric aṅgas and even amongst these the nirbīja samādhi is core-essence of the practical path of Patañjala Aṣṭāṅga Yoga. Therefore the only and assured means for reaching kaivalya is the practice of these esoteric aṅgas and particularly of sabīja and nirbīja samādhis, in the manner as suggested in sūtras I:20 to 23 till the goal is reached.

* * * * *

kaivalya cannot be reached through its practice alone, even if it be carried over any long period whatsoever. Kaivalya will make its appearance i.e. will become established after the practice of nirbīja samādhi carried over a very long period (may be even some years or till the saṁskāras cannot be done away with easily and quickly, even some lives) and only after it is perfected and culminates into the ultimate and highest samādhi viz. the Dharmamegha samādhi. By means of the saṁyamas, specially mentioned in the sūtras III-35, 47, 52 etc. and vibhūtis mentioned in the sūtras III-49, 53 etc., the yogī approaches only very close to kaivalya. As per the sūtra I-51, the nirodha (cessation) of all vṛttis (functional modifications) of the citta is the characteristic or definition of nirbīja samādhi, and as per sūtra I-12 practice (abhyāsa and here it means, of the samādhis) accompanied by high detachment (parama vairāgya) is the only and sure means for achieving cessation i.e. the nirodha of the citta. Thus out of the eight aṅgas (members) of Aṣṭāṅga Yoga the first five are preliminary and exoteric and the three viz. dhāraṇā, dhyāna and samādhi (which includes sabīja and nirbīja both) are the esoteric aṅgas and even amongst these the nirbīja samādhi is core-essence of the practical path of Patañjala Aṣṭāṅga Yoga. Therefore the only and assured means for reaching kaivalya is the practice of these esoteric aṅgas and particularly of sabīja and nirbīja samādhis, in the manner as suggested in sūtras I-20 to 23 till the goal is reached.

Blank

४ कैवल्य पादः

4 KAIVALYA PĀDAḤ

(Section of Kaivalya i. e. Absoluteness)

SS. - जन्मौषधिमन्त्रतपःसमाधिजाः सिद्धयः ।।४:१।।

TL. - janmauṣadhi-mantra-tapaḥ-samādhijāḥ siddhayaḥ - IV:1

WM. -

janma	=	birth;
auṣadhi	=	medicine;
mantra	=	mantra, a sacred formula of one or more letters;
tapa(ḥ)	=	tapa, austerities (nominative case);
samādhi (jāḥ)	=	samādhi (born of, produced through);
siddhi (>ayaḥ)	=	siddhi (s = plu. suffix), perfection, accomplishments, miraculous powers.

TR. - Siddhis are produced through birth, medicines, mantras, austerities (and) samādhi.

CE. - Patañjali enumerates here the various means through which siddhis i.e. miraculous - like powers are produced in a person.

In some persons such strange and miraculous abilities, e.g. clairvoyance, clairaudience, prophesying or doing some abnormal and almost impossible feat etc. are present naturally, These abilities are thus congenital and the only cause for their presence, which may be given, is that they are 'by birth'. No doubt the phenomena are explained in the Indian way of thinking on the basis of karma-siddhānta (= Theory or Law of Karma).It is postulated that such special power is the result of puṇya (= meritorious acts), particularly practice of Yoga, in some past lives (cf. Bhagvad Gītā, VI:37-45). Some commentators have interpreted birth, as the birth in a particular species e.g. a bird or a fish etc., giving rise to special qualities, e.g. flying in birds and underwater living and floating over water in fishes, which they look upon as siddhis. But these innate abilities can be explained in a rational manner and so are not considered as abnormal or miraculous. For this reason these examples as of birth being the cause of siddhis do not seem to be very fitting.

From ancient times medicines are recognised as possessing potentialities to give results which seem miraculous and so can be and are actually called siddhis. Examples are often seen, where almost improbable feats of physical strength have been performed by the use of medicines or sick persons, almost on the point of death, have been revived to almost normal condition and activities, at least for some hours, by giving them medicines. (The present commentator has himself seen some instances of such miraculous happenings). It is claimed that if by treatment with some herbal medicines the mercury can be solidified (the process is called pārada-bandhana i.e. binding of mercury) and a pellet of such solidified mercury is kept under the tongue, a man can make himself or even can fly through the air. Claims of temporarily gaining powers of clairvoyance or clairaudience and other extraordinary experiences through use of drugs have been made even in recent times.

Mantra is a sacred formula composed of letters, (= varṇas i.e. sounds which can be and are represented by letters i.e. akṣaras) usually more than one and these forming meaningful words, but occasionally even of a single letter. The mantra is usually a prayer to some deity or some sacred statement, but it may sometimes be just a grouping of letters or words , which ordinarily does not have any conventional meaning, but is supposed to have a mysterious and mystical force hidden in it. It is believed that by recitation and repetition (= japa) of these mantras, sometimes accompanied by a specific ritual, siddhilike miraculous results are produced. Very well known examples are the claims of removing the ill-effects of poisonous snakebites and insect-stings, curing of acute diseases and other miraculous results. These are actually called 'Mantra-siddhis'. Such effects are not claimed only in India, but in other countries and cultures also.

Tapa i.e. performing austerities is believed, all the world over, to give great miraculous powers to its practicant. As said in sūtra II:43, this is the result of removal of impurities. Very trustworthy instances of such powers being possessed by some persons, who have obtained them through observance of some type of austerity are known in India and also elsewhere. Purāṇas abound in legends of gods and demons who got such miraculous powers through tapa.

The vibhūtis gained through saṃyama, which is an instantaneous sabīja samādhi (dhāraṇā and dhyāna having also become instantaneous and so merged into the sabīja samādhi) can be looked upon as siddhis, if and when they are exploited for worldly gains and selfish benefits, as said in sūtra III:37. Popularly also it is believed and claimed that yogīs can do many miraculous things through siddhis gained through the practice of samādhi.

It can be easily seen that out of the five means for gaining siddhis, the value from the yogic and spiritual aspect goes on increasing from the first towards the fifth.

Some commentators think that the sūtra has no pertinent connection with the subject-matter of this fourth pāda and with the sūtras following immediately. They think, therefore, that the sutra is an interpolation. But as per our view the next few sūtras (IV :2 to 8) indicate the process by which an advanced yogī exhausts all his karma-saṃskāras accumulated till then, by performing compensatory activities for nullifying the effects of these, which he gets done through the agency of innumerable citta-body complexes, as if produced only for this specific purpose. This potentiality of the yogī is a super-miracle, a super-siddhi. So the sūtra seems to be an apt introduction to the topic.

SS. - **जात्यन्तरपरिणामः प्रकृत्यापूरात् ।।४:२।।**

TL. - jātyantara-pariṇāmaḥ prakṛtyāpūrāt - IV:2

WM. - jātyantara = (jati (→y) = (1) birth, (2) species + antara = difference, change)
(1) different births
(2) different species;

pariṇāma (ḥ)	=	transformation, change (is);
prakṛti (→y)	=	prakṛti, here creation;
āpūra (→āt)	=	abundance, overflow (from).

TR. - (The material needed for) The transformation from one ... (1) ...birth,...(2)...species...to another (is ready and is availed) from overabundance (of it) in prakṛti.

CE. - One very important and fundamental query arises in connection with the hypothesis about the advanced yogī's way of quickly exhausting his karma-saṃskāras through compensating actions carried out by means of innumerable body-citta complexes, referred to heretofore. Can and does the yogī create completely newly the material needed for producing these many bodies accompanied each by its respective citta? If he does that, then he becomes a creator, in a way Greater-God or super-īśvara. But as per Sāṃkhya-yoga matter falls under the realm of prakṛti and this is eternal, neither creatable nor destroyable by anybody. So even the yogī cannot create the material needed by him newly. He gets it ready-made from the inexhaustible overabundant stock of matter present in prakṛti. Just as removal of any amount of water from the sea does not apparently reduce its stock of water in any appreciable degree, so also prakṛti can supply any amount and type of material needed by the yogī without getting affected in the least manner. Indeed, from the next (IV:3) sūtra, it can be speculated that the yogī gets not only crude material for producing the extra bodies (nirṃāṇa kāya), but requisitions also and uses the bodies of the particular species as needed for his purpose, from the pool of the bodies of all the various species, which are being produced continuously in the natural course in the prakṛti. There is such an overflow of these that what the yogī needs and uses is only an insignificant and infinitesimal fraction of the spillings.

SS. - **निमित्तमप्रयोजकं प्रकृतीनां वरणभेदस्तु ततः क्षेत्रिकवत् ।।४:३।।**

TL. - nimittam-aprayojakaṃ prakṛtīnāṃ varaṇa-bhedas-tu tataḥ kṣetrika-vat - IV:3

WM. -

nimitta (ṃ)	=	cause (immediate or incidental) (is);
aprayojaka (ṃ)	=	(a = non+pra = intensive + yojaka = stimulator) one not directly stimulating, intro-ducing result;
prakṛti (→īnāṃ)	=	prakṛti, here natural process, law or tendency (of, possessive plu. suffix);
varaṇa	=	a material impediment, lump of earth etc. used for damming, and thus preventing water from flowing further in a channel or gutter;
bheda (ḥ→s)	=	break through, here removal (is);
tu	=	indeed, verily;
tataḥ	=	thence, from that;
kṣetrika	=	farmer;
vat	=	like, same as.

TR. - The (incidental and immediate) cause (here the yogī's desire) is verily not the stimulating factor (directly leading to the desired effect, here another birth or birth with a change of species). It merely removes the impediments, thence it is like a farmer (who wants to water a bed in his farm and so removes the obstacles from the channel taking water to that bed).

CE. - This sūtra is an amplification and clarification of the last sūtra IV:2. The nimitta i.e. incidental cause for producing new bodies (nirmāṇa-kāya) and cittas (nirmāṇa-citta) appears to be the yogī's desire to have these. In other words the yogī seems to create new bodies and new cittas as he needs them. But the yogī cannot and so does not bring out any kind of creation or transformation against the laws of nature. If he adopts a new body (produced through a new birth) or a body of another species, he has not broken any natural law and so has not wrought any miracle. Nature (prakṛti) is ever producing any number of such bodies in its regular course and as said in the preceding (IV:2) sūtra, the yogī only borrows and appropriates some of these for his own purpose according to his needs.

Specially the ability to adopt any body-form of any species (and for the non-believer in the doctrine of rebirth, even another human body) may seem a thing very hard to accept for a man of modern rationalistic outlook. For him and even for a common man it is hard to believe. And yet if at all it takes place, then it is a miracle.

Though the sūtra in the present context is more pertinently concerned with the jātyantara pariṇāma i.e. transformation into another body, either human or of other species, the wording and the statement in the sutra explain the rationalistic view point about all transformations which appear as miracles at the first sight.

A particular substance or system can undergo a number of possible alternative transformations respectively giving rise to a number of products or a number of different new systems. Let us take a simple example of wheat. This can be turned into flour of different grades which again can be transformed into various tasty dishes. A very clever housewife prepares from this very same wheat, a dish, which has such super taste that it sometimes even actually is praised a 'divine' or 'miraculous'. But a number of other women, on the other hand, are never able to prepare such a dish or even one tolerably comparable dish from the same materials. Nobody thinks that in producing that superfine dish from wheat, this clever woman has wrought any miracle, though the feat is almost worthy of being so designated, since rarely another woman is able to duplicate it. It is understood by everybody that though incomparable, the feat is due to the brilliant culinary skill and knowledge of that particular woman, who knows how to put everything to the best use to have the desired end product. The yogī is just like this woman, a knowledgeable person in his own special field, who has the skill to utilize the prakṛti for achieving his purpose (sūtra II:18) in the best possible manner.

Even if a particular transformation may seem miraculous, what it really means is that it is a transformation, which is very rare, may be one which might not have taken place any time before and so seems almost miraculous, because, no one knows the mechanism or the channel of reaction by which the result has been wrought. Patañjali explains this by giving an illustration of a farmer watering different parts or beds in his field. The water naturally flows from a higher lever to a spot at lower level. When the farmer wants the water to flow into a particular bed, which may be even a little higher than another slightly lower bed into which the water is at the moment flowing, he amasses a lot of earth and puts it like a dam in the channel, which is taking water into the lower bed and makes this barrier even higher than the other high level bed. He also opens, clears and deepens the channel meant for carrying water to this higher bed. The barrier prevents the water from flowing through the former channel to the lower bed and the height of the barrier is so great that the flowing water has thc only course left open, that of flowing into the higher bed. The farmer thus only removes the impediments from the path and facilitates the flowing of water in that particular bed. But the water actually flows of its own, according to the natural law about its flowing.

To elaborate this illustration a little more : - We usually express this law about the flowing of water as : - 'Water flows from a higher level point to a low level point'. So if water is made to flow in a reverse manner from lower place to a higher place, it should be really considered a miracle. But that is what is being done in pumping water at the top of a multistorey building or in a hill-top reservoir. And yet not even a rustic villager looks upon this as a miracle. Though he may not understand the whole thing clearly, he at least is vaguely aware that the thing is worked by some natural means or principle. In fact, the more correct statement of that law would be that 'The water flows from a point at high pressure to a point at low pressure,' which an engineer or scientist knows well. When the yogī seems to perform miracles, his case is like the culinary-expert woman mentioned above or this engineer. He is exploiting advantageously a particular mode of transformation which is rarely known or a prākṛtika principle little understood by most others.

As explained above, when the yogī wishes to exhaust his past karma-saṃskāras quickly, he does not produce the needed bodies himself (even though they are called nirmāṇa-kāya = Created body), but appropriates these from the routine production of these in the prakṛti. At that time there is no citta present in these bodies and consequently there is no karmāśaya i.e. the storage of the past karmasaṃskāras. In fact there is no past life for these bodies, because it is the citta's part, particularly the karmāśaya, which passes successively into the bodies in which the being is reborn and forms a link in these successive lives. As said in the next sūtra IV:4 the provision of the cittas in these bodies is made by the yogī out of his asmitāmātra (=Mere i.e. pure I-am-ness i.e. I-consciousness). The other things (elements or principles) needed even for these nirmāṇa-cittas, he takes from the abundant supply of prakṛti. His asmitā-mātra regulates the activity of these innumerable nirmāṇa - citta nirmāṇa-kāya combinations as per the design of the yogī, so as to get a definite number of his past karma-saṃskāras exhausted and this, no doubt, without accumulation of new saṃskāras again from this. But these nirmāṇa-cittas also have no karmāśaya and so no past saṃskāras besides those apportioned to each of them for exhausting these. The citta is thus free from the burden of saṃskāras. This is something akin to the fanner's clearing and removing the dirt and obstacles from the water-channel in the above noted example. Because the citta present ordinarily in a body in regular course of prākṛtika birth carries in it the karma-saṃskāra storage (=karmāśaya) and this compels the attached body to behave (do fresh karmas) in consonance to those saṃskāras. The yogī has removed (indeed has not given chance to arise) this coercive cause i.e. binding (i.e. bond or restraining thing = varaṇa) from the nirmāṇa citta. This nirmāṇa body and nirmana citta complex will perform only those actions, which are necessary to exhaust the saṃskāras which have come as its portion. But the performance of those (counter-) actions is taking place in such a way that they leave no saṃskāras in their own turn, because these actions are not being done with any expectation of any fruit i.e. result, and if there is no desire and expectation of any fruit, there is no reason that the action be stored in the form of saṃskāra till that fruit is gained. If this does not happen and these counter-actions leave behind their own saṃskāras, then the whole thing will be purposeless and in vain, because then the karma (= action)→saṃskāra (= residual impression or effect)→ (prati-) karma (= counter action)→ saṃskāra... chain will continue. Therefore the highly advanced yogī is able to exhaust all his past karma-saṃskāras in one single life by requisitioning as many artificial bodies as needed from the stock of prakṛti in the above said manner.

SS. - **निर्माणचित्तान्यस्मितामात्रात् ।।४:४।।**

TL. - nirmāṇacittānyasmitāmātrāt - IV:4.

WM. - nirmāna-citta (āni→āny) = artificially created citta (plural end suffix, nominative case = are);

asmitā-mātra (→āt) = (asmitā = as-mi-tā = (i) am-ness + mātra = Mere i.e. pure asmitā i.e. (1) am-ness or I consciousness (from, out of).

TR. - The artificially created cittas (seem to be produced by the yogī) from (his) asmitā-mātra (i.e. pure I -consciousness).

CE. - The Karma-siddhānta or Law of Karma is accepted by most of the Indian Darśanas. Yoga darśana and so Patañjali also implicitly accept it. According to it the fruit i.e. result or consequence of each and every karma done by one is inevitably to be faced and received by him. One has to enjoy the pleasant fruits of good karmas and suffer the painful consequences of evil karmas (sūtras II:12 to 14). This is unavoidable and none can escape from this law. When this is so, even the yogī cannot be any exception.

The difficulty then arises as to how the yogī can have apavarga (= emancipation) and attain kaivalya and get out of the cycle of birth and death very quickly, probably even in one life-span, after he takes to the path of Yoga. How can the saṃskāras of as yet unexhausted karmas of probably a very large number of past lives be done away with, within a short span of one (or at the most very few) life ?

The answer to this, given by the Yoga-philosophy, is very

tersely stated in this and the following sūtras (5 to 11). It is that the yogī creates or rather appropriates for his specific purpose (as explained in sūtra IV:2) the various bodies and no doubt accompanying citta-material (since a body without a citta i.e. potentiality to be conscious and stimulate action in the body, would be purposeless) as needed for exhausting totally all the saṃskāras (i.e. residual impressions of actions). It may be that he thus utilizes one kāya-citta complex for each karmasaṃskāra stored up in the karmāśaya. The exhaustion of a past karmasaṃskāra is accomplished by having the final phala= fruit i.e. result of that past karma. This phala is to be had in the form of a bhoga i.e. experience, which may be a painful suffering or pleasure-giving enjoyment depending on respectively that karma being evil (pāpa = sin) or meritorious (puṇya = virtuc) (cf. sūtra II:13, 14). Depending on the specific nature of the phala, the body of the appropriate species will be requisitioned from the prakṛti's stock by the yogī (cf. Jātaka-kathā of Buddha).

But every experiencing is as good as doing a karma afresh. This then would leave behind its own new saṃskāra in the karmāśaya. This is avoided by keeping the new karma, undergone in experiencing the phala of the past karma, niṣkāma i.e. desireless or without expectation of any further fruit from it. This knack (= kauśala) is well recognised in Yoga (cf. Bhagvad-Gīta, IV : 14 ff, VI: 7 ff., XVIII: 17,49 etc.) and is very concisely expressed hereafter in sūtras IV : 6 to 11.

Creation of artificial bodies (nirmāṇa-kāya) is explicitly mentioned in Buddhistic yogīc writing. Patañjali does not mention it. But nirmāṇa citta cannot function meaningfully without the support of a body. So for efficient functioning a nirmāṇa-citta would need a nirmāṇa-kāya i.e. a body and so its creation is to be implicitly assumed. Patañjali refers to the nirmāṇa-citta only, because karmasaṃskāras can be stored in the karmāśaya portion of citta only and in the consideration of the process of exhaustion of these, only their psychic (citta) aspect is of importance and not the body i.e. kāya aspect.

Another question may arise in the mind of a reader about the creation of numerous cittas, specially about the source of their potentiality of consciousness. The natural citta of an individual gets its power of consciousness from the puruṣa principle. But the yogī cannot create and allocate such a puruṣa for each of the numerous nirmāṇa-cittas. Moreover provision of such one puruṣa for each citta would each mean or cause a puruṣa-prakṛti saṃyoga, which leads to the chain:- saṃyoga→avidyā→bhoga-duḥkha-bondage (sūtra II:23 ff.). How then these nirmāṇa-cittas become conscious and active ? The clarification of this is that the asmitāmātra, the pure I - consciousness is the source of the consciousness arising in these nirmāṇa-cittas. The asmitāmātra is different from asmitā-the kleśa. It is an early stage in the evolution of the citta, where the consciousness of the individuality and so of distinctness from others first appears. It being non-material and ajaḍa (potentially active) can expand in any measure and thus can contribute the ability of consciousness in general and in this case particularly that of yogīs own individual consciousness potentiality to all the new nirmāṇa-cittas, whatever be their number. The other material needed for the development of this nirmāṇa-citta into functionally a full-fledged cittta, with its mahat i.e. buddhi, manas (= mind) and other aspects, as said before (sūtra IV:3), the source is the abundant stock of prakṛti.

SS. - **प्रवृत्तिभेदे प्रयोजकं चित्तमेकमनेकेषाम् ।।४:५।।**

TL. - pravṛtti-bhede prayojakaṃ cittam-ekamanekeṣām - IV:5

WM. -

pravṛtti	=	(intensive or specific) mode of functioning or tendency (of citta);
bheda (→e)	=	differentness (in);
prayojaka (ṃ)	=	stimulator, impeller, driving force (is);
citta (ṃ)	=	citta (is);
eka (ṃ)	=	one (is);
aneka (→eṣām)	=	(an = not + eka = one) many (in, plural).

TR. - The driving force behind the difference (seen) in the tendencies of the many (different nirmāṇacittas) is the one (original or innate) citta (of the yogī).

CE. - The nirmāṇa-citta-kāya complexes are needed for carrying out compensatory counter-actions (= pratikarmas), which are to be undertaken or rather undergone as the bhoga (= experience), which is the phala (fruit) of a (or a few) past karma. Depending on the specific nature of this compensating karma to be undergone for the exhaustion of the saṃskāra of the past karma through expiation, by means of this new karma, the specific tendency of the nirmāṇa-citta will be quite different from the specific tendencies of the other nirmāṇa cittas, who have to do their own quite different compensatory karmas. If all these nirmāṇa-cittas begin to work each one according to its own special tendency, with total disregard for the others and their works, there can be occasions when some cittas may be working even on contrary lines from some others. There would be a confusing situation- nay may be even chaos. In that case the whole plan for the exhaustion of all the karmasaṃskāras in the karmāśaya would go awry. It is therefore essential that there is good co-ordination and smooth co-operation in the working of all the nirmāṇa cittas. For this, the driving and guiding force behind all of them must be one. The sūtra tells that there is such a single co-ordinator force or agency and that can be only the innate or natural citta of the yogī.

SS. - तत्र ध्यानजमनाशयम् ।।४:६।।

TL. - tatra dhyānajam-anāśayam - IV: 6

WM. - tatra = there, in them;
dhyānaja (ṃ) = produced by means of dhyāna (is);
anāśaya (m) = (an = not + āśaya = content, storage), not having a storage (i.e. karmāśaya).

TR. - There (i.e. in those nirmāṇa-cittas) (the citta) created by means of dhyāna (is) without a storage (of karma-saṃskāras i.e. karmāśaya).

CE. - Although for the procurement of the nirmāṇa-cittas, the prākṛtika material needed will, as said, be available to the yogī from the stock of prakṛti, the consciousness would be imparted to them from the asmitāmātra aspect of the yogī's natural citta. This bestowing of the potentiality of consciousness to these nirmāṇa-cittas is accomplished by the yogī only by concentrating all the power of his natural citta along with a one-pointed desire of transferring the power of consciousness of this original natural citta partially to the other i.e. the nirmāṇa-citta. For having such intense one-pointedness, the stage of dhyāna as defined in sūtra III:2 has to be attained by the yogī. Thus the nirmāṇa-citta gets its ability of consciousness i.e. its citta-tva (= citta-hood) though the process of dhyāna. In this manner, this nirmāṇa-citta is dhyāna-ja i.e. born out of dhyāna. As said, these dhyānaja nirmāṇa-cittas will have no āśaya (= storage, here that means of karma-saṃskāras, therefore it is the karmāśaya), since they are produced completely newly, artificially and only temporarily for the specific purpose of the annulment of one or a few past karma-saṃskāras and not in the normal manner, as a result of rebirth, caused by the past lives and karmas (sūtras II:12 and 13).

The word 'āśaya' has another meaning viz. intention. Some commentators have assumed this sense of the word here. Therefore they interpret that the action done by the dhyānāja citta is without intention i.e. desire and so is niṣkāma. The same conclusion is reached also through the previous interpretation, as when there is no karmāśaya, there would be no predisposing desires (vāsanās) for and so no expectation of any fruit from the karma and thus the karma done by the dhyānaja nirmāṇa citta would be niṣkāma.

SS. - **कर्माशुक्लाकृष्णं योगिनस्त्रिविधमितरेषाम् ।।४:७।।**

TL. - karmāśuklākrṣṇaṃ yoginas-trividhamitareṣām - IV:7

WM. -

karma	=	karma, action (associated with its maturation, storage as saṃskāra and fruit);
aśukla	=	(a = not + śukla = white, pure) not pure, not meritful, non-virtuous;
akrṣṇa (ṃ)	=	(a = not + krṣṇa = black, sinful not sinful, non-vicious (is);
yogin (aḥ->as)	=	yogī (of);
trividha (ṃ)	=	(tri = three + vidha = variety) of three varieties or types (is);
itara (->eṣām)	=	other (of, plural).

TR. - Karmas (actions) of the yogī are neither white (= meritful) nor dark (= sinful). In other persons (these are) of three types (namely white i.e. meritful, dark i.e. sinful and mixed i.e. partly meritful and partly sinful).

CE. - As per sūtras II: 13,14 karma (= action) leaves behind an impression (saṃskāra) or residual effect in the karmāśaya portion of the citta, which gives its phala (fruit) after its maturation in due time. This phala may be pleasure-giving, if the karma be puṇya i.e. meritful or extremely agony-giving, if the karma be pāpa i.e. sinful.

The karma of a common man in most cases will be an admixture of these two categories i.e. it will be partly meritful and partly sinful. Depending on the dominance of the merit or the sin, however, it may be stamped as meritorious or sinful. In rare instances a karma of a common man might be either totally full of merit or totally sinful. These three are the possibilities of the typification of the karmas of a common man. But indeed a karma can be and is adjudged as meritful or sinful and accordingly the phala is respectively pleasing or painful.

Whether a particular karma will give pleasure or agony will depend on the expectation about the desire for the phala of that karma, which the person performing that karma will be having in his mind. If the expectation and the desire is fulfilled, the person will be pleased, but when it will not be so, he will be pained. In this way the threefold typification of the karmas will be ultimately dependent on the expectation and desire about the phala and its nature, which a person might be holding in his mind.

When the yogī is getting karma done through the agency of a nirmāṇa-citta-kāya complex, it is done only for the expiation and through this the annulment of the saṃskāras of the past karmas. He has neither any further expectation nor desire for any sort of phala. These karmas of his, got done through the nirmāṇa-citta-kāya, are thus from his point of view and in effect, neither śukla (i.e. puṇya =meritful) nor kṛṣṇa (i.e. pāpa= sinful), since he is neither expecting a pleasant nor a painful phala indeed he does not expect nor want any phala at all. All his karmas, whether done through the nirmāṇa-citta-kāyas or through his natural citta-body, with which he was born, are truly totally desireless i.e. niṣkāma. The well-recognised theory as to how this niṣkāmatva (= desirelessness) in the karma results into naiṣkarmya i.e. non-karmaness (i.e. a condition where an action, even when actually done, does not become a 'karma'. That means there is no storage and preservation of the after-effect of that karma in the form of saṃskāra, which in its due time i.e. after its period of maturation produces the phala i.e. fruit or final result of that karma, which itself is or leads to another karma. If this saṃskāra-preservation and phala - production is there, then the unending cycle of karma - saṃskāra→phala (another karma)→saṃskāra→phala (= karma) .... ad infinitum, continues. In other words the chain of birth-life-experience-birth also continues endlessly) and how the cycle of karma→phala (which takes the form of birth→life→ experience or suffering)→karma ... is finally broken and done away with, is summarized in the following sūtras.

SS. - **ततस्तद्विपाकानुगुणानामेवाभिव्यक्तिर्वासनानाम् ।।४:८।।**

TL. - tatas-tad-vipākānuguṇānām-evābhivyaktirvāsanā-nām-IV:8

WM. - tataḥ (→as) = from those, from that;
tad = of that;
vipāka = maturation, fructification;
anuguṇa (→ānān) = according to (in consonance to, as necessary and suitable to) the nature of, plural);
eva = only;
abhivyakti (ḥ→r) = manifestation (is).
vāsanā (nām) = inclinations, tendencies, intentions, impulses leading to desire (of, plural).

TR. - From those (karmas i.e. here karmasaṃskāras) (there is) the manifestation of only those (in the form of) tendencies (or desires), which are necessary and suitable for the fructification of those (karmas).

CE. - Two meanings of the word tataḥ (→s) are possible and also applicable here. (1) From that i.e. out of those (karmas or karma-saṃskāras). (2) From that i.e. on account the characteristics of karmas being of the types as described in the preceding sūtra IV:7. We have accepted the meaning (1) in the translation above. But the meaning (2) could be very well adopted. Nevertheless, whatever meaning of the word 'tatas' be taken, the main purport of the sūtra remains unaltered.

As said the karma→phala is an eternally continuous chain. It can be elaborated thus :--karma→saṃskāra→phala, which is a bhoga i.e. experience in the shape of a new karma, which creates its own→saṃskāra→leading to its phala (a karma) .....and this ad infinitum. In this process every karma is stored up and preserved in the form of a saṃskāra i.e. some kind of impression or effect on some part of citta. This is designated as 'karmāśaya.' Where and what it exactly is nowhere has been clearly explained, but this does not cause any difficulty for understanding the theory.

As said in sūtra III:22, different karmas need different periods for their maturation to produce their final phala. When this period of fructification of a particular karma is complete, the proper vāsanā, which may be necessary in accordance with the nature of that karma and the nature of the phala due for that karma, becomes manifested in the citta. At this first appearance, the vāsanā is purely an inclination to perform the (new) karma, which is fitting with or rather equivalent to the phala. In other words the vāsanā is at first only a stimulus for the happening of that karma which gives, or rather which is itself, the phala. But in a common man the vāsanā does not remain only that much i.e. a pure vāsanā only. It gets associated with an expectation an hankering, usually for a phala, which may be quite different from the legitimate and the natural phala, which is due for that first karma, as per the law of karma. This is why the vāsanā seems to be a wish and so such a meaning is often given to the word vāsanā. The association of a wish for an extraneous phala is on account of the existence of the numerous other saṃskāras lying in the karmāśaya, which also affect and give their colouring to the particular vāsanā.

In the case of a yogī such association of vāsanā with icchā (= wishes or desires) does not take place, firstly because the yogī, who has advanced to such a high stage, will be having also a very high degree of vairāgya; and so will have no desires left in him, secondly since only one or a very few karmas of a similar nature are being expiated through the agency of one nirmāṇa-citta-kāya, there is no admixture of the vāsanā, specifically having the expiation of a past karma-saṃskāra as its aim, with the desires for extraneous phalas, since all the remaining saṃskāras are also simultaneously being expiated through other nirmāṇa-citta-kāyas.

Since the vāsanā in the yogī is thus pure and only serves as a stimulus for activating a saṃskāra, so as to start the process of its fruition and since there is no wish attached for any other extraneous fruit, either good or bad, the fresh karma, undertaken by the nirmāṇa-citta-kāya or even by the cittta-kāya natural by birth of the yogī, is thus totally niṣkāma (=devoid of expectation and desire). Since there is no expectation and wish about the fruit's being either pleasant (= hlādaka) or agonising (paritāpada), the nature of this fresh expiatory karma, undergone as the phala, is neither meritful (= puṇya) nor sinful (= apuṇya or pāpa) (cf. Sūtra II:14), because the nature of the karma, whether good (i.e. puṇya = meritorious) or evil (i.e. pāpa = sin) is determined by the nature of its phala. But in the yogī's view the phala is neither good nor evil, as for him neither of these exist or in other words he looks upon these both as the same. Therefore for him the karma is 'no-karma' (= niṣ-karma) and this mode of having action accomplished is known as 'naiṣkarmya'. Action done or better said, undergone, with this sort of attitude does not lead to bondage (= karmabandha), because, as there is no expectation for any further phala, there is no reason that its saṃskāra may take place and be preserved upto maturation. The yogī has undergone the karma as an expiation and through this the total abolition of a past karma-saṃskāra. Since the karma is not transformed into saṃskāra nor preserved in karmāśaya for the further process of fructification, the karma→saṃskāra→phala (=another karma) →saṃskāra .....chain is broken and thus discontinued.

SS. - **जातिदेशकालव्यवहितानामप्यानन्तर्यं स्मृतिसंस्कारयोरेक-रूपत्वात् ।।४:९।।**

TL. - jāti-deśa-kāla-vyavahitānām-apy-ānantaryaṃ smṛti-saṃskārayor-eka-rūpatvāt - IV:9

WM. -

jāti	=	birth;
deśa	=	country, region, locality;
kāla	=	time, period;
vyavahita (→ānāṃ)	=	separated by (of, plural);
api (→y)	=	even;
ānantarya (ṃ)	=	unseparatedness, closeness, close relationship;
smṛti	=	memory;
saṃskāra (→yoḥ→r)	=	saṃskāra i.e. residual impression or effect of a karma, remaining in the karmāśaya portion of the citta (of the two, dual possessive);
ekarūpatva (→āt)	=	(eka=one+rūpa=form + tva = ness) oneness, (from, on account of).

TR. - On account of the identicalness of the two, namely smṛti (= memory) and saṃskāra (= residual impression of the action i.e karma), there is closeness (i.e. immediate conversion) (of saṃskāra into smṛti) even when (the two are) separated by birth, locality or time.

CE. - As soon as an action is done or an experience (which is a passive action in the view of the karma-siddhanta i.e. Law of Karma) is undergone by a person, there is produced an effect or a lasting impression or record of it in the citta. This impression or record is preserved for a long time in a part of the citta, which has this special function of maintaining the record until it is required for giving its (final) fruit i.e. phala, with the gaining of which the original karma is compensated or expiated and thus, so to say, the account is closed. In other words the karma is fully exhausted and so its saṃskāra in karmāśaya is abolished. The record is technically called the saṃskāra of the karma and the store-house of these karma-saṃskāras is called karmāśaya. Where this karmāśaya is and in what manner it gains the karma-saṃskāras and maintains and preserves them is not known and no attempt has been made by anyone to explain this. The only ground for assuming the production of the saṃskāra and the existence of the karmāśaya is the phenomenon of the memory itself. When a person can remember an experience of several years ago, sometimes correct even in every detail, it should be obvious to anyone that this past experience must have been recorded and preserved in some form somewhere. Modern science in recent decades has begun to accept that even pre-natal experiences, really consciously undergone by the mother alone, are imprinted in the mind of the off-spring in the fetus state also. This theory was to be accepted because the origin of certain complexes could not be explained otherwise in a rational manner acceptable to modern science. Extrapolating on the same lines the Ancient Indian sages postulated that certain traits and peculiarities, seen in some persons, could be reasonably explained as arising from the saṃskāras from past lives only.

Even the common man easily understands and knows that the remembrance of an experience, undergone sometime ago in the present life, is a partial or total revivification of that experience, because he has an innate ability to connect this revival to the original experience. It can, therefore, be easily assumed and accepted that upto the moment of this revival, the experience must have been preserved in some kind of record in the organism and very possibly this recording is made in some subtle manner in the mind, or according to the Indian sages in the citta, in the karmāśaya portion of this, in the form of a karmaśaṃskāra. When some circumstance helpful for such a revival is present, the saṃskāra is brought up into the current consciousness and this is what is called remembering, recollection or memory. Ordinarily this is possible to a very great extent for the current life only. Most often even when the incident has been experienced at a place or region (= deśa) or at a time (= kāla) too far removed from the present ones, the revival or remembrance (smṛti) can be easily connected to that incident or experience, which was the source of this memory.

But if the experience was undergone in some past life, it cannot be so linked with its revival in the present life, because a common man has not got the ability to remember the past lives. Ancient sages of India (many of whom were advanced yogīs) and yogīs, who had conquered the time and so transcended its limitation or bondage (cf. sūtras III:52 and IV: 12), can recollect the experiences of previous lives* also.

---

* Note : - The savants of modern natural sciences are, in this respect, on par with the common man. They also have no ability to remember past lives. Moreover most of them are adherents of Christianity and again like a common follower of Christianity, staunch believers in the dogmas of that religion. Accepting the notion of rebirth is a hearsay for them and so almost improbable for them to accept it. This is the main reason why such quite rational explanations, based upon a belief on and acceptance of the theory of rebirth have not become acceptable to the modern science, which means to modern scientists, who are most often Christians.

Even a common man in his ordinary life has very probably such recollections or revivals of experiences of past lives, may be even in wakeful condition, but more particularly in dream state. But since he is unable to link them with the original experience, which his citta had in some past life, he is indeed confused and considers them as some weird creations or wayward vagrancies of the mind. The revival or recollection of such experiences of past lives stored in the form of saṃskāras in the karmāśaya is easily seen in meditational processes, specially in the vitarka and vicāra samāpattis, as has been already explained (cf. sūtras I:17 and 41 to 44 etc.)

Since vāsanās i.e. inclinations or tendencies to do a particular action (= karma) is on account of activation or arousal of some saṃskāra, the process is somewhat akin to revival or recollection of memory (= smṛti). The only difference is that very often the person is not aware that this is a smṛti or arousal of a saṃskāra of past experience, particularly if this latter be of some earlier life. Again the vāsanā may not be having any nature of icchā (= desire), since the arousal of the saṃskāra is purely for the purpose of making the sādhaka perform the compensating karma, which is to be done for only nullifying the past karma through gaining of its phala. To make the yogasādhaka clearly comprehend the mechanism through which an advanced yogī exhausts all the saṃskāras lying in the karmāśaya rapidly and in one life, this close relationship, in fact the identity, of smṛti with saṃskāra should also be well understood by the sādhaka.

Patañjali in the present sūtra affirms that the smṛti and corresponding saṃskāra are ekarūpa (= identical). Thus even when the two, having been separated from each other by a great geographical distance or long time interval or even one or more births (lives), may not be easily connected and so recognised as identical, yet on account of their identicalness the saṃskāra, stored in the karmāśaya, is, as if, at once changed into smṛti, as and when a situation facilitatory for this is present. This arousal of saṃskāra and its transformation into smṛti is so vivid, as though there is no gap of distance, interval of time or differentness of lives at all. The phenomenon of transformation of saṃskāra into smṛti therefore, seems as though, the saṃskāra has become smṛti at the very moment that it was recorded and stored in the karmāśaya. In other words the effectiveness of the change is so good that for practical purposes there was no time interval in between the two. If the sādhaka comprehends this well, then at the time of his becoming a yogī on the very threshold of kaivalya, he can have his vāsanās very pure without any admixture of desires for any extraneous phala. These then will serve only as stimuli to arouse a former saṃskāra, which will lead to the performance (or experiencing) of the phala, which will be in a way a fresh karma, but which is niṣkāma (= devoid of desire).This then would only nullify the saṃskāra and will not produce in its turn another fresh saṃskāra of this fresh karma, because it is niṣkāma. Thus the chain reaction of karma→phala (= karma)→phala (= karma) ceases.

SS. - तासामनादित्वं चाशिषो नित्यत्वात् ।।४:१०।।

TL. - tāsām-anāditvaṃ cāśiṣo nityatvāt - IV: 10.

WM. - tāsām = of those;

anāditva (m)	=	(an = not+adi = first, beginning + tva = ness) beginninglessness (is);
ca	=	and;
āśiṣa (ḥ→o)	=	(as = to exist + is = to desire) will or desire to live (is);
nityatva (→āt)	=	everness, eternality (from, on account of).

TR. - And (there is) beginninglessness of those (i.e. smṛti and saṃskāras) on account of the eternality of the will to live.

CE. - A question may be asked as to why these saṃskāras are produced in the cittta and preserved long-even through many lives-in the karmāśaya part of the citta. The answer given to it in this sūtra is almost on the same lines as of the modern science. According to this latter, every action in a living organism is directed in such a way as to help the preservation of life. Even disease is a protective mechanism. It serves as a forewarning of a possible and more dangerous situation and of death and its purpose is that the organism can be saved from these by adopting proper measures. The process or mechanism of karma → saṃskāra → phala (i.e. karma) → saṃskāra → phala (= Karma)...., also serves the same purpose of perpetuation of life, not only the maintenance of a single life, but continuance of the entity through many lives. The driving force behind this is the āśiṣa (= will to live). This force is eternal that is beginningless. The saṃskāras need also be supposed to be beginningless since they are produced and preserved in the karmāśaya by this force of āśiṣa, through which the cycle of life after life is perpetuated.

Patañjali has used two different terms having the meaning 'the will to live', namely 'āśiṣa' and 'abhiniveśa' (cf. sūtras II:3 to 9). The former is a benign force essential for maintenance of life activities and so also for Yoga. The abhiniveśa is a kleśa, which causes troubles, as it is associated with egotism i.e. āsmita, another kleśa.

Just as there is a very subtle difference between the benign 'āsmita-mātra' (= mere and pure I -consciousness, of sūtra IV:4) and asmitā, a kleśa (= egotism), so also there is a difference between the benign āśiṣa (mere will to live) and the trouble-causing kleśa abhiniveśa (= will to live manifested in an obnoxious domineering way, admixed with and dominated by egoism). Avidyā, the first and supermost kleśa is eternal (cf. sūtras II:3 ff.) and so also the other four kleśas, which are just like its variations or aspects, are almost lifelong. In the same way saṃskāras and the karmāśaya, in which they are preserved are eternal. As already said (cf. sūtra II: 13), the question, which of them was the first, is ever unanswerable. But in this sūtra, though not explicitly expressed, the statement is, as if, the āśiṣa is the cause and saṃskāras, which are identical to smṛtis (=memories), which give rise to vāsanās. (= arousal of saṃskāras, leading most often to desires), are the consequences. Thus the conversion :-- saṃskāra→smṛti→vāsanā→desire, is caused due to āśiṣa (= will to live).

SS. - **हेतुफलाश्रयालम्बनैः संगृहीतत्वादेषामभावे तदभावः ।।४:११।।**

TL. - hetu-phalāśrayālambanaiḥ saṃgṛhītatvādeṣām-
-abhāve tad-abhāvaḥ - IV: 11

WM. - hetu = purpose, cause;
phala = fruit, result, effect;
āśraya = place of refuge, (safe) reservoir;
ālambana(→aiḥ) = means of support (through, by);
saṃgṛhītatva (→āt→ād) = (saṃgṛhīta = put or held together + tva = ness), the property of being held together (as one-whole or a unit) (from, on account of);
eṣām = of these;
abhāva (e) = absence, disappearance (in);
tad = its or their;
abhāva (h) = absence, disappearance (is).

TR. - On account of the property (i.e. ability) of being held together...... (1) through the means of supporting this togetherness and wholeness (namely) cause which here is (a) āśiṣa (= desire to live) and (b) kleśas, the effect (here phala = fruit or result) and reservoir (here karmāśaya)........or,............(2) through the cause, the effect, the reservoir and the support (which here would be subjects or objects in the world) .... (when there is) absence of these [i.e. factors supporting or holding together a thing, which as per (1) are three and as per (2) are four] there is absence of those also (i.e. of saṃskāra-vāsanās also).

CE. - A karma (= action) is preserved in the form of saṃskāra, because the person performing this karma has an expectation and desire of some kind of phala i.e. result from this karma. This desire for karma is aroused by the force of āśiṣa as per one view (a) or due to the impelling force of kleśas as per second viewpoint (b) and it, so to say, converts the saṃskāra into vāsanā, which serves as a stimulus for activation of the saṃskāra of that karma, when the period of maturation of that karma is over and its phala is going to appear. This karma-phala-ākāṅkṣā (expectation and desire for the fruit of the action) or vāsanā is produced, as said above, on account of (1) āśiṣa or (2) kleśas, which thus is the real cause (hetu) which leads to the record and preservation of the saṃskāra of that karma in the karmāśaya. After due time, when the circumstances are facilitatory, the phala or effect of the karma is produced. Till then the karmasaṃskāra is preserved in the reservoir (=āśraya) of karmāśaya. Thus the whole chain of saṃskāra to phala is dependent on these supporting factors (= ālambanas) and becomes an integral process on account of these. If these (in fact even one of these) ālambanas are absent, the whole mechanism will break down, since everyone of these factors is equally essential to hold it together.

If it be assumed that aśaṣa is the cause (= hetu) then for doing it away para-vairāgya (= extreme detachment) is the remedy. If it be assumed that the cause is kleśas, the remedy is kṛiyā-yoga, as explained in pāda II (sūtras 2 ff.). For abolishing the effect (phala), the desire for fruit (phala-ākāṅkṣā) is to be given up, as is well recognised and beautifully expounded in Bhagavadgītā. Obviously for this also, therefore, high vairāgya is necessary. When no phala is desired, the action(= karma) becomes niṣkāma (= desireless). Thus the reason for converting the karma to saṃskāra and this into vāsanā does not exist and so its storage in the reservoir of karmāśaya becomes unnecessary. With vairāgya the ālambana (separately counted as the fourth factor for holding together the karma-phala chain, in translation (2) of the sūtra) viz. the subject or object in the world becomes meaningless for the yogī and so plays no part in maintenance of the chain of karma-saṃskāra-phala (i.e. karma)........ Thus vairagya is the master-remedy for abolishing all (the three or the four) factors holding the process of saṃskāra-vāsanā formation and storage and stopping the karma-saṃskāra-vāsanā-phala chain from going on eternally.

When the desires (= icchās) causing the storage of saṃskāra disappear and the chief cause (hetu) of theirs viz. the will to live (aśaṣa) also disappears, the yogī has nothing to achieve hereafter and so no desire to live any further. Now he is ready to step out of the wheel of birth after birth and to set himself free of the bondage and suffering of life and death and to enter into kaivalya--The Absoluteness.

The word ālambana means support and we have understood the terms 'ālambanaiḥ saṃgṛhītatvāt' in the sūtra as meaning - 'on account of the means supporting this togetherness and wholeness'. We therefore accept the meaning of the sūtra as in TR (1), that the means (= ālambanas) maintaining this togetherness are three viz. the cause (=hetu), fruit (= phala) and reservoir (āśraya). But many commentators interpret by this term ālambana another additional and so a fourth factor in holding the process of saṃskāra→vāsanā together i.e. as an integral process. They mean by ālambana the support, which they think as being the worldly objects or subjects with which the experience or action (=karma) and so the saṃskāra is concered. Even if this interpretation, as given in TR (2), be accepted, the general purport and practical significance of the sūtra does not change much. Since, as said, absence of any one of these is as good as absence of all and also disappearance of the saṃskāra-vāsanās, it does not matter whether these factors are assumed to be three or four.

As per our understanding and the context of the sūtras, āśiṣa [as in TR. (1)] seems to be the best explanation as being the cause [= hetu]. But others understand it to be kleśas [as in TR. (1)], probably on the basis of sūtra II:12, as therein kleśas are said to be the origin of karmāśaya. Nevertheless even this explanation of the cause (= hetu) really does not differ from that of (1) (a) significantly, as abhiniveśa, which is almost the same as āśiṣa [only asmitā gets admixed with it, when it appears as abhiniveśa], is included in kleśas and so the explanation in (1) (b) may be acceptable, though that of (1) (a) seems preferable interpretation to us.

SS. - **अतीतानागतं स्वरूपतोऽस्त्यध्वभेदाद्धर्माणाम्** ।।४:१२।।

TL. - atītānāgataṃ svarūpato'sty-adhvabhedād-dharmāṇām - IV:12

WM. -

atīta	=	gone away, past;
anāgata	=	(an = not+āgata = come) not yet come, future;
svarūpataḥ (→o)	=	from or by its own (real) nature (nominative);

asti (→y)	=	is;
adhva	=	path, direction;
bheda (→āt→ād)	=	difference (due to);
dharma (→āṇām)	=	fundamental properties or qualities (of, plural).

TR. - (The feeling, perception or notion of) The past and future is in its nature (i.e. really a feeling produced merely) due to the difference of the directionalities of the dharmas (i.e. the basic properties of things).

CE. - Many of the commentators have divided the sūtra in two parts, which they look upon as two independent statements. Therefore the sūtra meaning is generally given as : - "The past and future exist in their own form (i.e. they exist as such, which means that they exist as two independent entities or two realities). The differentness of dharmas is on account of the difference in the paths of dharmas". (cf. Taimni and others).

But this understanding of the sutra seems to be quite wrong. If the past and future were looked upon as two separate realities, their mention should have been in dual number as 'atītānāgatau'. So also the verb should have dual form 'staḥ' and not the singular 'asti' = is, as it is at present in the sūtra. Again the last part of the sūtra viz. 'adhvabhedād-dharmāṇām' is clearly a subordinate phrase to the first part, showing the reason for the arising of the feeling of the past and future being as separate entities. The confusion seems to be caused by the wrong understanding about the meaning of the term 'svarūpataḥ' as 'in reality' or 'as real'. But the syllable 'sva' means 'one's own' i. e. 'one's basic or real' and 'rūpa' means 'form' or here 'state or nature'. The whole term thus means : - 'in its real nature' and not as 'in reality' or 'as real'. So our meaning (TR.) is linguistically more precise and correct.

The meaning of the sūtra, therefore, according to us, is diagonally opposite to that given by most of the earlier commentators. Indeed the sūtra seems to state that the notion of the past and future i.e. of a continuously flowing time is not real. It is a mere notion caused by the different directionalities of the dharmas i.e. basic properties, which determine the nature of the particular thing or substance. It is a well-recognised fact that everything is ever undergoing a change and this leads to a total disappearance (destruction or end) of the thing one day. According to Sāṃkhyayoga (cf. Bhagavadgītā, II: 16), however, nothing is ever destroyed. (Modern science has also the same view.). The destruction or disappearance is in reality a drastic change, where dharmas are changed so much that the resultant thing or substance is not recognizable as the original one and so a feeling of disappearance of the thing is caused.

In these processes of destruction and disappearance i.e. of drastic transformation., what happens is that some dharmas go back into the unmanifested state from their manifest condition and we say that they have gone and feel that they have become 'past'. Other fresh dharmas will become manifested from their unmanifest sate and we say and feel that they will come up later i.e. in future. Thus there is no any reality to time. It is a conception created merely by the two directions of the movement of dharmas, from manifest to unmanifest and inversely from unmanifest to manifest. This view, expounded millenniums ago by our sages, is what modem science has been approaching in very recent decades. As per this view, the corollary arises that the whole course of evolution of the Creation must be, as though, fully charted. What happens for a person is that his consciousness is, as if, traversing over this charted expanse. Just as a traveller going by a railway train sees the places passing away and new places approaching, the person notes the disappearance of old dharmas (of things) and arising of new dharmas (in that thing transformed). This leads to the feeling of the passage of time, with a sense about the past, present and future and thus time is not real but only a consequence of the two-fold progression of the dharmas.

After describing the method by which the yogī exhausts all his past karmasaṃskāras, simultaneously precluding any further accumulation of saṃskāras, Patañjali has to explain the true nature of time, because a clear comprehension of this illusoriness of time removes the bondage of time, which is a great constraint on the freedom of the citta and the most difficult hurdle in the path to kaivalya. The total abolition of this constraint of time is accomplished by the saṃyama on kṣaṇas (= time quanta) and their sequentiality (cf. sūtras III : 52 ff.). This, as said there, leads to vivekaja-jñāna, which helps the yogī to realize the reality behind things and phenomena and through this to attain kaivalya. This also becomes clear from the sūtras which are to follow.

Moreover it makes it possible to understand how the yogī can operate the vibhūti of atīta-anāgata-jñāna and in general how the prophesies could become feasible. The yogī and prophets only take their consciousness in the so called future time, which, as per this theory, is existing at the current moment, but is in an unmanifest state for others.

SS. - **ते व्यक्तसूक्ष्मा गुणात्मानः ।।४:१३।।**

TL. - te vyakta-sūkṣmā guṇātmānaḥ - IV: 13

WM. -

te	=	they;
vyakta	=	manifest;
sūkṣma (→āḥ →ā)	=	subtle, unmanifested (plu.);
guṇa-ātmāna.(→ḥ)	=	of the nature of guṇas.

TR. - They are manifest and unmanifested (and) of the nature of guṇas.

CE. - They (= te) refers to the dharmas of the preceding sūtra. These are guṇātmāna i.e. guṇaika or prākṛtika in their nature and can be vyakta i.e. manifested at the present moment or sūkṣma i.e. subtle, latent that have been manifested and gone in the past and as yet (i.e. in future) are to be manifested. Since the twofold aspect of time, viz past and future, is merely a feeling caused by this dual directionality of the progression of dharmas, the description, particularly the first part 'vyaktasūkṣma' can become applicable to past and coming up dharmas i.e. in other word to the past, present and future times also.

SS. - **परिणामैकत्वाद्वस्तुतत्त्वम् ।।४:१४।।**

TL. - pariṇāmaikatvād-vastu-tattvam - IV: 14

WM. -

pariṇāma	=	transformation;
ekatva (āt →ād)	=	(eka - one + tva = ness); uniqueness (from, on account of);

vastu = object, thing;

tattva (m) = (tat--that + tva -- ness) essence, individuality-principle (is, exists, is established).

TR. - On account of uniqueness of the transformation (the existence of) the essence of a thing (is established).

CE. - Prakṛti being pariṇāmī(everchanging), every object or thing (vastu) is also constantly undergoing changes. In things or objects of the same kind (i.e. of one class or species) there is a close similarity or identicalness of dharmas (fundamental characteristics determining the nature and species of a thing), yet all the individuals of one species or class differ one from the other in some subtle manner. Due to this subtle difference the thing is recognised as one individual different from another of the same class or species. These pariṇāmas i.e. transformations which may be pertaining to its dharmas, lakṣaṇas (external or secondary characteristics) or avasthās (states) or all these three (cf. sūtra II: 13), though broadly similar in all members of that class, are unique for each individual member of that class. This is the meaning of 'pariṇāma-ekatva'.

The word 'tattva', as shown in WM. literally means 'That-ness', which, therefore, indicates that quality or speciality, which makes a thing 'that particular thing' distinct from others. The usual English words used to translate it are : -- principle essential element, property or nature, reality etc. Thus, on account of the uniqueness of the transformations is produced or established the essential nature of reality or true and essential principle behind that thing. This reality or essence is not the Ultimate

Reality behind the thing, but what may be designated as the individuality principle or often called the personality in the case of a living being or a human. Thus the sūtra affirms that in spite of all kinds of changes, which a thing may undergo, there is a subtle principle or element present in it, which gives it its uniqueness or specific individuality. This vastutattva is very closely related to that principle, which is indicated by the term 'dharmī' in sūtra III:14. No doubt, dharmī is subtler and has a greater personification, while vastutattva is grosser, more concerned with material aspect of the thing and has less of personification.

SS. - **वस्तुसाम्ये चित्तभेदात्तयोर्विभक्तः पन्थाः ।।४:१५।।**

TL. - vastu-sāmye-citta-bhedāt-tayorvibhaktaḥ panthāḥ - IV:15

WM. -

vastu	=	thing, substance;
sāmya (→e)	=	sameness, oneness (in);
citta-bheda (→āt)	=	differentness of cittas (due to, on account of, from);
tayoḥ (→r)	=	of the two;
vibhakta (ḥ)	=	separate;
pantha (→āḥ)	=	path (s), directionality (→ties).

TR. - In the sameness of a thing (i.e. even in a condition when a thing is one and the same), due to the differentness (i.e. different natures) of (individual) cittas (there exist) separate directionalities of the two (i.e. the thing and the citta).

CE. - Although the time in which the Pātañjala Yoga Sūtras were compiled is not precisely known, the consensus of the scholarly opinions about it seems to be about two to three centuries after Buddha. By this time the various schools of Buddhistic philosophies had become well established and very probably highly popular. These four sūtras (IV: 14 to 17) seem to be a refutation of the momentariness of the creation and the view that the things are only a production of mind and as such have no real existence of their own, which has been propounded by idealistic schools particularly Vijñānavādins. The main argument put forth in support of this view is that the one and same object or thing appears (i.e. is experienced) differently to different persons. They argue that if the thing had a real existence, it should have appeared the same to one and all. Since that is not the case, they claim the things have no real existence but are just creations of mind. Patañjali explains that the thing or object perceived by the citta is itself undergoing transformations in its own independent way. But different cittas on account of their individual different natures (i.e. specific proportions of sattva, rajas and tamas in them) perceive and so experience these transformations, each one in its own separate manner, because that perception by a citta is admixed with and so coloured by its own individual transformations.

So, according to Patañjali having the different perceptions by different cittas of one and the same thing does not go against the thing having a real existence. A very significant and revealing example of how different persons i.e. cittas have widely different perceptions of one and the same thing can be a snake. Even when it be completely non-poisonous and so harmless, it is generally looked upon as a terrible and dangerous thing by most of the people, but for a snake -charmer or a person who recognises their species, it can be quite a pleasant thing; some of these may even carry it on his or her own body as a play-thing or even as an adornment or show-piece. On the other hand a child, who is quite innocent and may treat it as a pitiable animal can and does handle it as such, as long as the child has not been warned about it and thus tutored by the ideas and fears of the grown ups. There have been a number of incidents when infants and small children have played with snakes, even poisonous ones, without being bitten by the snake, which very often is even handled roughly by the infant. The saṃskāras on the cittas of these different human beings are vastly different in nature. The same one object snake is quite a different thing to each one of them according to each one's past saṃskāras and the proportion of trigunas in their personalities.

SS. - **न चैकचित्ततन्त्रं वस्तु तदप्रमाणकं तदा किं स्यात् ।।४:१६।।**

TL. - na caika-citta-tantraṃ vastu tad-apramāṇakaṃ tadā kiṃ syāt- IV: 16

WM -

na	=	not;
caikacittatantra (ṃ)	=	(ca = and+eka = one+ citta + tantra = control) and, under the control of (i.e. governed by) one citta (is);
vastu	=	thing, object;
tat (d)	=	that;

apramāṇaka (ṃ)	=	(a = not+pramāṇaka = proved thing, fact, reality) unproved, unreal, non- existent;
tadā	=	then;
kiṃ	=	what, often a particle indicative of a question, just like a sign of interrogation;
syāt	=	be, become (showing probability).

TR. - And the thing (or object) is not governed by (any-) one citta. Does it, therefore, become unreal (non-existent) when that (one particular citta) is not perceiving that thing or object?

CE. - This sūtra is a continuation of the preceding one (IV: 15) and is an amplication and corroboration of the argument refuting Vijñānavāda of Buddhism. An object does not undergo transformations as per the desire of any person i.e. it is not under the control of any one citta. To bring out pointedly the absurdity of such an erroneous view that things are mere creations of citta, Patañjali puts forth a very pertinent question: - "What becomes of a thing at that time, when a particular citta is not measuring i.e. not perceiving it ? Would it become nonexistent? The answer is obviously, "No".The common and universal experience is that when one person i.e. his citta is not perceiving or not paying attention to a thing, others are perceiving it. As though there will be some differences in the perceptions of the same thing by different cittas, there would be seen an overall similarity or commonness among all of them, which will be existing because the thing has this in its own nature. This, therefore, is a further proof of the existence of a vastu-tattva i.e. an essential principle or reality-element in that thing.

Every citta is vaguely aware of the thing as being still existent, even when it is not paying any attention to that particular thing, which again refutes the Vijñānavāda. If the things were mere creations of the citta, at least those, which were troublegiving and so the citta would have them done away with, they would have disappeared immediately the citta wished thus about them. But it does not happen so. On the contrary, due to the troubles produced by them the citta is still more aware about them. All this goes totally against the presumptions of Vijñānavādins.

SS. - **तदुपरागापेक्षित्वाच्चित्तस्य वस्तु ज्ञाताज्ञातम् ।।४:१७।।**

TL. - tad-uparāgāpekṣitvāc-cittasya vastu jñātājñātam

WM. -

tat (→d)	=	(of, by) it;
uparāga	=	taking up colours (of), being coloured (by);
apekṣitva (→āt→āc)	=	(apeksā = (i) expectation, want, need; (ii) relation, reference + tva = ness + āt→āc = From due to) (i) due to the necessity of, as a result of ; (ii) in proportion to, relatively to;
citta (sya)	=	the citta (of);

vastu	=	thing, object;
jñāta	=	known;
ajñāta (m)	=	(a = not + jñāta) not known (is).

TR. - (I) (For the knowing i.e. cognition of a thing) it is necessary that there is a colouring (i.e. taking up or grasping of its qualities) of the citta by it (the thing), as a result of which that thing becomes known, otherwise (it remains) unknown.

or

(II) The thing becomes (relatively) known or unknown in proportion to the degree of coloration of the citta by it.

CE. - The Western and modern concept about the mechanism of perception is that some type of energy or vibration coming from a thing affects the pertinent sense organ, when it reaches the latter, e.g. the sound waves coming to the ear, light waves coming to the eye, vaporous molecules reaching the olfactory bulb inside the nasal cavity and affecting it by chemical energy etc. The stimulation caused is carried by the nerves from this outer organ-station e.g. the eye, to the pertinent centre in the brain e.g. visual centre in the back part of the brain. This then goes further and affects the mind* in a way, which is not yet known. This results in the perception of that object by the senses and the mind.

---

* Modern science is rather uncertain about and reluctant to accept the existence of such an entity fully independent of body. But it has nevertheless to use this term and a total rejection of some such notion is also not possible for modern science.

Ancient Indian thinkers believed that it is the citta (the apparatus or agency of consciousness, which , as already explained in sūtra I:2, is much extensive than mind in its sphere of activity) which goes out through the doors of senses, grasps the object and takes up (so to say, absorbs) the qualities of the object to a greater or lesser degree. The perception and knowledge about the object will be better, more is the absorption of the qualities of the object (i.e. colour-absorption or colouring as said in the sutra) by the citta. This colour absorption i.e. quality-uptake of the citta is called its upa-rāga (= upa= secondary + rāga = colouring) by the object.

The word 'apekṣā' has two meanings : - (1) expectation, needed thing etc., (2) in comparison or relation or reference to. Two translations of the sutra, (I) and (II) as above, can be made as per these two meanings of apekṣitva. Though there is a little difference in the two translations, from the practical utility point of view the general purport of the sūtra remains the same in both. In (I) the uparāga (= colouration) of the citta by the object (= vastu) is said to be necessary for having the knowledge of the object, which otherwise would remain unknown. In (II) this necessity of the uparāga of citta by the vastu is no doubt implied, but it is further clarified that the vastu would become known (or remain unknown) in proportion to the degree of colouration (= uparāga-apekṣitva) of the citta by the qualities of the object.

Nevertheless, out of the two translations the IInd translation is preferable, because if Patañjali wanted to tell that the object became known only when colourisation of citta by it happened, then the term 'apekṣi' and the term 'ajñātam' in the compound 'jñātajñātam' become superfluous. The wording 'taduparāgatvāt-cittasya vastujñātam', (=If there be colourisation of citta by the vastu i.e. thing, then it becomes known would be enough). It is obvious that if there be no colouring of the citta by the thing, it will remain unknown and so there remains no need of mentioning the term 'ajñātam' additionally. Yet Patañjali has added it. This, therefore, must be only to point out that the thing would remain unknown in relation to its qualities which would cause no colourisation of citta. Moreover, this IInd translation gives another clarification of the difficulty raised by the question in the sūtra IV: 15, viz. - "Why are the same things seen differently by different persons?" The colouring (uparāga) by the thing of different cittas occurs in different proportions, depending on the nature (guṇa-proportions) of each citta. So the knowledge of the thing in different cittas is variable and therefore each citta will perceive the same thing differently.

SS. - सदा ज्ञाताश्चित्तवृत्तयस्तत्प्रभोः पुरुषस्यापरिणामित्वात् ।।४:१८।।

TL. - sadā jñātāś-citta-vṛttayas-tat-prabhoḥ puruṣasyā-pariṇāmitvāt - IV: 18

WM. -

sadā	=	ever, always;
jñāta (→āḥ→āś)	=	known, cognised (are);
cittavṛtti (ayaḥ→ayas)	=	vṛtti of citta (plural);
tat	=	their;
prabhu (→oḥ)	=	master, superior, controller (possessive case);

puruṣa (sya)	= puruṣa (of, possessive case);
apariṇāmitva (→āt)	= (a = not + pariṇāmī = changeable + tva = ness) unchangeability, immutability (on account of).

TR. - On account of immutability of puruṣa, the citta-vṛttis (the functional modifications of citta) become known (cognised) to (this puruṣa, which is) their master.

CE. - For measuring or evaluating anything correctly the scale i.e. the measuring instrument or standard should remain constant. If this standard or reference-gauge itself goes on changing, correct measurement and evaluation would become impossible. This is true also for the evaluation of changes or activities taking place in a thing.

For man the means of cognition is his citta or mind. But these are constantly undergoing modifications i.e. vṛttis. The citta, due to its potentiality to know, can know even these modifications taking place in itself. But as said in the preceding IV: 17 sūtra, it gets the knowledge in the proportion it takes up the colouring of the thing, it is cognising. Thus the knowledge got by citta is always relative and so imperfect. As is a very well known fact, this is still more true in the case of the knowledge about one's own self and one's activity. This knowledge is always distorted by various factors intrinsic to the knower i.e. here the citta, e.g. certain stubborn preconceptions, likes and dislikes etc. Therefore the cognition and evaluation of its own vṛttis by the citta is quite imperfect. Specially with regard to controlling and ultimately having the total cessation (= nirodha) of the citta-vṛttis, the citta itself cannot do it to perfection, on account of this imperfect cognition of these by the citta. For this, therefore, recourse will have to be taken to something which is immutable. On account of the immutability (= apariṇā-mitva) of puruṣa, which has a (latent or unmanifest) potentiality to produce consciousness, this serves as the stable standard or gauge for reference, with the help of which the vṛttis of the citta can be adjudged in their totality. So this fact is explained in the sūtra, where the puruṣa is referred to as the master of citta and its vṛttis, an impartial supervisor or witnesser of the activities i.e. functional modifications of citta. The puruṣa can, therefore, observe these cittavṛttis without being involved in them and so can know about them in their totality.

SS. - **न तत्स्वाभासं दृश्यत्वात् ।।४:१९।।**

TL. - na tat-svābhāsaṃ dṛśyatvāt - IV: 19

WM. -

na	=	not;
tat	=	that;
svābhāsa (ṃ)	=	(sva = one's own + ābhāsa = illumination) self-illuminating self-enlightening (is);
dṛśyatva (→āt)	=	(dṛśya = a thing perceived + tva = ness) perceptibility, its nature being such that it could be perceived (on account of).

TR. - On account of its nature being that of a dṛśya (i.e. something that could be perceptible), it (i.e. the citta) is not self-enlightening.

CE. - Just as the physical light makes it possible to see things, consciousness is the inner illumination, which potentiality of citta makes it able to perceive and cognise things. But this potentiality is not intrinsically citta's own. The citta seems to have consciousness, but that is a reflection of the potentiality of the puruṣa, just as the moonlight is the reflected light of the sun, but which also makes the things visible.

The reason given in support of the statement is that the citta is itself a thing perceived, as explained in the preceding IV: 18 sūtra. When a thing is perceived, the perceiver must be other than this thing. In the case of the citta, when it is perceiving the things in the external world, it is doing this due to the potentiality of perception and cognition gained from and so a reflection of the similar (but latent) potentiality of the puruṣa, just like the light of the sun falling on the surface of the moon and reflected from there to the objects making them visible. But the moon itself is seen as a luminous object, not by its own light, but again by the sun's light reflected from its surface. Parallel is the case of the citta and its relation to the puruṣa, the source of its consciousness.

The terms illumination, perceiving etc. here are not concerned with the visible physical light. They are all used here in connection with consciousness and its functioning and effects. In the case of the physical light, the self-luminous things e.g. the sun, the lamp etc. are themselves also dṛśya (=perceptible).

But anything which is jñeya (= knowable) is itself never self-knower i.e. one having the capacity of knowing one's 'self '(i.e. the essential principle). Therefore the citta, which is itself dṛśya (perceptible, knowable) is not self-enlightening or self-knower. Most commentators have spoken of puruṣa as 'consciousness', 'conscious principle' and so on. But purusa is said to be 'citi' or 'citi-śakti' (sūtras IV:22, 34), which means it has the potentiality of consciousness. That means it is not (actively) conscious or active-consciousness, but it can give rise to consciousness in something else viz. the citta. Puruṣa's potentiality of consciousness is thus 'latent'. Through it, in fact through its mere presence and vicinage, the citta (cit = to ignite, to incite, to enlighten + ta = suffix to make a past participle) is incited and able to get enlightened i.e. to know. This is the full import of thc sūtra.

SS. - एकसमये चोभयानवधारणम् ।।४:२०।।

TL. - eka-samaye cobhayānavadhāraṇam, IV:20

WM. - eka = one;
samaya(→e) = time (at);
cobhayānavadhāraṇa (m) =(ca = and + ubhaya = both + an = not + avadharana = knowing, cognising) and, impossibility of cognising both (nominative neutral singular case - ending).

TR. - And (because of) the impossibility of cognising both (citta itself as perceiver and also a thing perceived) at one and the same time.

CE. - The conjunction 'and' shows that this sūtra is an extension of the preceding (IV: 19) one. This is another argument to support the statement that the citta is not self-knower i.e. not able to know its 'self-principle'. By its nature itself the citta is always cognising things. But even in this the citta is able to have knowledge of only one thing at a time. When it is felt that the citta is cognising a number of things at the same time, then if minute observation is made of such activity of citta, it becomes clear that really that is not the case. The citta cognises different things one after another with such rapidity, that an impression is created that it is cognising all those things simultaneously. If cittta could have the ability to tackle simultaneously a number of subjects, there would have been no necessity of developing one-pointedness (= ekāgratā) in it and special effort would not have become necessary for achieving it. But by its basic nature citta (and also its part mind) is very fickle and vagrant. It is ever running from one thing to other and how ekāgratā is to be established taking advantage of this very vagrancy itself of the citta is already explained under the sūtra III:12 describing ekāgratā-pariṇāma (=Transformation-of citta-into one-pointedness). That efforts have to be specially made for attaining ekāgratā of the citta, is, therefore, a strong point supporting the view that the citta cannot cognise simultaneously more than one subject. The purpose of the affirmation of this everyday experience about the citta in the present sutra is to support, as said, the statement of sūtra IV: 19.

The citta is constantly experiencing the external world. We feel that the citta has at the same time the awareness that it itself is undergoing that experience. But as explained above, it is not possible for the citta to have these two awarenesses simultaneously. Why is such an impression then created ? The answer is that this awareness is a reflection of the (latent) awareness of the puruṣa. But due to the 'saṃyoga' (sūtra II:17) there is a false sense of superimposition or identity of the citta with the puruṣa, which produces this feeling that the citta cognises itself at the same time when it is cognising the external world. The sūtra thus brings to the notice the truth that the draṣṭā-principle, which perceives and cognises the citta and its activities (vrttis), is not the citta itself, but it is puruṣa-principle.

SS. - **चित्तान्तरदृश्ये बुद्धिबुद्धेरतिप्रसङ्गः स्मृतिसंकरश्च ।।४:२१।।**

TL. - cittāntara-dṛśye buddhi-buddheratiprasaṅgaḥ smṛti-saṃkaraś-ca - IV:21

WM. -

cittāntara	=	(citta + antara = difference) different cittas;
dṛśya (→e)	=	being perceived (in);
buddhi	=	intelligence, cognition;
buddhi (→eḥ→er)	=	cognition (of);
atiprasaṅga (ḥ)	=	excessive stretching of a circumstance or principle, superfluity of data or arguments, reduction-ad-absurdum (is);
smṛti	=	memory;

saṃkara (ḥ->ś)	=	a mixture causing confusion (is);
ca	=	and.

TR. - And in (presuming the phenomenon of) the perception of one citta by another different citta, it would become a case of reduction-ad-absurdum viz. cognition of (another) cognition of (still another) cognition ....ad infinitum, (which moreover would lead to) mixing of memories, causing confusion.

CE. - The 'and' shows that this is another argument to strengthen the preceding three sūtras IV: 18 to 20. If it be assumed that the activity of one citta is perceived by the cognition-power (= buddhi) of another citta, then continuing this argument it will have to be assumed that the activity of this second citta will have to be perceived by the cognitive power (=buddhi) of a third citta and of the third citta by the buddhi-portion of a fourth citta and so on. The chain of the cittas and their buddhis will have to be extended infinitely and there could be no end to the argument. Any discussion will then become impossible and an absurd situation will result. So such an assumption would be a barrier to any fruitful discussion, which alone can lead to any purposeful and practically useful conclusion and so such assumption is to be discarded totally.

Moreover our practical experience also stands against such assumption. If an infinite series of cittas, one perceiving another, is assumed, there would be as many karmāśayas (= storehouses of saṃskāras and of memories arising out of these)as there are cittas. Because these cittas are not the nirmāṇacittas mentioned in sūtra IV:4. These would be natural cittas and so will have their respective karmāśayas one each separately for each citta. With this, the first difficulty would be that if here be so many cittas per person, in which of these innumerable karmāśayas the saṃskāra of a karma of that person would be stored would become quite indeterminate. Secondly, as said in the sūtra, if even one saṃskāra from each of these karmāśayas be aroused to become a memory, there would be innumerable memories jostling one another in the consciousness of that person at one single moment and they would create a chaos, as they may be very often conflicting with each other. But such a thing never happens- at least in a normal healthy person. Therefore such a chain of cittas cannot be accepted.

There is no clear mention of it here in the sūtra, yet another argument is suggested which also goes against the assumption of a chain of cittas perceiving one another. The citta exists and functions in and with the body. So these innumerable cittas should have their innumerable bodies. But that is not the case. If it be presumed that all these cittas are in one body, then, since these are not nirmana-cittas, but are natural cittas, each one of them will try to control and manipulate that body independently and irrespective of the others. Then there should and would arise conflicts, at least on some occasions, among them. But such a thing has never occurred. Taking all these arguments into consideration it is to be concluded that the citta is perceived and cognised by another and ultimate entity. This observer of citta is the puruṣa as per Sāṃkhya-Yoga.

SS. - चितेरप्रतिसंक्रमायास्तदाकारापत्तौ स्वबुद्धिसंवेदनम् ।।४:२२।।

TL. - citer-apratisaṃkramāyās-tad-ākārā-pattau svabuddhi-saṃvedanam - IV: 22.

WM. -

citi(→eḥ→er)	=	citi (ś), the (latent) potentiality of consciousness (suffix for possessive case, singular), puruṣa-tattva (ś);
apratisaṃkrama (→āyāḥ→āyās)	=	(a = not + prati = towards + saṃkrama = crossing or going over towards (the subject to be comprehended) (by reason of);
tadākārāpattau	=	(tad = its+ākāra=shape, form+ā = in+patti (=au) = falling or merging (into), in the condition of merging into i.e. taking up the form of it (i.e. of citi or puruṣa);
sva	=	one's own;
buddhi	=	cognition;
saṃvedana (m)	=	knowing, knowledge (is).

TR. - By reason of the citi's nature of not crossing over towards (the subject to be comprehended), (the citta) gets its own knowledge through the power of cognition (which is enhanced) in the state of merger into it (the citi).

CE. - The term 'puruṣa' has been explained by most of the English commentators as consciousness or consciousness-principle. Some have even translated the word puruṣa by these English words. But as explained (cf. sūtras I:3 ff) puruṣa is neither conscious nor consciousness- principle. Since it is apariṇāmī (= immutable), akartā (= actionless) etc., it itself cannot directly perceive or know, as that perceiving and knowing itself involves a change and an action. It therefore is merely the cause of consciousness. The faculty of consciousness is manifested only by the citta. Puruṣa is the 'background principle' of the consciousness and has a latent or unmanifest potentiality for producing consciousness. The term citi (and citi-śakti in sūtra IV:34) is used to indicate this aspect of puruṣa, distinguishing it from citta, the active consciousness-principle.

As per the ancient Indian viewpoint the citta goes over to the subject to have uparāga (colouring, cf. sūtra IV: 17) from it, through which it knows the subject. The question then comes forth : - When the puruṣa knows the vṛttis (functioning) of the citta, does it also similarly go over and has uparāga from the citta? No, it cannot and does not do so. Because this would be against its nature of apariṇāmītva (= changelessness) and akartṛtva (= actionlessness). Then how does the knowledge of cittavṛttis become possible? The answer to this is given in this sūtra.

As per the wording of the sūtra the citta 'falls into (or merges into) the form of puruṣa' i.e. it takes up the same form (since puruṣa has really no form, this means here, puruṣa's nature) and thus becomes an exact copy or reflection of puruṣa. In this condition its buddhi aspect (the part of citta having the power of cognition) becomes so acute and limitlessly powerful that it becomes, as if, the citiśakti of puruṣa, which has become manifest and active. The knowledge about the citta itself and its vṛttis, which the buddhi (which is itself the cognitive function of citta i.e. itself part and parcel of citta) gets, is virtually the knowledge, as if, gained by that citi or puruṣa. This is what has been otherwise expressed in such terms as : - 'The puruṣa perceives through the agency of the citta-buddhi' or' The puruṣa gets the pratyaya i.e. experience through the medium of 'citta' (sūtra II:20). The draṣṭātva (literally seer-hood, i.e. witnessing) on the part of the puruṣa in respect of the citta is of this kind. When the final Realization of puruṣa (vivekakhyāti, sūtra II:26 and 28, puruṣakhyāti, sūtras I:16; III:35) is accomplished in the nirbīja and dharmamegha samādhis, at that time also there occurs perfect purification of citta, so that it is almost as pure as puruṣa (cf. śuddhisāmya, sūtra III:55) and it becomes as though a replica of the puruṣa. This is what is meant by the term 'puruṣa-jñāna' or 'puruṣa-khyāti'. This is not mere knowledge i.e. knowing about an extrinsic subject. Rather it is a Realization i.e.'the becoming oneself that subject'. The start toward this 'Realization' of the reality of puruṣa begins with such svabuddhisaṃvedana (knowing of itself i.e. of the citta through its own cognitive power) which takes place when citta becomes a replica of the puruṣa. [N. B. - This, in a way, is a very round-about way of saying that citta (or mind) is perceived by the same citta (or mind). But there is a subtle distinction in the two types of expression and in the two clarifications of the phenomenon. This had become necessary for Patañjali to clarify as per the fundamental view point of the Sāṃkhya and the Yoga about the natures of the puruṣa and the citta].

SS. - द्रष्टृदृश्योपरक्तं चित्तं सर्वार्थम् ।।४:२३।।

TL. - draṣṭṛ-dṛśyoparaktaṃ cittaṃ sarvārtham - IV:23

WM. - draṣṭṛ = draṣṭā, seer, perceiver;
dṛśya = dṛśya, seen, perceived, manifested world;
uparakta (ṃ) = coloured (by the perceived subject);
citta (ṃ) = citta (suffix for nominative neutsing);
sarvārtha (m) = (sarva = all + artha = purpose) all purposeful, all-comprehending (is).

TR. - The citta, becoming coloured by the draṣṭā (= the seer, the puruṣa) and also dṛśya (= the seen, the world) is all-comprehending.

CE. - The citta, as per sūtras IV: 19 and 20, being itself dṛśya cannot, on its own power, perceive even its own activity. Perception of thc background principle of perception itself, namely puruṣa, is still more beyond the capacity of the citta. How then the knowledge, or better still, the realization of puruṣa will ever be possible?

As said in the preceding (IV:22) sūtra, the citta develops this ability, when it, so to say, becomes identical with or a replica of the puruṣa. No doubt, due to its basic nature of apariṇāmitva (= immutability) the puruṣa ever remains totally unaffected by and unconcerned with the citta- a product of the prakṛti. But when there is perfect purification of the citta to such a degree that it is a replica (śuddhisāmya, cf. sūtra III:55) of the puruṣa, then there remains no barrier to its power of cognition, comprehension and realization (sūtra IV:22). It then becomes absolutely all-comprehending and can grasp and comprehend not only the external world, but also its own nature and activities (vṛttis), as though it is an extension of the puruṣa and can even realize the puruṣa itself, since it has itself become a replica of the puruṣa.

SS. - **तदसंख्येयवासनाभिश्चित्रमपि परार्थं संहत्यकारित्वात् ।।४:२४।।**

TL. - tad-asaṃkhyeya-vāsanābhiś-citram-api parārthaṃ saṃhatya-kāritvāt - IV:24

WM. -

tat (→d)	=	that;
asaṃkhya (eya)	=	(a=not + saṃkhya=countable) innumerable (3rd, instrumental case suffix, sing);
vāsanā (bhiḥ→bhiś)	=	subliminal desires (3rd, instrumental case suffix, plural = by, due to);
citra (ṃ)	=	variegated (is);
api (→ya)	=	even then;
parārtha (ṃ)	=	(para = the other+artha = for the sake of) For the sake of the other;
saṃhati (→ya)	=	assemblage, collection together;
kāritva (→āt)	=	production, creation (from, on account of, because).

TR. - That (citta) is variegated due to innumerable vāsanās (= subliminal desires); even then (it can be understood that) it is for the sake of the other (i.e. puruṣa), because it is a creation of an assemblage (viz. of vāsanās, saṃskāras etc.)

CE. - Just as the archeologists infer about the existence of an ancient civilization, when they find some remains of constructions showing a well designed plan, so also whenever there is seen any assemblage of things, put in a certain orderly arrangement, which at once gives an indication of a purpose behind this, it has to be assumed that there must be some entity, which ought to have created this orderly arrangement of things to serve some objective of that entity. This is the type of argument which is very often put forward as an evidence of the existence of a Creator God by the believers.

The citta is also such a purposeful and productive assemblage. Every karma that is undergone by the individual is recorded as a saṃskāra and this record or impression is preserved in the citta in its karmāśaya section. These saṃskāras comeup into the current consciousness as smṛtis (= memories). In this process the memories are associated with the pertinent subliminal desires i.e. vāsanās. The number of these vāsanās is countless. Yet in the variegation and infinitude of vāsanās, there is evidenced an orderliness in their arousal and this leading to a purpose, which on the biological plane is often broadly referred to as preservation of life and in spiritual sphere as 'Liberation or Salvation.' (N.B. This latter is the view, which is more explicitly put forth in the school of theosophy than in others). This 'saṃhatyakāritva' (an assemblage with a design) is a clear indication, that it (citta, with its multifarious saṃskāra-vāsanās and its well organised sections e.g.. manas, buddhi etc.) has been put together to serve the purpose of something else, viz. its lord or supervisor, the puruṣa (sūtra IV: 18).

SS. - **विशेषदर्शिन आत्मभावभावनाविनिवृत्तिः ।।४:२५।।**

TL. - viśeṣa-darśina ātma-bhāva-bhāvanā-vinivṛttiḥ - IV:25

WM. - viśeṣa-darśin

(→aḥ→a)	=	(viśeṣa = special + darśin = one who is seeing) one who is seeing in a special way (i.e. realizing the distinction of puruṣa from citta) (6th, possessive suffix = of);
ātma-bhāva	=	(ātma = belonging to oneself + bhāva sense, here = ness) one's ownness, sense of being the(one) self;
bhāvanā	=	feeling;
vinitvṛtti (ḥ)	=	(vi = viśeṣa, i.e.. particular, here total + nivṛtti = cessa -tion, end) total cessation (is).

TR. - There is total cessation of the feeling of the ownness (i.e. of self-ness, about various entities e.g. body, citta etc.) in that person, who is seeing in a special way (i.e. has realized the distinction of the puruṣa from all other things).

CE. - Man wrongly identifies many things with the real principle or essence of self, which as per Sāṃkhya and Yoga is the puruṣatattva in man. This misidentification of self, in the garb of 1 and mine, can be with the nation, society, country, region, town, family, wife, son and so on. As per sūtra II:5 this misidentification is the ultimate aspect of avidyā. But the distinction of most of these things from the self or I, is very easily recognised. In fact usually one is aware that none of these is really the self. But the common man usually identifies the body with the self. Yet even he can be easily made to see that the body is not the 'self', particularly when he uses an expression such as 'my body'. No doubt, this understanding on merely intellectual level is not enough to eradicate the sense of self regarding the body, totally and for ever. It takes a long time and great efforts (in higher yogāṅgas) to achieve this finally.

Still more difficult is to remove such feeling about an inner entity like the mind or its wider aspect the citta being the self. Since we use the expression 'my mind (or citta)', it is not so very difficult to make an intelligent person to understand that the mind and citta also are not the essential 'self' element. But again such an intellectual understanding does not totally abolish the avidyā of superimposing the activities and the identity of citta on the puruṣa -principle-the real-self. Even in an advanced yogī this ātmabhāva-bhāvanā about the citta is not permanently obliterated. It is only in the highest state of samādhi-the dharmamegha samādhi (sūtra IV:29) that this realization of the puruṣa as distinct from even the citta is finally totally and permanently established. The yogī then becomes a 'viśeṣa-darśin' i.e. he is able to see what no one else, who has not attained this stage, has ever seen, namely the real and utter distinction between citta and puruṣa. He is now on the threshold of kaivalya and then only there is vinivṛtti or total disappearance of ātmabhāvabhāvanā, the last bastion of avidyā.

Nevertheless this ātmabhāvabhāvanāvinivṛtti is only intermittently present, when the citta transcends asmitā and enters nirbīja samādhi, but there it is not firmly established for ever. However the yogī who has attained nirbīja samādhi also gets a foretaste of kaivalya, as and when he has disappearance, for a time-being of the ātmabhāvabhāvanā, at intervals in this samādhi. This is clarified in the next two sūtras.

SS. - तदा विवेकनिम्नं कैवल्यप्राग्भारं चित्तम् ।।४:२६।।

TL. - tadā viveka-nimnaṃ kaivalya-prāgbhāraṃ cittam - IV:26

WM. -

tadā	=	then;
viveka	=	the discrimination, here between the puruṣa and the citta (cf. sūtra III:52);
nimna (ṃ)	=	bent down;
kaivalya	=	kaivalya-the goal of Pātañjala Yoga and Sāṃkhya, absolute-ness;
prāgbhāra (ṃ)	=	(prāk (→g) = fore, pre, anticipatory + bhāra = burden, weight) fore-burdened, pre-loaded;
citta (m)	=	the citta (is).

TR. - Then (i.e. at the time ātmabhāvabhāvanāvinivṛtti is established) the citta is bent down by (the gravity of) viveka and fore-loaded with (the weightiness of) kaivalya.

CE. - As explained above in sūtra IV:25, the ātma-bhāvabhāvanā, i.e. the feeling of 'self' extrapolated to those things, which are 'belonging to self' i.e. are looked at as 'mine', disappears even in the nirbīja samādhi, since asmitā i.e. I-consciousness has been already transcended. But this disappearance of the ātmabhāvabhāvanā may last only during the intervals for which the state of nirbīja samādhi lasts and so it is intermittent (sūtra IV:27). However the effect of this temporary disappearance of ātmabhāvabhāvanā persists in the citta for a long time, even after the termination of the nirbīja samādhi.

With the disappearance of ātmabhāvanā, viveka i.e. the ultimate discrimination between the puruṣa and the citta arises. This is such an important or grave thing that the yogī's citta is awed by the gravity of this viveka and in metaphorical sense, bent down by this heaviness of viveka. Nimna = bent down can have also another sense here, though it can-not be affirmed that it is definitely meant in this sūtra. Since with the rising of viveka the last trace of asmitā = I-ness will be dissolved, there will be total absence of pride and egotism. The yogī, therefore, will be having the greatest humbleness of meekness, which, in a way, is the result of viveka.

In the expression 'prāgbhāra' also the same metaphorical sense of heaviness of weightiness is involved. The yogī gets a fore-taste or fore-glimpse of kaivalya even in the nirbīja samādhi, specially when this latter is firmly established by a long abhyāsa and is almost approaching its culminatory stage of the dharmamegha samādhi. This foretaste or preview of kaivalya is also quite awe-inspiring and the yogī realizes : 'what a weighty thing is kaivalya!'

SS. - तच्छिद्रेषु प्रत्ययान्तराणि संस्कारेभ्यः ।।४:२७।।

TL. - tac-chidreṣu pratyayāntarāṇi saṃskārebhyaḥ - IV :27

WM. - tacchidra (→eṣu) = (tat (→c) = That + chidra=Hole, gap + eṣu = Plural suffix for 7th, locative case = In) In the gaps in that (i.e. ātmabhāvabhāvanā-vinivṛtti);

pratyaya = experience or content in the citta;

antara (→āṇi) = different, other (plural nominative suffix);

saṃskāra (→ebhyaḥ) = saṃskāra i.e. residual effect of karma (Though, due to).

TR. - In the gaps in that (i.e. disappearance of the false feeling of self about extraneous things) (there arise) other pratyayas (contents in the citta) due to saṃskāras (karma-residues).

CE. - The ātmabhāvabhāvanā (i.e. the feeling about different non-self entities as being the self) does not disappear permanently all at once at the beginning of the nirbīja samādhi. This disappearance gradually goes on lasting for longer and longer durations, as the yoga-sādhaka repeats his practice of the nirbīja samādhi again and again. In sūtras I:50 and 51 it is stated that all the saṃskāras (other than that of the sabīja samādhi itself) are counteracted and made ineffective in the sabīja samādhi and even this sabīja-samādhi-saṃskāra is abolished in the nirbīja samādhi and sarva-nirodha (= cessation of all, viz. vṛttis and saṃskāras) is attained, which establishes the nirbīja samādhi. From this an impression is produced that all saṃskāras are totally done away with for ever at the start itself of the nirbīja samādhi. (Even our TR. and CE. on these sūtras have this tone of expression). But it becomes evident here that it is not so. Here it is explicitly stated that what is meant by the statement of sūtra I:51, viz. 'on account of nirodha of all saṃskāras there is achieved nirbīja samādhi', is that at the final accomplishment i.e. in the perfection of the nirbīja samādhi only there is the sarva-nirodha (= the cessation all viz. saṃskāras, vṛttis etc.)

While the sādhaka is continuing his practice of nirbīja samādhi from day to day, there are often breaks in it, particularly in the earlier days, even while the sādhaka is having his daily seance of practice. During these intervals of break the sense of self about non-self entities, particularly about the citta and some times even the body, often overpoweringly rises up in the sādhaka. Then again the sādhaka cannot and does not for all the twenty four hours remain in the samādhi. Even in these days his citta reverts to the ordinary awareness, when he has to meet the demands of the body for its life-maintenance and do other duties in his worldly life. At these times also the feeling of self, perhaps very feeble and vague, about the citta and body still lingers in him. These interruptions in the absence of the false feeling of self about nonselves (ātma-bhāvabhāvanāvinivṛtti) occur because (1) the saṃskāras curbed for the time being in the sabīja samādhi surge up again even in the early days of the practice of nirbīja samādhi and (2) there are created fresh saṃskāras when the sādhaka's citta returns to ordinary day to day awareness, as said above. The citta undergoes different experiences (= pratyayas) during such breaks.

In short the sūtra tells that the nirbīja samādhi is not permanently established all at once, as may perhaps be misunderstood from the sūtra I:5 1 . It has frequent interruptions in the beginning. From this it can also be inferred that it must be getting permanently and perfectly established by continuous practice and then only the ātmabhā-vabhāvanā also will be for ever abolished. Such a special development and the culmination of the nirbīja samādhi is designated as the dharmamegha samādhi.

SS. - **हानमेषां क्लेशवदुक्तम् ।।४:२८।।**

TL. - hānam-eṣāṃ kleśavad-uktam - IV:28

WM. -

hāna (m)	=	destruction, annihilation (is);
eṣām	=	of these;
kleśa	=	kleśas, the ultimate causes of pain and misery (cf. sūtras II:3 to 12);
vat (→d)	=	like, in the same manner as;
ukta (m)	=	said, described (is).

TR. - The annihilation (permanent removal) of these (is to be achieved) in the same manner as is described for kleśas.

CE. - The word 'eṣām' could mean saṃskāras, pratyayas or chidras (gaps) from the preceding IV:27 sūtra. As per usual rules of the sūtra interpretation it should be referring to the last word saṃskāra. But by context it can be better interpreted as referring to chidras or the prayayas appearing in those chidras. However whatever of these three meanings be given to 'eṣām', it does not distort the total statement in the sūtra, since all these three are so intimately linked to each other that the presence of anyone of them during the breaks in the nirbīja samādhi would mean essentially the presence of the others also.

The remedial measure prescribed for doing away with these breaks, during which the feelings of pseudo-self in respect of the citta etc. reappear, caused by the saṃskāras and giving rise to the pratyayas, is the same, as prescribed for the total removal of the kleśas. This measure, as per sūtra II:10 is the 'pratiprasava' i.e. counter-evolution or reversal of the process of evolution (as described in the Sāṃkhya-Yoga darśanas). As explained by us under sūtra II:10 and as is clear from sūtra IV:34, the fulfilment of this pratiprasava is kaivalya, which is accomplished only through following the practice of the whole system of the aṣṭāṅga yoga. In other words, thc total annihilation of saṃskāras is accomplished only in the state of kaivalya. So, what the sūtra purports is that the kaivalya is established through the total annihilation of saṃskāras, which can be achieved only through the practice of Yoga and specifically through the repetition of abhyāsa i.e. through the anuṣṭhāna of the nirbīja samādhi.

Incidentally, this sūtra also confirms that our interpretation of the term pratiprasava given in the sūtra II:10 is correct and that the view, put forth by some commentators is untenable, namely that the meaning of pratiprasava in that earlier sūtra is the pratiprasava of kleśas, by which they mean that each kleśa is to be dissolved in the one preceding it in their enumeration (sūtra II:3) or that the latter four kleśas are to be dissolved in the first one i.e. avidyā. The present sūtra says that method of doing away with saṃskāras or pratyayas is the same as that for the kleśa i.e. as described in sūtra II:10. Obviously this in the way as explained by these commentators cannot be applicable here, because there is no hierarchy or fixed sequence in the saṃskāras or pratyayas as it is in the case of the kleśas. Strangely these very commentators, who interpret pratiprasava in sūtra II:10 as that of kleśas, here interpret pratiprasava as that of guṇas i.e. prakṛti, just like us, without bothering about the fact that the present sūtra recommends the same procedure for annihilation as prescribed in sūtra II:10, which obviously is not applicable here, if understood in the way as explained by them.

SS. - **प्रसंख्यानेऽप्यकुसीदस्य सर्वथा विवेकख्यातेर्धर्ममेघः समाधिः ॥४:२९॥**

TL. - prasaṃkhyāne' py-akusīdasya sarvathā viveka-khyāter-dharmameghaḥ samādhiḥ - IV:29.

WM. -

prasaṃkhyāna (→e)	=	(pra = prakarṣeṇa = with intensity + saṃ = saṃpūrṇatayā = wholly + khyāna = act of knowing) the thorough and complete knowledge (in);
api (→y)	=	even;
akusīda (sya)	=	(a = not + kusīda = usurer) one not taking undue interest or benefit (of);
sarvathā	=	in every way;

viveka	=	discrimination (here between puruṣa and citta);
khyāti (→eḥ→er)	=	knowledge, (here better meaning would be) actual realization (of);
dharmamegha (ḥ)	=	name of a stage of samādhi, meaning the cloud of dharma (nominative case);
samādhi (ḥ)	=	samādhi (is).

TR. - (The samādhi state) of one (yogī), who is not taking any interest (or benefit) even in the prasāṃkhyāna (=the complete and thorough ultimate knowledge) (and is possessed) in every way of vivekakhyāti (Realization of the utmost distinction of the puruṣa from everything prākṛtika, including the citta) (is designated) the dharmamegha samādhi.

CE. - When the yogī has the viveka-khyāti (Realization of the extreme contra distinction between puruṣa and prakṛti) in every way i.e. in perfection, in every aspect and for all time, he would obviously have the highest knowledge or the ultimate realization, which is the aim of Yoga and the goal of the search of every yogī. He would already have the perfect mastery over saṃyama (sūtras III:4 and 5). He may and will not exploit this mastery over the saṃyama for gaining any vibhūti, specially if vairāgya of the highest order (the vaśīkāra vairāgya would, no doubt, be already possessed by him and in this stage he will be developing almost to the guṇavaitṛṣṇya vairāgya (cf. sūtras I:15 and 16) is imbibed in him. On account of this absolute disattachment being ever awake in him due to the perfectly established vivekakhyāti, he is not concerned or interested even in the vibhūtis of omnipotence and omniscience, mentioned in sūtra III:49, nor in any other vibhūti. At this stage he may not even be interested in salvation (= mokṣa) or liberation from duḥkha (= misery) nor from the cycle of births and deaths. Thus he has no expectation of any kind of benefit from this realization. As said in sūtra II:50, he enters into the Absolute-State of Kaivalya directly. This last stage of development of the samādhi is given a special name of dharmamegha samādhi.

After going into the nirbīja samādhi, even when the seed of asmitā (= I-am-ness) is destroyed and so there is no possibility that the yogī may again be tempted by the allurements of the world and may get entangled, yet his citta has to and does revert to the ordinary consciousness off and on, as explained under sūtra IV:27. But once the citta goes into dharmamegha samādhi there is no such reverting. Thereafter the only way and end is Kaivalya.

The meaning of the term dharma here is not clear. The name dharmamegha also, therefore, is not easily explainable. Dharma is usually rendered into English as religion or with the closely allied meanings as merit or virtue. But with both these meanings the samādhi-name does not give any sense, relevant to this high state of samādhi, which leads to the Ultimate goal of Yoga.

Patañjali has used the word 'dharma' in the sense of the fundamental properties or essential attributes (sūtras II:13 and 45 and IV: 12). Taimni (in 'Science of Yoga, p.433, Theosophical Publishing House, Adyar, S. India, 1961) has tried to explain the name, taking this sense of the word 'dharma'. But this also is not satisfactory, because to think the name of the samādhi, "In which", according to his wording, "the yogī shakes himself free from the world of dharmas", to be as the 'cloud (i.e. a mystifying and obscuring thing) of dharmas' seems self-contradicting in its sense.

If, however, 'dharma' is understood in a broad sense of religion i.e. almost a universal religion and not any sectarian religion with its dogmatism, fanatical beliefs and hide-bound official organisation etc., then every religion, from the most crude to most developed, has one essential and common aspect, that of getting an inner and highly mystic experience i.e. a spiritual realization. Then this highest samādhi, mentioned in Patañjali's yoga-system, just like a cloud loaded with water (=the megha) showering water, showers this essence or the jīvana (=water, as well as the vital thing) of dharma (quintessence of religion-in the above noted broad sense) on the yogī. Here it is called kaivalya, but it may be named differently in other systems.

SS. - **ततः क्लेशकर्मनिवृत्तिः ।।४:३०।।**

TL. - tataḥ kleśa-karma-nivṛttiḥ - IV:30

WM. - tataḥ = from that (i.e. dhramamegha samādhi);
kleśa = kleśas, the primordial causes of misery;
karma = karma, action with chain of saṃskāra (impress) and phala (fruit) accompanying it;
nivṛtti (ḥ) = termination, cessation (is).

TR. - From that there is termination of kleśas and karmas.

CE. - As per the wording in the sūtra, through the dharmamegha samādhi (or sarvathā viveka khyāti) kleśas and karmas are totally abolished. That is, the abolition is, as if, the fruit or result of the dharmamegha samādhi. But this statement can be reversed also. In fact the abolition of kleśas and karmas is the essence of the dharmamegha samādhi. Only according to our customary way of thinking and speaking we say that dharmamegha samādhi leads to kleśa karma nivṛtti and the statement in the sūtra is made in this fashion. But it can also be affirmed that the total abolition (= nivṛtti) of kleśas and karmas results into the dharmamegha samādhi.

When vivekakhyāti (= Realization of the distinction of puruṣa from prakṛti) is perfectly and permanently established in the dharmamegha samādhi, the most fundamental aspect of avidyā, viz. the misidentification of non-self (= anātma) with the self (= ātma) is done away with. The remaining four kleśas will automatically disappear, as they can exist only on the ground i.e. support of avidyā (sūtra : II:4). The past karma saṃskāras will, if need be, quickly exhausted by the yogī, by the method explained in IV:4 to II sūtras. In sūtra IV:29 it has been pointed out that the yogī, who will enter the dharmamegha samādhi will have the highest vairāgya (= disattachment) and so will not have the least desire or expectation for anything. Any action that the yogī may have to do now will be 'niṣkarma' (= Non-karma) because:- (1) the kleśas having been done with, the root-cause of the formation of the karmāśaya is removed (cf. sūtra II:12) and (2) as the yogī does action without any expectation of phala (= fruit) from it, the action leaves no saṃskāra and so does not become the 'karma' (in its technical sense).

Thus through vivekakhyāti the kleśas are done away with and the accumulated saṃskāras are exhausted through nirmāṇa citta-kāyas (cf. sūtras IV:4 to 11), while new karma-saṃskāras can not take place, as the yogī's kṛtis (actions) are non-karma due to his utter desirelessness and so there happens total abolition of kleśas and karmas in the dharmamegha samādhi.

SS. - **तदा सर्वावरणमलापेतस्य ज्ञानस्यानन्त्याज्ज्ञेयमल्पम् ।।४:३१।।**

TL. - tadā sarvāvaraṇa-malāpetasya jñānasyānantyāj-jñeyam- alpam - IV:31

WM. -

tadā	=	then;
sarva	=	all;
āvaraṇa	=	coverings, shrouds;
mala	=	impurities;
apeta (sya)	=	one- free from (of);
jñāna (sya)	=	knowledge (of);
ānantya (→āt→āj)	=	endlessness, limitlessness, infmiteness, (from, on account of, due to);
jñeya (m)	=	worth-knowing (is);
alpa (m)	=	little i.e. almost nothing (is);

TR. - Then, on account of the limitlessness of the knowledge of that one (yogī), who is free from all shrouds (i.e. obscuring factors) (and) impurities, there is (i.e. remaining) little (i.e. nothing more) worth-knowing.

CE. - The omniscience of the yogī, who has reached very high levels of samādhi, has already been referred to in sūtras III:49 and IV:29. This is reiterated in the present sūtra, but with an elaboration of the nature and the causal factors of this potentiality of the yogī.

The omniscience is developed in the yogī, even if he may not employ the saṃyamas recommended in sūtras III:44 ff. as he is not even interested in the power of omniscience. The development of this potentiality in him is a side-product of the perfect and permanent vivekakhyāti developed in the dharmamegha samādhi. The reason why this power is developed is that perfection of vivekakhyāti is disappearance of avidyā and consequently of all the other kleśas (cf. sūtras II:4 and IV:30) and the kleśas are the obscuring factors or shrouds, distorting and hindering the gaining of knowledge. Even in regard to worldly knowledge, any one of the four secondary kleśas, viz abhiniveśa, dveṣa, rāga or asmitā, produces distortion of reality. This can be easily seen in the udāra (i.e. generously abundant) stage of these kleśas. That is why very often it is remarked, 'he has been blinded by his ego (= asmitā) or by love (= rāga) or by hatred (dveṣa)' etc. In respect of the knowledge, really significant in the spiritual sphere, the kleśas work like opaque screens, making it almost impossible to gain any such knowledge as long as they are not curbed (tanukaraṇa, cf. sūtras II:2 ff.) adequately. In dharmamegha samādhi, as vivekakhyāti is established, avidyā and with it all kleśas disappear and thus these screens or barriers in the path of realization of truly spiritual knowledge are removed.

Karma leaves its residual effect in the citta (i.e. in karmāśaya) in the form of saṃskāra. These saṃskāras are the malas or impurities which also interfere in the gaining of knowledge by obscuring inner illuminative faculties, just like the dirt on the glass-chimney of a lantern. The saṃskāras also cause interference and distortion even in the worldly knowledge. The viewpoint of a person is coloured by his saṃskāras. That is why it is often said of a person that he cannot see the things in a proper light as his saṃskāras are like that. They cause still more obscuration in gaining of spiritual knowledge.

When these hindering screens (āvaraṇas) of kleśas and obscuring impurities (= malas) of saṃskāras are removed in the dharmamegha samādhi, there remains not the slightest obstruction in the path of the inner illuminating faculty viz. the ṛtaṃbharā prajñā (cf. sūtras I:48,II:27 etc.). It, therefore, shines forth in its full brilliance and the yogī can know the reality of every thing and any thing. On account of such power of omniscience, the moment the yogī wants to know about a particular subject, that knowledge of any thing and everything what-so-ever it may be, as if, flashes in his citta. Thus his capacity for knowledge would be boundless and there would be very little or rather nothing, which remains unknown to him and that he is yet to know.

There may be a slightly different meaning applicable to the sūtra. The yogī has gained the highest i.e. the most valuable knowledge, that he or any other man may want to have. Any other knowledge, even if it is yet not gained by the yogī, will be of little (alpa) value in comparison to what he has already gained.

SS. - ततः कृतार्थानां परिणामक्रमसमाप्तिर्गुणानाम् ।।४:३२।।

TL. - tataḥ kṛtārthānāṃ pariṇāma-kramasamāptir-guṇānām - IV:32

WM. -

tataḥ	=	from that;
kṛtārtha (→ānāṃ)	=	(kṛta = accomplished+artha = purpose) (those whose) purpose has been accomplished (plural possessive suffix = of);
pariṇāma	=	changes, transformations;
krama	=	sequence, process;
samāpti (ḥ→r)	=	finish, end, termination (is);
guṇa (→ānām)	=	trigunas, the three fundamental characterising components of prakṛti (of).

TR. - From that (i.e. limitlessness of knowledge) (results) the termination of the process of transformations of guṇas, (whose) purpose has been accomplished.

CE. - According to the Sāṃkhya and Yoga view about the evolution of prakṛti, the mūla-prakṛti or pradhāna is the state of equilibrium (= sāmyāvasthā) of the three guṇas. In this state the three guṇas are in such an ideal balance that neither of them is manifest. This equilibrium is disturbed, the moment the influence or vicinage of the puruṣa affects the pradhāna and a delusion of an association, technically called 'saṃyoga' (sūtra II:23), of puruṣa with prakṛti is produced. The pradhāna begins to evolve. The first transformation is to the stage of 'mahat' (On individual level this same is the element called 'buddhi'-- an aspect or section of the citta) and the three guṇas--so to say-- the fundamental characteristic fibres of the pradhāna-- lose their equilibrium and become manifested, with dominance of one over the other two, according to which the resultant product is called sāttvika or rājasika or tāmasika. As is customary to express, the cause of the saṃyoga is avidyā, but looked in another way it can also be said that saṃyoga is itself the most important and the ultimate form or aspect of avidyā. The strongest point and so the most difficult to remove aspect of avidyā is the delusion of the identicalness of the citta (an evolute of prakṛti) with puruṣa and this is nothing else but the 'saṃyoga'.

With the limitlessness of knowledge in prasāṃkhyana (IV:29), achieved in the dharmamegha samādhi, there is realization of the utter alienness and aloofness of puruṣa and the prakṛti i.e. specifically here the citta. As per sūtra II:23 this is the purpose of the saṃyoga, which latter had triggered the evolution of prakṛti i.e. the process of transformations of the three guṇas. Since this purpose behind the process of transformations of the three guṇas has been fulfilled and the saṃyoga has disappeared, because its cause avidyā has been removed, its last stronghold, that of misidentification of the citta with puruṣa having fallen away, there also comes an end of the process or chain of transformations of the guṇas.

Incidentally it may be pointed out that kṛtārtha can be interpreted as yogīs who have accomplished their purpose i.e. who have reached the goal of yoga. Then the sūtra could be rendered as : - 'From that there results the termination of the processes of transformations of guṇas in the case of the yogīs, who have accomplished their purpose.' Nevertheless, even then, the general purport and explanation of the sūtra remain substantially the same.

SS. - **क्षणप्रतियोगी परिणामापरान्तनिर्ग्राह्यः क्रमः ।।४:३३।।**

TL. - kṣaṇa-pratiyogī pariṇāmāparānta-nirgrāhyaḥ kramaḥ - IV:33.

WM. -

kṣaṇa	=	instant, a point or smallest unit or a quantum of time;
pratiyogī	=	(prati = opposite, counter, antagonistic + yogī = cooperator, one who helps). One who really helps in finishing an activity, but apparently doing something which seems antagonistic, counter-co-operator;
pariṇāma	=	transformation, change;
aparānta	=	(apara = ultimate + anta = end) ultimate endpoint;
nirgrāhya (ḥ)	=	(niḥ (→r)=without remainder, total+grāhya = grasped, graspable) totally grasped or comprehended (is).
krama (ḥ)	=	krama, sequentiality (is).

TR. - Krama (sequentiality producing a feeling of continuity) is the counter-co-operator (= pratiyogī) of the ksana (= instant) (and) is comprehended in its totality (only) at the ultimate end-point of transformations (= parinamas) (of guṇas of prakṛti).

CE. - It is often seen that two things seem to be antagonistic, as they appear to produce opposite effects and yet their combined action produces a desired result, which anyone of them could not have produced singly in an efficacious manner. They are called 'pratiyogī, which can be rendered in English by the term 'counter-co-operator'. Examples of these are : (1) raja ↔ tamas; (2) accelerator ↔ break etc. In an extreme case of prati-yoga (= antagonistic-co-operation) the two things may be so contradictory and incompatible, that if they come even close to each other they may annihilate one another. And yet one cannot exist without the other. A very good and well-known example of this is that of the two poles of a magnet. They cannot be in one and the same point, as this would do away with the magnetism i.e. their own existence. Yet one pole of a magnet alone also cannot exist. There needs to be an opposite pole somewhere, to counterbalance, as can be evident from the existence of the south and north magnetic poles of the earth.

Kṣaṇa, which is often translated by English words such as instant or moment, is, in fact, the smallest unit of time. That the concept of time, specially the notion about its continuousness, is an illusion has been already explained under sūtras III:52 and IV: 12. How and why this illusion about the continuity of time is created has been discussed there and needs no repetition here. Kṣaṇa is comparable to an atom of matter or a quantum of energy in modern science. On the same lines it may even be called time-atom or better still time-quantum.

The antagonism in between the kṣaṇa (= time-quantum) on one side and krama (time sequentiality) on the other side can be easily understood. Kṣaṇa is discrete, while krama and kāla (= time) have the notion of continuousness behind them, and discreteness is discontinuousness, i.e. exactly contrary to continuousness .Therefore as soon as the concept of kṣaṇa is taken up by the citta, the reality of krama and kāla i.e. of a continuity breaks down and vice versa. And yet the kāla and krama are made up of and exist because of the kṣaṇas. Just as the human eye is not able to perceive the gaps in between the pictures in a cinema-film being screened, because they last for less than one-tenth second and so cannot grasp the dis-continuity of the pictures, in the same way the innumerable kṣaṇas follow each other so rapidly that the ordinary man's citta is not able to grasp their discreteness and so an illusion of the continuousness of krama and kāla is created. Thus it can be seen that krama (and also kāla) is pratiyogī i.e. a counter-co-operator of kṣaṇa.

As said under sūtra IV: 12, to have no limitation to freedom, the yogī's citta should transcend the barrier of the notion of the inevitableness and coerciveness of time i.e. kāla and also of krama. This notion is so deeply ingrained in our citta that for an ordinary man it is impossible to totally discard this notion and transcend its barrier. However, the yogī can do this easily and quite early on his path of yoga by directing saṃyama on kṣaṇas and their krama, as recommended in sūtra III:52.

But if the yogī has extreme vairāgya and so has become unconcerned (cf. akusida, sūtra IV:29) about the eternal removal of duḥkha or even salvation (= mokṣa (etc., he may not take trouble to apply that saṃyama of sūtra III:52, even for transcending the constraint of krama and kāla. But even for entering kaivalya (the Absolute state, in which most probably eternal annihilation of duḥkha, moksa and such others are implicitly included) he has to transcend the barrier of kāla and krama. This happens in his case automatically, when there is pariṇāma-krama-samāpti (= end of the sequentiality of transformations of guṇas, IV:32) in prasaṃkhyāna and jñānasyānantya (IV:29 and 31) in the dharmamegha samādhi. The end of the sequence of transformations of guṇas is of course also the ultimate end-point (= aparānta) of transformations (= pariṇāmas) of guṇas. Without resorting to any saṃyama, e.g. that of sūtra III:52, the absurdity and unreality of krama (and also kāla) is realized by him through his omniscience, since these are antipodic and non-coexistent with kṣaṇa and as kṣaṇa is the really directly perceived entity for him. As soon as pariṇāma-krama ceases, kṣaṇa alone remains as real entity and thus the true nature of nonreality (= vikalpa) of krama and its antipodic relationship to kṣaṇa becomes very clear to the yogī.

(N.B. Incidentally it may be noted that Patañjali has not used the word kāla (= time) in the three sutras (viz. II:52, IV: 12 and 33) concerned with this unique theory of the illusoriness of the continuous movement of time. Because very probably for him kāla or time, at least its aspect of inevitability and coerciveness, does not exist. Kṣaṇas are only really existing and their raid sequence (= krama) produces the false feeling of the motion of kāla, which is therefore an illusion. It is, who have inserted the word kāla in this discussion as it was convenient).

SS. - **पुरुषार्थशून्यानां गुणानां प्रतिप्रसवः कैवल्यं स्वरूपप्रतिष्ठा वा चितिशक्तिरिति ।।४:३४।।**

TL. - puruṣārtha-śūnyānāṃ guṇānāṃ pratiprasavaḥ kaivalyaṃ svarūpa-pratiṣṭhā vā citiśaktir-iti - IV:34.

WM. -

puruṣārtha	=	(puruṣa + artha = purpose), purpose of puruṣa;
śūnya (ānām)	=	devoid (of, plural);
guṇa (ānām)	=	trigunas (of, plural);
pratiprasava (ḥ)	=	(prati = counter + prasava = birth and development, evolution) counter-evolution (nominative singular suffix);
kaivalya (ṃ)	=	kaivalya (absoluteness) (is);
sva	=	one's own;
rūpa	=	form, state;
pratiṣṭhā	=	(re-) establishment, reinstatement;
vā	=	or;
citiśakti (ḥ->r)	=	(citi = citi, the latent source of consciousness + śakti = potentiality) potentiality of citi, unmanifest potentiality for consciousness (is);
iti	=	the end, finish.

TR. - The pratiprasava (counter-evolution) of guṇas, which are (now) devoid of any purpose (yet) to be served for puruṣa, (is) kaivalya, (which is) reinstatement (of the primordial principles viz. prakṛti and puruṣa) in their own state or (which is) the potentiality of citi (= the source of consciousness in latent condition). Finish.

CE. - Two meanings are here applicable to 'puruṣārtha-śūnya'. Puruṣārtha = (1) ability to do some specially important work and (2) for the purpose of the puruṣa. So puruṣārthaśūnya would also mean 'so feeble that they cannot do any worthwhile work', besides the meaning given above (WM. and TR.). This triguṇas in the yogī in dharmamegha samādhi are so enfeebled that they are unable to do anything, because the stimūlating force behind them has disappeared (cf. sūtra IV:32). As per the meaning (2) of 'puruṣārtha' the purpose of the existence of the guṇas i.e. prakṛti is for the puruṣa (sūtras II:18 to 21). The draṣṭā (= supervisor, witnesser) of the bhoga = (experiencing) of the citta is the puruṣa. The attainment of kaivalya means the termination of the draṣṭṛtva (= supervising status) of the puruṣa and achievement of apavarga (= absolution, liberation, II:18) and regainment of the pristine pure puruṣa status. With this there remains no further need of the process of the transformation of guṇas i.e. need of the guṇas for serving the purpose of the puruṣa has become void (= śūnya).

The sūtra seems to give some synonyms of kaivalya, the summum bonum of Patañjali's Yoga system. This is clearly indicated by the term 'vā' in the sūtra. As is usually the case with synonyms, each of these sheds a light on a different aspect of kaivalya and in a way thus describes it. No doubt the description of this transcendental state is beyond of even comprehending and also beyond the scope of words. It can be only realised and experienced and this also in a very subtle mystic manner. The puruṣārthaśūnyatā becomes thus the first synonym and partial description of kaivalya.

The second synonym of kaivalya is pratiprasava (of guṇa-pratiprasava). Due to saṃyoga (II:17 & 23). The mūla-prakṛti or pradhāna, which means the three guṇas, begins to evolve. The products of the transformations in the evolution are called 'vikṛtis' (= deformations, distortions). From pradhāna i.e. mūla-prakṛti are produced seven prakṛti-vikṛtis, which are cause-effects i.e. origins as well as products and twenty-three vikṛtis, which are end products, i.e. they do not give rise to further products. This is the prasava (=development, evolution) of prakṛti as per Sāṃkhya view. Just as an unrolled map or roll of cloth is rolled up again, in the same manner this spread out of guṇas i.e. prakṛti is folded in and the reversion of the distorted or transformed prakṛti back again into its original state (mūla-avasthā) takes place. Simultaneously the puruṣa-tattva, as said above, also loses its draṣṭṛtva and becomes pure puruṣa of its primordial status. This infolding or reversal of the evolution of prakṛti is indicated by the term pratiprasava (counter-evolution).

Prakṛti and puruṣa take up their own original status in kaivalya, so svarūpāvasthāna (I:3) and svarūpa-pratiṣṭhā (this sūtra) are the two synonyms indicative of this. The puruṣatattva, as often explained is neither conscius nor consciousness, yet it has the potentiality of passively inciting the citta to develop active conciousness in the citta by its mere presence and this is its nature for all time and so even in kaivalya. Indicating this characteristic of the puruṣa is the synonym citi-śakti (or even mere 'citi' in IV:22).

As already pointed, there have occurred other terms, which are similarly just like other synonyms of kaivalya, the delusion of the linking of the puruṣa and prakṛti, particularly the citta, which is also a product of prakṛti, is the greatest avidyā and is designated saṃyoga. In kaivalya there is disappearance of avidyā i.e. avidyābhāva or avidyānāśa and also dissolution of saṃyogābhāva (or saṃyogaviyoga, as per Bhagavad-Gītā, VI:23) and so both these are like synonyms of kaivalya (cf. II:25) Hāna i.e. permanent abolition of duḥkha (= pain, misery) is also mentioned alongwith these two as synonymous to kaivalya. Guṇavaitṛṣṇya vairāgya and puruṣakhyāti (I:16), puruṣajñāna (III:35) vivekakhyāti (II:26, 28) and vivekajñāna (III:52, 54) are notions approaching very close to the concept of kaivalya and so can be looked upon as almost synonymous to the latter.

The last term 'iti' indicates the end of the discussion of Yoga in this sūtra-text.

*****

INDEX

C

D

L

M

N

O

R

S

* * * *